Brent E. Dickson

JUSTICES

of the

INDIANA SUPREME COURT

★ ★

JUSTICES
of the
INDIANA
SUPREME
COURT

Edited by LINDA C. GUGIN *and* JAMES E. ST. CLAIR

Published by the Indiana Historical Society Press
in cooperation with the Indiana Supreme Court
Indianapolis 2010

Printed in the United States of America

This book is a publication of the
Indiana Historical Society Press
Eugene and Marilyn Glick Indiana History Center
450 West Ohio Street
Indianapolis, Indiana 46202-3269 USA
www.indianahistory.org
Telephone orders 1-800-447-1830
Fax orders 1-317-234-0562
Online orders @ http://shop.indianahistory.org

The paper in this publication meets the minimum requirements of American National
Standard for Information Sciences—Permanence of Paper for Printed Library Materials,
ANSI Z39. 48–1984

Library of Congress Cataloging-in-Publication Data

Justices of the Indiana Supreme Court / edited by Linda C. Gugin and
James E. St. Clair.
    p. cm.
Includes bibliographical references and index.
ISBN 978-0-87195-288-2 (cloth : alk. paper)
1. Judges—Indiana—Biography. 2. Indiana. Supreme Court—Officials
and employees—Biography. 3. Indiana. Supreme Court—History. I.
Gugin, Linda C. II. St. Clair, James E.
KF354.I56J87 2010
347.772'03534—dc22
[B]
                    2010017352

Table of Contents

Editors' Notes and Acknowledgments

Linda C. Gugin and James E. St. Clair

This work on the judges and justices who have served on the Indiana Supreme Court was inspired by the Honorable Randall T. Shepard, chief justice of Indiana, who wanted to provide an invaluable resource about the history and operation of Indiana's highest court for students, citizens, and lawyers. In this volume, the history of the Court is told through the lives and accomplishments of the 105 men and one woman who were members of the Court up through 2010. The reader will find not only standard biographical information about each justice, but also interesting personal stories that give additional insight into the lives and times of the justices. Thanks to the diligent work of its sixty-six contributors, readers should be able to more fully appreciate the legal expertise, as well as the human dimensions, of the justices.

Few readers will consume this book from beginning to end, so we want to provide the reader with some important historical background about the Court that will help in understanding the context of each essay.[1] The Court today is significantly different than the state's first Supreme Court that was established in 1816 when Indiana became a state. The first court began operations on May 5, 1817. It consisted of three judges appointed by the governor with "advice and consent" of the Indiana Senate. They served seven-year terms.

In 1850 a constitutional convention was held, primarily to deal with the problem of the state's bonded debt, but the convention delegates also made important changes in the organization of the Court in terms of method of judicial selection, length of terms, and size. Election of judges by the people replaced gubernatorial appointment. Terms were limited to six years, but there were no limits on the number of terms. With partisan elections, however, the length of judicial tenure was shortened by tides of party strengths or weaknesses, unpopular court rulings, and the whims of the voters. The Indiana Constitution of 1851 also stipulated that the Court would consist of no less than three nor more than five judges. In 1852 the Indiana General Assembly increased the size of the Court to four judges, each of whom was elected from one of four districts on a statewide ballot, and they began their terms on January 3, 1853. In 1872, due to an increasing caseload, the size of the Court was expanded to five. Despite various efforts to increase the size of the Court since then, it remains at five.

Due to what some considered undue partisanship in judicial decisions and instability caused by frequent turnover on the Court, advocates of judicial reform began lobbying as early as the 1950s to remove partisan politics from the judicial selection process. The general assembly, responding to these efforts, drafted an amendment to the state constitution that would substantially reform the Court. This amendment, approved by the voters in November 1970, brought about several significant changes. It replaced partisan elections of appellate court judges with a merit-based system of gubernatorial appointment coupled with nonpartisan retention elections. Under this process, a Judicial Nominating Commission, comprised of citizens and attorneys, screens candidates for both the Supreme Court and the Court of Appeals and recommends three to the governor, who then appoints one of

INDIANA SUPREME COURT

The Indiana Supreme Court circa 1870. From left to right: James S. Frazer, Jehu T. Elliott, Robert C. Gregory, and Charles A. Ray.

the three to a two-year term. At the end of that term, voters participate in a retention election to decide if the justice should be retained. If a majority of voters favor retention, the justice serves for a ten-year term, when another retention election must be held. As of 2010 no justice has ever lost a retention election, which has lengthened considerably the amount of time that justices serve on the Court.

The 1970 amendment also changed the title of Court members from Supreme Court judges to Supreme Court justices. In the essays in this volume the term "judge" is used for those who served prior to 1970 and "justice" for those who have served since then. Even so it has been difficult to stick to this "rule of thumb," so that the term "justice" is used at times to encompass all who have served on the Court, as is the case with the title of the book.

Another important change brought about by the 1970 amendment was the method for selecting the chief justice. Prior to 1970, the chief justice was chosen in a variety of ways. At one time, according to Leander Monks in his seminal work on Indiana courts and lawyers, the members of the Court elected one of their own to be chief justice, with the stipulation that each would serve no more than one term until all members had presided. At some later date the position was rotated among the members by district. It was not unusual for one person to serve as chief justice several times during his tenure on the bench, and also on occasion a person who was newly elected to the Court became chief justice because he replaced the sitting chief justice who came from his district. Under the revised judicial article, the chief justice is elected by the members of the Judicial Nominating Commission from among the sitting justices. The title of the office was changed to Chief Justice of Indiana, which parallels the title at the national level of the Chief Justice of the United States. Since 1970, three men have served as chief justice—Norman F. Arterburn (1972 to 1974), Richard M. Givan (1974 to 1987), and Randall T. Shepard (1987 to present). The term for a chief justice is five years, but he or she may be reappointed.

The 1970 judicial reform amendment also reorganized the appeals court, which was originally established by the Indiana legislature in 1891 as a temporary court and made permanent in 1901. The amendment in 1970 made the appeals court a constitutional court and formally named it the Court of Appeals. Throughout its history the jurisdiction of the Court of Appeals has been altered, either by expanding or reducing its powers of review. In 1988 another constitutional amendment expanded the jurisdiction of the Court of Appeals to hear appeals in criminal cases, reducing the mandatory criminal jurisdiction of the Supreme Court. This shift, which greatly reduced the Supreme Court's criminal caseload, made it truly a court of last resort.[2] Today the Court of Appeals has fifteen judges who represent five state districts. They are appointed and retained in the same manner as justices of the Supreme Court. The retention elections, however, are not the same for all Court of Appeals judges. Retention elections for nine judges, three each from the first, second, and third districts, are limited to voters in those districts. The retention elections for judges of the fourth and fifth districts, each consisting of one judge from each of the three other districts, are held on a statewide basis. The Court of Appeals has been a stepping-stone for nine men who went on to become Supreme Court justices.

The editors are indebted to many people for the successful completion of this publication. First and foremost, we want to acknowledge the financial support from the Indiana Bar Foundation and the Indiana Supreme Court, whose generous contributions were critical to this undertaking. We are grateful to Chief Justice Shepard for giving us the opportunity to edit this work and for having the confidence in us to do the job. The chief justice and Elizabeth Osborn, assistant to the chief justice for court history and public education, have been tremendously helpful from beginning to end by assisting us in identifying and recruiting contributors and by responding quickly to any questions, no matter how thorny or trivial, as we worked our way through the process of editing 105 essays. This volume would not have been possible without their help. Others at the Supreme Court also made important contributions. In particular, Terri Ross at the Supreme Court Library responded graciously and quickly to any and every question we presented her. Erin Gobel, Supreme Court intern, tracked down cases and citations and developed the chart of judicial succession found in the appendices. Sarah Hachey, Webcast coordinator, did yeoman work pulling together the pictures for this volume. Several staff members at the Supreme Court wrote essays for the book, and their contributions are found throughout the work.

We are indebted to all of the contributors for their excellent scholarly work. We asked a lot of these very busy people, and they more than met our expectations. Their strong research and writing efforts are evident in each essay. At the end of each essay there is a "Selected Bibliography." In most cases authors searched far more sources than we could list. Their combined efforts provide an engaging and colorful portrait of Indiana's highest court.

A work such as this requires a lot of research, and as editors we were constantly trying to track down information and verify facts. The staff at the Indiana State Library was especially helpful to us in our own search for information as well as that of the other contributors. Special thanks also go to those at numerous libraries throughout the state who assisted with research efforts. Many of the families of justices were generous in providing information to contributors and also in sharing photographs and other resource materials. We hope that they will find the final product a fitting tribute to those who have served on the Court.

We also benefited from the assistance of staff at our own institution, Indiana University Southeast. Lesley Deal compiled and revised the author/subject list so many times she probably knows the authors and their subjects as well as we do. Mike Ellis helped in handling technical processing of photographs. A former student, Margaret "Peggy" Fukunaga, saved us untold hours by learning the arcane rules of the *Chicago Manual of Style* and lent her expertise in the details of editing.

The Court's conference room provides a formal setting for the justices' weekly meeting. It is also used for other judicial and legislative committee meetings. The justices sit with the newest member of the Court directly to the chief justice's left and proceed clockwise around the table in reverse seniority: (left to right) Frank Sullivan Jr., Brent E. Dickson, Randall T. Shepard, Robert D. Rucker, and Theodore R. Boehm.

Finally, our heartfelt thanks go to the wonderful staff at the Indiana Historical Society Press with whom we had the pleasure to work on two previous publications. Paula Corpuz, Ray Boomhower, and Kathy Breen handled the demands of this extensive volume with their usual grace, good humor, competency, and efficiency. Their expertise and careful eye for details have improved upon our own editing efforts. Also, Stacy Simmer deserves recognition for his excellent design work.

We have come to the end of a long journey. This work has been three years in the making. We hope the readers will agree that it was well worth the combined efforts of all those whose hard work made it possible.

1. For a more thorough history of the Indiana Supreme Court see Jerome L. Withered, *Hoosier Justice: A History of the Supreme Court of Indiana* (Indianapolis: Indiana Supreme Court, 1998).

2. See Robert H. Staton and Gina M. Hicklin, "The History of the Court of Appeals of Indiana," *Indiana Law Review* 30, no. 1 (1997): 203–31.

Indiana's leading contribution to the nation's judiciary is the Chief Justice of the United States, John G. Roberts Jr. (middle), who grew up in Long Beach in the northwest part of the state. In addition to his duties as leader of the U.S. Supreme Court, Roberts collaborates with members of state supreme courts and other state court judges. He is shown here in November 2005 at an event hosted by the National Center for State Courts that honored both his predecessors, William H. Rehnquist and Warren E. Burger, with state chief justices Randall T. Shepard (left) of Indiana, Shirley S. Abrahamson of Wisconsin, and Ronald M. George of California. Indiana's only other member of the U.S. Supreme Court was Justice Sherman Minton of New Albany, Indiana, who served from 1949 to 1956.

Introduction

Chief Justice of the United States John G. Roberts Jr.

Within the pages of this book lie the stories of the remarkable individuals who have served on the Indiana Supreme Court from its creation in 1816 until the present. Each presents a captivating vignette. Collectively, they tell how public-spirited individuals have transformed a frontier court into today's dynamic and innovative institution.

The Indiana Supreme Court has always been a select body. It began as a three-member court, and today it consists of only five members. The 105 individuals who have had the privilege of sitting on the Court share the common bond of dedication to public service. They have distinguished themselves as jurists, but have also contributed to their profession, their community, their state, and their nation. For example, Judge Isaac N. Blackford responded to the shortage of printed legal works in the early 1800s by collecting and publishing judicial decisions, receiving praise from lawyers throughout the country. Judge Jesse Lynch Holman was a founder of Indiana University and, later, Judge Byron Elliott headed the Indiana Law School, which later became the IU School of Law in Indianapolis. Many of the justices—too many to mention—have held important executive and legislative positions in Indiana. And many of the justices have also answered their nation's call, through positions in the military and appointments to the federal bench.

Indiana is justly proud of the members of its Court, both past and present. Over nearly two centuries, those jurists have fostered a collegial institution dedicated to securing justice for Indiana's citizens. The accounts of their accomplishments, however, comprise only the opening episodes of a still developing story. I congratulate the editors and authors of this volume for inspiring others to take up public service and add new and compelling chapters to this unfinished history.

JOHN G. ROBERTS JR.

JOHN JOHNSON
December 28, 1816–September 10, 1817

THOMAS D. KOTULAK

John Johnson, considered the first judge of the Indiana Supreme Court, had an active political career during the state's formative era. After statehood was achieved, Johnson, James Scott, and Jesse L. Holman were nominated to the Court in December 1816 by the state's first governor, Jonathan Jennings, and conducted their first session in May 1817. Although Johnson's death that same year precluded any lasting impact on the Court's subsequent decisions, in his earlier public career he was influential in helping to create the institutional contours of Indiana's judiciary branch of government and in framing some of the political and legal issues confronting the new state.

Born outside of the state, with date and place of birth in dispute (Virginia, Pennsylvania, and Kentucky have been cited as the family's state of origin), Johnson moved to Vincennes at the beginning of the nineteenth century and began a law practice. In 1804 he actively supported the cause of changing the Indiana Territory to the "second grade" status, which when it was approved by voters that year, allowed a semirepresentative form of government and moved the territory one step closer to statehood. For Johnson, the success of the movement was the beginning of his political career. Having studied law and practiced law in the courts of the Indiana Territory, he was reputed to be "one of the finest lawyers in the territory." Not surprisingly, given his support of "second grade" status for the Indiana Territory and his reputation for effectiveness as an attorney, Johnson was elected to serve in the first general assembly as a state representative. He subsequently served as clerk of the Indiana House and as a member of the legislative council.

During his service with the territorial legislature, Johnson was one of two representatives (the other was John Rice Jones) charged with the task of revising and codifying the territorial laws. The resulting Revision of 1807 (also known as the Rice Jones Revision, though the division of labor now seems impossible to calculate), once it was adopted with additional adjustments and amendments, effectively became a major component of the statutory law in force in the Indiana Territory until statehood caused the general assembly to issue the Revision of 1824.

Another noteworthy aspect of Johnson's service in the territorial legislature, however, foreshadowed a major political and legal issue for the state. In 1805 he signed a petition to Congress asking that the Northwest Ordinance of 1787 be revised so that slaves could be brought into the territory. Perhaps because of the high-profile nature of these early involvements with Indiana's territorial government, Johnson's bid for reelection to the territorial legislature in 1809 was a resounding success, and he received more votes than any other candidate. Though he lost his bid for territorial delegate to Congress to Jennings in that same year, this loss did not appear to sully his political or legal reputation. Indeed, when Jennings later became president of the constitutional convention that met at Corydon in 1816, he placed Johnson on the committee to draft the section of the constitution dealing with the judicial department.

In this capacity, Johnson, representing Knox County and "considered the finest lawyer of the convention," was able to shape the institutional framework of the state's judiciary. Although alterations were later made to the wording he helped draft by a select committee of the convention, the most important change involved a designated term for judges of the state Supreme Court, rather than the original wording of "during good behavior." This change can be seen to reflect the fervor for increased democratization of political institutions during this era of Indiana's history. Otherwise, as one historian has characterized it, "the judiciary article proved remarkably well suited and resilient for the early years of statehood."

Johnson also helped to frame one of the most contentious political issues facing the creation of the new state. The Northwest Ordinance had prohibited slavery in the territory, and the convention of 1816, in the "amendment" section of the proposed constitution, had the words "no alteration of this constitution shall ever take place so as to introduce slavery or involuntary servitude in this State." Johnson moved to replace these words with "it is the opinion of this convention that no alteration of this Constitution ought ever to take place, so as to introduce slavery or involuntary servitude in this state." Although his motion was voted down, the attempt to replace the definitive word "shall" with the merely prescriptive word "ought" could arguably be interpreted as further evidence of Johnson's proslavery stance, which he had earlier revealed in his petition to Congress as a member of the territorial legislature.

Though Johnson's tenure on the Court was short-lived and uneventful, he is remembered as one of Indiana's leading figures in its formative era. In addition to his service in the territorial legislature and as a delegate to the constitutional convention of 1816, he also served as a special attorney general of the Indiana Territory and as clerk to the board of trustees at Vincennes University.

THOMAS D. KOTULAK, PhD, is associate professor of political science, Indiana University Southeast. He is the author of biographical profiles of former Indiana senator William Jenner and former congressman Ray Madden in *The Scribner Encyclopedia of American Lives*, "Litigating Civil Liberties Under the Indiana State Constitution: The Problematic Promise of Price v. State" (2001) and "Bush v. Gore: Two Competing Conceptions of Democracy" (2007) in the *Journal of the Indiana Academy of Social Sciences*, and the Paris C. Dunning profile in *The Governors of Indiana* (2006).

SELECTED BIBLIOGRAPHY

Bodenhamer, David J., and Randall T. Shepard, eds. *The History of Indiana Law*. Athens: Ohio University Press, 2006.

Buley, R. Carlyle. *The Old Northwest: Pioneer Period, 1915–1940*. 2 vols. Indianapolis: Indiana Historical Society, 1950.

Dunn, Jacob. *Indiana and Indianans*. New York and Chicago: American Historical Society, 1919.

Monks, Leander J. *Courts and Lawyers of Indiana*. Indianapolis: Federal Publishing Company, 1916.

Withered, Jerome L. *Hoosier Justice: A History of the Supreme Court of Indiana*. Indianapolis: Indiana Supreme Court, 1998.

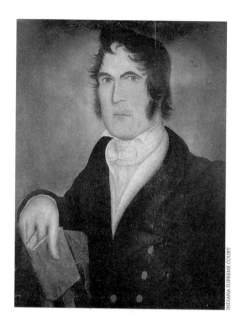

INDIANA SUPREME COURT

JAMES SCOTT
December 28, 1816–December 28, 1830

RAY E. BOOMHOWER

James Scott, one of the first three men appointed to the Indiana Supreme Court, was also one of the original forty-three delegates to the state's constitutional convention in June 1816 at Corydon, serving as chairman of the committee drafting the article on education and as head of the committee writing the constitution's provisions regarding the judiciary.

The committee on education recommended that it be the duty of the general assembly (as soon as circumstances permitted) to "provide by law for a general system of education . . . wherein tuition shall be gratis, and equally open to all." Indiana University granted Scott an honorary degree in 1844 in recognition of his work on behalf of education. The original draft issued by the committee on the judiciary was later revised by a select panel on which Scott did not serve. Scott was one of five delegates from Clark County to the constitutional convention, along with such notable figures as Jonathan Jennings, Thomas Carr, John Graham, and James Lemon.

Born on May 28, 1767, in Pennsylvania, Scott moved to Clark County, Indiana. Although not much is known about his early life, Scott was later described as "a stout, rugged and burly man, plain spoken with a vein of humor and pleasantry." In 1810 he received an appointment as the county's prosecuting attorney by William Henry Harrison, governor of the Indiana Territory. While living in Charlestown, Scott served as one of the founders of the community's Sunday school, which was held at the courthouse. In 1813 he won election to the territory's House of Representatives, resigning to take the position as a chancery judge.

In addition to Scott, those selected by Jennings to serve a seven-year term on the new three-judge Indiana Supreme Court that first met in Corydon on May 5, 1817, were John Johnson (who died in 1817 and was replaced by Isaac N. Blackford) and Jesse L. Holman. During the early years of their term in office the judges tackled the issue of slavery in the 1820 case of *Lasselle v. State*. The case centered on a woman named Polly, the daughter of a slave owned by General Hyacinth Lasselle of Vincennes. Although a Knox County court had ruled in favor of Lasselle, Scott, who wrote the unanimous opinion for the Supreme Court, ordered Polly to be set free, writing: "The framers of our constitution intended a total and entire prohibition of slavery in this State; and we can conceive of no form of words in which that intention could have been more clearly expressed."

Scott received high praise for his work from the Indiana legal community. In his history of the legal profession during the state's early days, Oliver H. Smith noted that many viewed Scott as "one of the purest men in the State, a good scholar, and a fine lawyer." According to Smith, Scott possessed a strong "common sense view" of the cases heard before him and was always able to "select the grain of wheat from the stack of straw, and say, holding it up to the parties without discussing the chaff, 'It is my opinion that this is a grain of wheat.'"

Reappointed to another seven-year term by Governor William Hendricks, Scott served on the Court until 1830, when he and Holman were replaced by Governor James B. Ray in a controversial decision that drew fire from the legislature, which fought against the governor's choices of two state senators, Stephen C. Stevens and John T. McKinney. The two men were eventually confirmed.

After leaving the Court, Scott returned to Charlestown to practice law, but also tried his hand at other professions, including publishing a newspaper called the *Comet* that had as its motto: "Ask not to what doctor I apply, for sworn to no sect or party am I." With the election of William Henry Harrison as president in 1840, Scott received a job as registrar of the federal land office at Jeffersonville. Removed when a new administration took office under President James Polk, Scott returned to Charlestown and opened a school for girls. During the last years of his life, Scott moved to Carlisle, Indiana, to live in the home of his adopted daughter. He died there on March 2, 1855.

RAY E. BOOMHOWER is senior editor, Indiana Historical Society Press, and editor of *Traces of Indiana and Midwestern History*. He is the author of numerous books on Indiana history, including *Gus Grissom: The Lost Astronaut* (2004) and *Robert F. Kennedy and the 1968 Indiana Primary* (2008). His articles have appeared in *Traces* and the *Indiana Magazine of History*.

SELECTED BIBLIOGRAPHY

Barnhard, John D., and Dorothy L. Riker. *Indiana to 1816: The Colonial Period.* Indianapolis: Indiana Historical Bureau and Indiana Historical Society, 1971.

Lewis C. Baird. *Baird's History of Clark County, Indiana.* Indianapolis: B. F. Bowen and Company, 1909.

Shepard, Randall T. "For Human Rights: Slave Cases and the Indiana Supreme Court." *Traces of Indiana and Midwestern History* 15, no. 3 (Summer 2003).

Smith, Oliver H. *Early Indiana Trials and Sketches: Reminiscences.* Cincinnati: Moore, Wilstach, Keys and Company, 1858.

CASES CITED

State v. Lasselle, 1 Blackf 60 (Ind. 1820).

JESSE L. HOLMAN
December 28, 1816–December 28, 1830

JOHN G. BAKER

An examination of Jesse Lynch Holman's legal career only provides limited insight into this Renaissance man's life. A novelist, poet, city planner, and preacher who was also active in the founding of Indiana University, Franklin College, and the Indiana Historical Society, Holman's legacy endures throughout Indiana.

Holman moved to the Indiana Territory from Kentucky in 1808 and settled on the banks of the Ohio River in Dearborn County. In 1810 Holman built his home and named it "Veraestau"—a reference to the Latin words for spring, summer, and fall. The Latin word for winter was noticeably absent from the moniker, reflecting Holman's vision that "the winter outside the house was never reflected within." That same year, at the age of twenty-six, Holman published a two-volume novel titled *The Prisoners of Niagara; or, Errors of Education*. The scandalous novel, which featured sexually active

teenagers, incest, prostitution, and rape, reportedly "gained a wide circulation for those days." Holman later attempted to destroy copies of the book,
claiming that "the morals of the book were not suitable for the minds of
young people."

Holman became a public official in 1814 when he was elected to the
lower chamber of the territorial legislature. Later that year he was appointed as a circuit court judge and traveled the southeastern region of the
Indiana Territory. Shortly after the Indiana Territory joined the Union in
1816, Governor Jonathan Jennings appointed Holman as one of the first
three judges of the Indiana Supreme Court.

In 1820 Holman, James Scott, and Isaac N. Blackford heard one of
the most contentious cases of the era—*State v. Lasselle*. Polly Strong was
a mixed-race female slave who had been brought to Indiana by Hyacinth
Lasselle. The state filed a writ of habeas corpus ordering Lasselle to disclose
the reason for Polly's detention. Lasselle filed a motion to dismiss the case,
and the Knox County Circuit Court ruled in Lasselle's favor after concluding
that Polly was his property. The Indiana Supreme Court reversed the lower
court and held that Indiana's constitution prohibited slavery. Relying on
the language of Article 11 that "there shall be neither slavery nor involuntary servitude in this State," the Court held that "it follows as an irresistible
conclusion, that, under our present form of government, slavery can have
no existence in the State of Indiana."

The Court reexamined the issue of slavery one year later in a case, *In re
Clark*, involving servitude disguised as a personal services contract. On
November 6, 1821, in an opinion penned by Holman, the Court held that
while all Indiana citizens could enter into contracts, contracts for personal
service could not be enforced through specific performance, which if enforced by law, "would produce a state of servitude as degrading and demor-
alizing in its consequences, as a state of absolute slavery; and if enforced
under a government like ours, which acknowledges a personal equality, it
would be productive of a state of feeling more discordant and irritating than
slavery itself."

Throughout his tenure on the Court, Holman remained active in the
southeast region of the state. In 1819 he helped create the plat for the town
in Dearborn County where he had built Veraestau. Holman later christened
the town "Aurora"—"as the Aurora comes before the Rising Sun"—to spite
the thriving community of Rising Sun located nine miles down the river.

Not content with simply founding the town, Holman also helped to establish the First Baptist Church of Aurora and the Aurora Public Library. Additionally, Holman served as the superintendent of Dearborn schools, cofounded the Indiana Bible Society, and successfully acquired financial support for the Aurora Seminary.

In 1830 Governor James B. Ray refused to reappoint Holman to a third term on the Court, apparently for political reasons. Holman ran for the U.S. Senate in 1831 but lost by one vote in the general assembly. During his vacation from politics, Holman was ordained as a pastor in 1834 and began preaching at the First Baptist Church of Aurora. President Andrew Jackson appointed Holman federal district judge for Indiana in 1835, and he served in that capacity until he died in 1842 at the age of fifty-eight.

An examination of Holman's life shows that he was a trendsetting jurist who was not afraid to tackle controversial issues. He was a man committed to developing and advancing Indiana through education and religion. U.S. Supreme Court Justice John McLean, speaking at a memorial service following Holman's death, said that what he admired most about Holman was his "singleness of heart;—he had no motive but to discharge his public duty uprightly. He has left behind him the influence of a high moral example."

JOHN G. BAKER, JD, LLM, is chief judge, Indiana Court of Appeals. He is the author of "Now or Never: Reforming Indiana's Court System," *Indiana Law Review* (2008); "Indiana Judges: A Portrait of Judicial Evolution," in *The History of Indiana Law* (2005); and "The History of the Indiana Trial Court System and Attempts at Renovation," *Indiana Law Review* (1997).

SELECTED BIBLIOGRAPHY

Baker, John G. "Indiana Judges." In *The History of Indiana Law.* Edited by David J. Bodenhamer and Randall T. Shepard. Athens: Ohio University Press, 2006, 303–24.
Blake, George. "Jesse Lynch Holman: Pioneer Hoosier." *Indiana Magazine of History* 39 (March 1943).
———. *The Holmans of Veraestau.* Oxford, OH: Mississippi Valley Press, 1943.
Davis, Abigail. Introduction to *The Prisoners of Niagara; or, Errors of Education,* by Jesse L. Holman. Westminster, MD: Heritage Books, 2006.
"Seeking a Federal Judgeship under Jackson." *Indiana Magazine of History* 35 (September 1939).

CASES CITED

In re Clark, 1 Blackf. 122 (Ind. 1821).
State v. Lasselle, 1 Blackf. 60 (Ind. 1820).

ISAAC N. BLACKFORD

September 10, 1817–January 3, 1853

RANDALL T. SHEPARD

It is not a disservice to the other hundred-odd Indiana justices to say that Isaac Newton Blackford, the fourth judge of the Indiana Supreme Court, still has no peer as someone of genuine international reputation.

Much of this reputation rests on Blackford's seminal contribution to nineteenth-century legal scholarship. In our nation's early decades, there was little printed American law, and most lawyers relied on works such as *Blackstone's Commentaries*. Blackford embarked on assembling a series of reports of the Court's decisions that marked Indiana as a place of respectable lawyering. He undertook this effort as a personal venture, editing all the decisions himself, paying for the printing, and selling the volumes.

When the first volume appeared in 1830, it was an instant hit in a very wide legal community. A young Washington Irving, then secretary to the American legation in London, wrote: "I meet with it frequently and am often asked as to the antecedents of its author, whose name is already quite familiar at Westminster." When Harvard librarian John Gage Marvin, regarded as the founder of American legal bibliography, first examined American law reports in 1847, he declared that Blackford's volumes "have the reputation of being among the best American reports." National figures such as Chancellor Kent praised the reports, and New York's *United States Monthly Law Magazine* called Blackford "the most accomplished reporter in the Union."

Blackford's demonstrated legal talent and his long tenure—longer even than John Marshall—propelled him to national prominence. When Dean William Draper Lewis, founder of the American Law Institute, undertook to write of the "Great American Lawyers" in 1907, he ranked Blackford as a figure of "permanent national reputation," alongside Joseph Story and Daniel Webster. When Kermit Hall did similar biographies a century later, Blackford was still featured as one of the leading figures in American law.

Blackford's work was known well beyond legal circles. Governor Albert G. Porter said that there was not a single Indiana community where Blackford was not "a household word." Citizens commonly quoted Blackford, rather than the statutes. To be sure, Blackford was part of the state's political establishment from the time Indiana was a territory. Territorial governor Thomas Posey named him the first clerk of Washington County in January 1814, and the territorial legislature engaged him as its clerk for successive sessions. In late 1815 Posey named him territorial judge, prompting his move to Vincennes. Blackford won election to the very first House of Representatives and became Speaker when it met in Corydon. Governor Jonathan Jennings named him to the Court in 1817.

Blackford's diligence, competence, and his connections led to roles in such early institutions as the Bank of Vincennes, designated by the first legislature as the state bank (indeed he became its second officer). This bank service reflected a lifelong interest in business. Usually living as a bachelor or widower under modest circumstances, Blackford accumulated assets and invested regularly in real estate and other ventures in southwest Indiana and in Indianapolis. The land surrounding today's Military Park was a Blackford real estate venture, still marked by Blackford Avenue alongside the park and the Indiana University School of Law. His most monumental project was a five-story office building at Meridian and Washington streets, demolished in 1912 to build what is now the headquarters of the law firm

Barnes and Thornburg. Of course, even his law reports were a business of sorts, a business of sufficient success that the Indiana Constitutional Convention of 1850–51 resolved to create a public office of reporter, presumably expecting that the state could profit from it.

Blackford played leadership roles in the major social movements of his time, opposing slavery and promoting education. He was a founder and president of Indiana's chapter of the American Colonization Society, which sponsored free blacks in returning to Africa. Modern generations view this effort with skepticism, but it once drew support from abolitionists, religious leaders, and people such as James Madison and Bushrod Washington. Blackford was also prominent in the "common school" movement, seeking to establish free and general education as a way of building Indiana's future. He allied himself with people such as Caleb Mills and presided at the common school convention of May 1847.

Blackford was born in Bound Brook, New Jersey, in 1786, and returned there after graduating from Princeton in 1806, part of a remarkable class that produced senators, governors, justices, and a vice president. He studied law in the offices of Colonel George MacDonald and Judge Gabriel Ford, later a member of the New Jersey Supreme Court. He migrated to Indiana in 1811 and was practicing law in Vincennes when MacDonald and his family arrived there in 1819.

Blackford married young Caroline MacDonald in 1820. She died while giving birth to their son, George, the following year. Blackford considered Vincennes home, though he lived in what was called the Governor's Residence on the Circle in downtown Indianapolis for some twenty years. It was there that he closeted himself in grief over George's death in 1846.

When Indiana began electing its judges in 1852, Blackford had been so long out of political circulation that the Democratic Party nominated instead a younger candidate, fellow judge Samuel E. Perkins. Blackford drifted a bit, until President Franklin Pierce appointed him to the new U.S. Court of Claims in March 1855, a choice that the nation's newspapers said drew "universal commendation." He became that court's chief judge and was serving there when he died in Washington on the last day of December 1859. His body lay in state in the chambers of the Indiana Senate. Upon Blackford's death, the editors of the *Indianapolis Journal* declared him "a giant." The *New York Times* called him "indefatigable" and "much esteemed." The verdict of history, rendered over and over, has been that they were right.

RANDALL T. SHEPARD, JD, LLM, is Chief Justice of Indiana. He is the former president of the Conference of Chief Justices and teaches periodically at Indiana University, Yale Law School, and New York University. Shepard is the author of "Jesse W. Weik: The Young Indiana Lawyer Who Made Herndon's Lincoln Possible," *Indiana Magazine of History* (2009) and coauthor (with David J. Bodenhamer) of *The History of Indiana Law* (2006).

SELECTED BIBLIOGRAPHY

Lupton, Suzann Weber, "Isaac N. Blackford: First Man of the Court." *Indiana Law Review* 30, no. 1 (1997): 319–28.

Marvin, John Gage. *Legal Bibliography; or, a Thesaurus of American, English, Irish, and Scotch Law Books.* Philadelphia: T and J. W. Johnson, 1847.

Thornton, W. W. *Isaac N. Blackford: The Indiana Blackstone.* Edited by Douglas Fivecoat. Indianapolis: Indiana Supreme Court, 2005.

———. "Supreme Court of Indiana." *The Green Bag* 4 (May–June 1892).

Vile, John R. *Great American Judges: An Encyclopedia.* Santa Barbara, CA: ABC-CLIO, 2003.

STEPHEN C. STEVENS
January 28, 1831–May 30, 1836

DOUGLAS K. FIVECOAT

The story of Stephen C. Stevens, the fifth judge to serve on the Indiana Supreme Court, is one of great accomplishment and tragic decline. He was a skilled, capable lawyer and jurist in his prime but has the distinction of losing both his wealth and a significant portion of his mind in his later years, dying a pauper in the Indiana Hospital for the Insane.

Stevens, born in Kentucky, came to Brookville in the Indiana Territory sometime prior to 1812. Like most early pioneers, Stevens pursued many professions in an attempt to make a living, having been both a merchant and a tavern keeper. As a storekeeper in 1811 he was indicted for selling a tin pan to an Indian, but managed to get the indictment quashed. Later, he took up banking, becoming president of the Vevay branch of the state bank, where Isaac N. Blackford served as a cashier.

In the winter of 1813–14 Stevens left Indiana and traveled to New Orleans on business, but then joined the American forces there in the war against Great Britain. He took part in the Battle of New Orleans on January 8, 1815. In the battle, General Andrew Jackson's force of nearly five thousand defeated a British expedition nearly twice its size. The victory was decisive, with American casualties small compared with those of British forces. Stevens unfortunately numbered among the wounded, taking a musket ball to the head during the fighting. After recovering from his injury, Stevens returned to Indiana and studied law. He was admitted to the Brookville bar on March 3, 1817. Stevens served several terms in both the Indiana House and Senate and was elected Speaker of the House in 1824.

Stevens was a passionate man and pursued several causes with vigor. He was a driving force in the founding of a local Masonic temple in Brookville in 1817. However, he left the Masons after the "Morgan excitement" in 1826, in which a disgruntled Mason from western New York, Captain William Morgan, threatened to expose the secrets of the organization in a book. Morgan was later taken away by a group of Masons never to be seen again. This event cast a pall over Freemasonry and inspired many, including pastors and politicians, to rally against the fraternity and its members. Many Masons, especially those in business or politics such as Stevens, had to abandon the fraternity to avoid the stigma associated with it.

Stevens, however, did not back down from issues of morality. He was an avowed abolitionist and was not afraid to share his views openly, even in southern Indiana, where there was significant sympathy for the institution of slavery. As a testimony to his abolitionist stance, Stevens represented blacks in court on several occasions and even drafted a resolution calling for the emancipation of slaves that the New School Presbyterian Synod later adopted. Stevens even ran for governor representing the Liberty Party in 1846, promoting a platform that incorporated the abolition of slavery.

As a lawyer, Stevens was known for his industry and his verbosity. One commentator, Judge John Test, who knew Stevens well from his early days at Brookville, wrote that he "was a very diffuse man and covered a good deal of paper to express a small idea." Oliver H. Smith wrote that he was "one of the strongest advocates in the State, but the diffuseness of his opinions left too many obiter dicta for other cases." Stevens attributed his verbose nature to a childhood experience in school in which he had trouble with an assignment. When his schoolmaster asked him about it, he did not elaborate on his difficulties. The schoolmaster beat him soundly for failing the assignment but later, after finding out the problems Stevens had encountered, told him that if he had offered all the details he would have escaped punishment. From then on, Stevens made it a rule to always tell the whole story.

Stevens was appointed to the Court when Governor James B. Ray, a fellow Mason from the Brookville lodge, refused to reappoint Jesse L. Holman and James Scott. Stevens served on the high court until resigning in May 1836 to return to private practice in Madison.

After leaving the bench, Stevens enjoyed a lucrative practice as a collections attorney, amassing a considerable fortune over the years. However, in 1851 or 1852, he invested his wealth in a railroad venture and lost it all. The loss was too much for Stevens to bear. In later years he imagined himself wealthy and bargained for real estate, homes, and other goods as he traveled around the state. By the 1860s Stevens was but a shadow of his former self, both intellectually and physically. On June 29, 1869, he was admitted to the Indiana Hospital for the Insane at Indianapolis.

After his admission to the hospital, Stevens was visited by Test, who found Stevens in his underwear having his trousers mended by another patient. Stevens first denied knowing Test but then admitted he knew him but said that "ever since the top of my head was cut off my memory is not as good as it used to be." Test was so struck by the former judge's poor state that he went to see Governor Conrad Baker about his encounter. The governor immediately pulled out a ten dollar bill and went around collecting money from others until he had accumulated fifty or sixty dollars. He sent the money to the superintendent of the hospital along with a request that a suit be made for Stevens and presented with compliments from the bar. After receiving the suit, Stevens is said to have given a fine speech to the superintendent expressing gratitude for being remembered by the bar.

Just days later, Stevens's precipitous decline reached an end. He died on November 7, 1869, and was buried in his new suit near his old homestead in Madison.

DOUGLAS K. FIVECOAT, JD, MA, is an attorney with Ladendorf and Ladendorf. He is the editor of William W. Thornton's *Isaac N. Blackford: The Indiana Blackstone* and coauthor (with Chief Justice Randall T. Shepard) of *Indiana's Supreme Court in the Civil War* (2007).

SELECTED BIBLIOGRAPHY

Palmer, John C. *The Morgan Affair and Anti-Masonry.* Whitefish, MT: Kessinger Publishing, 1992.

Reifel, August J. *History of Franklin County, Indiana.* Evansville, IN: B. F. Bowen, 1915.

Remini, Robert V. *Andrew Jackson: The Course of American Empire, 1767–1821.* Baltimore, MD: Johns Hopkins University Press, 1998.

Thornbrough, Emma Lou. *Indiana in the Civil War Era, 1850–1880.* Indianapolis: Indiana Historical Bureau and Indiana Historical Society, 1965.

———. *The Negro in Indiana before 1900: A Study of a Minority.* Indianapolis: Indiana Historical Bureau, 1957.

JOHN T. McKINNEY
January 28, 1831–March 4, 1837

JOHN J. NEWMAN

Knowledge of law and friendship with Governor James B. Ray made John Taliaferro McKinney an obvious choice as the sixth judge on the Indiana Supreme Court in 1831. McKinney successfully practiced common law and was experienced in criminal law, having served as prosecuting attorney in Brookville, Indiana, in 1822. As a state legislator, he worked to codify Indiana's statutes in 1831. McKinney practiced law with, and against, Ray in Brookville and supported him politically as governor.

Born on March 18, 1785, in Caroline County, Virginia, McKinney was one of five children of John and Sarah Taliaferro McKinney. He attended Charlotte Hall School, a military academy in Maryland, read law, and was admitted to the bar in Kentucky about 1815, most likely when he moved to Campbell County. There he married Sarah Augusta Mayo on June 11, 1821. Some sources say the couple had three children, but only two are known: Taliaferro, who died on June 23, 1836, at age fourteen, and Mary, who reached adulthood and married. After the death of his first wife, McKinney married Elizabeth Amanda Hall on June 26, 1834, in Cincinnati.

McKinney's exact arrival in Indiana is uncertain. He does not appear on the 1820 census for Indiana, and his first purchase of land in Brookville occurred on September 30, 1831. He was admitted to the Franklin County bar on March 3, 1822, and was appointed prosecuting attorney on October 7, 1822. His family continued to live in Newport, Kentucky, when McKinney settled in Brookville, most likely seeing the community, which had become an increasingly important political and economic center in southeast Indiana, as the place to advance his career.

Public service and politics dominated McKinney's career before his appointment to the bench. Although there is no proof of service, given his age and educational background, he probably served in the War of 1812.

On October 31, 1822, he was commissioned a captain in the Seventh Regiment of the Indiana Militia, which included Franklin and Rush counties. Judicial historian Leander J. Monks gave McKinney the title of "general" but no source for this rank has been found. On December 11, 1831, he was appointed a trustee of the Franklin County Seminary. As a Democrat, he served two terms in the Indiana House of Representatives (1826–27 and 1827–28) and three terms in the Indiana Senate (1828–31). It was as a member of the senate's judiciary committee that he participated in codifying Indiana's laws.

McKinney was a successful and colorful attorney. The practice of common law required the exchange of claims and counterclaims that were argued over several terms of court until both sides agreed upon a single issue and the court could render a judgment. Such winnowing down of the issues oftentimes led to fisticuffs. On March 24, 1826, McKinney was fined one dollar after pleading guilty to an assault and battery charge for fighting in the courtroom. The prosecutor, granting "mercy," waived his docket fee.

McKinney began purchasing large numbers of town lots in Brookville and farmland in surrounding townships in 1831. When he died, his estate was valued at $4,500 and included a bookcase and 207 books, valued at $250. In addition to an extensive law library, he owned books on the life of George Washington, histories of Greece and the United States, along with volumes on arithmetic, geography, and French and English grammar.

Ray's selection of McKinney and Stephen C. Stevens to the Supreme Court was political, according to some of the governor's critics. Indiana historian Donald F. Carmony noted that "some weeks before the legislature convened late in 1830, reports and accusations circulated that Governor Ray was trying to *bargain* appointments to the court in such a manner as to enhance his prospect for election to the United States Senate."

The terms of the then serving judges, Isaac N. Blackford, James Scott, and Jesse L. Holman, expired December 27, 1830. Ray failed to nominate any successors, and on January 8, 1831, the senate sent him a resolution requesting appointments. With "absence of official courtesy," the governor, on January 12, renominated Blackford and submitted the names of senators McKinney and Stevens to replace Scott and Holman. The senate rejected the latter two and admonished Ray for his lack of civility. The governor responded in a softer tone, resubmitting McKinney and Stevens as his nominees. On January 28 the senate approved them by a vote of 11 to 10.

The apparent politicalization of the process irked even a Ray ally, John Watts, who, on February 10, in a long discourse in the state senate, raised a number of issues regarding Ray's nominations. The senator claimed that McKinney "did not possess the superior qualifications required for so important a station." McKinney, who had more than fifteen years of experience as an attorney, including arguing cases before the Supreme Court, went on to serve for twelve sessions on the Court and was principal author of one-third of its decisions. Monks, in his 1917 history, noted of McKinney: "those who were well acquainted with his work call him a first-rate lawyer and his decisions are fair."

McKinney died of tuberculosis at his home in Brookville on March 4, 1837, and is buried in Brookville City Cemetery.

JOHN J. NEWMAN, MA, is retired and the former Indiana State Archivist and Director, Information Management, Indiana Supreme Court. He is the author of *American Naturalization Records, 1790–1990* and *Uncle, We Are Ready! Registering America's Men, 1917–1918.*

SELECTED BIBLIOGRAPHY

Brookville Indiana American. July 4, 1834, July 29, 1836, March 10, 1837.

Franklin County, Indiana. Circuit Court. Civil Order Book 3, p. 125. Order Book 4, p. 61.

———. Probate Court. Probate Order Book, Complete 5, p. 507. Probate Order Book, Complete 3, pp. 441, 444–46.

Indianapolis Journal, March 11, 1837.

Reifel, August J. *History of Franklin County, Indiana.* Indianapolis: B. F. Bowen and Company, 1915.

Riker, Dorothy L., and Gayle Thornbrough, eds. *Messages and Papers Relating to the Administration of James Brown Ray, Governor of Indiana, 1825–1831.* Indianapolis: Indiana Historical Bureau, 1954.

http://www.geocities.com/Taliferro_Family_2002/generations.

INDIANA SUPREME COURT

CHARLES DEWEY
May 30, 1836–January 29, 1847

DONALD B. KITE SR.

After moving his law practice from his hometown of Sheffield, Massa-chusetts, to Indiana in late 1816, Charles Dewey, the seventh judge of the Indiana Supreme Court, did not have to wait long to become involved in a significant dispute that drew on his legal training. In 1818 Governor Jonathan Jennings, Dewey's friend and political ally, became involved in a highly charged conflict following his appointment by President James Monroe to serve as a commissioner and negotiate a treaty with various Indian tribes. Jennings's lieutenant governor, Christopher Harrison, maintained that as a result of a provision in the Indiana Constitution prohibiting those who hold "any office under the United States" from "exercis[ing] the office of Governor," Jennings had abdicated his office and Harrison had become governor in his place. Jennings appointed Dewey to appear on his behalf before the legislative committee formed to resolve the matter. Following the testimony of several witnesses, the committee voted 15 to 13 that it was "inexpedient to further prosecute the inquiry," and Jennings should remain governor.

The growth of Dewey's practice and acclaim throughout the state soon followed his successful defense of the governor. In the same year of 1818, Dewey presented his first case before the Court, and in the nearly twenty years preceding his own appointment to the Court, he argued more than eighty cases before it, more than any attorney at that time. While he was called a model judge who "spoke with great dignity and decorum" on the bench, what he much preferred was "to urge a cause before a jury or court where he could unleash all his powers of forensic argument." Dewey, it was noted, "pursued his point with invincible logic, enlivened by wit and enforced with abundant sound sense."

While little is known about Dewey's early years and his upbringing, he did graduate with high honors from Williams College in Massachusetts and began practicing law there before his move to Paoli in Orange County. When the Indiana legislature approved the establishment of the state seminary, ultimately Indiana University, on January 20, 1820, Dewey was one of six men named to the school's first board of trustees. The university awarded him an honorary doctor of laws degree in 1844. In 1821 Dewey was elected a state representative from Orange County, and while defeated twice in races for Congress, first in 1822 and again in 1832, he served as U.S. attorney for the district of Indiana from 1825 to 1829 and prosecuting attorney for the Second Circuit from 1833 to 1836.

The pinnacle of his public service came during his eleven-year tenure on the Court from 1836 to 1847. For much of that period he served with Isaac N. Blackford and Jeremiah C. Sullivan, "who complemented each other and made for the finest Court under the old Constitution and perhaps in the entire history of the Indiana judiciary." Dewey, appointed to the Court by Governor Noah Noble to fill the vacancy created by the resignation of Stephen C. Stevens, had "accepted the office at the urgent and unanimous solicitation of the members of the bar, at a great sacrifice of pecuniary interest."

Dewey authored hundreds of opinions, a number of which shed light on the tenor of the times. In *Wyant v. Smith*, Dewey decided that Smith had not slandered Wyant by accusing him of stealing his hogs, butchering them, and

then selling the meat. His ruling in *Boyd v. Byrd* upheld a father's suit for se-
duction of his unwed daughter, who had yet to reach the age of twenty-one.
Until a woman reaches that age, Dewey wrote, "The relation of master and
servant must be supposed to exist between her father and her." Writing for
the Court in *Blanton v. State*, Dewey explained the Court's ruling to affirm
the defendant's conviction of "keeping a billiard table for the purpose of
gain," writing that "such an establishment can not but be deleterious to the
morals of the neighborhood in which it is situated." In *Fowler and Another
v. Throckmorton*, Dewey filed the Court's first dissent. The case involved a
contractual agreement for a $1,126 loan that carried $24 in interest.
Blackford's decision, joined by Sullivan, voided the contract because he
believed the interest rate amounted to usury. Dewey disagreed, arguing for
dropping the interest payment while enforcing repayment of the principal.

Dewey was as firm in his beliefs as he was blunt in expressing them.
For example, he rejected an opportunity to serve as a federal district judge
after being confirmed by the U.S. Senate, either due to the higher salary of a
Supreme Court judge or his unwillingness to accept an office under President John Tyler. Additionally, when he learned in early 1847 that he had
not been reappointed to the Court, he did not simply return quietly to his
law practice. Instead, Dewey wrote a letter to a newspaper that described
in detail how Governor James Whitcomb had not kept his word regarding
Dewey's reappointment. The letter, which was published in the February 1,
1847, *Indianapolis Journal*, concluded with the statement, "I have only to
add, that the Governor's word has not been kept, his pledge is unredeemed."
On one occasion, after Dewey informed a judge exactly what he thought of
the court's ruling, he reportedly said, "Now, damn you, fine me; send me to
jail, too; you ought to if you have any respect for yourselves." In April 1861
Dewey was sitting by the stove in the Charlestown courthouse with a group
of lawyers, waiting for court to begin. When they heard of the attack upon
Fort Sumter, Dewey, though no admirer of Andrew Jackson, nonetheless
raised his crutch and said, "I wish old Jackson could be brought up out of
purgatory just long enough to put down this rebellion, but then I would
want him sent straight back there again."

At sundown on April 25, 1862, Dewey died at his home in Charlestown
after a long illness. His friend, William T. Otto, who had been Clark County's first circuit judge, went to the house to see his colleague one last time.

Otto remarked, "The equal of Daniel Webster is in that coffin today." Dewey was buried in the Charlestown cemetery under a marker that observed he was "A learned and upright Judge." Dewey's wife, Sarah, lived for nearly three decades after his death, passing away in Indianapolis on April 21, 1890.

DONALD B. KITE, SR., JD, is a partner with Dean-Webster, Wright and Kite, LLP. He is coauthor of *Federal Justice in Indiana: The History of the United States District Court for the Southern District of Indiana* (2007), recipient of Defense Trial Counsel of Indiana Defense Lawyer of the Year Award (2005), and corecipient of the Indianapolis Bar Association's Dr. John Morton Finney Jr. Award for Excellence in Legal Education (2007).

SELECTED BIBLIOGRAPHY

Albert Gallatin Porter Papers, 1759–1934. Series 3, folders 18 and 19, and Series 5. William Henry Smith Memorial Library. Indiana Historical Society, Indianapolis, IN.

Biographical and Historical Souvenir for the Counties of Clark, Crawford, Harrison, Floyd, Jefferson, Jennings, Scott and Washington, Indiana. Chicago: John M. Gresham and Company, 1889.

McCullouch, Hugh. *Men and Measures of Half a Century.* New York: C. Scribner's Sons, 1888.

Roll, Charles. *Colonel Dick Thompson: The Persistent Whig.* Indianapolis: Indiana Historical Bureau, 1948.

CASES CITED

Blanton v. The State, 5 Blackf. 560 (Ind. 1841).

Boyd v. Byrd, 8 Blackf. 113 (Ind. 1846).

Fowler and Another v. Throckmorton, 6 Blackf. 326 (Ind. 1843).

Wyant v. Smith, 5 Blackf. 293 (Ind. 1840).

JEREMIAH C. SULLIVAN
May 29, 1837–January 21, 1846

BRANDON T. ROGERS

Jeremiah C. Sullivan, who served as the eighth judge on the Indiana Supreme Court, was a representative to the 1820 Indiana General Assembly, where his colleagues greeted him with laughter for suggesting the name "Indianapolis" for Indiana's new capital city. Born in Harrisonburg, Virginia, on July 21, 1794, to Roman Catholic parents, Sullivan grew up in the Shenandoah Valley. He attended William and Mary College in Williamsburg before enlisting during the War of 1812. After attaining the rank of major, he left the military to join the Virginia bar when the war ended. Deciding not to settle in his native commonwealth, Sullivan ventured out into the frontier in 1817 to establish new roots and begin his new career. Once in the Ohio valley, he heard that the people in Madison, Indiana, could use a lawyer so he headed there—and made it home for the rest of his life.

Just three years later, Jefferson County elected Sullivan as a representative to the general assembly. During the course of the 1820 session, the legislature moved the state capital from Corydon to a town in the center of the state. When Senator William Polke announced a bill establishing a commission for laying out the capital, he left a blank for the name of the new city. Debate ensued as to how the blank should be filled. One member urged the selection of an Indian name, such as "Tecumseh." Another proposed "Suwarro." Polke, no doubt aware of the irony in his suggestion after the spirited exchanges, offered "Concord." All of these names were voted down, and the legislature adjourned for the night. In a letter he wrote to Governor Conrad Baker many years later, Sullivan said the discussions were marked by "some sharpness and much amusement."

That night, Sullivan suggested a name to Representative Samuel Merrill of Switzerland County, who immediately gave his assent. They took Sullivan's idea to Governor Jonathan Jennings, who also approved. When the house returned and went into committees, Sullivan moved to fill the blank with "Indianapolis." The committee members initially responded with "a shout of laughter." But Merrill seconded the motion, and after some discussion, the committee approved and the name was accepted. Sullivan later explained that he believed the name's "Greek termination would indicate the importance of the town."

Sullivan only served in the state legislature for one term, but following the death of Judge John T. McKinney, Governor David Wallace nominated Sullivan to be the eighth judge of the Indiana Supreme Court alongside Isaac N. Blackford and Charles Dewey. In 1837 the Senate confirmed the trio, who served on the bench together for nearly nine years. Sullivan's opinions were always brief—"such an expression as would in plain English go to the point and there stop." His frankness and cogency earned Sullivan posthumous recognition as the best writer on the Court during his time.

Sullivan's private writings demonstrate the clarity of his pen, and surviving letters reveal that religion and family were perhaps most important to him. In a letter to his son Algernon, attending college at the time, Sullivan advised that "[t]he first great object with all of us should be the glory of God, which includes everything else. . . . [I]f we do, to mankind, all that he requires us to do, we shall be truly & extensively useful." Though Sullivan sometimes admonished Algernon in his letters, particularly for not writing home often enough and once for attending the theater, the younger

Sullivan's usefulness to mankind cannot be questioned. Algernon Sydney Sullivan eventually found his way to New York City, where he became involved in a number of charitable causes and joined forces with William Nelson Cromwell to start the law firm of Sullivan and Cromwell.

After he left the Court in 1846, Sullivan returned to private practice out of his Madison home, often consulting with Algernon on cases by mail. He remained engaged in public affairs and politics throughout the rest of his life, but he never returned to public office. Sullivan died on December 6, 1870, hours before he was to take the bench again as judge of the new Jefferson County criminal court.

Although he is remembered for his service on the Indiana Supreme Court, Jeremiah C. Sullivan's legacy unquestionably begins with the naming of Indianapolis.

BRANDON T. ROGERS, JD, is general attorney, Office of Chief Counsel, U.S. Customs and Border Protection. He is a former law clerk to Chief Justice Randall T. Shepard. Like Jeremiah C. Sullivan, Rogers is a graduate of Marshall-Wythe School of Law at the College of William and Mary.

SELECTED BIBLIOGRAPHY

"Algernon S. Sullivan: Death of One of New York's Noted Citizens." *New York Times*, December 5, 1887.

Indianapolis Star, January 14, 1940.

Schauinger, Joseph H. "Jeremiah C. Sullivan, Hoosier Jurist." *Indiana Magazine of History* 37 (September 1941): 217–36.

———. "Some Letters of Judge Jeremiah C. Sullivan." *Indiana Magazine of History* 37 (September 1941): 261–73.

Sullivan, Jeremiah C. Jeremiah C. Sullivan Collection (1843–1869), Box M-0270. William Henry Smith Memorial Library, Indiana Historical Society, Indianapolis, IN.

Woollen, William Wesley. *Biographical and Historical Sketches of Early Indiana*. Indianapolis: Hammond and Company, 1883.

SAMUEL E. PERKINS

January 21, 1846–January 3, 1865; January 1, 1877–December 17, 1879

MARISOL SANCHEZ

After two failed efforts to be seated on the Indiana Supreme Court, Samuel Elliot Perkins, the ninth and only judge to serve on both Supreme Courts created by Indiana's first and second constitutions, was given a temporary one-year appointment to the Court in 1846 by Governor James Whitcomb to replace Jeremiah C. Sullivan. He was then confirmed the following year by the Indiana Senate for a full term. Perkins was only thirty-four years old at the time of his appointment and served on the Court almost twenty-two years, albeit not consecutively. Interestingly after the constitutional change making Supreme Court judges elected officials, Perkins received the nomination of the Democratic Party over Isaac N. Blackford, the longest serving judge in Court history with thirty-five years of continuous service.

Five years after his confirmation to the Court and under this new regimen, Perkins was elected by popular vote to the bench, where he remained until his defeat at the polls in 1864. While Perkins resumed the practice of law after 1864, he did not stay away from the judiciary for too long. Instead, he served as judge of the Marion County Superior Court from 1872 to 1876, and was again elected to the Court, serving from 1877 until his death in late 1879. This determination was characteristic of Perkins.

Born on December 8, 1811, in Brattleboro, Vermont, Perkins was left as an orphan at the age of five and grew up living with friends near Conway, Massachusetts. Upon coming of age, Perkins took an interest in the law and began to study law at Penn Yan, New York. In 1836 he headed west on foot, and his journey led him to Richmond, Indiana, at the peak of the internal improvement boom. Here, he concluded his law course with J. W. Borden of Richmond, and a year later he was admitted to the Indiana bar.

Once in Indiana, Perkins became very active in Democratic politics and through this passion he helped to revitalize a party newspaper, the *Richmond Jeffersonian*, and became its editor. The focus of the newspaper was to recruit new members to the Democratic Party and cater to those "disgruntled over the failure of the state canals" and other government improvement projects. This endeavor strengthened his political positioning within the party, subsequently leading to his appointment as prosecuting attorney for Wayne County by Whitcomb in 1843. The view of Perkins's reputation, up to this point, was primarily political, which might help explain why the Senate twice refused to confirm him for the Court.

Perkins was known as a legal scholar. While serving on the Court, Perkins was appointed professor of law at Northwestern Christian University (later Butler University) in 1857 and was professor of law at Indiana University from 1870 to 1872. He also published two notable legal works: *A Digest of the Decisions of the Supreme Court of Indiana* in 1858, a work of eight hundred pages and known as the "Indiana Digest," and a treatise titled *Pleading and Practice . . . in the Courts of Indiana* in 1859, known as the "Indiana Practice."

Given his long service on the Court, Perkins left an extensive record of opinions. While many of his decisions were routine, others involved hot-button issues that attracted widespread attention and often searing criticism. Three of his decisions in particular cast such disapprobation. In *City of Lafayette v. Jenners*, Perkins declared unconstitutional a law authorizing cities and towns to levy taxes to support their school systems, a widely denounced decision that impeded the state's educational progress. Perkins also unleashed a torrent of outrage with his decisions in *Beebe v. State* and *Hermann v. State*, both of which held the prohibition act of 1855 unconstitutional.

Several of Perkins's decisions during the Civil War were likewise controversial and viewed by some as a partisan tug-of-war with the state and national Republican administrations. In *Ristine v. State ex rel. Board of Commissioners*, Perkins ruled that Governor Oliver P. Morton tried to exceed his authority by forcing an expenditure from the state treasury without a legislative appropriation. Two other decisions by Perkins, *Skeen v. Monkeimer* and *Griffin v. Wilcox*, declared unconstitutional attempts by the military to exercise control over civilians. While these decisions were unpopular at the time, historian Emma Lou Thornbrough wrote that Perkins "enjoyed a kind of vindication" later when the U.S. Supreme Court in the postwar period affirmed "some of the constitutional doctrines he had expounded during the war."

One summation of Perkins, as stated by Napoleon B. Taylor in his memorial to the judge and adopted by the Indianapolis Bar Association following his death in 1879, is filled with praise. Taylor, an Indianapolis attorney and former superior court judge, said that Perkins pursued his life with "fortitude and determination" and was successful in life, attaining "exalted position" and enjoying the "admiration and approval of his countrymen" due to his "excellent natural endowments" and his "pure motives." He added that Perkins "fell like a soldier—died at his post—crowned with the honors of his profession, and holding at the time its highest trust in the State."

A more nuanced assessment was offered by W. W. Thornton in his history of the Court. While crediting Perkins as "an indefatigable and never ceasing worker" and "a man of considerable vigor of mind," he also wrote that "it can scarcely be said that he was a learned man." He faulted Perkins for failing to grasp the "opportunities afforded him in being one of the first judges whose duty it was to interpret the Constitution of 1851."

MARISOL SANCHEZ, JD, is a partner with Bose McKinney and Evans LLP's Litigation, Appellate and White Collar Crime Practice Groups. She is a former law clerk for Chief Justice Randall T. Shepard. Sanchez is coauthor of "Appellate Civil Law Update," *Res Gestae* (2004–present).

SELECTED BIBLIOGRAPHY

Adams, Wendy L., and Elizabeth R. Osborn, eds. *In Memoriam: Glimpses from Indiana's Legal Past.* Indianapolis: Indiana Supreme Court, 2006.

Dictionary of American Biography Base Set. American Council of Learned Societies. Reproduced in *Biography Resource Center,* http://galenet.galegroup.com/serviet/BioRc.

Thornbrough, Emma Lou. "Judge Perkins, the Indiana Supreme Court, and the Civil War." *Indiana Magazine of History* 60 (March 1964): 79–96.

Thornton, William W. "The Supreme Court of Indiana." *The Green Bag* 4 (May–June 1892).

CASES CITED

Beebe v. The State, 6 Ind. 501 (1855).

City of Lafayette and Martin County Treasurer v. Jenners, 10 Ind. 52 at 55 (1857).

Griffin v. Wilcox, 21 Ind. 370 (1863).

Hermann v. The State, 8 Ind. 545 (1855).

Joseph Ristine, Auditor of State v. The State of Indiana ex rel. The Board of Commissioners of the Sinking Fund, 20 Ind. 328 (1863).

Skeen v. Monkeimer, 21 Ind. 1 (1863).

THOMAS L. SMITH
January 29, 1847–January 3, 1853

JAMES E. ST. CLAIR

Prior to his service as the tenth judge on the Indiana Supreme Court, Thomas Lacey Smith already had a host of considerable accomplishments, including such distinctions as a medical practice, high-seas adventurer, novelist, and newspaper editor. Born in Philadelphia on March 23, 1805, Smith obtained his medical degree from the University of Pennsylvania and shortly thereafter was selected as a surgeon on a ship traveling to various ports in the Orient. He spent nearly a decade in China, engaging in trade while at the same time acquiring vast knowledge of the Chinese people, their language, and culture. In the immediate years after medical school, Smith also published a novel, *The Chronicles of Turkeytown*, under the pseudonym of Jeremy Peters, which was a satire of small-town America.

After his sojourn in China, Smith returned to Pennsylvania, where he established a medical practice in Chester County, married a woman from the area, and served for a time as the county's representative in the state legislature. Soon, however, Smith was on the move again, venturing westward to Louisville, Kentucky, and eventually across the Ohio River in 1845 to New Albany, Indiana, which would be his home for the rest of his life. He died there on January 23, 1875. Smith apparently did not practice medicine in his new surroundings, instead turning his attention to studying law and for a short time becoming editor in chief of the *Louisville Weekly Democrat,* of which he was also part owner. He eventually concentrated his efforts on his law practice and Democratic politics, allying in both endeavors with Ashbel P. Willard, a future Indiana governor, and Michael C. Kerr, who became Speaker of the U.S. House of Representatives. Smith was defeated in his sole attempt for elective office in Indiana when in 1843 he lost a race for the state senate.

Smith's nomination to the Supreme Court by Democratic Governor James Whitcomb similarly seemed headed for failure. Whitcomb, who took office in 1843, was determined to replace the two Whig judges, Charles Dewey and Jeremiah C. Sullivan, with Democrats. After Smith was rejected for confirmation three times by the Senate, Whitcomb gave him an interim appointment and renominated him for a regular term for a fourth time in 1847, which the Senate finally acceded to by a twenty-six to twenty-two vote. It was widely believed that the governor's protracted struggle with the Senate to remake the Court was the result of Whitcomb putting partisanship above merit and that the judges being replaced, Dewey and Sullivan, were better qualified than their successors, Smith and Samuel E. Perkins. In any event, the Court, then consisting of Isaac N. Blackford, Smith, and Perkins, marked the end of an era. Under changes in the 1851 constitution, Supreme Court judges thereafter would be candidates for election statewide along with other state officials.

During his six years on the bench, Smith wrote more than two hundred opinions, the most notable of which involved a land dispute between the state and Vincennes University. Smith's decision, which found in favor of the state, was reversed by the U.S. Supreme Court in early 1853. While on the court Smith also wrote one volume of *Indiana Reports*, published in 1850, and a textbook for schoolchildren titled *Elements of the Law*, published in 1853. Later, he also wrote the lyrics to a Civil War song called "The Union Soldier's Hymn."

Smith resumed his law practice in New Albany after leaving the Court, but he was soon back in the state capital as a lobbyist and led the charge to charter a new state bank in 1855, later described as the most serious legislative scandal of the era. Smith drafted the legislation and was indefatigable in trying to win support among lawmakers, buttonholing them in the halls of the Senate and House and at their hotels. After the bank bill passed, over the governor's veto, Smith's rewards came from being granted subscription rights to stock in the bank and several of its branches. He was also appointed a member of the bank board that decided branch locations. Although a subsequent Senate investigation into the sordid affair did not result in any actions against Smith, the episode nonetheless left an indelible stain on what otherwise had been an extraordinary career.

JAMES E. ST. CLAIR, MA, is professor of journalism, Indiana University Southeast. He is coauthor of *Sherman Minton: New Deal Senator, Cold War Justice* (1997) and *Chief Justice Fred M. Vinson of Kentucky: A Political Biography* (2002) and coeditor of *The Governors of Indiana* (2006) and *Justices of the Indiana Supreme Court* (2010).

SELECTED BIBLIOGRAPHY

Lansing, Dorothy I., M.D. "Thomas Lacey Smith, M.D. (1805–75): A China Trade Physician Who Gave Up the Practice of Medicine." *Transactions & Studies of the College of Physicians of Philadelphia.* 4th ser., 42, no. 4 (April 1975).
New Albany Ledger-Standard, January 23, 1875.
Smith, Thomas Lacey. *Chronicles of Turkeytown.* Philadelphia: R. H. Small, 1829.
———. *Elements of the Law.* Philadelphia: Lippincott, Grambo, 1853.
———. *Reports of Cases in the Supreme Court of the State of Indiana.* New Albany, IN: Kent and Norman, 1850.
Walsh, Justin E. *The Centennial History of the Indiana General Assembly, 1816–1978.* Indianapolis: The Select Committee on the Centennial History of the Indiana General Assembly, 1987.
Withered, Jerome L. *Hoosier Justice: A History of the Supreme Court of Indiana.* Indianapolis: Indiana Supreme Court, 1998.

CASES CITED

State v. Trustees of the Vincennes University, 2 Ind. 293 (1850).
Trustees of the Vincennes University v. State, 55 U.S. 268 (1852).

ANDREW DAVISON
January 3, 1853–January 3, 1865

KATHRYN R. DOLAN

Andrew Davison, the eleventh judge of the Indiana Supreme Court, left his home in Chambersburg, Pennsylvania, in the spring of 1825, traveling west on horseback in search of a place where he could restore his health. He had intended to return to Pennsylvania, but on the journey back home he stopped in Greensburg, Indiana, for a few days of rest. With nearly five hundred miles to go, Davison instead decided to make Indiana his new home.

Born on September 15, 1800, Davison grew up as the son of an Irish Presbyterian minister, and he was sent to college to continue the family tradition. After graduating in four years from Jefferson College in Canonsburg, Pennsylvania, however, he admitted he did not feel a calling to the ministry and instead took up the study of law with Thomas H. Crawford. Under Crawford, who had served in both the Pennsylvania House of Representatives and Congress, Davison was not only schooled in the law but also in politics, becoming like his mentor, an Andrew Jackson Democrat. Davison was admitted to the bar in Franklin County, Pennsylvania, in 1823.

Shortly after he settled in Greensburg, Davison was admitted to the bar of the Decatur Circuit Court. In his years of practice on the circuit, Davison gained a reputation as a "careful, hardworking, technical lawyer, rather than as an advocate." His greatest strength, according to a close associate, "was in his masterly use of general principles, and unerringly he applied them to the given particular case." On April 15, 1839, Davison married Eliza Test, the widow of another lawyer and politician, John Test. The couple had a daughter, Jennie, who died in 1860, and a son, Joseph, who died a few years after his father's death in 1871.

As an attorney for the prosecution in 1849, Davison helped win a conviction in Decatur Circuit Court of Luther Donnell for aiding fugitive slaves. The conviction was reversed on appeal to the Supreme Court, with Samuel E. Perkins ruling in *Donnell v. State* that the state's fugitive slave law was unconstitutional. Just a few months after that decision was rendered, Davison himself joined Perkins and two other Democrats as the first Court judges elected to the Court under the change mandated by the 1851 Constitution. Although accounts say that Davison "mingled little with the magnitude" and "therefore lacked the popular manner which usually distinguishes the politician," he was still able to defeat his opponent in 1852, Charles Dewey, a Whig and Court judge from 1836 to 1847, by more than fourteen thousand votes. Davison won re-election for another six-year term in 1858, but he and his fellow Democrats on the Court were defeated in the Republican landslide of 1864.

Davison's second term overlapped with the Civil War, a time when the Court dealt with a number of highly contentious issues, the most prominent of which concerned the wartime powers of the executive branches of state and national governments. His hundreds of opinions, published in eighteen volumes of *Indiana Reports*, were also of less lofty matters such as his first, *Case and Wife v. Wildridge and Others*, which was a dispute over the inheritance of land, and his last, *Dale v. Moffitt*, a case of an unpaid promissory note.

After his defeat for a third term, Davison retired from public life. He died on February 4, 1871. His funeral was attended by Governor Conrad Baker as well as Court judges John Pettit, Alexander C. Downey, and Samuel H. Buskirk. Davison is buried in South Park Cemetery in Decatur County.

KATHRYN R. DOLAN is Indiana Supreme Court Public Information Officer. A former television news journalist, she conducts training for judges on how to work with the media and leads a public access committee for the Indiana Division of State Court Administration.

SELECTED BIBLIOGRAPHY

A Biographical History of Eminent and Self-Made Men of the State of Indiana.
   Cincinnati: Western Biographical Publishing Company, 1880.
Decatur Republican, January 15, October 22, 1858.
Decatur Press, November 22, 1852, February 11, 1871.
Kittochtinny Historical Society Papers, vol. 13. Chambersburg, PA, Kittochtinny
   Historical Society.

CASES CITED

Case and Wife v. Wildridge and Others, 4 Ind. 51 (1853).
Dale v. Moffitt, 22 Ind. 113 (1864).
Donnell v. The State, 3 Ind. 479 (1852).

ADDISON L. ROACHE
January 3, 1853–May 8, 1854

COLLEEN KRISTL PAUWELS

Addison Roache's father had big plans for his sons, so when Addison was eleven the family moved to Indiana so that the boys could attend Indiana University. Born on November 3, 1817, in Rutherford County, Tennessee, Addison Locke Roache, the future twelfth judge of the Indiana Supreme Court, was the eldest son of Doctor Stephen and Elmira Sloan Mc-Corkle Roache. Following his graduation from Indiana University in 1836, he studied law under Rockville, Indiana, attorney, Tilghman A. Howard, and established his law practice in Frankfort. After practicing for a few years, Roache toured the western United States for a year, returning in January 1842. In June of that year, he married Emily A. Wedding. They had seven children, one son and six daughters.

In 1847 Roache, a Democrat, was elected to the Indiana General Assembly, but served only one term. He returned to practice in Rockville until October 1852, when at age thirty-five, he was elected to the Indiana Supreme Court, taking office on January 3, 1853. Among the issues facing the Court during this period was the revision of the rules of pleading and practice, specifically abolishing the distinctions between actions at law and equity, substituting in their place the term civil action. Roache did not remain on the bench long enough to establish a judicial character, resigning on May 8, 1854, after only 490 days to become the president of the Indiana and Illinois Central Railroad. Alvin P. Hovey, then a Democrat, was appointed to fill his seat.

Roache formed a law partnership in 1859 with Joseph Ewing McDonald in Indianapolis. The firm of Roache and McDonald became one of the most well-regarded firms in the state, but after only eleven years Roache retired from the firm due to ill health. After a few years of rest, Roache's health was restored, and he began a law practice in Indianapolis in 1876 with his son-in-law, Edwin H. Lamm, creating the firm of Roache and Lamm. In 1887 Roache again retired, but continued to be active in business and public affairs. He was the president of the Manufacturers and Real Estate Exchange in Indianapolis, the agent and manager of the New York Mercantile Trust Company, and he was a member of the Masonic Lodge and the Presbyterian Church.

Perhaps due to his continued relationship with IU, Roache had a long-standing interest in the development of public education in the state. As a part of this effort, Roache sought to establish a public library in Indianapolis. He drafted the resolution for the library, saw to its passage in the general assembly, and developed a plan for the library's creation and support. The Indianapolis Public Library opened its doors in 1873.

Roache was elected to the IU Board of Trustees in July 1858, but served only briefly. He was forced to resign for jurisdictional reasons when he moved to Indianapolis to begin his law practice with McDonald. Roache was again elected as a university trustee on April 10, 1878, and served as the president of the board from 1879 to 1881. While on the board, he used his position to promote the university throughout the state as the "fountainhead" of the public school system, encouraging the training of scholar-teachers who would return to towns throughout Indiana to train the young. Although he was elected to another four-year term to begin in 1882, he resigned from the board on December 27, 1882.

Roache died at the age of eighty-eight in Alhambra, California, on April 24, 1906, after moving with his family to the area five years before. An editorial in the *Indianapolis News* after his death described him as "a man of kindly nature, an honorable gentleman, and a public-spirited citizen. . . . To say that he was a good man is to say the best thing that can be said of any one."

The Addison Locke Roache Lectureship was established at IU in 1956 from a bequest in the will of Roache's son, Addison Locke Roache Jr. The annual lectureship honors the elder Roache's achievements in the areas of law, business education, and letters.

COLLEEN KRISTL PAUWELS, JD, MLS, is associate professor of law and director of the Law Library, Indiana University Maurer School of Law, Bloomington. She is the author of *Hepburn's Dream: The History of the Indiana Law Journal* and coauthor of *Trustees and Officers of Indiana University, 1982 to 2010* (forthcoming 2011) and *Legal Research Today: Traditional Sources, New Technologies.*

SELECTED BIBLIOGRAPHY

Cashdollar, Hunter. *Marketing Farm Produce in 1847 in Dyer County.* Family letters of the Roache/McCorkle Families. June 3, 1847. http://tn-roots.com/tndyer/family/1847-mccorkle.html.

Indiana University Board of Trustees Resolution, May 10, 1956. Addison Roach File. IU Archives, Bloomington, IN.

http://en.wikipedia.org/wiki/IndianapolisMarion_County_Public_Library.

Indianapolis News, April 25, 1906.

Indianapolis Sentinel, April 17, 1877.

Myers, Burton Dorr. *Trustees and Officers of Indiana University, 1820 to 1950.* Bloomington, IN: Indiana University, 1951.

"Roache, Addison L." In *Biographical History of Eminent and Self-Made Men of the State of Indiana.* 2 vols. Cincinnati: Western Biographical Publishing Company, 1880.

WILLIAM Z. STUART

January 3, 1853–January 3, 1858

JONATHAN A. BONT

Exemplifying the sort of spirit that would mark his life, William Z. Stuart, the thirteenth judge of the Indiana Supreme Court, ran away from his home in Aberdeen, Scotland, at the age of fourteen to return to Massachusetts, his birth state.

He enrolled in Amherst College with the goal of following in his father's professional footsteps as a physician. During his time at Amherst, however, he became particularly skilled in debate and writing. As a result, he eventually decided to study law. He graduated second in his class in 1833, and later in life Amherst awarded him a doctor of laws degree. For a brief time following graduation Stuart served as a high school principal while continuing to study law.

In 1836 Stuart moved to Logansport, Indiana, where he was admitted to the Indiana bar. He became known for his clear and logical voice in the courtroom, and although his arguments were seldom impassioned, he had a knack for interjecting wit and irony at appropriate times. Stuart received notoriety, though not necessarily popularity, in 1838 when he defended James H. Harrison, a shoemaker who was new to the area, for the murder of David Scott, a popular local farmer. Stuart and Daniel D. Pratt, later a U.S. senator, were appointed by the court to represent Harrison. Pratt, as senior counsel for the defense and a legendary orator in the courtroom, was set to make the closing argument. However, after Stuart finished his last argument, Pratt whispered to another lawyer: "Stuart has exhausted every argument; there is not one word left for me to say."

From 1845 to 1846 Stuart was the prosecuting attorney for the Eighth Judicial Circuit and then returned to his career as a defense attorney. He was elected to represent Cass County in the state legislature in 1851 and was instrumental in forming the code of procedure that still governs the practice in Indiana courts. He also introduced legislation to establish a state bank under the 1851 constitution.

Stuart, a Democrat, was elected to the Court in 1852. His written opinions during his tenure on the high court were noted for their clarity, elegance, and conciseness. So impressive were they that legal scholar Theodore Sedgwick referred to them in his oft-quoted treatise on damages. Stuart was a proponent of judicial restraint and deference to the legislature. His opinions reflected his unwillingness to use the Court as a means for settling political disputes. For example, in *Bepley v. State*, a case involving the regulation of the sale of alcohol, Stuart wrote: "If the act is not a reflection of public sentiment, neither the responsibility nor the remedy lies with the courts." In a decision upholding a conviction for illegal liquor sales, *Maize v. State*, Stuart said that the judiciary looks to "the acts of the legislature with great respect and reconciles and sustains them if possible."

Stuart took a moderate stance on most politically divisive issues and often wrote separately or in dissent to the opinions of his fellow Democrat, Judge Samuel Elliot Perkins. In his decision ruling the 1855 prohibition statute unconstitutional, *Beebe v. State*, Perkins argued that the legislature overstepped its authority by oppressively regulating the constitutional rights of Hoosiers to own, manufacture, buy, and sell property, including alcohol. Stuart dissented, concluding that there are some "evils" that the legislature must regulate.

After resigning from the Court in 1857, Stuart was appointed attorney of the Toledo and Wabash Railway Company. He was the choice of his district to be elevated to the high court once again in 1870, but declined, preferring the higher income of his law practice.

Stuart's first wife, Minerva Potter, with whom he had three children, died in 1846. In 1849 he married Sarah Benedict of New York. They had four sons together, three of whom, Charles B., Thomas A., and William V., also became railroad attorneys and founded the Lafayette, Indiana, firm that today bears the name Stuart and Branigin.

In what little spare time he allowed himself Stuart read poetry. He was particularly fond of Robert Burns, whose poems he could recite by memory, as well as George Byron and Walter Scott. He also studied military history and talked at length about all of the leading American battles. In 1875 his health began to deteriorate rapidly, and in 1876 his family moved him to Clifton Springs, New York, hoping that he would recover. Stuart died on May 7, 1876, at age sixty-five.

JONATHAN A. BONT, JD, is law clerk to the Honorable Larry J. McKinney, U.S. District Court Senior Judge. He is a former summer associate at Stuart and Branigin, LLP.

SELECTED BIBLIOGRAPHY

Biographical History of Eminent and Self-Made Men of the State of Indiana, vol. 2. Cincinnati: Western Biographical Publishing Company, 1880.

Esarey, Logan. *History of Indiana from Its Exploration to 1922*. Dayton, OH: Dayton Historical Publishing Company, 1924.

Holliday, Joseph E. "Daniel D. Pratt: Lawyer and Legislator," *Indiana Magazine of History* 57 (June 1961).

Past and Present of Tippecanoe County, Indiana. 2 vols. Indianapolis: B. F. Bowen and Company, 1909.

Thurman, Suzanne. "Cultural Politics on the Indiana Frontier: The American Home Missionary Society and Temperance Reform." *Indiana Magazine of History* 94 (December 1998).

CASES CITED

Beebe v. State, 6 Ind. 501, 512 (1855).

Bepley v. State, 4 Ind. 264 (1853).

Maize v. State, 4 Ind. 342 (1853).

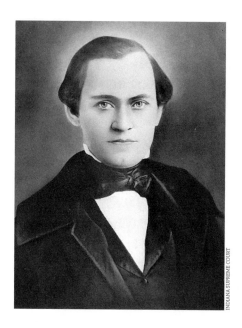

ALVIN P. HOVEY
May 8, 1854–January 1, 1855

JAMES M. REDWINE

Colonel Alvin Peterson Hovey was in command of the Twenty-fourth Indiana Volunteers at the Battle of Shiloh in Tennessee. In the confusion and darkness of the disastrous first evening, April 6, 1862, Hovey encountered unknown forces and was met with a sharp, "Who comes there?" Hovey improvised the password, "Hoosiers." He was greatly relieved to hear the response, "Welcome Hoosiers!" Promoted to brigadier general for his gallantry at Shiloh, Hovey then rose to the rank of major general due to his pivotal role in the siege of Vicksburg, Mississippi.

Grace under fire and a quick-witted ability to improvise marked Hovey's life from an early age. Other powerful people recognized Hovey's sound judgment and courage and often turned to him for public service, including his time as the fourteenth judge of the Indiana Supreme Court.

Hovey and Abraham Lincoln were contemporaries who had similar backgrounds. Both men were born in log cabins. For Hovey, it was in the small settlement of Farmersville in Posey County, Indiana, on September 6, 1821. Both died while in high office. Hovey's tenure as Indiana's twenty-first governor was cut short by his death on November 23, 1891. Hovey and Lincoln also had a direct connection through attorney and common pleas judge John Pitcher, who practiced law in Spencer County, Indiana, during Lincoln's residency there from 1816 to 1829. Lincoln borrowed Pitcher's *Blackstone's Commentaries on the Law*. When Pitcher moved to Posey County, Hovey read for the law in Pitcher's office using the same volume until he was sworn into the bar in the Posey Circuit Court in 1843.

Elected as a delegate to the 1850 Indiana Constitutional Convention, Hovey was instrumental in establishing Indiana's probate system. He also gained the attention of politicians throughout the state and was appointed by Governor Joseph A. Wright on May 8, 1854, to the Indiana Supreme Court, replacing Addison L. Roache, who resigned. Hovey, at age thirty-two, became the youngest person to serve on the Court up to that time.

Although he served less than a year, losing his bid for a full term in the election of 1854, Hovey was respected by his colleagues and the bar. On the Court, he did not lose sight of his own difficult childhood and poverty. In the case of *Falkenburgh v. Jones*, Hovey led the Court in guaranteeing that indigent defendants could obtain a transcript for appeal. He wrote:

> In arriving at our conclusions, we have felt constrained to give a liberal construction to our statutes in favor of the pauper, for we can scarcely conceive of a system of laws so inhuman and cruel that would consign the destitute and friendless to conviction and infamy, without affording full and ample means for investigation. Such a system would, in many cases, make poverty equivalent to crime; for without the means of procuring writs, witnesses and records, the innocent might, and frequently would be convicted; and that part of our constitution which provides that justice shall be administered freely, and without purchase, completely and without denial would be an empty boast, and worse than mockery to the poor.

Hovey, who had served as Posey Circuit Court judge before his appointment to the high court, returned to the county to practice law, eventually living and practicing law with his son-in-law, Gustavus Menzies, out of what is known as the Hovey House, which is across from the current courthouse.

Hovey, who had taught himself to be a stonemason when he was orphaned at age fifteen, was given the honor of laying the first brick for Posey County's historic courthouse on July 4, 1876.

Besides being in the thick of combat during the Civil War, Hovey also served as martial law commander in Indiana during the last year of the war. From 1865 to 1870, he was the U.S. envoy to Peru and served one term in Congress, 1886 to 1888, just prior to being elected governor.

Hovey's rise to positions of prominence and his close associations with other distinguished public servants did not cloud his clear vision of human nature. As he himself wrote in defense of his fellow Hoosier, General Lew Wallace, who had been unfairly maligned by biographers of Ulysses S. Grant and William Tecumseh Sherman, all people, including Grant and Sherman, are fallible and to ignore a hero's faults actually demeans his humanity. In that regard, Hovey's behavior concerning Posey County's darkest episode should not be ignored.

There is no hard evidence that Hovey was directly involved in the murder of five black men on the courthouse campus by a white mob consisting of hundreds of Posey County's leading citizens on October 12, 1878, nor in the subsequent successful cover-up and pogrom that drove out half of the county's black population. There is, also, no evidence that he tried to prevent it or seek justice for the victims. This remains one of the few question marks as to Hovey's public service and legal career.

Stonemason, attorney, trial judge, constitutional convention delegate, Supreme Court judge, major general, martial law commander, diplomat, and governor, Hovey was the consummate "Hoosier" public servant. He served on the Court but a short time, but served Indiana his whole lifetime.

JAMES M. REDWINE, JD, is judge of the Posey County, Indiana Circuit Court. He is the author of *Judge Lynch!* (2008), a historical novel, and *Gavel Gamut Greetings from JPeg Ranch* (2009), an anthology. Redwine is a faculty member of the National Judicial College.

SELECTED BIBLIOGRAPHY

Dickson, Brent E., Thomas A. John, and Katherine A. Wyman. "Lawyers and Judges as Framers of Indiana's 1851 Constitution." *Indiana Law Review* 30 (1997): 397–408.

Hovey, Alvin P. "Autobiography of Alvin P. Hovey's Early Life." With introduction and notes by Elfreida Lang. *Indiana Magazine of History* 48 (March 1952): 71–84.

London, Lena. "Homestead Exemption in the Indiana Constitution." *Indiana Magazine of History* 44 (September 1948): 267–80.

Phillips, Clifton J. *Indiana in Transition: The Emergence of an Industrial Commonwealth, 1880–1920*. Indianapolis: Indiana Historical Bureau and Indiana Historical Society, 1968.

CASES CITED
Falkenburgh v. Jones, 5 Ind. 296 (1854).

SAMUEL B. GOOKINS

January 1, 1855–December 10, 1857

B. MICHAEL McCORMICK

Newspaper editor and publisher, attorney, judge, state legislator, horticulturist, author, and poet, Samuel Barnes Gookins, the fifteenth judge of the Indiana Supreme Court, was one of Indiana's most esteemed and versatile men.

The youngest child of William and Rhoda Munger Gookins, Samuel was born on May 30, 1809, in Rupert, Vermont. His father died when he was five years old and, after a brief residency in upstate New York, his mother brought Samuel and older brother Milo to Vigo County in 1823, where she died in January 1825. During his late teen years, Gookins lived near Fort Harrison with the family of Captain Daniel Stringham, father of Rear Admiral Silas Horton Stringham. Milo moved to Vermillion County in 1826, the year Samuel apprenticed himself to pioneer Terre Haute newspaper publisher John Willson Osborn. On January 23, 1834, Gookins married Osborn's daughter, Mary Caroline.

After brief stints as editor of the *Vincennes Gazette* and the *Western Register and Terre Haute Advertiser*, Gookins studied law for four years with Amory Kinney, a progressive lawyer who freed Polly, the slave of Vincennes innkeeper Hyacinth Lasselle, by taking her case to the Supreme Court (*State v. Lasselle*). Admitted to the bar in 1834, Gookins became a partner with Kinney and Salmon Wright in Terre Haute and served briefly on the town council. On July 27, 1850, after the resignation of John Law, Governor Joseph A. Wright appointed Gookins judge of the First Judicial Circuit, which included Vigo and several other counties. The assignment lasted through January 1851.

Meanwhile, the Gookinses acquired thirteen scenic acres a mile south of Terre Haute, known as Strawberry Hill for its abundant wild fruit. An avocational horticulturist, Gookins adorned the estate with flora and made substantial improvements to the land. In 1851, following the adoption of a new state constitution, he was elected to the Indiana House as a Whig and, while serving a one-year term, worked diligently drafting the new civil code. In his initial effort to seek a seat on the Court in 1852, he was defeated by Democrat Addison L. Roache. However, running as a Republican in 1854, he was elected to the state's highest court by a large margin. On September 22, 1857, after earning a reputation for having a mind "of high order, clear, strong and concentrative," Gookins resigned, citing poor health and the inadequate $1,200 annual salary. The resignation was effective December 10. In 1858 Gookins founded the Chicago law firm of Gookins, Roberts and Thomas while commuting frequently to Terre Haute on weekends until 1875, when he closed the Chicago law office. During this time, his poetry was published in several national journals.

The Gookinses had four children but two died in infancy. Son James Farrington, cofounder of the first Indiana School of Art, became a distinguished artist. Daughter Lucy married George C. Duy, a New York lawyer, and the couple resided at Strawberry Hill. Upon returning to Terre Haute, Gookins formed a law partnership with his son-in-law and began writing a history of Vigo County, which became a part of H. W. Beckwith's *History of Vigo and Parke Counties*. Gookins died unexpectedly at Strawberry Hill on June 14, 1880, a few months before the book was published.

B. MICHAEL MCCORMICK, JD, is a semiretired attorney in Terre Haute, Indiana. He is a columnist with the *Terre Haute Tribune-Star*, the author of *Terre Haute: Queen City of the Wabash* (2005) and *Century: 100 Years in the Wabash Valley*, coauthor of *George W. Cutter, America's Poet Warrior* (2001), and a contributing author for the *Encyclopedia of Northern Kentucky*. McCormick is also the Vigo County Historian.

SELECTED BIBLIOGRAPHY

Abbott, Lyman. *Reminiscences*. Boston and New York: Houghton Mifflin Company, 1915.

Beckwith, Hiram W. *History of Vigo and Parke Counties*. Chicago: H. H. Hill and N. Iddings, 1880.

Condit, Blackford. *The History of Early Terre Haute, Indiana from 1816 to 1840*. New York: A. S. Barnes, 1900.

McCormick, Mike. *Terre Haute: Queen City of the Wabash*. Mount Pleasant, SC: Arcadia Publishing, 2005.

McKivigan, John R. *Abolitionism and American Law*. New York: Garland Publishing, 1999.

Oakey, Charles C. *Greater Terre Haute and Vigo County*. Chicago: Lewis Publishing Company, 1908.

Parker, Benjamin S., and Enos B. Heiney. *Poets and Poetry of Indiana*. New York: Silver, Burdett and Company, 1900.

CASE CITED

State v. Lasselle, 1 Blackf. 60 (Ind. 1820).

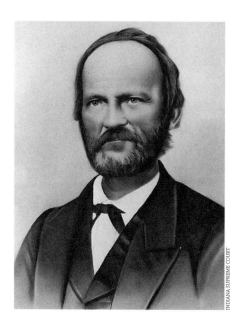

JAMES M. HANNA

December 10, 1857–January 3, 1865

JAMES R. WILLIAMS

James McLean Hanna, who served as the sixteenth judge of the Indiana Supreme Court, was a loyal Democrat active in antebellum and wartime Indiana politics. His private law practice was intermittent at best as he devoted considerable parts of his career to elective offices.

Born on October 25, 1816, into the prominent Hanna clan of Franklin County in the southeast part of the state, he spent most of his youth working on the family farm. Hanna had only a few months of formal education, but through reading books he "acquired a breadth of thought and . . . culture rarely attained by one of his age."

Trained in the law by an apprenticeship in Brookville, Hanna earned his law license in 1841 and then "packed his saddlebags full of clothes and books, and mounted a pony and started west." He chose Bowling Green, which was then the county seat of Clay County. It was there that he married Elizabeth Susan Burton, with whom he had a son and two daughters. Hanna's entry into Democratic politics began in earnest shortly thereafter with his appointment as private secretary to Governor James Whitcomb. Hanna was then elected prosecuting attorney for the Seventh Circuit (Sullivan, Parke, Knox, Vigo, Putnam, Clay, and Vermillion counties) for a single two-year term from 1844 through 1846. After losing his race for state representative in 1847, Hanna won three consecutive terms for the state senate, representing Clay, Sullivan, and Vigo counties from 1849 to 1852.

Hanna moved to Terre Haute in 1854 to set up a law practice and was then elected Vigo County Circuit judge a year later. Upon the resignation of Judge Samuel B. Gookins in 1857, Hanna was appointed to the high court by Governor Ashbel P. Willard. He was elected to serve a full term on the Court in 1858, defeating William D. Griswold of Terre Haute. The three other Democratic candidates for the Court also were elected, setting the stage for the highly contentious partisan battle waged between the Democratic judges and the strong-willed Republican governor Oliver P. Morton, who took office in 1861.

One of the most highly charged issues occurred when the Democratic-controlled general assembly adjourned in 1863 without approving an appropriations measure. With an interest payment on the state's debt coming due, the governor directed the state auditor, Joseph Ristine, a Democrat, to make the payment. He was advised by the attorney general, Oscar Hord, another Democrat, to refuse. In two decisions rendered on the same day, prompted by conflicting rulings of the Marion Circuit Court, the Court upheld Ristine's refusal to make the interest payment. Samuel E. Perkins wrote one of the decisions and Hanna the other (*Ristine v. State ex rel. Board of Commissioners of Sinking Fund* and *State ex rel. Board of Commissioners of Sinking Fund v. Ristine*).

Hanna and his Democratic colleagues lost their bids to stay on the Court in the election of 1864 as Republicans, led by Morton, won all major state offices, including the four Court seats, and regained control of the state legislature. After leaving the bench, Hanna was for a brief period the political editor of the *Indianapolis Sentinel,* a leading Democratic newspaper, and then returned to public office with his election to the state senate in 1868 representing Sullivan and Clay counties. Hanna, described as someone who sympathized with the South during the Civil War, resigned his seat in protest when the state senate deliberated ratifying the Fifteenth Amendment, giving blacks the right to vote.

In retirement, Hanna spent most of his time on his large farm in Sullivan County, which contained the first underground coal mine in the county. He died at his farm on January 15, 1872. In tribute on January 17, 1872, the *Franklin Democrat* wrote that he was "a genial, well-disposed man, of more than average abilities, and when once engaged, never tired until his work was completed."

JAMES R. WILLIAMS, JD, is a partner with Defur Voran LP. He was Union Circuit Court judge (1999–2005) and senior judge (2005–7).

SELECTED BIBLIOGRAPHY

Franklin Democrat, January 19, 1872.

Monks, Leander J., ed. *Courts and Lawyers of Indiana*. Indianapolis: Federal Publishing Company, 1915.

Thornbrough, Emma Lou. *Indiana in the Civil War Era, 1850–1880*. Indianapolis: Indiana Historical Bureau and Indiana Historical Society, 1965.

Thornton, William W. "The Supreme Court of Indiana." *The Green Bag* 4 (May–June 1892).

CASES CITED

Ristine v. State of Indiana ex rel. Board of Commissioners of Sinking Fund, 20 Ind. 328 (1863).

State ex rel. The Board of Commissioners of Sinking Fund v. Joseph Ristine, 20 Ind. 345 (1863).

JAMES L. WORDEN
January 16, 1858–January 3, 1865; January 3, 1871–December 2, 1882

ALLEN SHARP

The appointment of James Lorenzo Worden as the seventeenth judge to the Indiana Supreme Court in 1858 by Democratic governor Ashbel P. Willard followed a political battle that was decided by the Court itself. The trigger for the series of events that unfolded was the announcement in the summer of 1857 by Judge William Z. Stuart that he intended to resign effective January 1858. The political parties, therefore, nominated candidates for Stuart's position, and in the fall 1857 election Republican Horace P. Biddle won. But Willard, known as a fierce partisan, disavowed the election results, claiming that no vacancy actually existed on the Court at the time of the election. Biddle sued, and the Court, with a Democratic majority, supported the governor's position in deciding *Biddle v. Willard*.

Worden was appointed and then won a full six-year term on the Court in the fall 1858 election, as did the three other Democratic Supreme Court candidates. After moving to Indiana in 1844, Worden, who was born in 1819 in Massachusetts, spent most of his forty years in the state in public service. He was elected prosecuting attorney for the Tenth Judicial District a year after his arrival and continued being reelected to that position until becoming judge of the same circuit in 1855. After his defeat for re-election to the Supreme Court in the Republican landslide of 1864, Worden was elected mayor of Fort Wayne in 1865, a position he held for only a year, resigning due to the increased demands of his law practice. Worden was again elected to the Court in 1870 and reelected in 1876, resigning in early December 1882 after being elected judge of the Allen County Superior Court. He died less than two years later.

During Worden's first term, the Supreme Court was confronted with a series of acrimonious issues stemming from the Civil War, several of which dealt with the imposition of martial law and denial of habeas corpus. Most of the controversial decisions during that time were written by Judge Samuel E. Perkins, with concurrence of Worden and the other judges. Two cases in particular illustrate the legal wrangling. In *Skeen v. Monkeimer*, the Court issued a "stinging rebuke to the claims of military authority" when it found no evidence to support the arrest and jailing of a man accused of stealing a horse belonging to the U.S. government. The second decision, *Griffin v. Wilcox*, was another strike against martial law with the Court ruling that a saloon keeper arrested and imprisoned for violating an order by the military prohibiting the sale of liquor to enlisted men had broken no civil law. As historian Emma Lou Thornbrough noted, the principles articulated in these cases "received a lasting vindication" by the U.S. Supreme Court in *Ex parte Milligan*, an 1866 decision overruling the conviction of a northern Indiana lawyer by a military court.

When Worden returned to the high bench in 1871, he was again joining a four-member, all-Democratic Court. By 1875, after the general assembly created a fifth position on the Court to help alleviate the backlog in cases, the Court was composed of five Democrats with the election of Biddle, who had switched parties in the years following the decision that nullified his election to the Court as a Republican. Democrats continued their domination of the Court through Worden's final year as judge in 1882. This one-sided nature led to charges that the Court was playing politics with its 1880 *State v. Swift* decision that invalidated the results of the votes on seven constitutional amendments, which included changing the date of general elections from October to November. It was charged that the Court's motive was to help a Hoosier Democrat win the party's nomination for president at the upcoming convention because delegates would realize a probable October win in Indiana could provide the candidate with momentum going into November voting elsewhere. The conspiracy theory was discounted by Court historian Jerome Withered as "unlikely."

The assessments of Worden, who had the third-longest tenure of nineteenth-century Supreme Court judges, tend to be favorable, though Withered said that he "acquired a notorious reputation for reversing criminal convictions" because of his highly technical opinions. Another critic said that "more than one criminal has cheated the punishment he justly merited" because of this habit. One critique of the Court from 1857 to 1862, a period during which Worden served, called its work "slipshod," but singled out Worden for praise, calling him a superior judge "who often wrote, when the spirit moved him, a very able opinion." The observation, written in 1899, added that the Court had "reached its highest point in 1881" when it was composed of Worden, George V. Howk, William E. Niblack, William A. Woods, and Bryon K. Elliott.

ALLEN SHARP, JD, was senior judge of the U.S. District Court for the Northern District of Indiana at the time of his death, July 10, 2009. Sharp served as judge and chief judge of the Northern District and judge of the Indiana Court of Appeals before his appointment to the U.S. District Court. He was the author of several historical articles including "Justices Seeking the Presidency" and "Presidents as Supreme Court Advocates."

SELECTED BIBLIOGRAPHY

Stoll, John B. *History of the Indiana Democracy, 1816–1916*. Indianapolis: Indiana Democratic Publishing Company, 1917.
Thornbrough, Emma Lou. "Judge Perkins, the Indiana Supreme Court, and the Civil War." *Indiana Magazine of History* 60 (March 1964).

CASES CITED
Biddle v. Willard, 10 Ind. 47 (1857).
Skeen v. Monkeimer, 21 Ind. 1 (1863).
Griffin v. Wilcox, 21 Ind. 370 (1863).
The State v. Swift, 69 Ind. 505 (1880).
Ex parte Milligan, 71 U.S. 2 (1866).

JAMES S. FRAZER
January 3, 1865–January 3, 1871

DONALD B. KITE SR.

Described as "a man of more than national reputation," James Sommerville Frazer, the eighteenth judge of the Indiana Supreme Court, was either appointed or offered appointive office by Presidents Abraham Lincoln, Ulysses S. Grant, and Benjamin Harrison, and Grant seriously considered him for the U.S. Supreme Court. Given Frazer's accomplishments at both the national and state level, the superlative pertaining to Frazer's reputation hardly seems an exaggeration.

He was born on July 17, 1824, in Hollidaysburg, Pennsylvania, to parents of Scottish descent. Frazer, whose mother died when he was two years old, moved with his father to Wayne County, Indiana, in 1837. He later studied law in the Winchester office of Judge Moorman Way, teaching school during the winter months in order to cover his expenses. Frazer was admitted to the bar in 1845 and opened a law office in Warsaw. He began serving the first of three terms as a state representative in 1847.

Frazer married Caroline McLean DeFrees in 1848. One of her brothers, John D. DeFrees, was editor of the *Indianapolis Journal,* a leading Republican newspaper, and later served as the U.S. superintendent of public printing under Lincoln. Her other brother was Indiana congressman Joseph H. DeFrees. The Frazers, who were married for forty-five years, eventually had five daughters and one son.

In 1852 Frazer was elected prosecuting attorney of a six-county circuit and in 1855, while serving his last term in the Indiana General Assembly, chaired the House education committee that drafted the state's new school law to replace the 1852 act declared unconstitutional by the Court. The new law permitted townships to levy taxes to pay for school buildings and "Frazer's mode of equalizing the revenues to the townships prevailed for the balance of the nineteenth century."

In the summer of 1855 Frazer moved his family to Waukegan, Illinois, to escape the outbreak of various diseases then afflicting Warsaw. After health conditions in the city vastly improved, the Frazer family returned in 1862, and he formed a partnership with prominent Warsaw attorney George W. Frasier. Also in 1862, he was appointed by Lincoln to serve as assessor of internal revenue for the district that included Warsaw, a position he held for less than a year.

The Republican tidal wave of 1864 propelled Frazer and three other GOP candidates onto Indiana's then four-member Court. Although he served only one six-year term, Frazer, according to Court historian Jerome Withered, fundamentally changed how the Court operated by getting it to focus on the merits of cases "rather than refusing to review on the basis of procedural technicalities." Furthermore, the Court also stopped "the practice of reversing most appeals of criminal convictions."

During Frazer's years on the bench, the Court decided a number of noteworthy cases, including *Smith v. Moody,* which was clearly one of the most significant cases in the Court's history. In this decision, the four judges, sometimes referred to as "the Lincoln four," declared unconstitutional Article 13 of the state constitution that prohibited blacks and persons of "mixed race" from entering into or settling in Indiana and voided contracts entered into with such individuals. The judges ruled these provisions violated the privileges and immunities clause of the U.S. Constitution.

While Frazer had "earned wide respect for his abilities while serving on the bench," he declined renomination. He was hardly finished with public service. In January 1871 Grant appointed him to a three-member international commission charged with adjusting claims made by citizens of the United States and Great Britain that arose during the Civil War. From 1873 to 1875 Frazer was employed by the U.S. Treasury Department to adjust claims of cotton growers whose crops were captured or destroyed during the war.

In 1879, following the passage of legislation that called for the revision of Indiana statutes, Frazer was appointed to head a board of revision whose other members were John H. Stotsenberg and David Turpie, also distinguished lawyers with state legislative experience. The board's work led to the Revised Code of 1881, the Revised Criminal Code and Offense Act, and to at least one other codification. It was called "one of the most carefully prepared compilations of statutory law yet attempted."

Nearly two decades after he left the Court, Frazer was appointed by Governor Alvin P. Hovey in 1889 to be Kosciusko County Circuit judge. During the year he served as circuit judge, his decision regarding the method of obtaining and distributing standard textbooks was reversed by the Court in *State ex rel. Snoke v. Blue, School Trustee.* Also in 1889, Frazer was a candidate to be on a commission to settle American claims against Venezuela. On August 16, 1889, Harrison wrote to Secretary of State James G. Blaine, when another candidate was unable to accept the position, stating "I now only think of Judge Jas. S. Frazer of Ind.—one of the best Sup. Judges we have had in later years and once on a Com[mission] here." Frazer, too, declined because of his duties as circuit judge.

On February 20, 1893, Frazer died at his home of what was then known as Bright's disease (acute or chronic nephritis), after a two-month decline. The funeral was held at the family's home and was attended by a "large concourse of people that braved the fi[e]rce winds that prevailed." He was buried in Warsaw's Oakwood Cemetery in the family plot situated on a knoll overlooking a lake under a marker that provided no indication of Frazer's service on Indiana's highest court or his years of public service.

Nearly thirty years later, Frazer's wife, Caroline, died. She was memorialized by the Kosciusko Bar Association as having shared the "hardships and struggles of the backwoods circuit riding lawyers of Indiana." One of the Frazers' daughters, Harriet DeFrees Frazer, who died in 1944, served as court reporter for the Kosciusko Circuit Court for forty years and was said to be the first court reporter in Indiana.

DONALD B. KITE, SR., JD, is a partner with Dean-Webster, Wright and Kite, LLP. He is coauthor of *Federal Justice in Indiana: The History of the United States District Court for the Southern District of Indiana* (2007), recipient of Defense Trial Counsel of Indiana Defense Lawyer of the Year Award (2005), and corecipient of the Indianapolis Bar Association's Dr. John Morton Finney Jr. Award for Excellence in Legal education (2007).

SELECTED BIBLIOGRAPHY

British Parliament. "Report by Her Majesty's Agent of the Proceedings and Awards of the Mixed Commission on British and American Claims..." *Parliamentary Papers.* House of Lords: London, 1874.

Frazer, James Ristine. "Autobiography of James Ristine Frazer." Unpublished and undated. In possession of Eric T. Bailey, Scottsdale, AZ.

"The Kosciusko County Bar: Reminiscences of Its Early Days,"

Progressive Men and Women of Kosciusko County, Indiana. Logansport, IN: B. F. Bowen, 1902.

Ristine, Ben F. *Frazer, Defrees, and Ristine Families.* Lakeland, FL: Author, 1945.

Warsaw Northern Indianian (Mammoth Holiday Sheet), December 28, 1878.

Williams, Sandra Boyd. "The Indiana Supreme Court and the Struggle against Slavery." 30 *Indiana Law Review* 305 (Winter 1997).

CASES CITED

Smith v. Moody and Others, 26 Ind. 299 (1866).

The State ex rel. Snoke et al. v. Blue, Trustee, 122 Ind. 600 (1890).

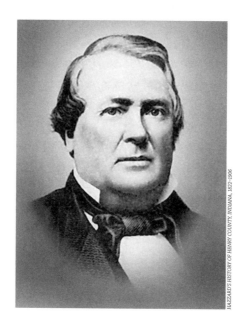

JEHU T. ELLIOTT
January 3, 1865–January 3, 1871

GRETA MORRIS SCODRO

Like many of his era, Jehu Tindle Elliott was born in a log cabin near a small settlement and received minimal formal education. But he lived in a period of great change. At the close of the Civil War, having sent his sons to college, he traveled by train from his now-populated county seat town of New Castle to take the bench as the nineteenth judge of the Indiana Supreme Court.

Elliott was born February 7, 1813, in Richmond, Indiana, into a Quaker family who, opposing slavery, had left North Carolina and moved North. In 1823 the family moved thirty miles west to settle near New Castle (population 150) in Henry County. They built a log cabin south of town. Money was tight for the large family, according to a brother, and as the twelve children grew, they "found it necessary to shift for themselves." Elliott made his own shoes for years.

After attending such local schools as were available, Elliott taught for two years, then studied law with Martin M. Ray in Centerville. He was admitted to the bar in 1833 at age twenty and began practicing with Ray. During the ten-year period from 1834 to 1844, Elliott held a series of public offices, including county treasurer, assistant secretary of the House of Representatives, prosecuting attorney (for Delaware, Fayette, Grant, Henry, Randolph, Rush, Union, and Wayne counties), and one term as state senator. He was elected judge of the Sixth Circuit (Henry, Jay, Randolph, and Wayne counties) by the legislature in 1844 and reelected in 1851. Elliott traveled the circuit by horseback, carrying law books and papers in one side of his leather saddlebag and clothes in the other.

Elliott resigned as judge to become president of a railroad and was soon sent East to obtain financing for a railroad proposed from Logansport through Kokomo, Elwood, Anderson, and New Castle to Richmond. In his book *Amazing Tales from Indiana*, Fred Cavinder writes that Elliott faced a tough sell because New Yorkers considered Hoosiers backwoods figures associated with hogs and ague. But because the judge was "quick and witty, Indiana acquired a railroad." Elliott won the day during a festive occasion when he was asked to name Indiana's favorite musical instrument. It was the swinette, Elliott declared, explaining that it was a long box divided into compartments. The story continues:

"A hog is thrust head first into each compartment from the open side and the aperture is closed with a door through which only the tail of the hog protrudes. In the largest compartment is a great old boar to represent the deepest brass. The next hog is slightly smaller and has a correspondingly higher squeal. The smallest is a little pig with a high-pitched squeak. The performer sits behind the box, places his music before him, and plays the instrument by pulling the tails in much the same way that a piano player strikes the keys. The hogs and pigs respond with proper notes and produce the most delightful music imaginable.

"The Easterners were charmed," Cavinder concludes, and invested the needed money. Painted on the side of the first engine (named Swinette), was a picture of Elliott carrying a pig under his arm.

His business with the railroad concluded, Elliott returned to public life. He ran again for circuit court judge (now the Tenth Judicial Circuit, encompassing Henry, Jay, Randolph, and Wayne counties) in a direct election as specified in the 1851 constitution, and won. He won again in 1861; no one ran against him.

In 1864, as the outcome of the Civil War became apparent, Republicans won landslide victories nationally and statewide. Elliott was one of the four new faces who took seats on the Court that year, along with fellow Republicans James S. Frazer, Robert C. Gregory, and Charles A. Ray. Their arrival may have been a breath of fresh air—four bright, forthright, hardworking men of judicial temperament. When President Abraham Lincoln was assassinated in April, Frazer, who had known Lincoln personally, and Elliott delivered a eulogy in the courtroom to mark the sad event: "[T]he death of Abraham Lincoln by the hand of an assassin, in view of the motive for the act, and the circumstances which surrounded both the victim and the deed, filled every mind with amazement and consternation, and every heart with inexpressible sorrow and grief."

Elliott did his share of the Court's business deciding cases and writing opinions. He authored some four hundred opinions during his six-year term, reading handwritten briefs and transcripts. A friend from New Castle had "known him to sit up all night . . . delving into law books, scattered about on desk and table and chairs, each opened at some particular page, writing and compiling his opinion in some important case." From all reports, he was respected and genuinely liked. One acquaintance described Elliott as "ruddy of face, an English beef-eating looking man with big round head and massive body, mild and genial in manner, a very sound and able lawyer, an honest, conscientious and capable man. . . . Scorning the quibbles and technicalities of the practice, he stood on the bedrock of general principles." Elliott's written court decisions seem plainly written and thoughtful, compact by today's standards. Most involved civil cases and addressed the issues of that day—Civil War bounty cases, actions on promissory notes, land disputes, actions for slander, and criminal charges that a person "desecrated the Sabbath" by selling a cigar on Sunday. He dissented only occasionally."

At the end of his single term in 1871, Elliott returned to New Castle and his law practice, having served twenty-four years as a judge. By that time, one son and several nephews were lawyers. Elliott died on February 12, 1876, at age sixty-three, in New Castle, survived by his wife, Hanna Branson, and several children. The judge's stately home near the courthouse is gone, but a small family cemetery on land that was known then as "the Elliott farm" and "Elliott Street" in New Castle remain.

GRETA MORRIS SCODRO, JD, is deputy administrator and staff attorney for the Indiana Supreme Court (since 1995). A native Hoosier, she is distantly related to Justices Jehu T. Elliott and Douglas J. Morris, and she was a law clerk to Justice Jon D. Krahulik.

SELECTED BIBLIOGRAPHY

Dailey, Joseph, Biographical and Historical Record of Adams and Wells County, "The Bar" (copied from www.rootsweb.ancestry.com/~inwells/bio/1887/586-597.html).
Hamm, Thomas, "Henry County's Three Migrations," *Henry County Historicalog* 18, no. 2 (1990).
Hazzard, George, *Hazzard's History of Henry County Indiana 1822–1906, Military Edition*. New Castle, IN: 1906.
Pleas, Elwood. *Henry County Past and Present*. New Castle, IN: 1871.

CASES CITED

Board of Com'rs of Fulton Co. v. Onstott, 29 Ind. 384 (1868).
Clegg and another v. Fithian, 32 Ind. 90 (1869).
Foltz v. State, 33 Ind. 215 (1870).
Heavilon v. Heavilon, 29 Ind. 509 (1868).
Mousler and wife v. Harding, 33 Ind. 176 (1870).
Reilly v. Cavanaugh and others, 32 Ind. 214 (1869).
Romig v. City of Lafayette, 33 Ind. 30 (1870).
Weaver v. Trustees of Wabash & Erie Canal, 28 Ind. 112 (1867).

CHARLES A. RAY
January 3, 1865–January 3, 1871

DAVID J. REMONDINI

Indiana's twentieth Supreme Court judge, Charles Andrew Ray of Indianapolis was an erudite man of letters who rubbed shoulders with the titans of the state's history and closed his lengthy career as a renowned legal scholar. Including tenures in Washington, D.C., and on Wall Street, his legal work spanned from the Civil War to the early days of the twentieth century, and he was the attorney of record on a case that was decided in 1906 by the U.S. Supreme Court.

It was almost inevitable that Ray would find a path to public service. Born in the Third Ward on the north side of Indianapolis on September 3, 1829, he was the son of an early settler, a prominent businessman and civic leader, and Marion County's first county clerk, James M. Ray, and his wife, Marie Rebecca Coe. The middle son between two sisters, Charles attended the Marion County Seminary and also the Sabbath School, founded by his father, where he was a classmate of Lew Wallace, author of *Ben-Hur*. It is quite obvious that the Ray family was well connected in Indianapolis. They were at times guests of Calvin Fletcher, a prominent Indianapolis attorney and businessman, and young "Charly Ray," as Fletcher called him, even stayed overnight as a youngster of eleven at Fletcher's home. Later, Ray attended Brown University in Providence, Rhode Island, for a brief period (1848–49), but returned to Indianapolis due to the illness of his father. On June 6, 1849, he married Laura Amelia Mills and the couple eventually had five children. To pursue his legal career, Ray studied at Harvard Law School, where he enrolled on September 2, 1853, before leaving sometime the following year.

Upon his return to Indianapolis, he entered the law practice with James Morrison, who had been Indiana's first attorney general and a Shelby County judge. Ray was named judge advocate of the Sixth Brigade Indiana on April 19, 1861, and later that year he was appointed by Governor Oliver P. Morton to the bench of the Twelfth Common Pleas Court to replace John Coburn, whom Morton had named colonel in the Thirty-third Regiment Indiana Volunteer Infantry. These actions prompted a lawsuit by a candidate for judge of the common pleas court in an election slated to be held shortly after Ray was named to the position. But the Supreme Court that Ray later joined ruled that no vacancy existed and Ray's appointment to the bench was valid. Ray was later elected to a four-year term to the same office as a Republican. Just over a year later, he accompanied Morton to the dedication of the cemetery at Gettysburg. He was even involved in the planning for a short-lived law school at what is now Butler University. While still on the local bench he signed a letter to Secretary of War Edwin M. Stanton along with Morton and other leading citizens urging that Indiana soldiers be allowed to return home to vote in the 1864 election. With fewer than a dozen years in practice, Ray was elected that year as one of the four Republican judges on the Indiana Supreme Court. It was the first time in the history of the Court that the four incumbent jurists were replaced by a completely new bench.

Ray, who served from January 3, 1865, to January 3, 1871, is listed in volumes 27, 30, and 33 of *Indiana Reports* as chief justice, a position that rotated at the time. One authority asserts the four judges focused largely on legal matters and for the most part avoided partisanship and political warfare. It was also the most productive court to date for a given six-year period, producing eleven volumes of cases. In 1869 Ray received a honorary doctor of laws degree from Indiana University. He was renominated at the state convention without opposition, but the entire state Republican ticket was swept out of office in 1870. During his legal career to this point, Ray had accumulated some wealth and reported assets of $25,000 in real estate and $10,000 in personal property.

With this measure of financial independence, Ray embarked on an extended overseas journey with his twenty-year-old daughter, Florence. Passport records show he applied in 1872 to travel to Ireland, England, Scotland, France, Italy, Germany, and perhaps even Switzerland. Noted Indiana legal scholar Leander J. Monks wrote that "it appears" Ray moved to California sometime in the 1870s and became a judge there, but there is no documentation to support the claim. In fact, the order book of the Marion Superior Court lists him as a member of the local bar in 1871. In the 1880s he did move to Washington, D.C., and was appointed a law clerk in 1881 of the post office by Postmaster General Thomas L. Lange. In congressional testimony regarding staffing levels at the Post Office Department, a ranking post office official, presumably Ray, was described as a "gentleman of very extraordinary talent and capacity and experience as a jurist." Ray also had some impact on the life of poet Walt Whitman when he interpreted mail regulations to mean that the widely censored book, *Leaves of Green*, was "mailable." Ray resigned in 1883 and returned to Indianapolis to practice law.

In the latter part of his legal career Ray worked on several legal treatises. The preface to one, dated March 1, 1892, indicates he became part of a New York City law firm located at 40 Wall Street. At least one of the four law books he authored, *Negligence Imposed Duties, Personal*, was well received. This 1891 tome by Ray, who described himself in the book as "Ex-Chief Justice of the Supreme Court of Indiana," was considered significant enough to be listed in *Appleton's Annual Cyclopaedia Register of Important Events* and rated a favorable citation as an "excellent work" in an 1893 Indiana Supreme Court opinion. Another editor declared that work "could not be improved upon." A reviewer in the *Harvard Law Review* was also impressed with Ray's work on this particular law book. He praised his handling of issues involving interstate commerce, but did note that at times it was a bit repetitious. Ray was also an editor of the *Western Reporter*, a legal publication based in Rochester, New York, which also published several of his law books.

Even at the age of seventy, Ray continued to review the law of the day. In 1899 he was listed as the editor for the Washington Law Book Company of "American practice reports" (1897–99), which is described as the "Official leading cases in all state and federal courts." In a review of that work, the author said Ray's "ability and reputation as Chief Justice of Indiana are acknowledged to be of the highest order." Ray also served as dean of the law department for the Columbian Correspondence College, based in Washington, D.C. Promotional material for the college described him as "one of the best known law-writers and jurists in the United States."

Ray did not limit his writing to legal writings, and he exhibited a touch of flair that even in a time known for flowery language seemed to exhibit just the right mix of literary license. A dedication in one of his law books is an ode to deceased acquaintances such as Fletcher and Samuel Merrill and other prominent residents of Indianapolis. He wrote with some eloquence, "Let not the limit of their lives, contract the circle of their influence."

Research did not reveal a date of death for Ray. However, he was still practicing law in 1906 and was listed that year as the attorney of record in a U.S. Supreme Court case that involved the Columbian Correspondence College and whether it was entitled to second-class mailing privileges.

DAVID J. REMONDINI is chief deputy executive director, Indiana Supreme Court, Division of State Court Administration. He is former counsel to Chief Justice Randall T. Shepard. Remondini, a former reporter for the *Indianapolis Star*, is the author of more than 1,600 newspaper articles and several magazine articles for local, state, and national publications.

SELECTED BIBLIOGRAPHY

Bodenhamer, David J., and Robert G. Barrows, eds. *The Encyclopedia of Indianapolis*. Bloomington and Indianapolis: Indiana University Press, 1994.

Dewey, Donald O. "Hoosier Justice: The Journal of David McDonald," *Indiana Magazine of History* 62 (Sept. 1966).

Dunn, Jacob P., Jr. *The History of Indianapolis*. Chicago: Lewis Publishing, 1910.

Foulke, William Dudley. *Life of Oliver P. Morton*. Indianapolis: Bowen-Merrill, 1899.

Ray, Charles A. *Contractual Limitations, Including Trade Strikes and Conspiracies, Corporate Trusts and Combinations*. Rochester, NY: Lawyers' Cooperative Publishing Company, 1892.

———. *Negligence of Imposed Duties*. Rochester, NY: Lawyers' Cooperative Publishing Company, 1891.

Thornbrough, Gayle, Dorothy L. Riker, and Paula J. Corpuz, eds., *The Diary of Calvin Fletcher*. 9 vols. Indianapolis: Indiana Historical Society, 1972–83.

Washington Post, August 18, 1891.

CASES CITED

Faris v. Hoberg et al., 134 Ind. 269 (1893).

Colombia Correspondence College v. Cortelyou, 200 U.S. 615 (1906).

ROBERT C. GREGORY
January 3, 1865–January 3, 1871

BRADFORD W. SAMPLE

The future twenty-first judge of the Indiana Supreme Court and the middle son of a farmer, trader, surveyor, and politician dreamed as a youth of being a successful merchant. His parents, James and Elizabeth Gregory, trekked from North Carolina to Kentucky, where Robert Crockett Gregory was born, and then into Indiana in 1813. James Gregory served as a state representative and a justice of the peace in several Indiana counties almost continuously from 1820 to 1839. All three sons—Robert, Leroy, and Benjamin—as well as a grandson, John, were Indiana legislators, giving the family three generations of service in the legislature during the nineteenth century.

At age sixteen, Robert clerked in the jobbing dry goods house of Samuel Hanna and Company of Fort Wayne. After marrying, Robert and his wife, Elizabeth, moved to Fountain County and then to Crawfordsville, where he continued to engage in trade until being admitted to the bar in 1838. Gregory first partnered with Alexander Thomson before moving to Lafayette in 1843. The Whig Party nominated him to finish the unexpired term of a state senator in 1841. Gregory won re-election to the general assembly from Montgomery County in 1842, but he was unsuccessful in other attempts at political office during the 1840s and 1850s, losing bids for a seat at the 1850 Indiana Constitutional Convention and in his 1852 race for Congress. At the age of fifty he briefly served in the Civil War as a member of the 108th Indiana Infantry Regiment.

In 1864 Gregory won a seat on the Court along with three others, termed "The Lincoln Four," in a Republican sweep of statewide offices. The Court dealt with a number of sensitive political issues arising from the Civil War and the end of slavery. The most significant action of the Court during this period was ruling Article 13 of the 1851 Indiana Constitution unconstitutional. This section prohibited those of African descent from settling permanently in the state and proscribed their ability to enter into contracts with Hoosier citizens.

The case, *Smith v. Moody and Others*, involved a Caucasian who refused to abide by the conditions of a promissory note made with an African American on the grounds that because the man moved to Indiana after adoption of the constitution he was ineligible to make contracts. Therefore, any agreement made was void. In a unanimous opinion, Gregory, then chief justice, wrote that "a free man of color born within the United States is a citizen of the United States, and as such is entitled to become a citizen of any one of the several states, by becoming a resident thereof." The Court thus established the idea that U.S. citizens could not be denied the right to live and work in a state since residency determines citizenship, basing its opinion on the Thirteenth Amendment and the Privileges and Immunities Clause of the Fourteenth Amendment of the U.S. Constitution.

Other cases in which Gregory wrote majority opinions included one, *Reams v. The State*, that overturned the Court's previous ruling on the constitutionality of a temperance law, and another, *Lower v. Wallick*, struck down a state law permitting the imprisonment of fathers for debt when they had not provided support for their illegitimate children. Gregory also wrote opinions concerning the need for railroads to accept their responsibility for damages, *The Indianapolis, Peru, and Chicago Railroad Company v.*

Bishop, and the ability of local governments to create and revise policies, with notice, at their discretion, *The City of Indianapolis v. Miller*.

During his tenure on the Court, Gregory served as the chief justice during three sessions. Typically, Gregory wrote efficient, brief opinions that included a large number of citations establishing precedent and lending credence to his arguments. He was renominated for the Court in 1870 but lost in the fall when Democrats captured all state offices, including the four seats on the Court. After leaving the bench Gregory returned to Lafayette and practiced law with his son, William B., until his death on January 25, 1885.

BRADFORD W. SAMPLE, PhD, is academic vice president, Bryan College. He was a contributor to *The Governors of Indiana* and the author of "A Truly Midwestern City: Indianapolis on the Eve of the Great Depression," *Indiana Magazine of History* 97 (June 2001).

SELECTED BIBLIOGRAPHY

Biographical Record and Portrait Album of Tippecanoe County, Indiana. Chicago: Lewis Publishing Company, 1888.

Bodenhamer, David J., and Randall T. Shepard, eds. *The History of Indiana Law*. Athens: Ohio University Press, 2006.

Shepherd, Rebecca A., Charles W. Calhoun, Elizabeth Shanahan-Shoemaker, and Alan F. January, ed. *A Biographical Directory of the Indiana General Assembly, Volume 1, 1816–1899*. Indianapolis: Indiana Historical Bureau, 1980.

Taylor, Charles W. *Biographical Sketches and Review of the Bench and Bar of Indiana*. Indianapolis: Bench and Bar Publishing Company, 1895.

CASES CITED

The City of Indianapolis v. Miller, 27 Ind. 394 (1866).

The Indianapolis, Peru, and Chicago Railroad Company v. Bishop, 29 Ind. 202 at 203 (1867).

Lower v. Wallick, 25 Ind. 68 (1865).

Reams v. The State, 23 Ind. 111 (1864).

Smith v. Moody and Others 26 Ind. 299 (1866).

JOHN PETTIT
January 3, 1871–January 3, 1877

GREGORY J. DONAT AND JOSHUA S. MALHER

When John Pettit, the twenty-second judge of the Indiana Supreme Court, was a delegate to the Indiana Constitutional Convention in 1850, there likely was some debate about whether he would one day go on to either fame or infamy, but there was no question whatsoever that he would achieve distinction. Throughout the convention, Pettit argued passionately, though ultimately unsuccessfully, against the incorporation of the ideas of racial equality into the revised constitution. Pettit called the statement that all men are created equal "a direct and unequivocal lie" and argued that the constitutional language concerning a defendant's right to trial "by his peers" was meant to "prevent such an anomaly as a white man being tried by Negroes." Despite his failure at altering the constitution, Pettit later expanded his argument, famously calling Thomas Jefferson's concept of equality a "self-evident lie" from the floor of the U.S. Senate. Abraham Lincoln, in the debates shortly before his election as president, condemned Pettit's words as "shameful."

Pettit also openly expressed his disdain for religion and, as a young man, ignored his parents' wishes for him to work in the ministry to pursue law. At the constitutional convention, he alone voted against the resolution to acknowledge God in the preamble. In addition to his strong opinions and fiery rhetoric, Pettit, according to one colleague, "had a mind and force of intellect which could successfully grasp great and mighty questions." Although known as "an uncompromising partisan," he was still "chivalrous and just to his foes."

Pettit's tenacity was on display during the constitutional convention when he persisted in arguing that Supreme Court judges should be elected statewide instead of by district, the method that initially was approved. "It is a mockery to tell me that you will elect a man in one district who is to administer laws for the whole State," Pettit said. Even after his amendment for such a change had been tabled by a decisive margin, Pettit did not surrender. After his vigorous appeal, delegates voted to ask the committee on courts to make the change Pettit suggested. Thus amended, the measure for voters of the state to elect Supreme Court judges was ultimately approved by the delegates.

Pettit was born in Sackets Harbor, New York, on June 24, 1807, and a life punctuated with service in the legislative, judicial, and executive branches of government followed. After passing the bar in 1831, he moved to Lafayette, Indiana, where he practiced law until 1837. He was then elected to the Indiana House of Representatives, serving one term. After this, he became a U.S. district attorney. Pettit then was elected to the U.S. House of Representatives and served for three terms. A loyal Democrat, Pettit was later a presidential elector and an interim U.S. senator, filling the vacancy left by the death of James Whitcomb in 1852. Pettit was defeated in his bid for re-election to the Senate.

After two years as a judge for the Twelfth District in Indiana, Pettit moved west and became chief justice for the Kansas Territories, one of few judges in U.S. history to have served on the high courts of two states. In his twilight years he returned to Lafayette to resume his legal practice and also served as city attorney for four years and as mayor until his election to the Indiana Supreme Court in 1870. Despite the rhetoric of his youth, he

was a fair and well-respected judge, given to judgments of deep contempla-
tion and eloquent expression. His opinions, one legal scholar wrote, were
notable "for the good common-sense often displayed in them." Pettit died
shortly after leaving the Supreme Court on January 17, 1877, in Lafayette,
where his legal career began.

GREGORY J. DONAT, JD, is judge, Tippecanoe Superior Court (Lafayette, IN). He
is a member of the board of directors of the American Judicature Society, the board
of managers of the Indiana Judges Association, and the advisory board of the U.S.
Department of Justice, Office of Victims of Crime. He has served on the faculty of the
National Center for State Courts, National Judicial College, Indiana Judicial Center,
and Indiana Continuing Education Forum.

JOSHUA S. MALHER, JD, clerked for Judge Gregory J. Donat, Tippecanoe Superior Court (Lafayette, IN) and Superior Court Judge William J. Boklund of La Porte
County. He was a member and executive justice of finance for the Valparaiso University School of Law Moot Court.

SELECTED BIBLIOGRAPHY

Basler, Roy P., et al., eds. *The Collected Works of Abraham Lincoln.* 9 vols. New Brunswick,
    NJ: Rutgers University Press, 1953–1955.
Carmony, Donald F. *Indiana, 1816–1850: The Pioneer Era.* Indianapolis: Indiana Histori-
    cal Bureau and Indiana Historical Society, 1998.
Dunn, Jacob Piatt, Jr. *Indiana and Indianans: A History of Aboriginal and Territorial Indi-
    ana and the Century of Statehood.* Chicago: American Historical Society, 1919.
Fowler, H. *Report of the Debates and Proceedings of the Convention for the Revision of the
    Constitution of the State of Indiana 1850,* vols. 1–4. Indianapolis: A. H. Brown, 1850.
Lafayette Journal and Courier, July 13, 1980.
Thornton, W. W. "The Supreme Court of Indiana." *Green Bag* 4 (1892).

ALEXANDER C. DOWNEY
January 3, 1871–January 1, 1877

TED R. TODD

Alexander Cummins Downey is the only Indiana jurist to serve as circuit judge under both Indiana constitutions and to serve on a state trial bench both before and after becoming a judge on the Indiana Supreme Court. Born September 10, 1817, in Hamilton County, Ohio, Downey and his family moved the following year to what is now Ohio County, Indiana, where he spent most of his life. His youthful occupations are described in Lincolnesque terms as farmer, carpenter, cabinetmaker, cooper, and flatboat builder. His formal education consisted of attending a log schoolhouse and the County Seminary School in Wilmington, the then county seat of Dearborn County.

Downey read law at Wilmington in the office of his first partner, J. T. Brown, and was admitted to the bar in 1841 at the age of twenty-four. With the creation of Ohio County in 1844 he moved his practice to the county seat of Rising Sun. In 1850 Downey was appointed judge of the Third Circuit Court, which then comprised the counties of Ohio, Switzerland, Jefferson, and Jennings. He was later elected to that post by both bodies of the legislature under the Indiana Constitution of 1816. In 1852, after the adoption of the 1851 constitution, he was elected by the voters to what became the First Circuit, consisting of the former Third Circuit plus the counties of Bartholomew, Brown, and Ripley. Downey rode this seven-county circuit twice a year, traveling by stagecoach and on horseback.

Finding the salary inadequate, Downey resigned as circuit judge and resumed practicing law in Rising Sun. He married Sophia J. Tapley in 1846, and from that union came seven sons and one daughter. His growing family may well explain the reason for seeking more remunerative employment.

A lifetime Methodist, Downey was an active member of the Methodist church in Rising Sun, and also had a long relationship with Methodist higher education in Indiana through his involvement with Asbury (now DePauw) University in Greencastle. There he taught on two different occasions in the law school, serving both as professor from 1854 to 1858 and, after his term on the Court, as dean. Even when not teaching law he mentored many who read law in his law office. Those who learned under his tutelage included Judges John G. Berkshire and Edwin P. Hammond of the Indiana Supreme Court and Justice John Works of the California Supreme Court.

Downey, who served on Asbury's board of trustees from 1852 to 1855 and from 1861 to 1887, was president of the board for fifteen years. He received an honorary doctor of laws from the university in 1858 and a similar degree from Indiana University in 1884. An active Mason throughout his adult life, Downey was first elected Grand Master of Indiana in 1851, a position he held for six terms.

Shortly after the Civil War began, Downey enlisted as a private in the Indiana Militia and was later appointed brigadier general of the Fourth Brigade, Indiana Legion. In that capacity he sent the Eleventh Regiment from Ohio County to aid in the pursuit of Confederate General John Hunt Morgan and his raiders as they cut a swath through southeastern Indiana in July 1863. The Ohio County unit was involved in the defense of the Jennings County courthouse and its treasury at Vernon, which was the one place in Indiana that Morgan was unable to plunder.

Downey served as a state senator from 1862 to 1866, having been elected as a War Democrat on the Union ticket. He was proud of his vote for the Thirteenth Amendment to the U.S. Constitution abolishing slavery, which was the first amendment to the federal constitution ratified by the Indiana legislature. The measure easily passed in the Republican-controlled House, but with the parties tied at twenty-five members each in the Senate, Downey's vote made the difference as the amendment was approved by the slim margin of twenty-six to twenty-four. Following his senate term, Downey was appointed a commissioner of the newly established Indiana House of Refuge for Juvenile Offenders. The group was responsible for selecting Plainfield as the site of that institution, which opened in 1868 and still serves as a juvenile facility.

In 1870 Downey was elected as a Democrat to a six-year term on the Court. He declined renomination in 1876 and returned to Rising Sun and the practice of law with his son, Samuel. They also had an office in Indianapolis. Six years later, Downey again sought his party's nomination to the high court, but he lost to his successor, George V. Howk, on the first ballot by ten votes.

During his tenure on the Court, the number of judges was expanded from four to five, with Andrew L. Osborn joining Downey, John Pettit, James L. Worden, and Samuel H. Buskirk in 1873. The Court had a November and May term and rotated the office of chief justice, with a different judge being selected for each term. Downey wrote more than one-third of the opinions published during his six years. The subject matter of these opinions was varied, and they tend to be logically sound, though at times a bit pedantic.

Downey returned to the trial bench in 1891, becoming judge of Indiana's Seventh Circuit, consisting at that time of the Dearborn and Ohio Circuit Courts and later expanding to include Switzerland County. Downey retired in the fall of 1897 at the age of eighty, though he was seen in his law office on a regular basis until he suffered a stroke and became homebound on February 4, 1898. He died on March 26 of that year.

Downey's funeral and burial included the honor of a Masonic band and escorts as his body was taken from his home to the Rising Sun Methodist Church for funeral services and then on to the local cemetery for burial. Both the local pastor, B. F. Rawlings, and the president of DePauw University, H. A. Gobin, presided over a large gathering at the church. Rawlings described Downey as a model citizen with a sound mind in a sound body. Reflecting on his life and his humble roots, he stated, "His cooper's adz is still preserved, which in his old age he prized more than did Ulysses his bow when his conflicts were over."

TED R. TODD, LLB, was judge of the Jefferson and Switzerland Circuit Courts (1989–2008) and is judge of the Jefferson Circuit Court (1989–present). His county seat law practice is in Madison, Indiana.

SELECTED BIBLIOGRAPHY

Baker, John G. "Which Way to Go: A Historical Analysis of the Indiana Court Organization and Judicial Selection Process." Unpublished thesis, University of Virginia, 1995.
History of Dearborn and Ohio Counties, Indiana. Chicago: F. E. Weakley and Company, 1885.
Monks, Leander J., ed. *Courts and Lawyers of Indiana.* Indianapolis: Federal Publishing Company, 1916.
Rising Sun Local, November 13, 1897, and April 2, 1898.

SAMUEL H. BUSKIRK

January 3, 1871–January 1, 1877

STEVEN M. FLEECE

Samuel Hamilton Buskirk, the twenty-fourth judge of the Indiana Supreme Court, was part of an extraordinary family of public servants. His father served as a justice of the peace and municipal judge, two brothers also became Indiana judges, and another edited a newspaper. Samuel and his brother, George, both served as Speakers of the Indiana House of Representatives and they shared a law practice, but not political parties. Samuel was a Democrat and George became a Republican. Never before or since have brothers from different parties served as Speakers. They served during bitter Civil War and Reconstruction times, yet remained friends.

Soon after Samuel's birth on January 19, 1820, in New Albany, his family moved to Monroe County. He graduated from the law department of Indiana University in 1841. While a diligent lawyer, Buskirk soon sought public office to augment his practice. He lost a bid for prosecutor in 1843, but was elected recorder in 1844. The following year he married Sarah J. Walters, with whom he eventually had seven children. Buskirk was first elected to the legislature in 1848 and then as prosecutor. Throughout the 1850s he served several more terms in the legislature, was a member of the electoral college in 1856, and appointed a director of the state prison in 1859. He was a delegate to several Democratic national conventions and became known as a powerful stump speaker.

Buskirk was also involved in civic affairs. Back in Bloomington, he helped organize an annual Old Settlers Meeting in 1857 to honor the area's pioneers. The next year he chaired a meeting to decide how to handle the town's assets after a majority of Bloomington citizens temporarily succeeded in dissolving the municipal government.

In 1862 Buskirk returned to the legislature to face his toughest opponent, wartime Republican governor Oliver P. Morton. Upon being elected Speaker for 1863, it became Buskirk's duty to defend the party against Morton's accusations that Democrats were too sympathetic to the South, too critical of Lincoln, and virtual traitors. On February 6, 1863, Buskirk responded, calling his fellow Democrats "a band of brothers" and vowing solidarity in opposition to the governor's quest for stronger executive powers. The legislature tried to curb Morton using the power of the purse, but the governor thwarted this attempt by running the state on borrowed money kept in his own office safe. Politics notwithstanding, on April 17, 1865, Buskirk was honored with the responsibility of eulogizing President Abraham Lincoln at a massive public memorial service in Bloomington.

In 1866 Buskirk lost his seat in the legislature, but by 1870 he was ready to mount a political comeback. This time it was as a candidate for the Court. He and three other Democrats prevailed over four incumbent Republicans and took office in January 1871. His many published opinions appear in *Indiana Reports* volumes 33 through 55. His writing style and legal knowledge are displayed in those cases and in his treatise on appellate procedure, *Buskirk's Practice*.

Unfortunately, in the light of history he erred in his most significant case, *Cory et al. v. Carter*. In that case, Buskirk reversed a Marion Superior Court decision that would have required the all-white school in Lawrence Township to admit black children. In his opinion he found that neither state law nor the Fourteenth Amendment gave the excluded children a remedy. Buskirk's reasoning, according to a 1977 article in the *Journal of Negro His-*

tory, "was reminiscent of the political theories of John C. Calhoun and not post Civil War social ideas."

In 1876 the Democratic Party dumped its incumbent judges, Buskirk included, rescinding their renomination due to outrage over reports of judicial chambers furnished at public expense with upholstered chairs, pillows, and velvet rugs. Buskirk then settled into private practice in Indianapolis and became president of the local bar association.

Buskirk died on April 3, 1879, at his home in Indianapolis. The Indianapolis and Bloomington bar associations adopted resolutions in his honor, and the *Indianapolis Journal* and *Bloomington Courier* printed laudatory obituaries. A special train bore his remains to Bloomington. Five hundred people turned out to pay their respects and escort him to his grave site in Rose Hill Cemetery. His obelisk looks out upon the taller monument of his Republican brother, law partner, and political rival. Farther down slope are the graves of sex researcher Alfred Kinsey and songwriter Hoagy Carmichael. History will judge who added more to the sum of human happiness, but none can deny that Judge Samuel Hamilton Buskirk led a productive and honorable life of service to his community, state, and country, even if at times blinded by the prejudices common to his era.

STEVEN M. FLEECE, JD, is Indiana senior judge. He previously served twenty-four years as judge of the County Court of Clark County and Clark County Superior Court No. 3.

SELECTED BIBLIOGRAPHY

Bishop, David W. "Plessy v. Ferguson: A Reinterpretation." *Journal of Negro History* 62, no. 2 (April 1977).

Blanchard, Charles, ed. *Counties of Morgan, Monroe, and Brown, Indiana.* Chicago: F. A. Battey and Company, 1884.

Bloomington Courier, April 12, 1879.

Indianapolis Journal, April 4, 1879.

Shepherd, Rebecca, Alan January, Elizabeth Shanahan, and Vincent A. Giroux, eds. *Biographical Directory of the Indiana General Assembly.* 2 vols. Indianapolis: The Select Committee on the Centennial History of the Indiana General Assembly in cooperation with the Indiana Historical Bureau, 1980–84.

CASES CITED

Cory et al. v. Carter, 48 Ind. 327 (1874).

ANDREW L. OSBORN
December 16, 1872–January 4, 1875

BRADFORD W. SAMPLE

When the Indiana General Assembly expanded the number of Supreme Court judges to five in a special session in 1872 in an effort to unclog the Court's backlog of cases, Governor Conrad Baker appointed Andrew Lawrence Osborn of La Porte to serve as the first judge of the Fifth District and the twenty-fifth judge on the Court. His service on the bench, which began just two years after he had been defeated in his race for a Court seat, was brief. He lost his bid for a full six-year term as judge in the 1874 election.

Osborn, who was born in Waterbury, Connecticut, traveled west to Chicago as a young man and started working as a printer for the *Chicago Democrat*. He also read law with the politically connected attorney William Stewart, later Chicago postmaster. In 1836 Osborn moved to Michigan City, Indiana, was admitted to the bar, and began practicing law with Judge Gustavus Evarts. He also married, joined the Presbyterian Church, and ventured into Whig Party politics. His next move was to La Porte in 1844, and he became a partner with Judge John B. Niles, one of the early settlers of the city. He then won successive elections to the general assembly, first to the House and then to the Senate, serving from 1844 to 1849. Although he did not seek elective office for almost a decade, he nonetheless retained his interest in politics with the Free-Soil Party and then the Republican Party. Osborn was elected judge of the Ninth Indiana Circuit, a position he held until 1870.

Osborn's appointment in 1872 made him the lone Republican on the Court but that did not seem to have limited his influence. During his tenure, cases concerned mostly property law and legal procedure, over which there proved to be little dissent among the judges. Osborn wrote numerous opinions and served as chief justice for the May 1873 term. His writing style was simple and straightforward. He conveyed the facts of the case, the legal issues involved, and then moved to review precedent before declaring the Court's verdict.

A review of those cases in which Osborn wrote the opinions reveals that they often fall into the categories of eminent domain and public roads, estate and family law, and cases in which mechanic's liens or voluntary associations appeared prominent. While all Court cases are important because they have the potential to set precedent, the eminent domain cases significantly restored a traditional restriction on government power.

An 1872 decision, *The Water Works Company of Indianapolis et al. v. Burkhart et al.*, written by Osborn, held that the abandonment of a public project does not entitle the former property owner to reclaim the land that was taken. The case strengthened the local use of eminent domain, but acknowledged that only legislative authority has the power of eminent domain and that it must be used for a public purpose. Going further in *Wild v. Deig et al.*, Osborn's opinion overturned a state law permitting local governments to use eminent domain for private roads, which he said illegally permitted local government to take the property of one person and give it to another for private rather than public use.

As he neared the end of his time on the Court, Osborn dissented in the *Cory et al. v. Carter* opinion, which overturned a lower court decision that would have allowed black children to attend an all-white school. While he agreed with the reversal, Osborn said that "there is very much in the foregoing opinion in which I do not concur," adding that in the short time he had left on the bench he could not "properly and satisfactorily consider the questions discussed, and must therefore content myself with this qualified dissent."

After leaving the Court, Osborn worked in Chicago as an attorney for the Michigan Central Railroad Company. He died in 1891 in La Porte.

BRADFORD W. SAMPLE, PhD, is academic vice president, Bryan College. He was a contributor to *The Governors of Indiana* and the author of "A Truly Midwestern City: Indianapolis on the Eve of the Great Depression," *Indiana Magazine of History* 97 (June 2001).

SELECTED BIBLIOGRAPHY

Bodenhamer, David J., and Randall T. Shepard, eds. *The History of Indiana Law*. Athens: Ohio University Press, 2006.

Daniels, E. D. *A Twentieth Century History and Biographical Record of La Porte County, Indiana*. Chicago and New York: Lewis Publishing Company, 1904.

Howard, Timothy E. *The Indiana Supreme Court, with Some Account of the Courts Preceding It: An Historical Sketch*. Publication no. 3. South Bend: Northern Indiana Historical Society, 1900.

Taylor, Charles W. *Biographical Sketches and Review of the Bench and Bar of Indiana*. Indianapolis: Bench and Bar Publishing Company, 1895.

CASES CITED

Cory et al. v. Carter, 48 Ind. 327 (1874).

The Water Works Company of Indianapolis et al. v. Burkhart et al., 41 Ind. 364 (1872).

Wild v. Deig et al., 43 Ind. 455 (1873).

INDIANA SUPREME COURT

HORACE P. BIDDLE
January 4, 1875–January 3, 1881

DOUGLAS B. MORTON

If any Hoosier justice can be called a true Renaissance man, Horace Porter Biddle, the Indiana Supreme Court's twenty-sixth member, fits the description. (The judge's name is sometimes listed as Horace Peters Biddle, especially by his prose and poetry publishers) Poet, musician, inventor, author, speaker, statesman, counselor, and jurist, Biddle compiled a list of accomplishments as varied as the masters of the Renaissance and much more attuned to current lifestyles.

Born Horace Porter *Beadle* on March 24, 1811, in what is now Hocking County, Ohio, he was the youngest of nine children of a farming couple. He attended local schools in the winter and farmed in the summer, but quickly determined that farm life was not for him. At the age of sixteen he started clerking in his brother's general store, educating himself through reading. He became fluent in several European languages, especially French. In 1836 he decided to become a lawyer, reading law for three years before being admitted to the Ohio bar in 1839.

Later that year he relocated to Logansport, Indiana, a place he had previously visited, and where he maintained his residence for the rest of his life. He began a practice of law under the name of Horace Biddle (he never explained the change in spelling) and, by 1845, was a partner with his nephew.

In his early years, Biddle was best known as a writer. Primarily a poet, his works were published in leading journals, including his translations of French and German poets. By 1882 he had published eight volumes of poetry. Biddle's prose was also widely published, and with the publication of *The Musical Scale*, he attained international renown for a work that became a standard in teaching musical theory. Biddle also invented a musical instrument he called a tetrachord, a four-stringed violin-style instrument that he played, often accompanying singers, for the rest of his life.

Biddle was always politically active. By 1844 he was the northern Indiana chairman for his friend and correspondent, Henry Clay, in his presidential campaign. Though sorely disappointed when Clay lost, Biddle remained a loyal Whig until the party's eventual unraveling. In 1846 Biddle was elected as the presiding judge of the Eighth Judicial Circuit, then covering Logansport and numerous surrounding counties, thus beginning the judicial career that dominated the balance of his work life.

On May 7, 1846, Biddle married Anna Maria Matlock, a woman of some wealth in her own right. After sixteen months, the couple separated amid accusations by her of abuse and by him of an affair. Though he filed for a divorce, none was ever finalized. The couple lived the rest of their lives separated and childless, residing in bitterness about seven blocks from one another.

Biddle, a Whig in a heavily Democratic district covering Howard, Cass, and Pulaski counties, was elected a delegate to the 1850 Constitutional Convention, no doubt due to his knowledge of constitutional issues. A highly visible participant in the convention, he served on the powerful rules committee and three other panels. At the behest of Howard County constituents, Biddle filed a petition that rights of suffrage "not be granted to Negroes" and that they should not be allowed to migrate to this state. On the convention floor, he remained silent on the topic while others championed the provision, which eventually passed. It was amended out of the constitution thirty years later. At the close of the convention in 1851,

Biddle returned to his judicial duties, only to resign shortly thereafter to accept the Whig nomination for Congress. He was defeated and returned to Logansport and the practice of law. Over the next eight years, Biddle developed his reputation as a successful attorney, working with a client base that included banks and railroads.

Biddle came close to joining the Court after William Z. Stuart announced in mid-1857 his intention to resign at the end of the Court's term in January 1858. Parties scrambled to find candidates to run in the off-year October election for the presumptive Court vacancy. Biddle, nominated by the Republicans, handily won the election, but Democratic governor Ashbel P. Willard refused to sign a commission upon his election. Biddle sued the governor in *Biddle v. Willard*, but ultimately the four members of the Court, all Democrats, sided with Willard, ruling that no vacancy had occurred in the office until after the election and therefore it was void.

In 1860 Biddle was elected judge of the then Eleventh Circuit Court. He was reelected to the position without opposition in 1866. While on the trial court bench, Biddle purchased a thirty-two-acre island and the mansion on it, property that came to be known as Biddle's Island. He expanded the home, adding "wings and furnishings expressive of his literary and artistic taste." Here he began his art and sculpture collections and his greatest treasure, his library. The Biddle House remained a Logansport landmark until it was razed in 1961.

Biddle retired in 1872, although he served briefly on the board of trustees of Purdue University, the newly created agricultural school. Then in 1874, "against his wishes and expectations," the Democratic Party nominated him as its candidate for the Court. He was elected by the largest aggregate vote and the largest majority given to any statewide candidate to that date. Biddle chose not to run for re-election in 1880.

Biddle's body of opinions while on the Court defies easy characterization. They lacked the literary touch one might have expected, and in fact they read much like those of his fellow judges. Biddle more than carried his weight in handling the caseload that came to the Court, writing 594 majority opinions, including a prodigious 102 opinions in the November 1877 term. Besides the majority opinions, Biddle also wrote responses for the Petitions for Rehearing on his own cases and on cases written by other judges, a role unique to him during his years on the Court. He served three terms as chief justice, the position at the time rotating among the judges for the biannual terms.

Biddle wrote in a day of collegiality when concurring opinions were virtually unheard of. He wrote only eight dissenting opinions, one of which concerned the closing of the Wabash and Erie Canal and whether the canal owned a fee (outright ownership) in the streambed or whether it merely had an easement in it. While this case will sound familiar to attorneys in today's world of the closing of railroad right-of-ways, the dispute also involved rights for the sale of millions of pounds of ice from the canal. Biddle's dissenting opinion in *Cromie v. Wabash and Erie Canal, Board of Trustees* accurately describes Indiana's present position on these difficult easement-fee issues. One of Biddle's own opinions, *State v. Swift*, sparked spirited dissent by two of his colleagues. His decision nullified approval by voters of seven constitutional amendments.

Following his years on the Court, Biddle retired to his island home. While he continued in the part-time practice of law, he spent most of his time writing and in his library with his "6400 friends." He maintained an active correspondence with many leaders of the day. On his death a letter from Henry Wadsworth Longfellow was discovered among his papers. After a lengthy and happy retirement, Biddle died on May 13, 1900, at his home. In keeping with his will, he was buried at Logansport's Mount Hope Cemetery with a plain stone. He had forbidden anyone else to be buried on the lot or for any other monument to be erected. He left his estate to six nieces, nephews, and friends equally. Not everyone was saddened about Biddle's death. Having outlived her husband of fifty-six years, Anna Maria sued his estate for her widow's share prior to her death in September 1900.

DOUGLAS B. MORTON, JD, was judge, Fulton Circuit Court 1979–2008, now senior judge. In 2001 he was the winner of the Kinsey Award for Juvenile Judge service and from 1994 to 2008 appeared as a regular guest on WROI's Legal Program.

SELECTED BIBLIOGRAPHY

Coggeshall, William Turner. *The Poets and Poetry of the West: With Biographical and Critical Notices*. Columbus, OH: Follett, Foster and Company, 1860.

Journal of the Convention of the People of Indiana to Amend the Constitution. Indianapolis: Austin H. Brown, Printer to the Convention, 1851.

Pioneers and Old Residents. Logansport, IN: Longwell and Cummings, Publishers, 1892.

Pratt, Sarah S. "Judge Horace P. Biddle." *Indiana Magazine of History* 32 (September 1936).

CASES CITED

Biddle v. Willard, Governor, 10 Ind. 47 (1857).

Cromie v. The Board of Trustees of the Wabash and Erie Canal, 71 Ind. 208 (1880).

The State v. Swift, 69 Ind. 505 (1880).

WILLIAM E. NIBLACK
January 1, 1877–January 7, 1889

ANDREW S. POTTS

Born in the sixth year of Indiana statehood on a farm in Dubois County, William Ellis Niblack, the twenty-seventh judge of the Indiana Supreme Court, was one of the earliest native-born Court judges and one of the last who could personally recall the state's frontier days. Early on he jettisoned his family's Whig politics in favor of Jacksonian democracy, eventually maturing into a conservative "Bourbon Democrat" whose populist roots and record of honesty distinguish him as a true Hoosier public servant.

Though Niblack, who was born on May 22, 1822, surely experienced frontier life, his family enjoyed a prominent status, albeit one diminished by his grandfather's Kentucky land speculations. Niblack sensed his family's "clipped pretensions" and vowed to "break away," a goal he realized in 1838 when he enrolled at Indiana University. His father's death a year later called him home, where he worked, studied law, and helped his mother. Niblack moved to Martin County in 1845 to begin his law practice.

Niblack's long career in Democratic politics began in 1849 with his election to the Indiana House and to the state senate a year later. There he worked on the Revised Statutes of 1852, which revolutionized Indiana legal practice. While some practitioners deplored the change, deft young lawyers such as Niblack benefited. In 1854 Governor Joseph A. Wright appointed Niblack judge of the Third Judicial Circuit. To combat doubts about his inexperience, he devoted himself to a busy docket of plank-road companies seeking damages, divorces, title cases, gaming offenses, and horse stealing.

In 1857, shortly after moving his family to Vincennes, Niblack battled his way to a nomination on the seventy-sixth ballot to fill a U.S. House of Representatives vacancy in the heavily Democratic First District. Elected, he left for Washington, D.C., pledged to oppose nativism and abolition and to support U.S. Senator Jesse Bright, Indiana's slave-owning state party boss. Niblack arrived to the "Bloody Kansas" maelstrom, where he voted for President James Buchanan's proslavery Lecompton plan. This sparked a bitter re-election fight in 1858, in which Niblack, prevailing over lifelong rival Alvin P. Hovey, was almost the only pro-Lecompton northern Democrat returned to Congress.

The Democratic Party split over Bright in 1860, but Niblack was not ready to break with him. Since Niblack had not sought re-election, Bright brokered a nomination for him to be territorial chief justice of Nebraska, but Senate Republicans balked. Bright was ultimately expelled from the Senate for disloyalty while Niblack emerged a pro-Civil War Democrat, later writing that Bright's Copperhead agenda had been dangerously misleading to young politicians such as himself. For the remainder of the Civil War, Niblack carefully balanced opposition to President Abraham Lincoln with Union loyalty. He returned to the Indiana House of Representatives in 1863 and helped lead Democrats in the fight against Governor Oliver P. Morton that resulted in the collapse of Indiana constitutional government. In 1864 Niblack was elected to the Thirty-ninth Congress, which met in the shadow of Lincoln's assassination.

Niblack supported President Andrew Johnson in the conflict over Reconstruction, favoring the right of "loyal States" to set their own racial policy, which in Indiana meant "antislavery" but also "antiblack." Niblack's parliamentary maneuvering delayed passage of the Civil Rights Act of 1866 but could not halt it or the Fourteenth Amendment. Further Republican gains in 1868 led to Johnson's impeachment and the passage of the Fifteenth Amendment, whose promise of enfranchisement Niblack rejected. Ironically, all out of procedural maneuvers, on February 25, 1869, it was Niblack who called the question on the amendment.

Despite his partisanship, Niblack had a conciliatory demeanor that gained the favor of Republicans such as President Ulysses S. Grant and Speaker of the House James Blaine. Niblack was named to the Poland Committee investigating the Credit Mobilier corruption scandal that had implicated Vice President Schuyler Colfax. When Niblack saw Colfax's failing attempt at self-defense, he warned his fellow Hoosier to "get a lawyer." Niblack narrowly won re-election in 1872, and did not seek another term. Before he left Congress in 1875, Blaine appointed him a director of what is now Gallaudet University, and he advocated for deaf education the rest of his life.

Niblack's return to private practice was brief, for in 1876 scandal helped elevate him to the Indiana Supreme Court. The judicial election that year was roiled by Republican charges that the Democratic incumbents enjoyed low caseloads and high living. Judge Samuel H. Buskirk took the brunt of the criticism, causing his own nephew to propose he be replaced on the ballot with Niblack, who went on to win two six-year terms. The scandal may have been invented by liquor dealers who feared the incumbents would uphold a law allowing wives to sue those who got their husbands drunk. If so, the gambit failed for Niblack himself supported the measure in *Schafer v. Smith*.

Niblack was twice the head of the Democratic caucus in Congress and helped manage the state and national parties. This prominence continued during his Court tenure. He aided Thomas Hendricks's unsuccessful presidential bid as an officer of the 1880 national convention, and when Hendricks was elected vice president in 1884, Niblack was considered for attorney general.

Still, Niblack was widely viewed as an impartial jurist. He dissented in *Swift v. State*, though its holding—that several constitutional amendments had failed to receive the required vote—was considered helpful to Hendricks's presidential effort. Niblack also twice ruled against Democrats when they sought to void the special election of a Republican as lieutenant governor (*Smith v. Myers* and *Robertson v. State ex rel. Smith*).

Niblack's economic views reflected his populist-inflected conservatism. A Bourbon on monetary policy, in the state senate he opposed the Free Banks Act of 1852 over specie issues and in Congress he provoked Indiana Greenbacks by opposing the Inflation Bill during the panic of 1873. Yet he also joined Hoosier populists in opposing the 1860 Morrill Tariff and introduced one of the first eight-hour workday bills in American history. On the Court, he showed concern for plaintiffs as in *New York, C. & St. L. Ry. Co. v. Doane*, when he chided a callous railroad that a passenger's maimed arm was "no trivial matter." Two opinions he authored in 1886 as chief justice were among the first to uphold the regulation of the nascent telephone industry (*Hockett v. State* and *Central Union Tel Co. v. State*).

Niblack suffered his only electoral defeat in 1888, narrowly losing his bid for a third term to Silas D. Coffey. The Democrat controlled general assembly responded "sorely" to what had been a Republican sweep by creating a legislatively appointed Supreme Court Commission to which Niblack was named. Hovey, then governor, rejected the usurpation, a result sustained in *Hovey v. Noble*. At age sixty-seven, Niblack took his place as an elder statesman of the bar, handling such matters as the Gas Boom-era case of *Jamieson v. Indiana Natural Gas & Oil Co.*, in which he defended the general assembly's efforts to reign in Elwood Haynes and others seeking to pillage Indiana's newly found reserves. A lifelong Episcopalian, Niblack died on May 7, 1893, in Indianapolis and is buried in Crown Hill Cemetery.

Widowed early, Niblack married his second wife, Eliza Ann Sherman, in 1849. One of their sons, Albert P., became a celebrated admiral and another, William C., a prominent lawyer, while daughters Eliza and Sarah were early benefactresses of the forerunner of the Indianapolis Museum of Art. Poignantly, just days after he shed the ermine in 1889, Niblack's middle son, Mason, was sworn in as Speaker of the Indiana House of Representatives, having been nominated in the very room where his father once presided.

ANDREW S. POTTS is a partner with Nixon Peabody LLP. A native Hoosier, Potts practices in Nixon Peabody's Washington, D.C., office in the area of historic preservation law. He is a former law clerk for Chief Justice Randall T. Shepard. He was the 2008 recipient of the John H. Chafee Trustees Award for Outstanding Achievement in Public Policy from the National Trust for Historic Preservation. Potts is the author of "Hidden Gems in Other Articles: Rights Language in the Indiana Constitution Not Found in the Bill of Rights," reprinted in *Litigation under the Indiana Bill of Rights* (Indiana Civil Liberties Union, 1994).

SELECTED BIBLIOGRAPHY

Barnes, William Horatio. *Biographies of Members of the House of Representatives of the Forty-Third Congress.* New York: Nelson and Phillips, 1874.

Frew, Ellen Niblack. *The Niblack Family, Chronicles and Genealogy Records.* Carmel: Guild Press of Indiana, 1997.

Gerichs, William C. "The Ratification of the Fifteenth Amendment in Indiana." *Indiana Magazine of History* 9 (September 1913): 131–66.

History of Warrick, Spencer and Perry Counties, Indiana. Chicago: Goodspeed Brothers and Company, 1885.

Niblack, William Ellis. *Congressional Globe*, 39th Cong., 1st sess., 1866, pp. 3211–3217 (his views of slavery and abolition and their roles in Indiana history).

Trissal, Francis M. *Public Men of Indiana: A Political History from 1860 to 1890.* Hammond: W. B. Conkey Company, 1922.

CASES CITED

Central Union Tel Co. v. State, 106 Ind. 1 (1886).
Hockett v. State, 105 Ind. 250 (1886).
Hovey v. Noble, 118 Ind. 350 (1889).
Jamieson v. Indiana Natural Gas & Oil Co., 128 Ind. 555 (1891).
New York, C. & St. L. Ry. Co. v. Doane, 115 Ind. 435 (1888).
Robertson v. State ex rel. Smith, 109 Ind. 79 (1887).
Schafer v. Smith, 63 Ind. 220 (1877).
Smith v. Myers, 109 Ind. 1 (1887.
Swift v. State, 69 Ind. 505 (1880).

GEORGE V. HOWK
January 1, 1877–January 7, 1889

DONALD B. KITE SR.

George Vail Howk's intellect and work ethic contributed to his rise to the top of his profession and ultimately to his election as the twenty-eighth judge of the Indiana Supreme Court. Of equal significance was the fact that Howk was born into a family that understood the importance of public service, and that Howk was mentored by Charles Dewey, a talented and seasoned lawyer, who served on the Court from 1836 to 1847.

Howk was born in Charlestown, Indiana, on September 21, 1824, to Isaac Howk, a pioneer Indiana lawyer and prominent member of the Indiana General Assembly, and Elvira Vail. His father was educated at Williams College, located in the county of his birth, Berkshire County, Massachusetts, and migrated to Charlestown in 1817, one year following Indiana's statehood. George was only eight years old when his father, "an Adams man" who had served as Indiana's Speaker of the House and was prosecutor for the Third Judicial District, died following an attack of "bilious colick." In his remarks to the Court upon Isaac's death, Dewey, also an alumnus of Williams College, stated that the bar was "shocked and awed" by Isaac's sudden death. Dewey was subsequently elected to succeed him as prosecutor.

After graduating from Indiana Asbury (now DePauw) University in 1846, Howk was admitted to the bar the following year. Following graduation, as was then the practice, Howk read the law under an established practicing attorney. Howk was quite fortunate as he was mentored by his eventual senior partner, Dewey.

Howk's connection to the Dewey family did not end with his mentor. Two years after he completed his studies, Howk married Dewey's daughter, Eleanor. They moved to New Albany, and Howk began practicing law there. Howk and Eleanor had two children who lived to adulthood. The Howks' oldest son, Charles Dewey, who also attended Williams College, later became a partner in his father's firm and subsequently opened his own law office in Louisville, Kentucky. Eleanor died on April 12, 1853, and many years after her death it was reported that it was her wish before she died that her husband marry "her bosom friend," Jane Simonson. True to Eleanor's wishes, Howk married Jane, the eldest daughter of General John S. Simonson, on September 21, 1854. They had six children.

In October 1876 Howk, a Democrat, was elected to the Court. Prior to his election, he had practiced law with such experienced lawyers as Colonel W. W. Tuley, his partner of seven years, and Dewey, his mentor and father-in-law, and with more than one of his sons. His experience also included two terms in the Indiana Senate, a term in the Indiana House, judge of the Sixth Circuit Court of Common Pleas, New Albany city judge, New Albany city councilman, and trustee of the New Albany Public Schools.

Howk's service on the Court, which included a period as chief justice, lasted twelve years. Among the notable opinions handed down during his two terms was the Court's decision in *The Western Union Telegraph Company v. McKibben* that found the telegram company negligent for failing to deliver a telegram that related to its intended recipient's prospective employment. Howk also wrote the unanimous opinion in *Kellum v. The State* that determined a lottery established by Vincennes University was legal. The Court noted that the lottery was intended to "ai[d] in procuring a library and the necessary philosophical and experimental apparatus" for the university. Four years after *Kellum* was decided, the Court reversed course in *The State v. Woodward*, reasoning that Article 15 of the state constitution prohibited lotteries.

One of the most controversial decisions during Howk's tenure was *Robertson v. The State, ex rel. Smith*, which arose out of a spirited dispute regarding the special election for lieutenant governor in 1886. While the majority held that the trial court lacked jurisdiction to prevent the newly elected official from taking office, Howk joined the vigorous dissent, penned by Judge Joseph A. S. Mitchell, which reasoned that the trial court did have jurisdiction in the case but nevertheless concluded that the injunction issued by the lower court should be dissolved.

Another Howk decision, *Brown v. State*, attracted national attention, which was most likely unwanted by the judge. He reversed the death sentence of a woman convicted of murdering her husband based on the incompetency of two jurors. However, the two men in question had been dismissed during voir dire and were not accepted as jurors. The attorney general filed a petition for a rehearing, but Howk, in upholding his original decision, ruled that the criminal code did not provide for a rehearing in a criminal case.

The late 1880s were an extraordinarily difficult time for Howk and his family. In 1888 the couple lost its daughter, Jennie, to consumption. She was by all accounts "the sunshine in the family circle." In that same year Howk lost his bid for re-election to the Court. One year later his son, George Jr., died. The father and son had worked closely in the family law firm.

Howk's level of professional and business-related activity remained high in spite of personal losses. He was appointed circuit judge in 1891 and also served as a director of New Albany's Merchant's National Bank and the New Albany Waterworks. Howk died of "the grip" in New Albany on January 13, 1892, after a brief illness. The press reported that Howk "fondly bid his aged wife good-bye, and, closing his eyes, as calmly as a child falling asleep he passed away, surrounded by sorrowing friends." Following the eulogy by the pastor of New Albany's First Presbyterian Church and a Masonic ceremony, Howk was buried in New Albany's Northern Cemetery (renamed Fairview Cemetery in 1896) in the family plot. Howk's monument reminds passersby of Howk's years of service as a Court judge and notes for posterity that Howk was a "Kind and Affectionate Husband and Father, and an Able and Eminent Jurist."

DONALD B. KITE, SR. JD, is a partner with Dean-Webster, Wright and Kite, LLP. He is coauthor of *Federal Justice in Indiana: The History of the United States District Court for the Southern District of Indiana* (2007), recipient of Defense Trial Counsel of Indiana Defense Lawyer of the Year Award (2005), and corecipient of the Indianapolis Bar Association's Dr. John Morton Finney Jr. Award for Excellence in Legal education (2007).

SELECTED BIBLIOGRAPHY

Biographical and Historical Souvenir for the Counties of Clark, Crawford, Harrison, Floyd, Jefferson, Jennings, Scott and Washington, Indiana. Chicago: John M. Gresham and Company, 1889.

History of the Ohio Falls Cities and Their Counties. Cleveland, OH: L. A. Williams and Company, 1882.

Nowland, John H. B. *Sketches of Prominent Citizens of 1876.* Indianapolis: Tilford and Carlon, 1877.

Robbins, D. P. *New Albany, Indiana: Its Advantages and Surroundings.* New Albany, IN: New Albany Ledger Company, 1892.

CASES CITED

Brown v. State, 70 Ind. 576 (1880).

Kellum v. The State, 66 Ind. 588 (1879).

Robertson v. The State, ex rel. Smith, 109 Ind. 79 (1887).

The State v. Woodward, 89 Ind. 110 (1882).

The Western Union Telegraph Co. v. McKibben, 114 Ind. 511 (1887).

JOHN T. SCOTT
December 29, 1879–January 5, 1881

MICHAEL J. SACOPULOS

Within twelve hours of the passing of Judge John T. Scott, the twenty-ninth judge of the Indiana Supreme Court, the Vigo County Bar Association assembled in the circuit courtroom to take action. Former U.S. Navy secretary Richard Thompson and other members of the bar were appointed to a committee to commemorate Scott's life and service. Former U.S. senator Daniel Voorhees was chosen to deliver the memorial address. It was further decided that local attorneys would assemble at the circuit courtroom and travel as one to attend the funeral and that the Vigo County Circuit Court would adjourn for several days out of respect for Scott.

Such immediate and expressive respect revealed the esteem that colleagues held for Scott, who began his law practice in Terre Haute in 1864. He was elected judge of the common pleas court in 1868, serving in this capacity until 1873, when these courts were abolished by the legislature. He returned to private practice and then became secretary of the Democratic State Central Committee in 1876. Scott was appointed by Governor James D. Williams on December 27, 1879, to fill a vacancy on the Court left by the death of Judge Samuel E. Perkins.

Shortly after Scott's appointment, the Court was presented with a thorny political issue in the case of *The State v. Swift*, which raised the question of whether a majority of voters had actually approved seven amendments to the state constitution voted upon in the spring election of 1880. All of the proposals received winning margins, but Judge Horace P. Biddle, in his opinion, ruled that the amendments had failed because a majority meant the total number of votes cast in the election and not the number of votes cast for the individual amendments, which were lower numbers in each case. In his dissent, Scott wrote, "Such a construction and interpretation would . . . lead to interminable trouble and confusion." Scott served on the Court only until January 1881, having been defeated for a full term in the election of 1880. He returned to Terre Haute to resume his law practice, which continued until his death on December 29, 1891.

Few residents of Glasgow, Kentucky, in May 1831 would have believed that Samuel and Sarah Scott's new son would ultimately rise to such prominence. At the age of fourteen, John left home without his parents' consent and apprenticed himself to a saddle and harness maker for five years. Four years into his apprenticeship, Scott happened to meet a young man who was teaching Latin, which he desperately wanted to learn. The saddle master, however, believed that Latin would distract Scott from his work and prohibited him from attending classes. Just three months shy of completing his five-year apprenticeship, Scott ran away from his master and immediately enrolled in Franklin College near Nashville, Tennessee, where he studied Latin, Greek, geometry, algebra, English, and rhetoric. Scott married Rebecca Jones of Edgar County, Illinois, and eventually the couple had five children, one of whom died in infancy. The Scott family moved from Montezuma, Indiana, to Terre Haute in 1864.

The Scotts' son, Charles, was admitted to practice law, but preferred engineering. He served as the building inspector for Terre Haute for many years. Another son, George, had a remarkable legal career by any standard. He studied in his father's law offices until being admitted to the bar in 1886. He practiced law in Terre Haute until his retirement in 1960. He died in 1964 at the age of 102.

A daughter, Sarah Scott, was such a beloved educator in Terre Haute that upon her death the Vigo County school system named a school after her, Sarah Scott Middle School, which continues to operate in Terre Haute. Scott's geology collection and portion of his library were donated to the school.

Throughout his life, Scott was an avid reader and amateur geologist, and his academic curiosity and vitality carried through to his children. Despite his death almost 120 years ago, John Scott's name is still remembered fondly in Vigo County.

MICHAEL J. SACOPULOS, JD, is a practicing attorney in Terre Haute. He is the author of numerous articles focusing upon medical malpractice and is general counsel for Medical Justice Services Inc.

SELECTED BIBLIOGRAPHY

Terre Haute Gazette, December 30, 1891.
Terre Haute Tribune, July 13, 1949, January 20, 1964.
Scott, George A. *Scott Family: John Scott and Margaret Thornton.*
———. *Sarah Scott: Biography.*

CASES CITED
The State v. Swift, 69 Ind. 505 (1880).

BYRON K. ELLIOTT
January 3, 1881–January 2, 1893

LINDA C. GUGIN

Byron Koscuisko Elliott was one of the most intellectually gifted and prolific judges to sit on the Indiana Supreme Court. His term of office as the thirtieth judge on the Court began exactly thirty years after the Indiana Constitution of 1851 was ratified, and during his tenure the Court wrestled with numerous significant constitutional questions. Elliott wrote many of the opinions involving constitutional interpretation. In particular, he was concerned about assuring that the principle of separation of powers was maintained and that the independence of the judiciary was protected.

Elliott's election to the Court in 1880 was the pinnacle of his distinguished career. He came to the Court with considerable experience as a lawyer and a judge. Elliott, born in 1853 in Butler County, Ohio, moved with his family to Indiana at the age of fifteen. He attended Marion County Seminary and then studied law. He was admitted to the bar in 1858 and in 1859, at the age of twenty-three, was appointed city attorney for India-napolis. His career was interrupted for four years of military service with the Union army during the Civil War, and upon his return he was chosen as city attorney in 1865, 1867, and 1869. He was elected judge of the Marion County Criminal Court in 1870, but two years later he again became city at-torney and served in that position until 1875. He returned to the bench in 1876 when he was elected judge of the Marion County Superior Court. He was nominated for a second term but declined it to accept the Republican nomination for the Supreme Court.

In 1880 Elliott was elected along with fellow Republican William A. Woods. Both men were recognized for the excellent reputations that they brought to the Court. The author of a critique of the first one hundred years of the Court's history (1816–1916) said that the Court in 1881, consisting of Judges George V. Howk, William E. Niblack, and James L. Worden, along with Elliott and Woods, had "reached its highest point [and that] no state court in the Union presented better opinions to the professions than did the Supreme Court of Indiana. Each judge was a host unto himself."

Described as a person of "untiring energy," Elliott wrote 1,632 opinions during his twelve-year court tenure. The opinions fill sixty volumes of *Indiana Reports*. He has been praised for the high quality of his opinions, which were shaped in part by his reading of philosophers Aristotle, John Locke, and Immanuel Kant. Among Elliott's most significant opinions were those that addressed constitutional issues about the roles of the three branches of government. In a trilogy of cases, Elliott's opinions clearly established judicial independence. His opinion in *Little v. State* enunciated the principle that the "court possessed the inherent power to punish for contempt inde-pendently of any legislation." The specific action provoking the contempt charges, he said, did not have to be included in any statutory definition.

In 1887 Elliott wrote the majority opinion invalidating a statute that required the Court to make a syllabus, or head notes, of each judicial opin-ion recorded, which he said was the responsibility of the reporter. In *Ex parte Griffiths, Reporter* he wrote: "Judges cannot be required to perform any other than judicial duties. This is a rudimentary principle of constitutional law." His opinion in *State ex rel. Hovey v. Noble et al.* overturned a legisla-tive statute that established the offices of commissioners, to be appointed by the general assembly, who would assist the Court with its duties. Elliott declared that the act was unconstitutional because it violated the principle of separation of powers. "The duty of maintaining the separation of the departments of government and the integrity and existence of the courts as established and organized by the Constitution, is one of the most important that the judiciary is required to perform," Elliott wrote. The courts, he added, could "yield no part of their right or authority."

While Elliott was determined to protect the independence of the judiciary, he was just as quick not to allow the judiciary to encroach on the powers of other branches. In *Smith v. Myers* the Court was confronted with a petition brought by the president of the Senate, a Democrat, who argued that he was next in line to become lieutenant governor after the sitting lieutenant governor had resigned. However, a Republican had won the special election for lieutenant governor. The senator filed suit to prevent the Speaker of the House from certifying the election results, which would have given the office to the Republican. Elliott, again demonstrating his strong commitment to the separation of powers, denied the petition for the injunction. "It is a principle of constitutional law, declared in our Constitution and enforced by many decisions of our own and other courts, that the departments of government are separate and distinct, and that the officers of one department shall not invade another," he wrote. Elliott said that the Court would violate this "fundamental principle" if it were to interfere in the case by issuing the injunction sought by the senator.

Another of Elliott's notable opinions was one that had far-reaching ramifications for public education in Indiana. *Robinson, Treasurer v. Schenck* involved a taxpayer challenge to an act of the general assembly that authorized local governments to levy school taxes, claiming that under the constitution only the legislature could levy school taxes and that it could not delegate that authority to the local school corporations. In a strongly worded opinion, Elliott said that nothing in the language of the constitution "forbids the Legislature from employing [political subdivisions] in securing revenues for the support of the common schools." In fact, he said, the constitution emphatically required the legislature the "use all suitable means to build up and maintain the system," and that failure to do so would be "a grave breach of duty." By overturning prior rulings that prohibited local school taxation, Elliott laid the groundwork for promoting a strong system of public education for the state.

Elliott won re-election to the Court in 1886, but in 1892, he and two other Republican judges were swept out of office by a Democratic tide. That ended Elliott's judicial career but not his engagement with law. After he left the Court he held the position of lecturer at Central Law School of Indianapolis and at the law schools of DePauw and Northwestern universities. He was one of the founders and the first president of the Indiana Law School of Indianapolis, now the Indiana School of Law at Indianapolis. He entered private practice with his son, and together they published several legal treatises. Among them were *The Work of the Advocates* (1888), *Roads and Streets* (1890), and *Appellate Procedure* (1892).

Elliott died on November 19, 1913. The state bar association paid tribute to Elliott's many contributions to the Indiana legal system: "For almost half a century he devoted himself to the study and practice of the law—to teaching it to young men, to collecting it in books, and to declaring it with the authority of a judge."

LINDA C. GUGIN, PhD, is professor emeritus of political science, Indiana University Southeast. She is coauthor of *Sherman Minton: New Deal Senator, Cold War Justice* (1997) and *Chief Justice Fred M. Vinson of Kentucky: A Political Biography* (2002), coeditor of *The Governors of Indiana* (2006) and *Justices of the Indiana Supreme Court* (2010), and author of "Sherman Minton: Restraint against a Tide of Activism," *Vanderbilt Law Review* (2009).

SELECTED BIBLIOGRAPHY

Stoll, John B. *History of the Indiana Democracy, 1816–1916*. Indianapolis: Indiana Democratic Publishing Company, 1917.
Thornton, W. W. "The Supreme Court of Indiana." *The Green Bag* 4 (1892).

CASES CITED

Ex parte Griffiths, Reporter, 118 Ind. 83 (1889).
Little v. The State, 90 Ind. 338 (1883).
Robinson, Treasurer, v. Schenck, 102 Ind. 307 (1885).
The State, ex rel. Hovey, v. Noble et al., 118 Ind. 350 (1889).
Smith v. Myers, 109 Ind. 1 (1887).

WILLIAM A. WOODS
January 3, 1881–May 8, 1883

JOHN DANIEL TINDER

Early struggles prepared William Allen Woods, the thirty-first judge of the Indiana Supreme Court, for the difficult challenges ahead at the intersection of law and politics. A month after his birth in rural Tennessee, his father died; seven years later, after the Woods family moved to slave-free Iowa in furtherance of their abolitionist beliefs, his first stepfather died. By age twelve, the necessity to support his family turned Woods into a sturdy farmer. Friction with a second stepfather drove Woods from the family home at fourteen, and he supported himself by driving oxen and operating a gristmill saw. Seemingly destined to a life of manual labor, a love for reading and a relative's loan allowed him the privileges of an education and a profession.

Woods moved to Indiana in 1855 to enroll at Wabash College. His abolitionist beliefs were soon tested in the form of the gift of a slave from a Tennessee relative. Urged to sell his gift for tuition, he instead freed the slave, announcing a preference for abandoning school rather than selling a human being. But frugality, hard work, and academic excellence earned Woods a Wabash diploma and a position on the faculty after graduation.

Woods began reading law while teaching, and in 1861 he was admitted to the Grant County bar. Rejection from Union army service because of an injury inspired him to move to Goshen to practice law and support the Union cause by collecting funds from conscripts who had bought their way out of service in the army. This accepted practice produced necessary revenue for Abraham Lincoln's government. Woods's collection success demonstrated his potential for political office. His abolitionist views estranged him from his Tennessee relatives, but inexorably drew him to the newly formed Republican Party. In 1866 he was elected a state representative and subsequently sponsored a bill regulating railroad freight charges, the first legislation in any state favoring the Granger movement. Woods preferred law practice to legislating, evidenced by his rejection of an offer to run for Congress. His practice thrived, and in 1873 he was elected judge of the Elkhart Circuit Court. Woods was known for fair, firm control of the courtroom and activity in Republican politics, then a widely accepted duality. Woods's affinity for law and politics earned his 1880 election to the Court.

Throughout the mid-1800s the Court's opinions were often long, tedious dissertations on technical procedure, leading to a substantial case backlog and criticism of the Court's maze of arcane procedural traps. Pledging reform, Woods helped refocus the Court by persuading his colleagues to avoid technical dispositions. During Woods's tenure, the caseload was expedited by a shift toward brief opinions going right to the disputed issues. Woods's writings were described as "clear, short, [and] luminous" and "destitute of verbiage.

Woods's Court tenure was brief: in 1883 an Indiana federal trial judgeship became available. Intraparty Republican squabbles about the appointment ended only when the outgoing judge recommended Woods's nomination, and President Chester A. Arthur agreed. Political strife surrounding Woods's selection foreshadowed turmoil that swirled around his bench after the 1886 and 1888 elections. In election fraud matters known as the "Tally Sheet" and "Blocks of Five" cases, Woods's decisions were criticized by the Democratic Party as favoring Republicans and expanding federal control over elections. Yet, Woods's greatest impact on the judicial process lay ahead.

He was next appointed to the newly created U.S. Court of Appeals for the Seventh Circuit in 1891. This contentious nomination produced an unprecedented 172 pages of U.S. Senate testimony; the Senate split purely on party lines. Confirmation succeeded only by the president pro tempore's tiebreaking vote.

Woods's strict interpretation of law and lucid explanations of legal principles carried over to the federal appeals court. The Pullman railroad strike of 1894 brought him national attention. Woods issued an injunction, breaking the strike and ordering imprisonment of labor leader Eugene V. Debs for contempt. The crippling strike posed such violent potential that federal troops were mobilized. A Chicago newspaper extolled Woods's "incisiveness of vision that saved this nation from the terrible menace of anarchy. He [did] more for the stability of this nation, for the orderly progress of labor, than has any other man." The labor movement was not so complimentary, contending that the case eviscerated the populist movement, swinging the judiciary toward management's view over labor.

Woods continued on the appeals court another seven years until his death, working continuously as he had since age twelve, to the very end.

JOHN DANIEL TINDER, JD, is a judge on the U.S. Court of Appeals for the Seventh Circuit. He previously served as judge for the U.S. District Court for the Southern District of Indiana.

SELECTED BIBLIOGRAPHY

Geib, George, and Donald Kite. *Federal Justice in Indiana: The History of the United States District Court for the Southern District of Indiana.* Indianapolis: Indiana Historical Society Press in cooperation with the District Court Library Fund and the United States District Court for the Southern District of Indiana, 2007.

History of Elkhart County, Indiana. Chicago: C. C. Chapman and Company, 1881.

Majliocca, Gerard. "Constitutional False Positives and the Populist Movement" 81. *Notre Dame Law Review* 821 (2006).

Memorial Meeting of the Bench and Bar of Indiana upon the Occasion of the Death of William Allen Woods. Indianapolis: Hollenbeck Press, 1901.

Papke, David Ray. "The Debs Case: Labor, Capital, and the Federal Courts of the 1890s." In *Federal Trials and Great Debates in United States History.* Washington, DC: Federal Judicial Center, 2008.

Solomon, Rayman. *History of the Seventh Circuit, 1891–1941.* Washington, DC: Committee of the Judicial Conference of the United States, 1981.

Research for this essay was conducted by Bradley J. Wombles, B.A. 1999 (Purdue University), J.D. candidate 2010 (Indiana University School of Law-Indianapolis.) The author is extremely grateful for Brad's assistance on this project.

WILLIAM H. COOMBS

December 2, 1882–January 1, 1883

SCOTT M. BUSHNELL

The shortest term served by a judge in Indiana Supreme Court history was the product of nineteenth-century politics and chivalry. William H. Coombs was said to be the oldest practicing attorney in Indiana when Governor Albert G. Porter appointed him to complete the term of Judge James L. Worden. The latter resigned after being elected to the Allen County Superior Court.

Coombs was not the governor's first choice, though. He had intended to nominate northeast Indiana's heroic Republican, Colonel Robert S. Robertson. A prominent attorney, former lieutenant governor, author of many works on the history of the Maumee valley, and recipient of the Medal of Honor for his valor in the Civil War, Robertson demurred. Instead, he asked Porter to appoint Coombs, a request that the governor publicly described as "most magnanimous and gallant."

Born in Brunswick, Maine, on July 17, 1808, Coombs had an extraordinary life for his time. He was raised on a farm outside Cincinnati and trained to be a carpenter. In 1831 he moved to Connersville, Indiana, where he studied law with Caleb B. Smith and was admitted to the bar in 1834. He practiced law in Wabash before moving to Fort Wayne, where he met and married Jane Edsall in 1837. It was a union that lasted fifty-seven years, and they were often referred to as one of Fort Wayne's pioneer families.

Perhaps attracted by the gold rush, the Coombs family sailed around Cape Horn to reach California in 1850 and lived there five years. They returned via the Isthmus of Panama and settled in Middleport, Ohio, in 1856, before returning to Fort Wayne three years later. Coombs continued an active practice with the firm of Coombs, Morris and Bell.

At the time of his selection to the Court, Coombs was seventy-four years old, an age thought to be reserved for retirement, not for service on the bench. Coombs did not apparently share that view. Instead of treating the appointment as honorific, he departed for Indianapolis the day after it was announced. Coombs has been criticized for writing only three decisions during his one month as a justice. Yet, it does not seem too modest of a record, given the time he needed to acclimate himself to the Court process, hear an appeal, research the law, and write an opinion. The first opinion written by Coombs, *Blake et al. v. Blake et al.*, was an affirmation of a lower court ruling involving the rights of collateral heirs where the deceased died intestate. It is not a groundbreaking decision, but it is—apparently typical of Coombs—clearly and concisely written.

Coombs died November 28, 1894, in Fort Wayne. He had been in declining health since his wife's death in June. He was recognized for his contributions to the early days of Allen County. In eulogizing Coombs, members of the Allen County bar described him as "emphatically a self-made man" who "was a clear, terse and effective speaker."

Yet, history has been unusually dismissive of this justice. He is the only member of the state's highest court to have his name misspelled for more than a century. In biographies of the Court judges, he is referred to as William H. Combs—only one *o* in his last name. The error is often accompanied by the statement that his date and place of death are unknown. Searching for these details apparently were stymied by the misspelling of Coombs's name.

SCOTT M. BUSHNELL is a former Associated Press writer and editor. He is the author of *Hard News, Heartfelt Opinions: A History of the Fort Wayne Journal-Gazette* (2007), *Historic Photos of Fort Wayne* (2007), *Historic Photos of Indiana* (2010), and coauthor of *Roanoke: The Renaissance of a Hoosier Village* (2003).

SELECTED BIBLIOGRAPHY

Fort Wayne Daily Gazette, December 3, 1885.

Fort Wayne Gazette, November 30, 1894.

Reports of the Cases Decided by the Supreme Court of Indiana, vol. 85. Indianapolis: Carlon and Hollenbeck, 1883.

Thornton, W. W., "The Supreme Court of Indiana," *The Green Bag* 4 (May–June 1892).

Withered, Jerome L. *Hoosier Justice: A History of the Supreme Court of Indiana.* Indianapolis: Indiana Supreme Court, 1997.

CASES CITED

Blake et al. v. Blake et al., 85 Ind. 65 (1882).

ALLEN ZOLLARS
January 1, 1883–January 7, 1889

SCOTT M. BUSHNELL

Allen Zollars of Fort Wayne, the thirty-third judge of the Indiana Supreme Court, was among the best-educated members of the legal profession in Indiana in the late nineteenth century and was recognized as a "just and learned judge." He held three degrees from Denison University in Granville, Ohio—bachelor of arts, honorary master of arts, and doctorate of law—as well as a law degree from the University of Michigan.

Born September 3, 1839, in Licking County in southeastern Ohio, Zollars was the seventh of eight children born to Frederick and Anna Whitmore Zollars. Only one of his siblings lived beyond childhood. Both of his parents were Prussian immigrants, and his father was a farmer and mill owner.

Following graduation from law school in 1866, Zollars moved to Fort Wayne to set up his practice. There he met Minnie Ewing, whom he married in November 1867. They had two sons and a daughter. Both sons became lawyers, and the oldest, Frederick L., was his father's law partner for about a decade. The other son, Charles E., practiced in Chicago.

Zollars was a Democrat when that party dominated Fort Wayne's political landscape. In 1868 he was elected to the legislature, but did not run for a second term. He served as city attorney from 1869 to 1875. When the superior court was created for Allen County, Zollars was appointed as its first judge in 1877. He resigned after a short term in office, however, "to resume the practice of his profession, which he found to be much more profitable than the judgeship."

In 1882 Zollars won his race for the Indiana Supreme Court and was the Democratic Party's leading vote getter in the northern part of the state. A re-election effort six years later failed when Indiana's Benjamin Harrison topped the Republican ticket and won the presidency on the strength of electoral votes of his home state and New York.

Zollars was one of the more prolific judges during his six years on the Court, writing more than four hundred opinions. His decisions, which were recognized for their clarity and vigor, also exhibited a modern touch. For example, when citing key points from the statutes, he used italics to emphasize the "portions which I regard as important in the case." It was also said of Zollars that he was not, and could not be, partisan in his demeanor or deliberations on the high court.

The nonpartisan nature of Zollars and his fellow judges was aptly demonstrated during the celebrated struggle by Lieutenant Governor Robert Robertson to preside over the Indiana Senate. Robertson, a Republican from Fort Wayne, had been elected in November 1886 to complete the term of Manlon Manson, who had resigned to take a federal position. The Democrats and, in particular, the president pro tem of the Senate, Alonzo Smith, sought to block Robertson from presiding over the senate. The Court, then composed of four Democrats and one Republican, twice ruled against Smith, thus "avoiding dragging the judiciary and its decisions into party politics."

In the first case, *Smith v. Myers*, Smith sued to prevent the certification of Robertson's election. The judges ruled unanimously that the state constitution gives the power to decide such matters to the legislature, not the courts. Smith then obtained a restraining order in Marion Circuit Court preventing Robertson from assuming the duties of his office. When the case reached the Court, Smith was again rebuffed.

Judge Byron K. Elliott, writing the majority opinion in *Robertson v. The State, ex rel. Smith*, found that the Marion court lacked jurisdiction. Judge Joseph A. S. Mitchell concurred, but expanded his opinion by writing that the Court was not "excused from giving its decision" on the question of whether the 1886 election for lieutenant governor was valid. Judge George V. Howk agreed with Mitchell. Judge William E. Niblack also believed that the lower court lacked jurisdiction, but then proceeded to examine the claims of both parties as to which one should preside over the senate. "The condition of things complained of is really one of disorganization between the two houses of the general assembly," he wrote.

Zollars agreed with Niblack and Elliott on their conclusion, but not their reasoning. He asserted that whether "there was a valid election is the very question in the contest," but noted that the Court should realize that the constitution made "the general assembly the exclusive tribunal for the determination of contested elections for governor and lieutenant governor." The separate opinions, according to Court historian Jerome L. Withered, "are notable for their reliance on judicial authority and lack of partisan rhetoric."

After leaving the Court, Zollars resumed his private practice in Fort Wayne. He was active until his final year of life. He died in Fort Wayne on December 20, 1909, at age seventy.

SCOTT M. BUSHNELL is a former Associated Press writer and editor. He is the author of *Hard News, Heartfelt Opinions: A History of the Fort Wayne Journal-Gazette* (2007), *Historic Photos of Fort Wayne* (2007), *Historic Photos of Indiana* (2010), and coauthor of *Roanoke: The Renaissance of a Hoosier Village* (2003).

SELECTED BIBLIOGRAPHY

Fort Wayne Journal-Gazette, December 20, 21, 1909.
Northeastern Reporter 10 (February 25–April 15, 1887).

CASES CITED

Robertson v. The State, ex rel. Smith, 109 Ind. 79 (1887).
Smith v. Myers, 109 Ind. 1 (1887).

INDIANA SUPREME COURT

EDWIN P. HAMMOND
May 14, 1883–January 6, 1885

ROBERT R. "GUS" STEVENS

Heroic soldier, skilled attorney, and wise jurist, Edwin Pollock Hammond, the thirty-fourth judge of the Indiana Supreme Court, lived a long and productive life serving his state and nation. He volunteered soon after the start of the Civil War and, except for brief periods back home, was in the thick of the fighting at the front until the war ended in 1865. Hammond, who began his legal career in 1857, served as a circuit court judge prior to and following his appointment to the Court in 1883.

Born November 26, 1835, in Brookville, Indiana, Hammond moved with his family in 1849 to Columbus, where he attended school and for a time a local seminary. At age nineteen he worked as a clerk in a wholesale dry goods store in Indianapolis, but soon moved to Terre Haute to serve as an apprentice in the law firm of his half brother, Abram Hammond, Indiana's twelfth governor, and his partner, Thomas Nelson.

Hammond entered Indiana Asbury (now DePauw) University in 1856 and after a preliminary examination was admitted to the senior law class. The following year he was awarded a bachelor of law degree, admitted to the bar, and moved to Rensselaer to open a law practice. It would not be long, though, before the rhythm of his small-town practice was interrupted by war.

Hammond's first tour of duty was as a lieutenant with the Ninth Indiana Volunteer Infantry Regiment, which saw action in western Virginia. After the unit's three-month enlistment ended, Hammond resumed his law practice and married Lucy J. Saylor on August 8, 1861. Two months later he was elected without opposition to the Indiana House, representing Newton, Jasper, and Pulaski counties. About a year later, however, he was back in uniform, having helped formed the Eighty-seventh Indiana Volunteer Infantry Regiment. He was commissioned as a captain and given a company command. Later, he was promoted to major and joined the regimental staff. In early 1863, while the regiment was camped near Gallatin, Tennessee, Hammond received the news that his wife of sixteen months had died.

The Eighty-seventh was deployed with the Army of the Cumberland during the summer and early fall of 1863, participating in fighting around Chattanooga, including the major battle at Chickamauga. The regiment suffered considerable casualties, including Hammond, who was struck by a spent rifle ball. While back in Indiana to recruit replacements, Hammond was promoted to lieutenant colonel and married Mary Virginia Spitler, daughter of Colonel George W. and Malinda Spitler.

By the fall of 1864 the regiment, now commanded by Hammond, had finished its steady and hard-fought advance to Atlanta. It then joined General William Tecumseh Sherman's "March to the Sea" and, following the surrender of Savannah, the regiment continued fighting through South Carolina and North Carolina. In April, near Smithville, North Carolina, Hammond was able to report that "we heard the last rebel bullet." At war's end, Hammond was promoted to brevet colonel, and he led the Eighty-seventh in a march down Pennsylvania Avenue during victory celebrations in Washington, D.C.

Following the war Hammond returned to Rensselaer and practiced law until becoming a circuit judge in 1873. He left that position in mid-1883 when he was appointed by Governor Albert G. Porter to the Court, filling the vacancy created when Judge William A. Woods was named to the federal district court for Indiana. Hammond was the Republican nominee to the

Court in 1884 from the Fifth District, but was defeated in a landslide Democratic victory. Despite his brief tenure on the Court, Hammond wrote nearly two hundred opinions on issues ranging from libel, blackmail, murder, probate, and liquor sales to minors. One legal historian called his opinions "clear and pointed; there is no mistaking what he decides."

After leaving the Court, Hammond returned to practicing law in Rensselaer and served another two years as circuit court judge, resigning in 1892. He then formed a partnership with Charles B. and William V. Stuart of Lafayette. Hammond handled the firm's business in Rensselaer and Jasper County for two years and then moved to Lafayette. The firm was first known as Stuart Brothers and Hammond and later became Stuart, Hammond and Simms.

Hammond was a longtime Freemason and a strong supporter of the Grand Army of the Republic, a fraternal organization of Civil War veterans. In addition, he was a trustee of Purdue University and was a delegate to the Republican National Convention in Philadelphia when President Ulysses S. Grant was nominated for his second term. Hammond was awarded an honorary doctor of jurisprudence by Wabash College in 1892.

When Hammond died at his home in Lafayette on January 27, 1920, the local newspaper wrote: "Judge Hammond was held in universal esteem in this community where he was known as a skilled and careful lawyer, an excellent citizen, a faithful friend and a modest and courteous man." He was married to his second wife, Mary Virginia, for fifty-five years. She died in 1927, and both are buried in the family plot at Weston Cemetery in Rensselaer.

ROBERT R. "GUS" STEVENS is retired director of the Lewis Historical Collections Library, Vincennes University and curator of the William Henry Harrison House in Vincennes. He is the author of numerous historical and sports articles.

SELECTED BIBLIOGRAPHY

Counties of Warren, Benton, Jasper and Newton, Indiana: Historical and Biographical. Chicago: F. A. Battey and Company, Publishers, 1883.

Cozzens, Peter. *The Shipwreck of Their Hopes: The Battles for Chattanooga.* Urbana and Chicago: University of Illinois Press, 1994.

Douglas, Samuel M. *Report of the Adjutant General of the State of Indiana*, vols. 2 and 3. Indianapolis: State Printer, 1866.

Martin, Charles Alexander, ed. *Alumnal Record, DePauw University.* Greencastle, IN: Published by the University, 1910.

The War of the Rebellion: Official Records of the Union and Confederate Armies. Washington, DC: U.S. Government Printing Office, 1891.

JOSEPH A. S. MITCHELL
January 6, 1885–December 12, 1890

TIMOTHY S. SHELLY

After receiving legal training in Chambersburg, Pennsylvania, Joseph A. S. Mitchell, the thirty-fifth judge of the Indiana Supreme Court, was admitted to the practice of law in 1859 and the following year established his fledgling legal practice in Goshen, Indiana. Mitchell's initial plunge into Indiana's legal practice was cut short when, in 1861, he was conscripted into the Union army, serving with the Second Indiana Cavalry. Mitchell's Civil War service proved to be his only significant time away from his newly adopted hometown of Goshen.

Mitchell, who was born in Franklin County, Pennsylvania, on December 21, 1837, spent his early years on his family's small farm near the borough of Mechanicsburg, eight miles west of the capital, Harrisburg. His father died when he was only a child, and at age sixteen Mitchell moved to Illinois, studying for two years at Blandensville Academy to become a teacher. After completing his studies there, Mitchell returned in 1856 to Pennsylvania, where he studied law at the firm of Riley and Sharp. At age twenty-two, following three years of apprenticeship in Chambersburg, Mitchell was licensed to practice law.

During the Civil War, Mitchell saw significant action in both Tennessee and eastern Kentucky, participating in the battles of Chickamauga, Chattanooga, Lookout Mountain, and Shiloh, among others. Despite a lengthy hospitalization because of a serious illness, Mitchell was promoted to captain. He then served under General Edward M. McCook as inspector general of the First Cavalry Division in the Army of the Cumberland, a post he held until the end of the war.

After the war, Mitchell returned to Goshen, resurrecting his nascent legal career. At that point he formed a partnership with fellow Methodist John Baker. Mitchell, a Democrat, and Baker, a Republican, practiced law together as well as actively participating in state and national politics. They maintained this partnership for nearly two decades, until Mitchell left upon his election to the Supreme Court. In the early part of his legal career, Mitchell also served as a deputy prosecuting attorney. During their association, Baker served six years in Congress and was appointed a judge of the federal district court for Indiana in 1892, two years after Mitchell's death.

Shortly after his return from the war, Mitchell married Mary Defrees in November 1865. Mitchell's interest in politics extended into his family life. Mary was the daughter of Joseph Defrees, a local political figure who was a member of the U.S. House of Representatives at the time. The Mitchells had two children, daughter, Harriett, and son, Defrees.

As a practicing attorney, Mitchell assisted considerably in the transformation of Goshen from a town to an incorporated municipality. He drafted the city's original ordinances in 1868, while serving as Goshen's first city attorney. After several years in that capacity, Mitchell was elected Goshen's third mayor, serving from 1872 to 1874. His experiences as city attorney and mayor, as well as his family and professional political ties, ultimately served Mitchell well among Hoosier voters. His first effort at securing a statewide elected position, however, proved unsuccessful. In the fall of 1880 Mitchell, running on the Democratic ticket for a seat on the Court, lost to Republican William A. Woods, a circuit court judge and fellow Goshen barrister. Woods resigned after two years to become a federal district court judge. Mitchell ran again for the Court in 1884, this time defeating Woods's replacement on the bench, Edwin P. Hammond.

In 1879 Mitchell was appointed to the board of trustees of Methodist-affiliated Indiana Asbury (now Depauw) University. Mitchell remained a trustee of the university for eleven years until his death in 1890, even earning a bachelor of law degree from DePauw's short-lived law school, which ceased operation in 1895. While a trustee, Mitchell advocated for professor salary increases, even if faculty size needed to be reduced to fund the increases. Shortly before his death, DePauw appointed Mitchell a lecturer at its law school.

As a Court judge for only six years, Mitchell earned not only the standard five thousand dollars annual salary, but also the respect of his fellow high court judges for professionalism and independent "judicial style," as Judge Byron K. Elliott later eulogized at Mitchell's funeral. Mitchell's opinions focused primarily on civil matters involving business transactions. In 1890 Mitchell was reelected to a second six-year term on the Court, but fell ill shortly after the election. He died at his home three weeks later, on December 12, 1890. Mitchell is buried in Goshen's Oak Ridge Cemetery.

TIMOTHY S. SHELLY, JD, is a partner with Warrick and Boyn, LLP. He is a board member of Indiana Landmarks and an adviser to the National Trust for Historic Preservation.

SELECTED BIBLIOGRAPHY

Deahl, Anthony, ed. *A Twentieth Century History and Biographical Record of Elkhart County, Indiana*. Chicago: Lewis Publishing Company, 1905.

Feeler, Horace W., ed. *The Green Bag: An Entertaining Magazine for Lawyers* 4 (1892) *Goshen Daily Times*, December 18, 1890.

Griffiths, John L. *Reports of Cases Argued and Determined in the Supreme Court of Judicature of the State of Indiana*, vol. 125. Indianapolis: Bowen-Merrill Company, 1891.

Howard, Timothy E. *A History of Saint Joseph County, Indiana*. Chicago: Lewis Publishing Company, 1907.

Report of Captain Joseph A. S. Mitchell, Company M. Second Indiana Cavalry. Nashville, TN: January 2, 1863.

Trissal, Francis M., *Public Men of Indiana: A Political History*. Hammond, IN: W. B. Conkey Company, 1922.

SILAS D. COFFEY

January 7, 1889–January 7, 1895

BRADFORD W. SAMPLE

The young man who carried a copy of *Blackstone's Commentaries* with him onto Civil War battlefields ascended to the Indiana Supreme Court as its thirty-sixth judge and served during a politically tumultuous period. Raised on a farm in Owen County by Hodge R. and Hannah Coffey, Silas Demarcus Coffey attended the local public school before enrolling at Indiana University in 1860. His stay was brief. After Fort Sumter fell, he joined the Fourteenth Indiana Infantry, serving until honorably discharged in June 1864.

After the war Coffey married Caroline Byles of Baltimore, and the couple settled in Clay County, Indiana, ultimately raising six children. *Blackstone* may have provided Coffey with his legal education, as there is no record of his having read law with anyone before joining in a law practice with Allen T. Rose upon arriving in Clay County. In 1868 Coffey became partners with William W. Carter, a fellow Civil War veteran. After leaving the Court, Coffey practiced with S. M. McGregor in Clay County until his retirement.

Coffey, a Republican, failed in his first two attempts at elective office, first losing in 1866 in his race for prosecuting attorney of a heavily Democratic circuit that included Owen, Clay, Putnam, and Greene counties. He was also unsuccessful in his bid for circuit judge in 1871. Solon Turman, however, the man who won, died while in office, and Governor Albert G. Porter, a Republican, appointed Coffey to the post in 1881. Coffey won over district Democrats and was reelected in 1882 to a full six-year term as circuit judge.

Republicans enjoyed a mixed year in 1888, winning many statewide offices, including the open seats on the Court, but losing the general assembly. Coffey was elected with fellow Republicans John G. Berkshire and Walter Olds and served as chief justice for three sessions. The Democratic-controlled legislature and Republican governor Alvin P. Hovey repeatedly clashed over the fundamental issue of separation of powers. Eventually, the disputes came before the Court. Coffey and his Republican brethren sided with the governor's positions over those of the general assembly's Democratic majority in a number of cases, leading the Democratic Party in its 1890 platform to denounce the Court's four Republican members as partisan judges who needed to be removed. Some of Coffey's opinions, however, also angered fellow Republicans.

Coffey, whose opinions were characterized by peers as unusually brief and "with few if any dicta," wrote three significant decisions during this heated political period. In *The State, ex rel. Jameson et al. v. Denny, Mayor*, Coffey and the Republican majority ruled unconstitutional legislation that gave the general assembly the power to appoint members of a city's board of public works. The legislation, Coffey said, "is subversive of all local self-government, a right that the people did not surrender when they adopted the Constitution." In the case of *The City of Evansville et al. v. The State, ex rel. Blend et al.*, the Court invalidated a similar measure that gave the legislature power to name members of a city's police and fire boards.

The second significant decision that Coffey wrote concerned the general assembly's assertion of authority to fill vacancies for the state geologist and state statistician rather than the governor. In *State, ex rel. Collett v. Gorby*, the Court determined that the vacancies should have been filled in the 1888 election, but that the state's chief executive had the authority to fill such vacancies. Coffey's third decision, *Parvin v. Wimberg et al.*, upheld the validity of the Australian or secret ballot, an elective reform measure enacted in 1889. His opinion, which angered Democrats at the time, overturned a lower court decision that had allowed a number of questionable ballots to be counted in an election for county auditor.

Other decisions reflected the era's politics in which some legislators pushed for what would later be designated Progressive legislation, while members of some courts questioned the constitutionality of the acts. Coffey, for example, wrote the opinion that approved increased licensing fees for retail liquor establishments in *Bush v. Indianapolis*.

The Republican Party refused to renominate Coffey at its 1894 convention. He had angered state officeholders, including Republicans, earlier that year with his decision in *Henderson, Auditor of State v. The State, ex rel., Stout, Sheriff of Vigo County*, that deprived them of extra compensation. Coffey continued to practice law after leaving the Court. When he died a decade after retiring from the bench, the Clay County Bar Association memorialized him as an affable and logical jurist who always befriended younger lawyers and served the state with honor.

BRADFORD W. SAMPLE, PhD, is academic vice president, Bryan College. He was a contributor to *The Governors of Indiana* (2006) and author of "A Truly Midwestern City: Indianapolis on the Eve of the Great Depression," *Indiana Magazine of History* 97 (June 2001) .

SELECTED BIBLIOGRAPHY

Blanchard, Charles, ed. *Counties of Clay and Owen, Indiana: Historical and Biographical.* Chicago: F. A. Battey and Company, 1884.

Taylor, Charles W. *Biographical Sketches and Review of the Bench and Bar of Indiana.* Indianapolis: Bench and Bar Publishing Company, 1895.

Thornton, W. W. "The Supreme Court of Indiana, II." *The Green Bag* 4, no. 6 (June 1892): 272–74.

Travis, William. *A History of Clay County, Indiana: Closing of the First Century's History of the County, and Showing the Growth of Its People, Institutions, Industries and Wealth.* 2 vols. New York and Chicago: Lewis Publishing Company, 1909.

CASES CITED

Bush v. The City of Indianapolis, 120 Ind. 476 (1889).

The City of Evansville et al. v. The State, ex rel. Blend et al., 118 Ind. 426 (1889).

Henderson, Auditor of State v. The State, ex rel., Stout, Sheriff of Vigo County, 137 Ind. 552 (1894).

Parvin v. Wimberg et al., 130 Ind. 561 (1892).

State, ex rel. Collett v. Gorby, 122 Ind. 17 (1890).

The State, ex rel. Jameson et al. v. Denny, Mayor, 118 Ind. 382 (1889).

WALTER OLDS
January 7, 1889–June 15, 1893

JAMES E. ST. CLAIR

Walter Olds's tenure as the thirty-seventh judge of the Indiana Supreme Court was brief but eventful. Following the election of Olds and two other Republicans to the Court in 1888, as well as the election of Republican Alvin P. Hovey as governor, the Democratic-controlled general assembly began passing laws designed to expand its powers while diluting those of the other two branches of state government and local government. Democrats, according to one historian, stung by the loss of three Court seats and all state offices, were determined "to save from the wreck of defeat" as much control as possible. One by one, however, their efforts were declared unconstitutional by the Court, with even the lone Democrat, Joseph A. S. Mitchell, occasionally siding with his brethren.

Addressing the festering issue of a clogged Court docket, the legislature resurrected the idea of a Court commission, an approach tried a few years earlier to help judges clear the backlog of cases. Under the previous system, the commissioners, each chosen by the five Court judges, acted as a clearinghouse in which they reviewed cases, wrote opinions, and then forwarded their recommendations to the judges for final action. This arrangement did not have the desired effect of efficiency because judges still had to review the work of the commissioners and the system was abandoned. The 1889 version of the commission adopted by the general assembly mirrored the earlier system with one important difference—the legislature, not the Court, would appoint commissioners. In *State ex rel. Hovey v. Noble*, a unanimous Court declared the act unconstitutional, noting the 1851 Indiana Constitution made it clear that only the courts can exercise judicial power. Ultimately, the creation of the appellate court in 1891 helped to ease the Court's logjam of cases.

Several legislative initiatives that had sought to shift power from local officials to the legislature were also struck down by Olds and his colleagues. Olds wrote the opinion in *State, ex rel. Holt v. Denny*, a suit resulting from a statute giving the legislature authority to manage and control city fire and police departments. Olds declared that such an act was "plainly in violation of the fundamental principles of government and the spirit of the Constitution" because it "seeks to take from the people the inherent and inalienable rights vested in them and to deprive them of local self-government."

The decisions that went against the general assembly unleashed a barrage of attacks on Olds and the other Republican judges by the Democratic press in the state and the state Democratic Party. The judges, according to Charles W. Taylor in his book, *The Bench and Bar of Indiana*, were hammered by partisan newspapers with "unusual violence of language and with charges of dishonesty and party subserviency." The platform adopted at the 1890 Democratic convention contained similar accusations. Taylor called the attacks unprecedented and said the charges were "wholly unfounded."

What effect, if any, the attacks had on the electorate is unknown, but Democratic fortunes in the state did shift swiftly, and after the election of 1892 the party controlled the governor's office and a majority on the Court. That advantage increased in mid-1893 when Olds resigned with about a year and a half remaining in his term and was replaced by Democrat Joseph S. Dailey. After leaving the bench, Olds moved to Chicago and formed a law practice with Charles F. Griffin, a former Indiana secretary of state. Olds said he resigned for financial reasons, noting that he was stepping into "an eight thousand dollar practice," an opportunity that might not be available had he served out his term on the Court. In Chicago Olds represented a number of railroads and large corporations, a clientele that he continued serving when he returned to Indiana in 1901 and established his practice in Fort Wayne. He announced in early 1915 his candidacy for the Republican nomination for U.S. Senate, but withdrew before the party's convention the following year.

Olds, who was born on August 11, 1846, in Mount Gilead, Ohio, enlisted at age seventeen with the 174th Ohio Infantry during the Civil War. His four brothers also fought in the war and two were killed. Following his discharge, Olds attended Capital University in Columbus, Ohio, and then read law with his brother, James. Shortly after being admitted to the bar in Ohio in 1869, Olds moved to Columbia City, Indiana, and began a law partnership with A. Y. Hooper, a state senator at the time. Olds was elected to the Indiana Senate in 1876 and then as circuit court judge for Kosciusko and Whitley counties in 1884, a position he held until his election to the Court four years later. While in practice in Columbia City, Olds supervised Thomas R. Marshall, later Indiana governor and U.S. vice president, in his study of the law.

Olds married Marie J. Merritt in 1873, and their son, Lee Merritt Olds, became a prominent lawyer in San Francisco. Olds was still active with his firm in Fort Wayne at the time of his death in 1925 at age seventy-nine.

JAMES E. ST. CLAIR, MA, is professor of journalism, Indiana University Southeast. He is coauthor of *Sherman Minton: New Deal Senator, Cold War Justice* (1997) and *Chief Justice Fred M. Vinson of Kentucky: A Political Biography* (2002) and coeditor of *The Governors of Indiana* (2006) and *Justices of the Indiana Supreme Court* (2010).

SELECTED BIBLIOGRAPHY

Goodspeed, Weston A., and Charles Blanchard. *Counties of Whitley and Noble, Indiana.* Chicago: F. A. Batty and Company, 1882.
Fort Wayne News Sentinel, July 30, 1925.
Fort Wayne Weekly Gazette, June 1, 1893.
Taylor, Charles W. *The Bench and Bar of Indiana.* Indianapolis: Bench and Bar Publishing Company, 1895.

CASES CITED

The State, ex rel. Holt et al. v. Denny, Mayor, et al., 118 Ind. 449 (1889).
The State, ex rel. Hovey v. Noble, et al., 118 Ind. 350 (1889).

JOHN G. BERKSHIRE
January 7, 1889–February 19, 1891

WILLIAM F. GULDE

John G. Berkshire was no stranger to hard work. From his early days as a blacksmith in Ohio County to his final days as the thirty-eighth judge of the Indiana Supreme Court, Berkshire worked hard to achieve his dreams.

Born in 1832 into an impoverished family in Millersville, Kentucky, Berkshire seemed destined for a hard life. His father, William G., a blacksmith, decided that the best way to provide for his family was to leave Kentucky. Around 1845 he moved the family to the Ohio River village of Rising Sun, Indiana. The youthful Berkshire must have thought Rising Sun to be an incredible change from Millersville, as its position on the river afforded him a chance to see dozens of flatboats and steamboats docking and departing daily.

While the town allowed for young Berkshire to dream about his future, his reality was a different picture. As early as age ten, he toiled at the forge alongside his father. Little is known of how often the boy attended school, but some sources indicate that his education was sporadic at best. At age sixteen, Berkshire suffered a heavy loss with the death of his mother.

How Berkshire first came to study under attorneys Alexander C. Downey and James J. Jelley is unknown, but what is known is that the young man begged his father to leave the family blacksmithing business to pursue the study of law under these men. Both lawyers had a profound impact on Berkshire's life.

Circuit Court Judge Downey mentored dozens of young lawyers throughout southeastern Indiana and later served as the dean of Asbury Law School (now DePauw University) and as a Supreme Court judge. It was Downey who noticed that Berkshire had talent, and he encouraged the young man to enroll in the newly formed law school in Greencastle. Despite the economic hardships that plagued his family, Berkshire managed to obtain a law degree in 1857.

Through the assistance of his mentor Jelley, Berkshire began to practice law in Versailles in 1858. The Versailles years were some of the most important in Berkshire's life—he established a successful business, became interested in Republican Party politics, and met and married Augusta Clendenning. During the Civil War, Berkshire remained in Versailles practicing law and selling insurance for the Phoenix Insurance Company of Hartford, Connecticut. Federal tax records reveal that Berkshire brought home an ample income. By 1866 he earned a yearly income of $1,079.

Berkshire's election as a circuit court judge in 1864 made him well known throughout southeastern Indiana. He earned a reputation as a fair judge, and he spent many days on the road away from his family, which by 1870 included two young daughters. When the state changed boundary lines for the circuit court districts, Berkshire moved his family to North Vernon in nearby Jennings County.

Soon after arriving to the new community, the family faced several health crises and one profound tragedy. In August 1877, while holding court in Vevay, Berkshire became very ill with cholera. He closed the court and went home to North Vernon to convalesce. Two years later a scarlet fever epidemic swept through North Vernon claiming the lives of thirty-three children. The Berkshire daughters came down with the fever and struggled to live. While Jennie, the oldest daughter, survived, eleven-year-old Bettie succumbed from the fever on May 23, 1879. Her death affected Berkshire for the rest of his life; as he lay dying twelve years later, he told family members that he planned to visit Bettie in heaven.

Berkshire had long been interested in politics, perhaps going all the way back to his boyhood days in Rising Sun. As a young attorney, he contributed articles to the *Versailles Dispatch,* and he attended the Republican National Convention in 1868. His many years as a circuit court judge likely gave him the confidence that he could run for the Court in 1882; and, while he lost his first race for that post, he could take comfort in the fact that he easily won Jennings County.

The Republican Party again recruited Berkshire to run for the Court in 1888. The politics of the country had changed dramatically since the last time he ran for public office, and Berkshire found himself swept into office in a Republican tidal wave that included the election of Benjamin Harrison as president.

Upon taking office, Berkshire, then fifty-seven, immediately plunged into work. The Court was several years behind, and there had been criticism from every corner of the state about the sluggishness of justice in Indiana. To help alleviate the Court's docket, a commission had been established to assist the judges, but Berkshire found himself in the middle of a political controversy when the legislature, controlled by the Democratic Party, chose all Democrats for the commission. Berkshire's election along with two other judges gave Republicans the edge on the Court, and they found the commission unconstitutional in *State ex rel. Hovey v. Noble.* The newly elected Republican court also began striking down Democratic Party appointments, causing a firestorm in the press. The Democratic-controlled legislature had attempted to thwart Governor Alvin P. Hovey, a Republican, by passing laws that gave them the authority to appoint the state geologist, statistician, and oil inspector. Berkshire and his fellow Republicans rendered the acts unconstitutional.

In making his mark on the Court, Berkshire labored many hours trying to wade through cases, reading late into the night. He worked on weekends and gave up his vacation time. Other judges also worked hard, but they became alarmed by Berkshire's office hours. In his first year in office, the Court heard more than a hundred cases, and Berkshire wrote the majority opinion in thirty-eight of them.

By all accounts, Berkshire should have rested. In early February at the start of the 1891 term, he developed a severe cold but remained at the

Court. Three separate physicians attended to him, but the cold turned into pneumonia. On February 19, 1891, with his wife at his side, he passed away at the age of fifty-nine. Although not in time to help Berkshire, the legislature created an intermediate appellate court in 1891 to alleviate the burden of Indiana's Court judges.

WILLIAM F. GULDE is curriculum coordinator and former chair, Social Studies Department, North Central High School, Indianapolis. He is the author of *Hopes, Dreams, and Books: The Story of North Central High School 1956–2004* (2004).

SELECTED BIBLIOGRAPHY

Griffiths, John L. *Reports of Cases Argued and Determined in the Supreme Court of Judicature of the State of Indiana.* Indianapolis: Bowen Merrill Company, 1889.
History of Ripley County, Indiana. Batavia, OH: Clermont Publishing Company, 1968.
Indianapolis Sentinel, February 21, 1891.
Indianapolis Times, April 10, 1937.
Trissal, Francis M. *Public Men of Indiana: A Political History.* 2 vols. Hammond, IN: W. B. Conkey Company, 1923.

CASES CITED
State ex rel. Hovey v Noble, 118 Ind. 350 (1889).

ROBERT W. McBRIDE

December 17, 1890–January 2, 1893

SUZANNE S. BELLAMY

During the Civil War, Robert Wesley McBride, the thirty-ninth judge of the Indiana Supreme Court, acted as a bodyguard for President Abraham Lincoln. McBride stood within twenty feet of the president when he delivered his second inaugural address on March 4, 1865, and was present when Lincoln met General Ulysses S. Grant for the first time that same month.

Born January 25, 1842, in Richland County, Ohio, McBride lived in Ohio as a youth and attended public schools there. Following the death of his father, McBride moved with an uncle to Iowa and continued his education at the common schools of Mahaska and Wapello counties and at a private academy in Kirkville from 1856 to 1858. In 1859 he received his license to teach in the public schools of Mahaska County, which he did for three years before returning to his home in Ohio. In the fall of 1863, as the Civil War intensified, McBride enlisted in the Seventh Independent Squadron of

Ohio Volunteer Cavalry, known as the Union Light Guard. He remained a member of this group until the war ended.

As a member of the Union Light Guard, McBride arrived in Washington, D.C., in late 1863 and learned for the first time that the special service for which he had enlisted was to act as a bodyguard or mounted escort for Lincoln. Initially disappointed at not being sent to the front, he later wrote, "We can also now realize, as we could not at that time, the honor of having been specifically chosen as the personal escort and bodyguard of one of the greatest of Americans and greatest of men." In writing about Lincoln's funeral more than a half century later, McBride reflected, "I feel certain that no more sincere mourners gathered around the bier or lamented the death of Abraham Lincoln than the men who had so long stood guard over him, and who, as I believe, would to a man willingly have given their own lives to save him."

After the war McBride moved to Waterloo, Indiana, and in 1867, after serving as clerk of the state senate, was admitted to the bar in DeKalb County based on his years of studying the law. He practiced law in Waterloo until 1882, when he was elected a circuit judge, a position he held until defeated for re-election in 1888. Two years later the Republican Party nominated McBride for the Court, but he was defeated. Upon the unexpected death of his opponent, McBride was appointed by Governor Alvin P. Hovey to fill the vacancy. McBride served on the Court from December 17, 1890, to January 2, 1893. Once again, he failed to be reelected.

McBride wrote a host of significant opinions during his term on the Court, including several that involved the power of cities and city officials. In *City of Frankfort v. State*, he upheld the city's method of assessing private landowners the cost of street improvements; he likewise affirmed the right of a city to supply private customers with electric lights in *City of Crawfordsville v. Braden*; and in *State v. Wolever*, McBride upheld the power of mayors to rule in civil and criminal cases. In *City of Rushville v. Rushville Natural Gas Co.*, however, McBride ruled that the city lacked the power to regulate the price of natural gas supplied to its citizens, and in *First National Bank of Mt. Vernon v. Sarlls* he decided that while a city could regulate building repairs it did not have the power to absolutely prohibit them.

After leaving the bench, McBride practiced law in Indianapolis and was one of the organizers of the State Life Insurance Company and counsel for its loan department. For nearly half a century, he was prominent in the Grand Army of the Republic, an organization of Civil War veterans, and served four terms as its judge advocate general. About a month before his death on May 15, 1926, at the age of eighty-four, McBride completed a brief book describing his observations of Lincoln while serving as a member of his guard. Upon McBride's death, the *Indianapolis News* of May 17, 1926, wrote, "One of the preeminent characteristics of the man was his ability to do, modestly and with the utmost fidelity, whatever was entrusted to him."

SUZANNE S. BELLAMY, JD, is a researcher and writer. She is the author of *Hoosier Justice at Nuremberg* (2010), a former editorial assistant of the Papers of Lew and Susan Wallace, and served as assistant general counsel, Anacomp Inc.

SELECTED BIBLIOGRAPHY

McBride, Robert W. *Lincoln's Body Guard, the Union Light Guard of Ohio: With Some Personal Recollections of Abraham Lincoln*. Indianapolis: Edward J. Hecker, printer, 1911.
————. *Personal Recollections of Abraham Lincoln*. Indianapolis: Bobbs-Merrill, 1926.
Pictorial and Biographical Memoirs of Indianapolis and Marion County, Indiana, Together with Biographies of Many Prominent Men of Other Portions of the State, Both Living and Dead. Chicago: Goodspeed Brothers, 1893.
Trissal, Francis M. *Public Men of Indiana: A Political History*. Vol. 2, *1890–1920*. Hammond, IN: W. B. Conkey Company, printer, 1923.

CASES CITED
City of Crawfordsville v. Braden, 130 Ind. 149, 28 N.E. 849 (1891).
City of Frankfort v. State, 128 Ind. 438, 27 N.E. 1115 (1891).
City of Rushville v. Rushville Natural Gas Co,. 132 Ind. 575, 28 N.E. 853 (1891).
First National Bank of Mt. Vernon v. Sarlls, 129 Ind. 201, 28 N.E. 434 (1891).
State v. Wolever, 127 Ind. 306, 26 N.E. 762 (1891).

McBride's papers are in the Indiana State Library, Indianapolis.

JOHN D. MILLER

February 25, 1891–January 2, 1893

ELIZABETH R. OSBORN

When the call came, John Donnell Miller, the fortieth judge of the Indiana Supreme Court, like thousands of other Hoosiers of his generation, dropped what he was doing and volunteered to serve during the Civil War. In 1861, with only a few months to go before his graduation, Miller left Hanover College to join Company G of Indiana's Seventh Infantry Regiment. Writing to his brother Robert from Kelly's Ford, Virginia, in 1863, Miller described life on the battlefield:

> John D. Miller and Henry were both struck by a shell, it just brushed Henry's shoulder and hit John a glancing lick on the head. He is not much hurt. Henry not at all. The sharpshooters came near fixing Henry and I both by one shot we were behind a tree skirmishing then one of them shot the ball passing just over our heads. 6 inches lower and we would both have been killed. I tell you I got some bully shots at the Greasers. Twice I shot with a good rest. And not over 40 yards at the

whole body of a man. I was not a bit nervous and shot cool and calm as I ever did at a squirrel.

After being assigned as a clerk to the adjutant in 1862, Miller started to study law in his spare time, "time that other soldiers gave to the frivolous amusements of the tented field." Unlike many of his comrades, Miller survived action at the Second Battle of Bull Run, Antietam, Fredericksburg, Chancellorsville, the Battle of the Wilderness, and Gettysburg, returning home to central Indiana at the end of his three-year enlistment.

Back home in Indiana, Miller completed his degree at Hanover and began his formal study of law in the Franklin, Indiana, firm of Overstreet and Hunter. He was admitted to the Johnson County bar in 1866 but returned home to Greensburg to begin his practice. He eventually joined Gavin and Miller, the firm of his former regimental commander, Colonel James Gavin. He continued in partnership with Gavin, and later his son, until he was appointed to the Court in 1891.

Miller was born December 2, 1840, on the family farm in Decatur County and, except for his Civil War service, spent his entire life in central Indiana. His grandparents were pioneers in the region, and on September 21, 1869, he married Mary J. Stevens, the daughter of another longtime Decatur County family. The Millers had two surviving children. Mary died in 1891 during the time her husband was serving on the Court.

Appointed to the Court by Governor Alvin P. Hovey following the death of John G. Berkshire, Miller had to stand for re-election in 1893 and, like many of his fellow Republicans, was defeated. Despite this relatively brief tenure on the Court, Miller's work was well regarded by his colleagues and the bar. The bar association resolution read at his funeral described him in this way: "His judgments were formed with care and expressed with vigor. He explored the authorities with diligence, and he sought the principles of right and justice with zeal and care."

Authoring 136 majority opinions during his 677 days on the Court, Miller spent much of this time writing on civil matters relating to land disputes, railroad claims, debt collection, employer liability, and resolving inheritance issues. He wrote only seven of his 136 opinions on criminal topics. He did write, however, on nine different cases involving women's legal standing in the courts. Surprisingly, cases regarding dower portions, coverture, and married women's limitations regarding the ownership of property were still arriving at the Court at the end of the nineteenth century.

Miller served his country and community not only as a soldier and Court judge, but also as a councilman, city clerk, county attorney, state legislator and, at the time of his death, judge of the Eighth Circuit, encompassing Rush and Decatur counties. Miller's election to the Eighth Circuit was not easy. It took two nominating conventions and 815 ballots to place his name on the ballot in 1894. This contentiousness was not a reflection of the suitability of Miller or his opponent, but of the competition between the Republicans of Rush and Decatur counties to place their own candidate in the office. Sadly, Miller's tenure as a circuit court judge was almost as brief as his time on the Court. He died on March 18, 1898, never recovering from a stroke he suffered on the bench while hearing a case about whether horse manure was real estate or personal property.

ELIZABETH R. OSBORN, PhD, is assistant to the Chief Justice of Indiana for court history and public education. She is responsible for the educational outreach programs of the Indiana Supreme Court, including the Indiana Supreme Court Legal History Series and Courts in the Classroom. Osborn is the author of numerous publications about the history and operation of Indiana's courts and a contributor to *The History of Indiana Law* (2006).

SELECTED BIBLIOGRAPHY

Greensburg Review, June 9, 1894, March 19, 23, 1898.

Hughes, John H. *Rush County Indiana: Chapter 2, 1822–1982; The Bench and Bar and Officials*. Rushville, IN: Wilkinson-Printing, 1983.

John D. Miller to Robert Miller. December 4, 1863. Letter held by the Miller family.

LEONARD J. HACKNEY

January 2, 1893–January 2, 1899

MARGRET G. ROBB

Leonard J. Hackney's ascension to become the forty-first judge of the Indiana Supreme Court at the relatively young age of thirty-seven was marked by detours, false starts, and years of acrimonious accusations that questioned his honesty, fitness for office, ethics, temperament, and manhood.

Hackney, born on March 28, 1855, never attended college or law school; his total formal education in an Edinburgh, Indiana, schoolhouse was a mere five terms—not particularly unusual in that era, but unthinkable today. Nevertheless, it did not disqualify him for a career in the law and a seat on the state's highest court, where he authored a precedent-setting decision that had national repercussions.

At the age of sixteen Hackney became a law clerk in the Shelbyville offices of Hord and Blair. In 1873 he was briefly employed in a Kokomo law office, and in 1874 he clerked in a law office in Indianapolis, where he was reunited with Kendall M. Hord. He was admitted to the Indiana bar at twenty-one and returned to Shelbyville to open his own law office.

Active in Democratic Party politics, Hackney was nominated in 1878 as the party's candidate for prosecuting attorney of Shelby County. The *Shelbyville County Atlas* that year hyperbolically attested to young Hackney's virtues: "In him are combined those rare elements of sociability, industry and physical and intellectual power so necessary to success in his profession." This is one of the more favorable comments about Hackney that found its way into print. After serving a single term as prosecutor, Hackney resumed his career as a lawyer.

He became Shelby circuit judge in November 1888 after a campaign that makes today's elections seem genteel by comparison. Hackney's predecessor on the court, Hord, his former employer and mentor, was accused of bribery and forced to resign. The *Shelbyville Republican* on July 10, 1888, charged that the nominations of Hackney and John McNutt, the party's candidate for prosecutor, "were procured by fraud and the corrupt use of money." A few days later the paper fired another salvo: "Len Hackney went to the convention with 12 delegates from this county who, he himself admitted, cost him $1000." The paper then righteously and rhetorically wondered, "What is to become of our courts if a few scheming politicians, and tools like Hackney and McNutt are permitted to violate their pledges and their manhood . . . and practice deceit?"

Hackney fought back. After delivering a speech on the tariff question in the Shelbyville Opera Hall attended by 103 people, Hackney used the occasion to respond, asserting, "Whoever says that I secured the nomination by corrupt methods is a white livered liar." According to the *Republican*, his remarks fell flat upon the silent crowd. Feigning outrage, the paper then editorially lectured Hackney for this outburst: "Such remarks as made by Mr. Hackney belong to the lowest dens of vice and crime."

Despite the *Republican*'s repeated attacks, Hackney won. After taking his seat on the Sixteenth Circuit on November 17, 1888, Hackney almost immediately set his sights on the Supreme Court. The charges against his impartiality and honesty continued. He was perceived as a tool of the Big Four Railroad, dating back to his days in private practice.

After serving as circuit judge until 1892, Hackney was named by the

Democratic State Committee to fill a vacancy on the party's Court slate caused by the suicide of Jephtha New. Predictably, the *Republican* opposed his candidacy, but the Shelbyville bar endorsed Hackney because of what "we conceive of his special fitness for the place. He is a young man, honest, competent, and industrious." Hackney's campaign was successful, and in November 1892 he was elected to the high court.

On June 14, 1893, at age thirty-eight, Hackney, who had been on the Court for only four months, was responsible for the majority decision in *In Re Petition of Leach, Ex Parte*, the case of Antoinette Dakin Leach, a woman seeking admission to the bar. It is no exaggeration to say that this decision had profound influence, both in Indiana and beyond. The decision reversed a circuit court ruling that held that women could not be lawyers because they could not vote. Breaking with tradition, Hackney wrote: "If nature has endowed women with wisdom, if our colleges have given her education, if her energy and diligence have led her to a knowledge of the law, and if her ambition directs her to adopt the profession, shall it be said that forgotten fictions must bar the door against her?" Hackney's decision was eloquent in its simplicity, forceful in its reasoning, and persuasive in its marshaling of evidence. Quite unexpectedly, because of Leach's personal skills in shorthand, stenography, and typewriting, she changed other aspects of the practice of law in Indiana by submitting one of the first typewritten briefs filed in the Court.

In 1897 Hackney was given another opportunity to take a stance on women's rights. Helen Gougar had been denied the right to vote in Tippecanoe County, and she sued for damages. The trial court ruled against her and she appealed. Although Hackney authored the opinion in *Gougar v. Timberlake*, affirming the trial court, he stated that many changes had occurred since the adoption of the Indiana Constitution, but suffrage is a political and not a natural right and therefore, "whatever the personal views of the justices upon the advisability of extending the franchise to women, . . . under the present constitution, it cannot."

Hackney was renominated for a second term but withdrew before the election. Upon leaving the Court, he became general counsel to the Big Four Railroad and moved to Cincinnati. He spent the remainder of his working life with the company, retiring in 1928. He died ten years later in Orlando, Florida.

MARGRET G. ROBB, JD, is judge, Indiana Court of Appeals. She is the chair of the Supreme Court Task Force on Family Court and a member of the American Bar Association, the Indiana Bar Association, and the Indianapolis Bar Association.

SELECTED BIBLIOGRAPHY

"A Plucky Indiana Woman: Antoinette D. Leach." *The Law Student's Helper* 1, no. 6 (June 1893).
Shelby County, Indiana: History and Families. Paducah, KY: Turner Publishing Company, 1992.
Shelbyville County Atlas.
Shelbyville Daily Democrat.
Shelbyville Republican.
Stoll, John B. *History of the Indiana Democracy, 1816–1916.* Indianapolis: Indiana Democratic Publishing Company, 1917.

CASES CITED

Gougar v. Timberlake et al., 148 Ind. 38 (1897).
In Re Petition of Leach, Ex Parte, 134 Ind. 665 (1893).

JAMES McCABE
January 2, 1893–January 2, 1899

GREGORY J. DONAT AND JOSHUA S. MALHER

James McCabe, the forty-second judge of the Indiana Supreme Court, was born July 4, 1834, in Darke County, Ohio, to modest beginnings as the son of a pious Whig father and doting mother. The family moved often while McCabe was young, and he worked the fields of Illinois for most of his childhood before finally moving to Indiana. Arriving in Crawfordsville, McCabe, then sixteen, began formal education for the first time, attending night school taught by a local judge while working as a section hand for the Monon Railroad during the day. After a year, McCabe had stopped attending school, married, and was working on a small farm.

One day, out of curiosity, McCabe attended a criminal trial where two prominent attorneys, Daniel Voorhees and Edward Hannegan, argued before the court. Struck by the lawyers' eloquence and poise, McCabe decided to pursue a career in the law. He studied diligently for several years while teaching school and working odd jobs. In 1861, at the age of twenty-seven, McCabe was admitted to the bar and set up practice in Williamsport where, after an initial struggle, he rose to prominence both as an attorney and as a citizen over the next twenty years.

He was nominated by the Democratic Party for Congress twice, only to suffer narrow losses in what was a strongly Republican district. Despite these setbacks, McCabe was well respected in his party and in 1896 was appointed as an Indiana delegate-at-large to the Democratic National Convention in Chicago. McCabe also developed a reputation for being a capable and passionate attorney. At the time, he had argued more cases before the Supreme Court than any attorney. It was, perhaps then, no surprise when, in 1892, McCabe was elected to the Court. He served for one six-year term, but lost his bid for re-election, as did the rest of the ticket.

Legislative apportionment, one of the liveliest political issues of the 1890s, came before the Court during McCabe's tenure. In *Denney et al. v. State ex rel. Basler*, a unanimous decision announced in early 1896, the judges, three Democrats and two Republicans, declared unconstitutional two apportionment bills passed the previous year by the Republican-controlled general assembly.

After retiring from the bench, McCabe returned to Williamsport, where he and his son, Edwin, opened a firm. They were quite successful, and McCabe was called upon on several occasions to sit as a special judge for the local court. After years of both struggle and prosperity, McCabe died on March 23, 1911, after a long illness. He was remembered for his eloquence, his intelligence, his alacrity of thought and expression, and his passion— much like the two lawyers who inspired him.

William Jennings Bryan, former Democratic presidential nominee and a close friend of McCabe's, delivered a speech at a memorial held in the judge's honor. Bryan, who described McCabe as a person of intense moral and intellectual commitment, saw McCabe's life as one spent tending to the four cornerstones that he held most sacred: God, home, society, and government. Bryan said that McCabe possessed "a remarkable power of clear statement and convincing logic," and that with his death, "our bar has lost the guidance of its oldest and wisest member."

McCabe's legacy continued long after his death. His son, Edwin, with whom the judge practiced in Williamsport, had three sons who practiced law, including one, Edward, who worked at the same firm as his grandfather. The family tradition continued with Edward's son, James, and James's daughter, Kimberly, both of whom practiced law in Williamsport. McCabe doubtlessly would have been proud of five generations of McCabes who felt the calling to which he had committed his life.

GREGORY J. DONAT, JD, is judge, Tippecanoe Superior Court (Lafayette, IN). He is a member of the board of directors of the American Judicature Society, the board of managers of the Indiana Judges Association, and the advisory board of the U.S. Department of Justice, Office of Victims of Crime. Donat served on the faculty of the National Center for State Courts, National Judicial College, Indiana Judicial Center, and Indiana Continuing Education Forum.

JOSHUA S. MAHLER, JD, clerked for Judge Gregory J. Donat, Tippecanoe Superior Court (Lafayette, IN) and Superior Court Judge William J. Boklund of La Porte County. He is a member of and executive justice of finance for the Valparaiso University School of Law Moot Court.

SELECTED BIBLIOGRAPHY

History of Montgomery County, Indiana, with Personal Sketches of Representative Citizens. Indianapolis: A. W. Bowen and Company, 1913.
Wallace, Leon, "Legislative Apportionment in Indiana: A Case History." *Indiana Law Journal* 42 (1966): 42–47.

CASES CITED
Denney, clerk et al. v. The State ex rel. Basler, 144 Ind. 503 (1896).

TIMOTHY E. HOWARD
January 2, 1893–January 2, 1899

FRANK SULLIVAN JR.

Service as the forty-third judge on the Indiana Supreme Court was but a tangent to the arc of Timothy Edward Howard's versatile and accomplished life. Barely escaping death in the Civil War, Howard became a popular professor at the University of Notre Dame and a creative legislator on the South Bend Common Council and in the Indiana Senate prior to his election to the Supreme Court in 1892. Following his defeat for re-election in 1898, Howard served on important state study commissions before returning to South Bend and teaching at Notre Dame. His contributions to both are memorialized in the city's Howard Park and the university's Howard Hall.

Howard was born on a farm in Northfield, Michigan, on January 27, 1837, to Irish immigrant parents. He enrolled at Notre Dame in 1859, teaching preparatory classes in return for scholarship assistance. On the eve of graduation, he enlisted in the Union army and was seriously wounded in the Battle of Shiloh on April 6, 1862. Throughout the rest of his life,

Howard played a leadership role in veterans' organizations and causes.

Howard returned to Notre Dame to receive his degree and received a faculty appointment. He later earned both a master's and a law degree from Notre Dame as well. As a popular member of the university's faculty, Howard taught many subjects, including astronomy, Greek, English, history, Latin, law, and mathematics.

In 1876 Howard began a series of forays into politics. In 1878, as an elected member of the South Bend Common Council, Howard proposed that a swamp along the Saint Joseph River be filled in and then landscaped to become the city's first public park. Howard Park was later named for the visionary councilman who proposed its creation.

As a Democratic state senator elected in 1886 and reelected in 1890, Howard was called "the most influential member of the senate." One statute he authored that endures to this day established the Appellate court of Indiana.

Howard was elected to the Supreme Court in the Democratic sweep of 1892. During his tenure, the Court produced more than two thousand majority opinions, and Howard himself authored more than four hundred. During his service on the Court, Notre Dame awarded him its prestigious Laetare Medal, conferred annually upon a distinguished American Catholic.

Howard was a member of a unanimous Court that held *In re Leach* (1893) that neither the Indiana Constitution nor state statute limited the right of Antoinette Dakin Leach to practice law. Yet he was also a member of a unanimous Court that held in *Gougar v. Timberlake* (1897) that "[w]hatever the personal views of the justices upon the advisability of extending the franchise to women, all are agreed that under the present constitution it cannot be extended to them."

In 1898 Howard was defeated in a Republican landslide. But the newly elected governor, Republican James A. Mount, and his successor, Republican Winfield T. Durbin, each appointed Howard to important state commissions, including one on compensation of public officials that recommended the pay of Court judges be increased from $4,500 to $6,000 per year. At the conclusion of this work, Howard sought reappointment to the Notre Dame faculty. As to compensation, "I do not believe that there would be any trouble," Howard wrote the school's president. "You would not wish me to have too little & I should not want to have too much."

One of Howard's great loves was history where, in his words, "the actors in the great drama of time seem to walk before us, and for our own amusement, upon the ever moving stage of human action." He authored histories of both Notre Dame and Saint Joseph County and served many years as president of the Northern Indiana Historical Society. Howard also wrote and lectured regularly throughout his life on a wide range of historical topics, including the Court and its prestatehood antecedents.

Howard died on July 9, 1916. In a eulogy, Father John W. Cavanaugh, Notre Dame's president, emphasized that Howard "was a profoundly spiritual man . . . with an enlightened sense of the presence, and the power, and the beauty of God."

A slim volume of Howard's poems was published in 1905. In one, called "Aristos," the poet—war veteran, professor, judge, and spiritual man that he was—meditates on the hero:

[S]trong, at ease, still smiling unto death, . . .

Dear life he yields, not truth, nor right, nor faith.

FRANK SULLIVAN JR., JD, LLM, is a justice of the Indiana Supreme Court. He was born in South Bend and raised in a neighborhood near Howard Park.

SELECTED BIBLIOGRAPHY

Archives, University of Notre Dame.
    Letter from Father Sorin to Howard (October 19, 1858).
    Letter from Howard to Father Cavanaugh (April 22, 1908).
Howard, Timothy Edward. *Musings and Memories*. Chicago: Lakeside Press, 1905.
———. *A History of St. Joseph County, Indiana*. Chicago: Lewis Publishing Company, 1907.
———. *The Indiana Supreme Court with Some Account of the Courts Preceding It: An Historical Sketch*. South Bend: Northern Indiana Historical Society, 1900.
Lyons, Joseph A. *Silver Jubilee of the University of Notre Dame, June 23rd, 1869* Chicago: E. B. Myers and Company, 1869.
Moore, Philip S. *A Century of Law at Notre Dame*. Notre Dame, IN: University of Notre Dame Press, 1969.
Scholastic, Notre Dame (formerly called The Scholastic Year). "The Laetare Medal" (March 19, 1898).
    [Howard's Opening Lecture on History] (February 1868).
    "Hon. T. E. Howard, Judge of the Supreme Court of Indiana" (November 12, 1892).
    [Howard's Lecture on the Centennial of Abraham Lincoln] (February 13, 1909).
    [President Cavanaugh's Eulogy of Howard] (October 28, 1916).
Sullivan, James C., "Role of Timothy E. Howard in History of South Bend," *South Bend Tribune Sunday Magazine*, September 21, 1975.

CASES CITED

Gougar v. Timberlake et al., 148 Ind. 38 (1897).
In re Petition of Leach, 134 Ind. 665 (1893).

INDIANA HISTORICAL SOCIETY

JOSEPH S. DAILEY
July 25, 1893–January 7, 1895

DONALD D. DOXSEE

In his first year of practice in Wells County, Indiana, in 1866, Joseph S. Dailey was elected district attorney of the common pleas court. That court existed from 1852 to 1873 and was limited to small claims, probate, guardianship, and misdemeanor jurisdiction. Except for his term on the Indiana Supreme Court as its forty-fourth judge, Dailey spent his entire life as a resident of Wells County.

Born on a farm in Wells County on July 25, 1844, Dailey was one of nine children born to James and Lydia Dailey; four of the children died in infancy. His brother, Lewis, died at age nineteen in command of the Twenty-second Indiana Volunteer Infantry during the Civil War. The local Grand Army of the Republic post was named in his honor.

Dailey was a fifth-generation descendant of Dennis Dailey, who emigrated from County Sligo, Ireland, to New Jersey in the early 1700s. Both of his grandfathers served in the War of 1812 and later moved to Indiana. Dailey's father, a farmer in Wells County, moved to Bluffton when he was elected county auditor in 1850.

After graduating from Wells County public schools, Dailey studied law with attorney Newton Burwell for two years. During that period he taught school in various parts of the county to raise money to attend Indiana University. He enrolled in the university's law department in 1865 and graduated in 1866. At that time few law schools or departments required any previous college education and required only one or two years for a certificate.

Dailey was admitted to the bar of the circuit court on February 8, 1865. In those days there was no bar exam, and it was common practice to "study law" in the office of a local attorney before being allowed to be an attorney at law. When that attorney felt that the apprentice was sufficiently educated in the law, he testified as to the candidate's qualifications before a local judge and moved his admission to the bar. It was not until 1931 that Indiana required law school and passing a law exam before being admitted to practice.

After his service as district attorney in the common pleas court, Dailey was elected prosecutor for the Tenth Judicial District, which consisted of Adams, Allen, Huntington, Wells, and Whitley counties. He served four consecutive two-year terms from 1868 through 1876 and was then elected to the Indiana House of Representatives in 1878. In 1882 he ran unsuccessfully as the Democrat candidate for Congress. While he lost, the newspaper reported that he did well enough with the voters of the other party to "reduce the number of Republicans from 1080 to 333."

In 1888 Dailey was elected as judge of the circuit court then consisting of Huntington and Wells counties. As the state grew and the business of the courts increased, the legislature from time to time reorganized the circuits, and now each of Indiana's ninety-two counties has its own circuit court. Dailey served as judge of the Huntington-Wells Circuit Court until he was appointed to the Court.

When Walter Olds resigned from the Court in 1893, Democratic governor Claude Matthews appointed Dailey to fill the unexpired term. Dailey was defeated for election in 1894. During his brief tenure on the court of a year and five months Dailey handed down more than eighty opinions. One case involved a citizen, acting as a private prosecutor, bringing a criminal charge against a candidate for county clerk for buying votes. The candidate countered that the vote fraud law was unconstitutional. On appeal Dailey sustained the constitutionality of the charge in *State ex rel. Beedle v. Schoonover* and sent the case back to the lower court to be tried. However, in *Kelsie v. Indiana*, Indiana no longer recognizes the right of private citizens to act as a private prosecutor to bring criminal charges.

On leaving the Court in 1895, Dailey returned to Bluffton to resume the practice of law with his son, Frank, under the firm name of Dailey, Simmons and Dailey. In the early morning of October 9, 1905, Dailey died at his home of an apparent heart attack. He was survived by his wife, Lydia, and four children. He is buried in Elm Grove Cemetery in Wells County.

DONALD D. DOXSEE, JD, is past president of the Allen County Bar Association. He is a board member of the Allen County Courthouse Preservation Trust. Doxsee practices in the association of Williams, Williams and Doxsee in Fort Wayne, Indiana

SELECTED BIBLIOGRAPHY

Biographical and Historical Record of Adams and Wells Counties, Indiana. Chicago: Lewis Publishing Company, 1887.
Biographical Memoirs of Wells County, Indiana. Logansport, IN: B. F. Bowen, Publisher, 1903.
Bluffton Evening News, October 9, 1905.
Bodenhamer, David, and Randall Shepard. *The History of Indiana Law.* Athens: Ohio University Press, 2006.

CASES CITED

Jenna Pauline Kelsie v. State of Indiana, 265 Ind. 363 (1976).
The State ex rel. Beedle v. Schoonover, 135 Ind. 526 (1893).

JAMES H. JORDAN
January 7, 1895–April 10, 1912

PATRICK L. BAUDE

Sometimes called Colonel Jordan before he was known as "Judge," James Henry Jordan, the forty-fifth judge of the Indiana Supreme Court, seems to have set the direction of his life during the Civil War. He was born in Woodstock, Virginia, in 1842, and his family moved to Corydon, Indiana, ten years later. Before his college years, he fought for the Union with the Third Indiana Cavalry. With the Army of the Potomac, he participated in all the major battles in the East, was wounded at Gettysburg in 1863, and gravely injured two months later at the Battle of Culpeper Court House. His commanding officer was Conrad Baker, a lawyer, later Republican governor of Indiana, and a supporter of Jordan's early political career in Morgan County.

After the war, Jordan began his studies at Wabash College but transferred to Indiana University at Bloomington, graduating in 1868. Back home in Corydon, he studied law under the tutelage of a local judge and another lawyer. He then returned to IU for formal law study and received a law degree in 1871. After practicing law a year in Missouri, he moved to Martinsville, where he established a successful practice and served as prosecuting attorney and city attorney. He maintained his connections with Wabash, which awarded him an honorary law degree in 1907, and with IU, serving on its board of trustees from 1891 to 1895.

Jordan first sought judicial office in 1882, but lost the race for circuit judge. He was also unsuccessful six years later in his first campaign for election to the Court, but in 1894, after a narrow victory in a contested ballot at the Republican state convention, he was elected to the Court and easily reelected in 1900 and 1906. Throughout this period, he was actively involved in Republican politics, serving as chairman of the state committee in 1892

Between the Civil War and World War I, Jordan and Leander J. Monks were the only judges to serve more than two terms. They were both first elected in 1894, creating a court composed of five Republicans. There continued to be a Republican majority until Jordan's death in office in 1912, nine months before the end of his third term. The political tensions between the Court and the political branches, and especially with Democratic governor Thomas R. Marshall, in that final year gave rise to what is probably Jordan's most important opinion, *Ex parte France.*

A 1911 statute had conferred final jurisdiction over some classes of cases on an intermediate appellate court, in effect "stripping" the Court of some measure of its ultimate authority. Had this legislative power been recognized, the rule of law would have been seriously strained. Jordan wrote for the Court's three-to-two majority, affirming that "the Supreme Court of this State is, in the full sense of that word, supreme over the other two departments of the state government."

One other of Jordan's 652 opinions has had a powerful influence on Indiana history. The issue was how to amend the state constitution, whose terms required a majority of electors to approve an amendment. In 1901 the majority in *Denny* defined the term "elector" as meaning the number of persons voting on any matter on the ballot. Since only a small percentage of voters actually vote on constitutional amendments compared to the number who vote for president or governor, it had become practically impossible to adopt an amendment. Jordan's forty-page dissenting opinion in *Denny* surveyed other states and examined the drafting history of the amendment clause in depth.

Thirty-four years later in *In re Todd* the Court reversed *Denny*, saying it had "no hesitancy to re-examine this question" in view of Jordan's "strong dissenting opinion." A substantial modernization of the Indiana Constitution soon followed.

PATRICK L. BAUDE, JD, LLM, is Ralph F. Fuchs Professor Emeritus of Law and Public Service, Indiana University Maurer School of Law, Bloomington. He is the author of *Judicial Jurisdiction: Reference Guide to the United States Constitution* (2007).

SELECTED BIBLIOGRAPHY

Adams, Wendy L., and Elizabeth R. Osborn, eds. *In Memoriam: Glimpses from Indiana's Legal Past*. Indianapolis: Indiana Supreme Court, 2006.
Cumback, Will, and J. B. Maynard, eds. *Men of Progress, Indiana*. Indianapolis: Indianapolis Sentinel Company, 1899.
Taylor, Charles W. *Biographical Sketches and Review of the Bench and Bar of Indiana*. Indianapolis: Bench and Bar Publishing Company, 1895.

CASES CITED

In re Denny, 156 Ind. 105, 59 N.E. 2d 359.
Ex Parte France, Clerk of the Supreme Court, 176 Ind. 72 (1911).
In re Todd, 208 Ind. 168 (1935).

INDIANA HISTORICAL SOCIETY

LEANDER J. MONKS
January 7, 1895–January 7, 1913

PATRICK L. BAUDE

Leander John Monks, the forty-sixth judge of the Indiana Supreme Court, served on the Court for eighteen years, longer than any judge elected under provisions of the 1851 constitution, a system changed by the 1970 amendment removing the office from direct election. During that time, he wrote eight hundred opinions, a remarkable production of one opinion every six weekdays. There was some speculation that President Benjamin Harrison might nominate him to the U.S. Supreme Court.

But Monks may be best remembered for a scholarly work, *Courts and Lawyers of Indiana,* published in 1916, three years after he left the Court. Monks was editor in chief for the three-volume work, and noted Indiana historians Logan Esarey and Ernest V. Shockley served as assistant editors. It is virtually certain that every contributor to this volume of essays relied on Monks's work in writing about the Court's first century. As a matter of style, the book is written without much personal commentary, mainly as a detailed accumulation of fact. It is invaluable to the researcher, although a contemporaneous review in the *Indiana Magazine of History* gave it back-handed praise with the description "as carefully done as time would permit." It is also a little disappointing to read Monks's own time on the circuit court bench briefly described as a "splendid record."

Monks was born in Winchester, Indiana, in 1843, where his father had been a pioneering settler and then a Whig legislator. He attended Indiana University from 1861 to 1863 and returned to Winchester, practicing law and becoming active in the Republican Party, serving as county chairman and member of the state executive committee. One observer described Monks's lawyerly skills as a "master" counselor but "not a public speaker." He was elected circuit judge in 1878 and continued until 1894, when he ran for the first of his three terms on the Court, defeating an incumbent Demo-crat as part of a unanimous Republican victory in that year.

The following eighteen years on the Court were a time of political tension and constitutional challenge in Indiana, presenting judges with such issues as women's suffrage, legislative apportionment, judicial inde-pendence, and the constitutional amendment process. During this period, however, Monks's opinions are primarily notable for their modest scope, their thorough research, and their attention to procedural niceties—in a word, for their judicious quality. In an era marked at the federal level by the doctrine of substantive due process in decisions such as the U.S. Supreme Court's in *Lochner v. New York* (1905), Monks's decisions reflect his high esteem for property and contract. A recurrent theme of his judicial output is an unwillingness to recognize new tort causes of action, even when directly authorized by the legislature.

When a statute, for example, attempted to protect workers by requir-ing a "safe place" for corporate employees, Monks wrote for the Court in *Bedford Quarries* in 1907, holding it unconstitutionally irrational to impose liability on corporate employers but not on sole proprietorships. At this point in the Industrial Revolution, it seems almost bizarre to equate cor-porations with small private firms. And he also wrote for the court in 1895 striking down a long line of precedents holding counties liable for negligent maintenance of roads and bridges in *Allman*.

Decisions such as these are now seen as typical examples of unjustifi-able exercises of judicial discretion hostile to the modern view of tort law.

Bedford Quarries in particular has been described by one historian as an "outlier" even for its time. In any case, these opinions are clear, carefully reasoned, and closely argued.

Monks was defeated for reelection in 1912, and the Republican Party lost its hold on the Court. In the end, the body of his work shows him as a guardian of the law if not one of its trailblazers.

PATRICK L. BAUDE, JD, LLM, is Ralph F. Fuchs Professor Emeritus of Law and Public Service, Indiana University Maurer School of Law, Bloomington. He is the author of *Judicial Jurisdiction: Reference Guide to the United States Constitution* (2007).

SELECTED BIBLIOGRAPHY

Adams, Wendy L., and Elizabeth R. Osborn, eds. *In Memoriam: Glimpses from Indiana's Legal Past*. Indianapolis: Indiana Supreme Court, 2006.
"Reviews and Notes," *Indiana Magazine of History* 12 (December 1916).
Witt, John Fabian. "The Long History of State Constitutions and American Tort Law." *Rutgers Camden Law Journal* 36 (2005).

CASES CITED

Bedford Quarries Company v. Bough, 168 Ind. 671 (1907).
Board of Commissioners of Jasper County v. Allman, Administrator, 142 Ind. 573 (1895).

ALEXANDER DOWLING
January 2, 1899–January 2, 1905

MARIA D. GRANGER

Alexander Dowling was elected as the forty-seventh judge of the Indiana Supreme Court in 1898 in a Republican landslide that resulted in the party winning all state offices, as well as taking control of the five seats on the high court. Dowling had been offered an appointment to the Court seven years earlier by Governor Alvin P. Hovey upon the death of John G. Berkshire, but he declined.

Shortly after Dowling's birth on December 19, 1839, in Hillsboro, Virginia, his parents moved to New Albany, Indiana. He completed his early education in the New Albany public school system, then studied law under Judge John S. Davis in the offices of Otto and Davis, and was admitted to the bar in 1858 at the age of twenty-one. He was later appointed prosecuting attorney in New Albany and served as city attorney from 1861 to 1865, from 1871 to 1875, and from 1883 to 1885. Dowling was described as an average speaker whose vast knowledge of the law outweighed his skills as an orator. His lack of eloquence did not affect his success in the courtroom. He successfully litigated a number of murder cases, with one client being acquitted and another receiving only a brief sentence.

In addition to his commitment to the practice of law, Dowling was one of the original stockholders of the Mutual Trust and Deposit Company and assisted in its organization in 1904. He served as chairman of the bank's board of directors and as its president. He was a charter member of the board of Trinity Methodist Church, which was founded in 1888. In addition to serving his church, each Christmas Dowling asked a secretary to make a list of needy people in the city, and he anonymously sent them food, clothing, and other items. It was said of Dowling that "as his money bag swelled his heart did not shrivel." Dowling also served as president of the board of regents of Fairview Cemetery and as a trustee of DePauw University in Greencastle.

During his six-year term on the Court, Dowling wrote hundreds of opinions, including many regarding claims of negligence by railroads. At the turn of the century rail lines were expanding to accommodate the increased demands of passenger and commercial traffic. This development inevitably led to a large number of tort claims filed against railroad companies. One such case resulted from a collision between a wagon driver and train. Dowling's decision in *The Baltimore & Ohio Southwestern Railway Company v. Young* upheld the verdict of the trial court, which found the railroad guilty of failing to maintain a proper speed at the crossing and failing to give adequate warning signals.

Perhaps Dowling's most notable decision on the high court was *Gray v. Seitz*, which involved John B. Seitz, a candidate for Brown County auditor in the Democratic primary of 1901. Seitz paid another candidate $300 to withdraw from the primary and had the candidate ask two of his supporters to use their influence to dissuade others from entering the primary. After Seitz won in the general election, the losing candidate, Arthur L. Gray, sued, claiming that Seitz was ineligible to hold office because of the bribe. In his opinion, Dowling wrote that the state constitution only prohibited the payment of bribes for a general election, not a primary, and that the state's 1901 primary law that made bribery illegal only applied when a candidate had been charged and convicted of the offense.

After completing his term on the Court, Dowling returned to New Albany and resumed his law practice. On the morning of December 11, 1917, Dowling, then age eighty-one, made his usual walk of several blocks from his home to his downtown law office. When his stenographer entered his office later that morning, she found him on the floor beside his desk, apparently having suffered a fatal heart attack as he took off his overcoat. In reporting the death, the *New Albany Daily Ledger* wrote, "Truly his life is an inspiration to the community; an example of usefulness and a life lived in the performance of full duty wherever placed."

MARIA D. GRANGER, JD, is judge, Floyd Superior Court 3 (New Albany, IN). She served as adjunct professor of business law at Indiana University Southeast from 2001 to 2005. Granger is on the Advisory Board for the Indiana Conference on Legal Education Opportunity.

SELECTED BIBLIOGRAPHY

History of Ohio Falls Cities and Counties. Cleveland, OH: L. A. Williams and Company, 1982.

McLauchlan, William P. *The Indiana State Constitution: A Reference Guide.* Westport, CT: Greenwood Press, 1996.

New Albany Daily Ledger, December 11, 12, 1917.

CASES CITED

The Baltimore & Ohio Southwestern Railway Company v. Young, 153 Ind. 163 (1899).

Gray v. Seitz, 162 Ind. 1 (1904).

JOHN V. HADLEY

January 2, 1899–January 2, 1911

LIBBE K. HUGHES

In the early hours of January 10, 1895, a crime occurred in the small Hendricks County town of Belleville, Indiana. A young woman's life ended violently, a Methodist minister was accused of murder, and subsequent newspaper headlines focused national and state attention on the courtroom of Hendricks County Circuit Court Judge John Vestal Hadley. Long active in Republican politics and having written a popular narrative about his experiences as a Union soldier during the Civil War, Hadley was already a familiar name to Hoosiers. Soon, Hadley was propelled from Hendricks County judge to the forty-eighth judge of the Indiana Supreme Court.

Hadley was born October 31, 1840, in Guilford Township, Hendricks County, to Jonathan and Ara Carter Hadley, who were early settlers in the township. Hadley was raised on the family farm and attended the local common schools. He continued his education at Northwestern Christian (now Butler) University in Indianapolis, completing two years there before interrupting his studies in August 1861 to fight for the Union in the Civil War. Enlisting in Company B, Seventh Regiment Indiana Volunteer Infantry for three years of service, Hadley was quickly appointed corporal. He fought in the Battles of Winchester and Port Republic and was wounded at Second Manassas on August 30, 1862. A convalescence of several weeks caused him to miss the regiment's engagements at Antietam and Fredericksburg. Promoted to lieutenant, Hadley saw further action at Chancellorsville and Gettysburg. Homesick and weary of war, he wrote home in August 1863: "No mortal has a more consuming desire to live to see the Armed Minions of our Government returning to their friends and families and to be one of them. Im tired of war. Im tired of wearing away my life in loneliness when it might be blessed with Angelic society. I watch, I hope, I fear, I wait anxiously for the Angel of peace."

As the regiment approached the end of its three-year enlistment in 1864, Hadley decided not to reenlist. Dissatisfied with the infantry, he hoped to return home at the end of his enlistment to organize a unit of cavalry or resume his studies. Reassigned to the brigade staff of Brigadier General James C. Rice to serve out the balance of his enlistment, Hadley was wounded again during the opening stages of the Battle of the Wilderness on May 5, 1864. This time he fell into Confederate hands. Instead of anxiously counting the weeks until the expiration of his enlistment, Hadley spent the next seven months a prisoner of war. On November 4, 1864, he and three fellow prisoners escaped from Camp Sorghum in Columbia, South Carolina. They made a perilous trek through some two hundred miles of Confederate territory, reaching the Union lines around Knoxville, Tennessee, on December 10, 1864.

Hadley was discharged from the army and returned home. He married Mary Jane Hill of Pittsboro, Indiana, on March 15, 1865. Resuming his studies, this time at Indianapolis attorney and Judge David McDonald's private law school, Hadley settled on a legal career. He was admitted to the bar in Hendricks County in 1866 and began practicing in the county seat, Danville. Years later he attributed his success as a lawyer to the fact that there were more than two hundred Hadleys living in Hendricks County at the time and as he was related to all of them, they brought their legal business to him. During his twenty-two years in private practice, his many associates included Enoch G. Hogate, Indiana University Law School dean from 1906 to 1917; Cassius Clay Hadley, Indiana Appellate court judge from 1907 to 1911; and James L. Clark, who served on the Indiana Public Service Commission from 1913 to 1917.

Politically, Hadley was a Republican, and in 1868 he was elected state senator representing Hendricks and Putnam counties, serving three terms. While continuing his legal practice, Hadley also served as president of the First National Bank of Danville for eleven years, beginning in 1877. He was a delegate to the 1888 Republican National Convention and that same year was elected circuit court judge of Hendricks County. He was reelected to the bench in 1894.

By the time Reverend William E. Hinshaw was brought to trial for the January 10, 1895, murder of his wife, Thirza, public opinion was sharply divided as to the charismatic Methodist minister's guilt or innocence. The crime made headlines in newspapers throughout the state, and the trial, beginning in September 1895, focused public scrutiny on Hadley and his courtroom. Hinshaw was found guilty of murder in the first degree and sentenced to life imprisonment. The conviction, based solely upon circumstantial evidence, was appealed to the Indiana Supreme Court and upheld in April 1897. Hadley's rulings on the admissibility of such evidence and his instructions to the jury were cited in numerous other cases.

Hadley was no stranger to publicity. Early in his career he wrote an account of his wartime experiences that was published in the Danville newspaper. In 1868 the story was reprinted by Indianapolis publishers J. M. and F. J. Meikel under the title *Seven Months a Prisoner; or, Thirty-Six Days in the Woods*. The book proved to be a popular one, and Charles Scribner's Sons of New York released an expanded version in 1898. Hadley was also active in local and state chapters of the Grand Army of the Republic and was a noted speaker at GAR encampments, regimental reunions, and veterans' relief events throughout the state.

In 1898 Hadley won on the first vote the Republican nomination for judge of the Indiana Supreme Court for the Third District. The Republicans won the majority of state offices in the November election, and Hadley assumed his duties with the high court on January 2, 1899. His nomination was unopposed at the Republican convention in 1904, and he was reelected to the bench in November.

The cases brought before Hadley reflected the social reforms being enacted by state government, such as prohibition and workmen's compensation laws. It was later noted that his "decisions were characterized by a clearness, candor and broadness of vision which have made them authority on many fine points of law." Hadley and his wife lived in Indianapolis during his years on the Court but returned to Danville after his retirement in January 1911.

Hadley remained active in retirement, continuing a rigorous schedule of public appearances. In 1913 he served on the Indiana commission organizing the Fiftieth Anniversary Reunion of the Battle of Gettysburg and presided over the Indiana Day portion of the event. He also undertook editing *The History of Hendricks County, Indiana: Her People, Industries, and Institutions* published in 1914.

Hadley died on November 17, 1915, at his Danville home, survived by his wife and three children. He is buried at Maple Hill Cemetery in Plainfield, Indiana.

LIBBE K. HUGHES is a local history researcher, writer, and lecturer residing in Hendricks County, Indiana.

SELECTED BIBLIOGRAPHY

Hadley, John V., ed. *History of Hendricks County, Indiana: Her People, Industries, and Institutions.* Indianapolis: B. F. Bowen and Company, 1914.

———. Private Papers. Civil War Letters. Lilly Library. Indiana University, Bloomington, IN.

———. *Seven Months a Prisoner; or, Thirty-six Days in the Woods.* 1898. Reprint, with an introduction by Libbe K. Hughes. Hanover, IN: Nugget Publishers, 1998.

A Portrait and Biographical Record of Boone, Clinton, and Hendricks Counties, Ind. Chicago: A. W. Bowen and Company, 1895.

Robertson, James I., Jr., ed. "An Indiana Soldier in Love and War: The Civil War Letters of John V. Hadley." *Indiana Magazine of History* 59 (September 1963).

FRANCIS E. BAKER

January 2, 1899–January 25, 1902

DORIA M. LYNCH

Francis Elisha Baker came from a family of distinguished jurists and politicians. His father, John H. Baker, served three terms in Congress (1875–81) and was a federal district court judge in Indiana from 1892 until 1902. Two uncles, James S. Frazer and Joseph A. S. Mitchell, were Indiana Supreme Court judges, and a third uncle, Lucian Baker, was a U.S. senator from Kansas. Francis achieved the most of the Baker family in the legal realm, becoming the forty-ninth judge of the Court and also serving on the U.S. Court of Appeals for the Seventh Circuit.

Born on October 20, 1860, in Goshen, Indiana, Baker attended local public and private schools and departed for Indiana University at age sixteen, eventually graduating in 1882 from the University of Michigan. Upon graduation he returned to Goshen, where he read law with his father and uncle in the family firm of Baker and Mitchell. Father and son continued in private practice together until the elder was appointed to the federal bench.

Francis Baker quickly established himself as a well-respected member of the Goshen bar and "was recognized as one of the best judges of law in northern Indiana. His ability was such that the prestige of the firm was not seriously affected when the father retired to assume his duties as a Federal judge." He continued to build his firm and twice was offered the Republican nomination for Congress, which he declined.

The only office Baker ever ran for was the Fifth District seat on the Court, a nomination he sought in 1898. After winning the nomination on the first ballot, he defeated the incumbent judge, Timothy Howard, soundly that November. Baker ran as a Republican, and his election helped make the Court entirely Republican. It remained so until 1911.

During Baker's service, the judges dealt with issues including railroads, mining safety, liquor licensing, and defendants' rights. Baker authored nearly 150 opinions, including *In re Denny*, one of the most important of the early twentieth century. The case resulted from a vote about a constitutional amendment that would have allowed the general assembly to change the requirements to become a lawyer in Indiana. According to the 1851 constitution, "Every person of good moral character, being a voter, shall be entitled to admission to practice law in all courts of justice." The legislature found these requirements to be lax, and in November 1900 an amendment was on the ballot during the general election.

The final tally on the amendment was 240,031 for and 144,072 against, and the state attorney general assumed the amendment had passed. However, George L. Denny filed suit after being denied admission to practice before the courts in Indiana, claiming that because the number of votes for the amendment was less than half the number of all votes cast in the election (655,965), the amendment had not been ratified.

Baker agreed, writing for the Court that a majority of all voters in an election, not just those voting on the amendment, needed to vote in favor of a constitutional amendment for ratification. While the state claimed that the amendment was voted on in a special election, and that only the votes for and against the amendment mattered, Baker wrote, "On November 6, 1900, there was but one election in Indiana, and that was the 'general election' at which the general assembly of 1899 determined to submit the proposed amendments to the electors of the state; and every person who voted at that election thereby furnished proof that he was an elector of the state." This opinion clarified the means by which amendments to the Indiana Constitution could be ratified. Ultimately, *In re Denny* was overturned in 1935, ironically via another case involving admission to the bar, *In re Todd.*

Baker's term on the Court was cut short by his appointment to the U.S. Court of Appeals for the Seventh Circuit in 1902. U.S. Senator Albert J. Beveridge, the junior Indiana senator, brought Baker to the attention of President Theodore Roosevelt as a means of thanking Baker and his father for their support during Beveridge's 1898 campaign, and Roosevelt selected Baker for the federal bench. Baker was confirmed by the U.S. Senate on January 21, 1902, and took the oath on February 4 of that year.

Baker's service on the Seventh Circuit was tainted by scandal in 1905 when he admitted in testimony before the U.S. Civil Service Commission to forcing postal employees to contribute money to the Republican Party in 1902. The commission did not have authority to take action against the judge, and the investigation was handed over to the U.S. Justice Department. In the end, Justice Department officials determined that the statute of limitations in the case had expired, and Baker was never charged or impeached in connection with the scandal. Instead, he went on to serve as presiding judge of the Seventh Circuit. In 1922 he was one of three finalists considered to fill a vacancy on the U.S. Supreme Court, but the appointment went to Pierce Butler. Baker remained on the Seventh Circuit until he died from a heart condition on March 15, 1924.

DORIA M. LYNCH, MA, is administrative specialist and historian at the U.S. District Court for the Southern District of Indiana. She is a contributor to *The Hoosier Genealogist: Connections* magazine, worked as an editorial assistant for *Finding Indiana Ancestors* (2007), and compiled the Name Index to the *U. S. District Court Order Book, District of Indiana, 1817–1833.*

SELECTED BIBLIOGRAPHY

Chicago Record-Herald, October 13, 16, November 14, 1905.
Chicago Tribune, December 12, 1901, October 12, 13, 15, 1905.
Indianapolis Journal, December 11, 1901, September 12, 1903.
Indianapolis News, December 18, 1901, October 12, 1905, April 17, 1906, March 15, 1924.
Indianapolis Star, October 20, 1914.
Presentation of Portrait and Resolutions in Respect to the Memory of the Honorable Francis E. Baker, U. S. Court of Appeals for the Seventh Circuit. June 10, 1924.
Solomon, Rayman L. *History of the Seventh Circuit, 1891–1941.* Washington, DC: Under the auspices of the Bicentennial Committee of the Judicial Conference of the United States, 1981.

CASES CITED

In the matter of the Petition of Denny for Admission to Practice Law, 56 Ind. 104 (1901).
In re Todd, 208 Ind. 168 (1935).

JOHN H. GILLETT
January 25, 1902–January 4, 1909

RICHARD STITH AND MARCUS C. FLINDERS

To recount the life of John Henry Gillett (pronounced "Gillette"), the fiftieth judge of the Indiana Supreme Court, is to tell three stories of great achievement: those of respected teacher, renowned scholar, and chief justice. Yet two of these narratives come to abrupt and startling conclusions.

Born in Medina, New York, on September 18, 1860, Gillett moved with his parents a year later to Valparaiso, Indiana; Hammond became his permanent home in 1891. There in northwest Indiana he had already become an accomplished law professor, legal scholar, and judge, when in early 1902 he was appointed to the Court. Forced to abandon the Court in 1909, he returned to a teaching career of great acclaim until that, too, ended suddenly in 1920.

While living in Valparaiso, young Gillett was introduced first to the-courtroom and then to the academy. Soon after the family's arrival in

Indiana in 1861, his father, Hiram A., was elected judge of the common pleas court and in 1873 was appointed judge of the Thirty-first Judicial Circuit (comprising Lake, Starke, and Porter counties). His father left that court a few years later to become one of the three founding faculty of the law department of the Northern Indiana Normal School—later transformed into Valparaiso University School of Law. The elder Gillett, who taught there until his death in 1904, was joined in 1898 by Florence Higgins, one of America's first female law school professors.

After a three-year tutelage under his professor father, and an eighteen-month partnership with Edgar D. Crumpacker, who later joined the law faculty and then became a member of Congress, Gillett taught law four years with his father. Following a short stint as Valparaiso city attorney, four years as deputy attorney general of Indiana, and a two-year partnership with Peter Crumpacker in Hammond, Gillett was appointed in 1892 judge of the same circuit court over which his father had presided. Gillett held the position until called in 1902 to the Fifth District seat on the Court, winning election to the position on the Republican ticket later that same year.

Gillett's early years of teaching were also ones of tremendous scholarship. His first major work, *A Practical Treatise on Criminal Law and Procedure in Criminal Cases with Direction and Forms* (1888), is nearly eight hundred pages and has been cited in more than 120 state cases, one as late as a 1994 Indiana Appeals Court decision, *Toops v. State*. In 1897 Gillett completed another massive (four hundred pages) work, *A Treatise on the Law of Indirect and Collateral Evidence*, cited in numerous states including the 1956 case of *Clifton v. Arnold*, and (with approval) by the U.S. Supreme Court in *Throckmorton v. Holt* (1901).

Never an ivory-tower elitist, Gillett's purpose was to serve his fellow attorneys and judges. The title to his first treatise begins with the word "practical," and at the close of the preface to his second, he "contemplates this effort, in its relation to the science of the law, as [someone] who feels, as he gazes upon a noble cathedral . . . that he helped to build that structure, for did not his faithful back carry mortar to the skilled workmen? May worthier minds find use for the material this book contains."

Appointed to the Court at age forty-one by Governor Winfield T. Durbin to replace Francis E. Baker, Gillett served for nearly seven years, five as chief justice. His was a time when many of the cases dealt with railroad issues, especially during his early tenure. He dissented only three times, one of which was really a concurrence in the result. He also wrote two opinions later reversed by the U.S. Supreme Court.

Although he wished to continue on the Court, and enjoyed political support at least in northwest Indiana, the Republican Party preferred to nominate Quincy A. Myers of Logansport. At the April 1, 1908, Republican gathering, Gillett withdrew a third of the way through the roll call, its outcome being apparent. Court judge and historian, Leander J. Monks, considered the manner in which Gillett's judicial career ended "an unusual proceeding."

In 1909 Gillett returned to practice law in Hammond and to serve as lecturer on the law faculty in Valparaiso, teaching real property, code remedies, and criminal law and evidence. Quite popular as a teacher, he commanded perhaps too much respect as reflected in this comment by a student: "The University Circuit Court, presided over by the Honorable John H. Gillett . . . gave us an opportunity to actually practice, during our school career, under Code Procedure. . . . [W]e soon gained courage but never enough to question the rulings of him whom experience has so eminently qualified to adjudicate upon finer points of law."

Because of the loss of students fighting in World War I, and also because of academic mismanagement, the university entered a many-year financial decline that diminished the quality of the law library, student body, and faculty. No doubt already depressed with this turn of events, Gillett lost his wife Agnes in 1918. In ill health at age sixty-three, Gillett hanged himself in the attic of the Hammond home of his son, Gerald, on March 16, 1920.

RICHARD STITH, JD, PhD, is professor of law, Valparaiso University. He is a member of the advisory council, doctoral program in philosophy of law, Universidad de los Andes, Santiago, Chile and is the author of "On the Legal Validation of Sexual Relationships," *The Jurisprudence of Marriage and Other Intimate Relationships* (2010).

MARCUS C. FLINDERS, JD, is a candidate for LL.M in taxation. He is the coauthor of *"The Flag Means More than Death": Comparing the Hitler Youth to Sierra Leone's Child Armies* (2008).

SELECTED BIBLIOGRAPHY

Cannon, Thomas H., H. H. Loring, and Charles Robb, eds. *History of the Lake and Calumet Region of Indiana*, vol. 1. Indianapolis: Historians Association, 1927.
Chesterton Tribune, March 18, 1920.
Hammond Lake County Times, November 2, 1907.
Howat, William Frederick. *A Standard History of Lake County, Indiana and the Calumet*

Region, vol. 1. Chicago: Lewis Publishing Company, 1915.

Swygert, Michael Irven. *"And We Must Make Them Noble": A Contextual History of the Valparaiso University School of Law*. Durham, NC: Carolina Academic Press, 2004.

Valparaiso Porter County Vidette, January 30, 1902.

CASES CITED

Laura Fussell Clifton v. Sam Arnold, d/b/a/ Arnold's Sawmill, 87 So.2d 386 (1956).

Throckmorton v. Holt, 180 U.S. 552 (1901).

Terry Toops v. State of Indiana, 643 N.E.2d 387 (1994).

OSCAR H. MONTGOMERY
January 2, 1905–January 2, 1911

JAMES M. BEEBY

Oscar Hilton Montgomery was regarded as a lawyer of unusual ability and a leading member of the bar in Indiana. He enjoyed a distinguished career, culminating in his one term as the fifty-first judge of the Indiana Supreme Court during the first decade of the twentieth century, but he also suffered several tragedies in his personal life.

Montgomery, who was born in Jackson County on April 27, 1859, graduated from Hanover College with a bachelor's degree in classics in 1881 and later earned a master's degree from Hanover. As an undergraduate, he was president of the Inter-State Oratorical Association.

Montgomery's years after college were full of hard work. For three years he taught at several schools in southern Indiana while also studying law in the office of Albert P. Summers in Seymour. After being admitted to the bar in 1884, he joined the firm of Reynolds and Montgomery in Greenfield, but remained there for just a year before returning to Seymour in 1885 to set up his own law practice. He married Ida Harding a year later.

Montgomery was active in local Republican politics, quickly rising through the leadership ranks. He was the party's candidate for mayor of Seymour in 1886, but lost. He did score a victory soon thereafter, however, winning the office of city attorney. Although he campaigned with Republicans, speaking on the stump throughout the 1890s, Montgomery continued to focus on his law practice and court cases, so that by the end of the decade he was known as the leading attorney of Jackson County.

In 1904 Montgomery ran on the Republican ticket for the Court from the Second District. In the Republican landslide of that year, Montgomery easily won. As news of his election swept the county, more than five hundred supporters, a band, and local dignitaries appeared at Montgomery's house to stage a surprise party.

Montgomery was an extremely active judge, writing more than 240 opinions, and some newspapers noted that this was a record at the time. It appears from all accounts that Montgomery had a fine reputation as a jurist. The *Indianapolis Star* noted, "He has been eminently fair in his decisions and courageous in his interpretation of the law." During this period the Court, controlled by the Republicans, was actively involved in a myriad of cases, particularly on Progressive Era issues such as voting rights, child labor, worker's compensation, regulations of monopolies, and public health issues.

The Republican-dominated Court, according to one historian, was not especially partisan. Indeed it unanimously struck down a partisan attempt to reapportion legislative seats. Ultimately the Court shifted from Republican dominance to a more politically divided institution. As the political winds changed direction, Montgomery, who was highly respected, lost to Democrat Douglas J. Morris in 1910. The defeat stunned locals. The *Seymour Daily Republican* noted, "The attorneys of the state will feel the loss of Judge Montgomery as they knew that when a case was determined by him the decision would be right and that justice would be given to all parties concerned."

Although Montgomery lost his re-election bid in 1910, he did not end his civic service. In 1912, for example, he served as president of the Indiana State Bar Association. He was also active in the Rotary, a trustee at Hanover College, and a member of the Knights of Pythias Lodge in Seymour and

Columbia Club in Indianapolis. However, personal tragedies began to hit Montgomery. In 1912 his father committed suicide. Despite his anguish, Montgomery continued to practice law and remained involved in politics. In 1912 he was a delegate to the Republican National Convention and held a prominent position in the Republican state committee. But he suffered personal tragedy again when his brother, Amazona, was brutally murdered just outside Seymour in 1921. In 1929 one of Montgomery's sons died at the young age of thirty-six. Throughout all these difficulties, Montgomery continued to practice law in Seymour (the law firm he established is still there). He died on May 5, 1936, after a year of ill health.

JAMES M. BEEBY, PhD, is a fellow of the Royal Historical Society. He is an associate professor of history, Indiana University Southeast. Beeby is the author of *Revolt of the Tar Heels: The North Carolina Populist Party, 1890–1901* (2008) and several scholarly articles, chapters, and essays on the Gilded Age and Progressive Era, African American history, and U.S. political history.

SELECTED BIBLIOGRAPHY

Madison, James. *The Indiana Way: A State History*. Bloomington: Indiana University Press; Indianapolis: Indiana Historical Society, 1986.

Monks, Leander J., ed. *Courts and Lawyers of Indiana*. Indianapolis: Federal Publishing Company, 1916.

Seymour Daily Democrat.

Seymour Daily Republican.

Seymour Daily Tribune.

Stoll, James B. *The History of the Indiana Democracy, 1816–1916*. Indianapolis: Democratic Publishing Company, 1917.

Taylor, Charles. *The Bench and Bar of Indiana*. Indianapolis: Bench and Bar Publishing Company, 1895.

QUINCY A. MYERS
January 4, 1909–January 4, 1915

JULIAN L. RIDLEN

Whether by twist of fate or by political design, both the Republican and the Democratic parties nominated Logansport lawyers as their 1908 standard-bearers for the Indiana Supreme Court from the Fifth Judicial District. For the Republican convention to nominate fifty-five year old Quincy Alden Myers, who became the fifty-second judge of the Court, it meant rejecting the bid for renomination of incumbent John H. Gillett. As the roll call of delegates advanced, the desire for change became apparent, and Gillett withdrew his name before the roll call reached one-third. Democrats had convened a week earlier and selected forty-nine-year-old Moses B. Lairy. Both were highly respected members of the local bar.

Myers was born September 1, 1853, in Clinton Township, Cass County, Indiana, the eldest son of Isaac and Rosanna Justice Myers. The Myers family story is traced to Huguenot ancestors who left Holland to settle in the British colonies of Virginia and Maryland nearly a century before the American Revolution. Three Myers brothers served under the direct command of General George Washington, and Quincy's grandfather, John Myers, left Virginia to become one of the early pioneers in Cass County.

Myers was prepared to depart for Princeton University but his mother's lamentations persuaded him to spend his first year at Northwestern Christian (now Butler) University in Indianapolis. He entered Dartmouth College in 1873, where he was a crew member of the varsity rowing team and honed his communication skills by serving as editor of the college paper, *The Dartmouth*.

Upon graduation in 1875, Myers returned to Logansport and began studying law in the offices of McDonnell and Winfield and with Dewitt C. Justice. Justice made Myers his deputy city attorney, a capacity in which he served for fourteen months before enrolling in Union Law School in Albany, New York. After graduating in 1877 as class valedictorian of his eighty-nine-member class, Myers returned again to his hometown to enter into a partnership with his mentor, Maurice Winfield, a relationship that continued until Winfield was elected to the Cass Circuit Court bench in 1882. Myers then formed a partnership with Judge John C. Nelson, who had returned to private practice upon the termination of the Cass Superior Court. The partnership continued until Myers was elected in November 1908 to the Indiana Supreme Court. Prior to his election to the Court, Myers served as Logansport city attorney from 1885 to 1887, two terms as county attorney (1895–97 and 1903–9), and as a Republican presidential elector in 1904. Myers's practice and political involvement extended to Indianapolis, and on March 3, 1886, he married Jessie D. Cornelius of Indianapolis.

Active in the community and interested in both state and local history, Myers served for thirteen years as a member of the school board and was also involved in the organization of the Cass County Historical Society in 1907, serving on the society's first executive committee. The society's museum is currently housed in the judge's former home.

Myers authored numerous Court opinions covering a broad spectrum of issues, including combinations in restraint of trade, contracts, probate, taxation, employer liability, and intoxicating liquor. On the latter topic, Myers wrote a number of opinions, the issue of Prohibition being a social and political battleground in the years preceding the adoption of the Eighteenth Amendment to the U.S. Constitution.

In the fall of 1915, a year after being defeated for re-election to the Court by his opponent six years earlier, Lairy, Myers joined in a three-way contest for the 1916 Republican gubernatorial nomination, only to lose to James P. Goodrich. Goodrich went on to win the governorship, and was succeeded four years later by the third contestant, Warren T. McCray.

After leaving the Court, Myers opened a law practice in Indianapolis in association with Edward Gates. Shortly after the completion of his term as governor, Samuel M. Ralston joined the practice, under the firm name of Myers, Gates and Ralston, a relationship that continued until Myers's death. During his stint on the bench and, later in his subsequent period of law practice, Myers was actively involved in the state and community through his memberships in the Century, Columbia, Woodstock, and Marion clubs in Indianapolis. Myers, a member of both the Indiana and American Bar Associations, was active while on the bench in the American Institute of Criminal Law and Criminology, an early and innovative group seeking improvement in the field of criminal justice. In his address as president of the institute in 1914, he observed:

> It has been the frequent inquiry, if not the conviction, of those charged with the administration of the criminal laws, whether the accused is not often one who requires treatment rather than punishment. If courts are to be directed by legislative enactment, it is important that the enactment itself be not merely legislative empiricism, but scientific deduction from reliable sources of information.

Myers served as president of the institute in 1913 and 1914 and was local chair when Indianapolis hosted the annual meeting in 1920. He remained involved with the Cass County bar throughout his life, attending a local bar meeting a few weeks before his death; the bulk of Myers's holdings in land, business, and residential properties were in Cass County at the time of his death. Myers had been ill for less than a week when he was taken to Saint Vincent Hospital, Indianapolis, on Christmas Day. He died on December 28, 1921.

JULIAN L. RIDLEN, JD, is senior judge and former Cass County Circuit Court Judge. He is a former Treasurer of Indiana and has taught courses at Indiana University, Kokomo; Anderson University; University of Indianapolis; and Indiana–University Purdue University, Indianapolis. Ridlen is the author of the essay, "Oliver Hampton Smith," in *The Encyclopedia of Indianapolis* (1994).

SELECTED BIBLIOGRAPHY

Adams, Wendy L., and Elizabeth R. Osborn, eds. *In Memoriam: Glimpses from Indiana's Legal Past*. Indianapolis: Indiana Supreme Court, 2006.

Journal of American Institute of Criminal Law and Criminology 5 (October 22, 1914).

Logansport Morning Press, December 30, 1921.

Powell, Jehu Z. *History of Cass County, Indiana*. Chicago: Lewis Publishing Company, 1913.

Seeds, Russell M., ed. *History of the Republican Party*. Indianapolis: Indiana Historical Company, 1899.

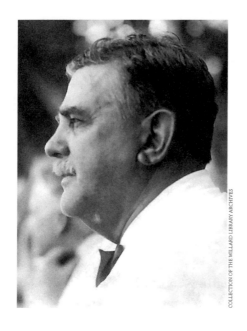

JOHN W. SPENCER
April 15, 1912–January 7, 1919

JAMES M. REDWINE

John Wesley Spencer was known for his forcefulness and his forthrightness as an attorney, a prosecutor, and a judge. He also had a reputation as a "strong and eloquent partisan in any case which he espoused . . . in the courtroom or on the political platform." His reputation and his active role in the Democratic Party at both the state and county level were key factors behind his political and legal successes. Governor Thomas R. Marshall twice appointed him to judgeships—once to fill a vacancy on the Vanderburgh County Circuit Court, and once to a vacancy on the Indiana Supreme Court as its fifty-third judge. On the Court Spencer's votes in critical cases were often aligned with those of the governor and his party.

Born in Posey County on March 7, 1864, Spencer was destined to become a lawyer. He graduated from Mount Vernon High School in 1880 and attended Central Indiana Normal College at Danville for one year before returning to Posey County to read in the law office of his father, Elijah. On his twenty-first birthday in 1885, Spencer was admitted to the Indiana bar, and after practicing law for five years he began his climb up the judicial ladder. In 1890 he was elected prosecuting attorney for the First Judicial Circuit, which encompassed Vanderburgh and Posey counties, and served two full terms. In 1896 he was elected district chair for the Democratic Party and also as a member of the Democratic State Committee. He made an unsuccessful bid in 1902 as the Democratic nominee for the U.S. House of Representatives.

His first judicial post came in 1911 when Marshall appointed him judge of the Vanderburgh County Circuit Court. Spencer's son, John W. Jr., following in his father's footsteps, later also serving as Vanderburgh circuit court judge. In 1912 Spencer was chosen by the Democratic State Convention as a candidate for the Supreme Court. In April of that year, before the election was held, a sitting Court judge died, and Marshall appointed Spencer to complete his term. In the general election of that year Spencer won a seat on the Court in his own right.

In his seven years on the Court Spencer wrote 253 opinions. One of his most significant was in the case of *Board of Election Commissioners of City of Indianapolis v. Knight*. In this case the Court majority struck down the Partial Suffrage Act of 1917, which was an attempt by the general assembly to expand voting rights for women for municipal officials such as mayor, city judge, city clerk, and members of the common council, as well as school board members. Writing for the Court, Spencer relied heavily on precedents by both the U.S. Supreme Court and Indiana Supreme Court. He wrote that "the right of suffrage is not a natural or an inherent right, but a political privilege, and it is held only by those on whom it is bestowed, either by virtue of express constitutional grant or through authorized legislative provision." Spencer said that the issue was one that only the people "in their capacity as creators of the Constitution" could decide and "never one for the consideration of the legislature" unless authorized to do so. Spencer demonstrated his loyalty to Marshall, his political benefactor, by dissenting in the famous case of *Ellingham, Secretary of State et al. v. Dye*, when the Court struck down the "Marshall Constitution" as an unconstitutional attempt by the legislature to make substantive changes in the state constitution.

In many of his decisions on the Court, Spencer's forceful personality comes through. A good example is his opinion in *Marietta Glass Mamufac-*

turing Company v. Pruitt when he took on a saw manufacturer's appeal from a jury verdict. In upholding the plaintiff's award of damages for injuries from an unguarded saw, Spencer discussed at length the issues that would become the heart of American tort law for the rest of the century. Spencer's strong leadership in Indiana's tort law during the critical years at the beginning of the twentieth century laid the foundation for Indiana's protection of individuals from rapacious industrial expansion. Spencer's advocacy from the bench might not sit as easy today, but when Indiana was developing its doctrine of negligence law, he led the way.

Although Spencer served on the Court for seven years that included intermittent terms as chief justice, he was much better known for his twenty years of trial practice after he left the bench. His colorful and vociferous courtroom demeanor swayed laymen and intimidated opponents. In one of his most famous final arguments, Spencer held up a heart-shaped stone and told the jury it represented "the heart of the bank trying to sell out the farmer, cold, hard and lifeless." The jury ruled in Spencer's farmer client's favor, and Spencer kept the stone on his desk the rest of his life.

A eulogy by his hometown bar association paid tribute to Spencer's tenacity. It said, "there were no half measures to the man. You either liked him or you didn't like him. . . . Judge Spencer never knew the meaning of fear, either physically or morally. When he went into a fight he went into it with everything he had, determined to win." Spencer died on June 28, 1939, and is buried in Bellefontaine Cemetery in Mount Vernon near another of Posey County's Court judges, Alvin P. Hovey.

JAMES M. REDWINE, JD, is judge of the Posey County Circuit Court. He is the author of *Judge Lynch* (2008), a historical novel, and *Gavel Gamut Greetings from JPeg Ranch* (2009), an anthology. Redwine is a faculty member of the National Judicial College.

SELECTED BIBLIOGRAPHY

Evansville Courier, June 29, 1939.
Evansville Press, June 29, 1939.
Nolan, John J. "History of the Democratic Party of Vanderburgh County." In
   History of the Indiana Democracy, 1816–1916, by John B. Stott. Indianapolis: Indiana
   Democratic Publishing Company, 1917.

CASES CITED

Board of Election Commissioners of City of Indianapolis v. Knight, 187 Ind. 108 (1917).
Ellingham, Secretary of State et al. v. Dye, 178 Ind. 336 (1912).
Marietta Glass Manufacturing Company v. Pruitt, 180 Ind. 434 (1913).

DOUGLAS J. MORRIS
January 2, 1911–January 1, 1917

GRETA MORRIS SCODRO

Douglas J. Morris, who served one term from 1911 to 1917 as the fifty-fourth judge of the Indiana Supreme Court, was an ardent Democrat. Most Court judges at this time were involved in party politics because being elected was the only avenue to the high court. Morris's election to the Court in 1910, along with fellow Democrat Charles E. Cox, gave the party seats on the Court for the first time in twenty years. A year later, a vacancy was created when James H. Jordan died, and Governor Thomas R. Marshall appointed Democrat John W. Spencer as his replacement. This gave the Democrats a three-to-two majority on the Court. Even so, Morris ended up dissenting in many cases. Most notable was his dissent in the famous case in which the Court ruled that a new state constitution, proposed by Marshall, passed by the Democratic-controlled general assembly, and submitted to the voters for approval was unconstitutional. Morris's dissenting opinion in this case has been called "his most notable achievement on the Court."

Morris was born January 5, 1861, in Knightstown, Indiana, in Henry County, the son and grandson of farmers, some of whose descendants live in that county still. He attended the county's public schools and graduated in 1882 from Asbury College (now DePauw University), where he became a lifelong member of the Delta Kappa Epsilon social fraternity. He taught for a single school term and began studying law in Indianapolis under the supervision of Benjamin Harrison. After being admitted to the Indiana bar in 1883 at age twenty-two, he spent two years practicing in Tennessee, then settled in Rushville, the seat of Rush County, and became active in Democrat politics, serving many years on the county's Democratic Central Committee. He ran for Congress in 1888, but lost. Ten years later he was elected judge of the Eighth Circuit Court, comprised of Rush and Decatur counties. He served one six-year term, but was defeated in the 1904 general election. In 1910 he was nominated by the Democratic Party convention to run for a seat on the Court from the Second District. After a successful campaign, he began his only term on the Court in 1911.

Morris authored some 278 majority opinions during his six-year term, a striking number of which dealt with probate matters, and many of which were but a few pages in length. Few words were required to dispose of some arguments. The issue of the "Marshall Constitution" was another matter. At this time in the state's legal history the judiciary usually bowed to the will of the legislature or the executive branch when their decisions were challenged, but the Court's response to Marshall's proposed constitution was an exception to the Court's typical posture of deference to the political branches. The "Marshall Constitution" contained substantial changes in the 1851 constitution. Among these were expanding the powers of the governor, increasing the size of both houses of the state legislature and the Court, and establishing such populist measures as the initiative, referendum, and recall. When the legislature submitted these changes to the voters, Republicans succeeded in getting the Marion County Circuit Court to issue an injunction to prevent the issue from being placed on the ballot for the election in 1912. On appeal the Court sustained the lower court decision by a vote of three-to-two, with Morris's fellow Democrat, Cox, writing the opinion in *Ellingham, Secretary of State et al. v. Dye.* The majority ruled that the proposed changes were unconstitutional because the legislature lacked the authority to propose a new constitution, and that the procedures for amending the constitution, which required that proposed constitutional amendments be approved by two separately elected legislatures, had not been followed.

Morris wrote a lengthy and stinging dissent that dissected in great detail both state and federal court precedents. The heart of his argument was that the circuit court had no authority to intervene in the case because the question before the Court was "purely political, and one over which the courts have no jurisdiction." Morris thought that the Court had overstepped its boundaries. He said "holding elections and voting, involve the exercise of political powers only, and this injunction is really against the voters of the state."

Morris also authored other notable dissents in a series of cases addressing efforts by the legislative and executive branches to reorganize state government. The plan included making the decisions of the relatively new appellate court final in certain types of cases. This change would have eliminated any opportunity for the parties to obtain further review by the Court, in effect rendering the appellate court, which was created by statute and controlled by the legislature, the state court of last resort in many cases. The first case, *Ex Parte France, Clerk of the Supreme Court*, arose just months after Morris took office. A Court clerk, Fred France, filed a petition directly with the Court requesting direction on whether to follow the new statute. The majority ruled the statute unconstitutional, declaring it "manifest" that the state constitution did not allow the legislature to establish a court equal in rank to the Court. Morris dissented on grounds that the legislature had the constitutional authority to establish the jurisdiction of a court it had created, a view shared by Marshall. Twice more, Morris dissented, siding with the legislature and the governor in other government reorganization cases.

Morris ran for a second term on the Court in 1916, but lost to David A. Myers, a Republican from Rush County. It was a banner year for Republican candidates for most state offices, and the election results shifted majority control of the Court back to the Republicans. Following his defeat Morris returned to private practice in Rushville. By this time, both of his children, son Douglas Jr. and, uncommon at the time, his daughter, Hannah, were lawyers. In the partnership Morris and Morris and Morris, the three practiced together until the former judge died on July 9, 1928, at the age of sixty-seven in Rushville. He was survived by his children and his wife, Pamela Spann. His children continued to practice in Rushville for many years.

GRETA MORRIS SCODRO, JD, is deputy administrator and staff attorney for the Indiana Supreme Court (since 1995). A native Hoosier, she is distantly related to Justices Jehu K. Elliott and Douglas J. Morris, and she was a law clerk to Justice Jon D. Krahulik.

SELECTED BIBLIOGRAPHY

Hughes, John N. *Rush County, Indiana: Chapter 2, 1822–1982; The Bench and Bar and Officials*. Rushville, IN: Wilkinson Printing, 1983.

Indianapolis Star, June 21, 1911, July 10, 1928.

Newhouse, Julie. Conversations with a Rush County attorney about the Morris family. October 2008.

Rushville Daily Republican, July 9, 1928.

Withered, Jerome L. *Hoosier Justice: A History of the Supreme Court of Indiana*. Indianapolis: Indiana Supreme Court, 1998.

CASES CITED

Ellingham, Secretary of State et al. v. Dye, 178 Ind. 336 (1912).

Ex Parte France, Clerk of the Supreme Court, 176 Ind. 72 (1911).

CHARLES E. COX
January 2, 1911–January 1, 1917

RYAN T. SCHWIER

Charles Elbridge Cox, fifty-fifth judge of the Indiana Supreme Court, was as much a product of the Indiana Constitution as he was a shaper of it. More than 170 published opinions distinguish his juristic agility on issues ranging from charitable trusts to labor and employment. His record of dissent reveals a conservative trend of opinion of which he remarked in *Hyland et al. v. Rochelle* that "the futility [of such] is so apparent that I am sometimes led to refrain.."

Born February 21, 1860, to Aaron and Mary Ann Cox, "Charlie" spent his youth with elder brothers Millard and Jabez on a farm near Westfield, Indiana. After attending common schools at Noblesville and Tipton, he followed fraternal tradition to pursue a career in law. Cox forged a successful practice during a period of legal-cultural transition and political volatility. His professional diversity, in a career spanning nearly six decades, illustrates a resourcefulness that left a unique imprint on Indiana legal history.

In 1877 Cox began the study of law in Indianapolis, where he apprenticed under former judge William E. Niblack. Cox served concurrently as assistant librarian of the Court. He was promoted to head librarian in 1883, and in 1889 the state published his expanded edition of the Court library catalog, a practical guide for many jurists of the day.

Lacking formal institutional training, Cox entered the practice of law in 1889 as a "constitutional lawyer," a term applied to those attorneys admitted under the early liberal qualifications of the 1851 Indiana Constitution. Cox was chief deputy prosecuting attorney of Marion County from 1890 to 1894. He subsequently served two consecutive two-year terms as city judge of Indianapolis. Upon returning to the bar, Cox practiced for several years with Charles Remster, an attorney who would later become Marion Circuit Court judge and whose opinions Cox often reviewed upon appeal.

Cox was elected to the Court in 1910 and was sworn in on January 2, 1911. During his tenure as judge, constitutional reform was a frequent issue on the court docket. In 1913 Cox wrote the majority opinion in *In re Boswell*. The court ruled that a proposed "Lawyers Amendment" to the state constitution, which would have given the general assembly power to set bar-admission requirements, failed voter ratification. Although the measure received a majority vote of electors, it did not receive a majority of those qualified at the time of election. The constitutional provision providing any Indiana voter "of good moral character" with a qualified admission standard remained in effect for another eighteen years. In 1931 a legislative enactment gave the Court exclusive jurisdiction over admitting attorneys to the bar.

Cox's most important and oft-cited opinion undoubtedly remains the "Marshall Constitution" case, *Ellingham, Secretary of State et al. v. Dye*. The controversy arose over the method of reforming the state's fundamental law by act of legislation rather than by a constitutional convention. Cox, a Democrat, was the sole justice to cross party lines in a politically divided court. The court's majority ruled that a new constitution proposed by Democratic governor Thomas R. Marshall and passed by the Democratic-controlled general assembly was unconstitutional. The "Marshall Constitution," as it was known, would have expanded the governor's powers, enlarged the House of Representatives and the Court, and strengthened the legislative authority to adopt laws providing for the initiative, referendum, and recall of elected officials. Republicans had sought and obtained an injunction to prevent the proposed changes from being submitted to voters in the 1912 general elections. According to the opinion, the enactment exceeded legislative authority by failing to meet the constitutional prerequisite of approval by two separately elected sessions of the general assembly before submission to popular vote. The decision to overrule the act preserved methods of constitutional construction in Indiana that remain in effect today.

At the close of his judicial tenure in 1917, Cox resumed private practice. He argued a case, *Rooker et al. v. Fidelity Trust Company et al.*, in front of the U.S. Supreme Court in 1923. In 1924 he presided over the Indianapolis Bar Association. Under his leadership, the IBA drafted trial court reform legislation for Marion County. Adopted by the general assembly in 1925, the "Municipal Court Bill" replaced the Indianapolis City Court with the Marion County Municipal Court. Ironically, Cox later assisted the IBA in defending the legislation over a lawsuit that challenged its constitutionality.

In 1925 Cox served as assistant prosecuting attorney in the infamous D. C. Stevenson trial. Stevenson, Grand Dragon of the Ku Klux Klan and highly influential in Indiana politics, was prosecuted for the murder of Madge Oberholtzer, a young statehouse worker. Cox presented the prosecution's opening statement, introduced medical testimony, and cross-examined the defense's expert witnesses. The events following Stevenson's murder conviction revealed political corruption and Klan infiltration at the highest levels of Indiana government.

A glimpse of Cox's personal life reveals a commitment to both family and community. He was a member of the Sons of the American Revolution, Indiana Democratic Club, and First Congregationalist Church. He married his wife, Emma Cooley, in 1884. Together they raised three children: Elinor (Karsten), Samuel, and Charles Jr. Emma and Charles spent their later years together at Boulder Brook Farm, their country estate in Lawrence Township. Cox died on February 3, 1936.

RYAN T. SCHWIER, MA, MLS, is librarian, Indiana University School of Law, Indianapolis. Schwier is the author of "The Bricks and Mortar of Information: Preserving Indiana's Historic Public Libraries," *Indiana Libraries* (2008) and contributing author for the *Encyclopedia of American Reform Movements* (2010).

SELECTED BIBLIOGRAPHY

Baker, John H. "The History of the Indiana Trial Court System and Attempts at Renovation." *Indiana Law Review* 30, no. 1 (1997): 233–61.

Busch, Francis Xavier. *Guilty or Not Guilty? An Account of the Trials of the Leo Frank Case, the D. C. Stevenson Case, the Samuel Insull Case, the Alger Hiss Case.* Freeport, NY: Bobbs-Merrill Company, 1970.

Maley, Robert J., and John R. Maley. "More Than Arbiters of Cases and Controversies." In David J. Bodenhamer and Randall T. Shepard, eds. *The History of Indiana Law.* Athens: Ohio University Press, 2006.

"News of Bench and Bar, Seventh District." *Indiana Law Journal* 2, no. 3 (December 1926): 286–90.

"Regular Meeting Minutes, 1918–1933." Indianapolis Bar Association, *Records, 1878–1987.* Bound volume 2437, Indiana Historical Society.

Walsh, Justin E. *The Centennial History of the Indiana General Assembly, 1816–1978.* Indianapolis: Published by the Select Committee on the Centennial History of the Indiana General Assembly in cooperation with the Indiana Historical Bureau, 1987.

CASES CITED

Ellingham, Secretary of State et al. v. Dye, 178 Ind. 336 (1912).

Hyland et al. v. Rochelle, 179 Ind. 671 (1913).

In re Boswell, 179 Ind. 292 (1913).

Rooker et al. v. Fidelity Trust Company et al., 261 U.S. 114 (1923); 263 U.S. 413 (1923).

RICHARD K. ERWIN
January 6, 1913–October 5, 1917

ANGELA M. QUINN

The early days of one's professional career often set the tone of the accomplishments to come. Such is the example of Richard Kenney Erwin and the Lige Holland trial in Adams County, Indiana. This case in 1891 involved Erwin's defense of two men, Lige Holland and Andy Pickering, who were charged as accomplices in a failed abortion attempt that left a young woman dead. The crime enraged local citizens, and many called for the lynching of Holland, an African American. Erwin, along with two other attorneys, represented the two men, who were found guilty. Despite the public outcry and rage against the defendants, Erwin worked to ensure that they received a fair trial. Following Erwin's death in 1917, a memorial tribute noted: "He saw the merits of the controversy with an eye which applied the never failing test in appellate judicial procedure,—Has substantial justice been done?"

The fifty-sixth judge of the Indiana Supreme Court, Erwin was born in Union Township, Adams County, on July 11, 1860. His parents, David and Mary Ellen Erwin, had been among the early settlers of the area, arriving sometime before 1845 when David first appeared on the Adams County tax records. Erwin was raised on the family farm and attended the local schools. At age twenty, Erwin was working as a teacher and still living with his mother in Union Township. She died soon after, and Erwin was left with the care of his younger siblings and the family farm. Erwin enrolled at the Methodist College in Fort Wayne for a term and continued to teach school in Adams and Allen counties as he studied law in the office of France and Merriman in Decatur, Indiana.

After his admission to the bar in 1886, Erwin practiced law for several years. In 1890 and again in 1892 he was elected to the Indiana House of Representatives. Concurrent with his term in the legislature, Erwin also served as the county attorney for Adams County from 1891 to 1897. His younger brother, Dore, studied law with him for a period of years before becoming a prominent attorney in Adams County. Erwin also served as a judge of the Twenty-sixth Indiana Judicial Circuit from 1901 to 1907.

In 1883 Erwin married Luella Waas at Monroeville, Allen County, and the family relocated to Fort Wayne in 1907. Erwin was an unsuccessful candidate to the Supreme Court in 1906. He was beaten by the distinguished jurist Leander J. Monks, who was running for a third consecutive term. In 1912 the tables turned, and he defeated Monks in a landslide, winning by more than 120,000 votes, the largest vote ever given to a Court candidate at that time.

In his fifth year on the bench, Erwin and the Court were confronted with two important and controversial constitutional cases. Erwin wrote the majority opinion in one of those—*Bennett v. Jackson, Secretary of State*. At issue was an act passed in 1917 by the Indiana General Assembly calling for the election of delegates to a constitutional convention. A challenge to the law was denied by the Marion County Superior Court, and on appeal the Court invalidated the law. Relying on established precedents limiting the legislature's authority to alter or amend the constitution, the majority opinion held that only "the people" possessed the power to call for a constitutional convention. Erwin wrote that the law was "null and void" because it was in conflict with section one of the state Bill of Rights and took "from the people the right to say when they desire a change in the fundamental law." In a second constitutional case in 1917, *Board of Election Commissioners of City of Indianapolis v. Knight*, Erwin voted with the majority to strike down another legislative statute. That opinion invalidated a partial suffrage act passed by the general assembly that allowed women to vote in certain elections not specified in the state constitution because it conflicted with language in the constitution about voter eligibility.

Erwin's term on the Court ended prematurely when he died in Fort Wayne on October 5, 1917, after an illness of several weeks. He was serving as chief justice at the time of his death. Erwin was a productive member of the Court, having participated in 180 cases and authoring 169 majority opinions. A fellow judge said that his opinions were "concise and clear, his reasoning sound, and his diction perfection." His career on the Court was termed "notable and honorable."

ANGELA M. QUINN, MA, is executive director of ARCH, Fort Wayne's historic preservation nonprofit organization, since 1996. She is the author of *The Underground Railroad and the Antislavery Movement in Fort Wayne and Allen County, Indiana* (2001), several National Register nominations, and articles in *History of Fort Wayne and Allen County*.

SELECTED BIBLIOGRAPHY

Adams, Wendy L., and Elizabeth R. Osborn, eds. *In Memoriam: Glimpses from Indiana's Legal Past*. Indianapolis: Indiana Supreme Court, 2006.

Heller, Dick, ed. *The 1979 History of Adams County, Indiana*. Dallas, TX: Taylor Publishing Company, 1979.

CASES CITED

Bennett v. Jackson, Secretary of State, 186 Ind. 533 (1917).

Board of Election Commissioners of City of Indianapolis v. Knight, 187 Ind. 108 (1917).

MOSES B. LAIRY
January 4, 1915–January 3, 1921

JULIAN L. RIDLEN

Moses Barnett Lairy, the fifty-seventh judge of the Indiana Supreme Court, thought he was going to be a schoolteacher. Born August 13, 1859, on the family farm in Cass County, the first of two sons of Thomas and Eliza Barnett Lairy, he was educated through the eighth grade in a one-room school. It was not uncommon for a student "of promise" to combine winter season teaching with warm-weather farming after little or no further training beyond eighth grade. Thus, when his father died in 1877, seventeen-year-old Moses assumed the farming responsibilities and attended the Northern Indiana Normal School (now Valparaiso University), to prepare himself to teach. Lairy taught for nine years and was reportedly being groomed for the post of county superintendent of schools. In the meantime, however, he had begun to study law under the tutelage of Judge Dudley H. Chase. In 1888 Lairy began law studies at the University of Michigan, finishing in the following year and returning to Logansport to open a solo practice. After four years, Lairy partnered with veteran attorney Dewitt C. Justice and later with M. L. Mahoney for fourteen years.

In 1894 Lairy ran for Cass County Circuit Court judge against Chase, his first law mentor, who had an understanding with sitting Judge D. B. McConnell that in the event of Chase's success at the polls, McConnell would resign and Chase would be appointed to serve the remainder of Mc-Connell's term. Chase was victorious, and McConnell resigned; however, Governor Claude Matthews, a Democrat elected in 1892, found Democrat Lairy more imminently qualified for the interim appointment. Two years later, Chase assumed the judgeship to which he had been elected, only to be defeated for re-election in 1902 by Lairy's younger brother, John.

Lairy's first marriage to Mazetta Rogers in 1892 ended in divorce shortly after his elevation to the Supreme Court in 1915. Lairy later married Nina Justice, daughter of his former law partner.

Active in the Masonic Order, the Elks, and the Democratic Party, Lairy was in demand as a speaker. By 1908 he had gained sufficient stature in the bar and in political circles to seek the nomination for the Fifth Judicial District. After three ballots, Lairy emerged victorious over Timothy E. Howard, former Court judge, and Jabez Cox, brother of Court judge Charles E. Cox. However, Lairy lost the general election to Quincy A. Myers, a fellow member of the local bar, in a cliff-hanger that was not resolved until three days after the election. Myers was a next-door neighbor to Lairy's brother. The adjoining homes of Myers and Lairy were later given to the Cass County Historical Society.

Despite the loss, the attention and name recognition gained in the closely contested election served Lairy well. In 1910 he was successful in seeking a seat on the Indiana Appellate court. Four years later, Lairy reversed the tables of 1908, defeating incumbent Myers, who along with the GOP found himself in the backwash of the 1912 Theodore Roosevelt split that pitted the conservatives against the progressives within the Republican Party.

In 1951 another member of the Cass County bar and former Court judge, Michael L. Fansler, reflecting upon Lairy's influence upon him as a young lawyer, observed, "He taught me what the college professors—didn't seem to know when I got on the bench, that the rules of equity and the common law in most respects, the law of torts, doesn't grow. The rules are what they should be—what they ought to be. The cases, the opinions, are only evidence of the law. The judges grow and learn, and the lawyers—the law, equity and most of the common law is and always has been what it ought to be."

Lairy left the Court in January 1921, and shortly thereafter joined the Indianapolis law firm of Myers, Gates and Ralston. He replaced Myers, who had died the previous month, just as he had succeeded his friend and colleague on the Court. Thus, the law firm took a distinctly Democratic political flavor, for in addition to Lairy and former governor Samuel M. Ralston, the reorganized firm also added Frederick Van Nuys, who later became a U.S. senator.

While Lairy earned a reputation as a hardworking judge during his single term on the Court and for his well-reasoned opinions, the cases that brought him more personal attention were those in which he was involved as counsel. In the 1920s the crosscurrents of movements such as the Ku Klux Klan and issues of Prohibition and its enforcement had sensitized the Hoosier State. When Edward S. Shumaker, Methodist minister, and others involved with the Indiana Anti-Saloon League were brought before the Court in *State v. Shumaker*, an original action charging them with indirect contempt based upon the distribution of a critical publication, Lairy, at the invitation of the Court, was one of two former Court judges to serve as amici curiae, or friends of the court, and to submit a brief on the questions involved.

In a case that garnered national press, Lairy was retained to defend Delaware Circuit Judge Clarence W. Dearth in the first impeachment proceeding heard in the Indiana Senate since 1835. Dearth was in an ongoing conflict with the editor of a local paper, who had charged him with jury manipulation, making "goats" of a few bootleggers and criminals, and being friendly to the Klan. The editor fled to Ohio to avoid appearing on a charge of criminal contempt. Responding to petitions from Muncie citizens, the House of Representatives approved seven formal articles of impeachment. In the trial before the Senate Lairy and his cocounsel prevailed for their client—two votes short of the two-thirds necessary to convict.

Lairy died at Logansport on April 9, 1921, little more than one week following the conclusion of the Dearth trial. He died in the presence of Fansler, having spent the afternoon together working on a case.

JULIAN L. RIDLEN, JD, is senior judge and former Cass County Circuit Court Judge. He is a former Treasurer of Indiana and has taught courses at Indiana University, Kokomo; Anderson University; University of Indianapolis; and Indiana–University Purdue University, Indianapolis. Ridlen is the author of the essay, "Oliver Hampton Smith," in *The Encyclopedia of Indianapolis*.

SELECTED BIBLIOGRAPHY

"Extemporaneous Remarks of Honorable Michael L. Fansler to Cass County Bar Association." Transcript of Cass County Bar Association Meeting, April 5, 1961. Recorded by Frank Tolbert.

"In Indiana." *Time*, April 11, 1927. http://www.time.com/time/magazine/article/0,9171,730339,00.html.

"Indiana's Dearth." *Time*, April 4, 1927. http://www.time.com/time/magazine/article/0,9171,723020,00.html.

Logansport Pharos Tribune, November 7, 1908, April 11, 1927, June 7, 1937.

Powell, Jehu Z. *History of Cass County, Indiana.* Chicago: Lewis Publishing Company, 1913.

CASES CITED

State of Indiana v. Shumaker et al., 200 Ind. 623 (1927).

DAVID A. MYERS
January 1, 1917–December 31, 1934

JAMES R. WILLIAMS

David Albert Myers, who served on the Indiana Supreme Court as its fifty-eighth judge, was a Republican politician and consummate legal fixture in the state of Indiana. His career was marked by remarkable achievement and longevity.

Myers was born on August 5, 1859, in Cass County, Indiana. He was educated at Smithson College, Danville Normal College, and Union University before receiving his law degree from Albany Law School in New York in 1882. Thereafter, he began practicing law in Greensburg, Indiana, being elected city attorney in 1886. In 1890 and 1892 he was elected prosecuting attorney of the Decatur-Rush Judicial District, before his 1899 appointment as judge of the Bartholomew-Decatur Circuit by Governor James A. Mount.

In October 1904 Myers was appointed judge of the appellate court from the First District by Governor Winfield T. Durbin. In November of 1904 and 1908 respectively, he was elected to the appellate court and served in that capacity until January 1913. Myers was first elected to Indiana's highest court in 1916, a year when Republicans won all of the top state offices on the ballot. He was reelected in 1922 and again in 1928, another big year for Republicans. He ran for re-election in 1934 but was unable to weather the Democratic tide that had begun to sweep the state in 1932. He was defeated by another Greensburg attorney, George L. Tremain. In his total of thirty-two years on Indiana's highest two courts, Myers served under eleven governors. Remarkably, the astute Republican politician was reputed to be as amicable with Democrats as he was with members of his own party. During his time on the bench, Myers was on two occasions the only elected Republican in the Indiana Statehouse.

In his first year on the Court Myers grappled with the other justices over some key constitutional issues. In 1917 in *Bennett v. Jackson, Secretary of State et al.*, he sided with the Court majority in preventing the general assembly from calling for election of delegates to a constitutional convention. The Court ruled that only the voters had the authority to call a constitutional convention. Myers also joined the Court majority in the case of *Board of Election Commissioners of City of Indianapolis v. Knight* to invalidate the Partial Suffrage Act that would have given women voting rights in some municipal and school board elections.

In his seventeen-year tenure on the Court, Myers wrote a total of 292 opinions. Close to 60 percent of Myers's opinions were about criminal appeals. At the time the Court was bogged down with a backlog of cases, due in part to the large number of criminal appeals the Court had to hear.

After retiring from the Court in 1935, Myers returned to Greensburg and practiced law until shortly before his death. He was believed to be the oldest practicing attorney in the Midwest, practicing up until the age of ninety-five. At the age of ninety-two, Myers reflected on a U.S. patent law case that he had recently successfully litigated for which he said he "had to buy an entire new set of law books and 'cram' for more than a month."

Aside from his involvement in political and public affairs, Myers helped to found the Indiana State Bar Association and was a lifelong member and supporter. In 1948 he was presented a life membership certificate along with the other four surviving founder-members of the association. Additionally, for more than a half century he was a member of the Knights of Pythias, the Masons, and the Columbia Club in Indianapolis.

The *Greensburg Daily News* wrote in a tribute to Myers's ninety-fifth birthday that he was "[m]aintaining his usual busy schedule . . . at his desk, smoking the inevitable cigar, with things other than his remarkable longevity and state of health uppermost in his mind." Myers died on July 1, 1955, at his Greensburg home.

JAMES R. WILLIAMS, JD, is a partner with Defur Voran LP. He was judge, Union Circuit Court (1999–2005); and senior judge (2005–7).

SELECTED BIBLIOGRAPHY

Greensburg Daily News, May 10, 1951, August 5, 1954.

CASES CITED

Bennett v. Jackson, Secretary of State et al., 186 Ind. 533 (1917).
Board of Election Commissioners of City of Indianapolis v. Knight, 187 Ind. 108 (1917).

LAWSON M. HARVEY
January 1, 1917–June 25, 1920

LINDA C. GUGIN

Lawson Moreau Harvey, the fifty-ninth judge of the Indiana Supreme Court, was as well known for his community service outside of the legal profession as he was for his service on the bench. He was born into a family whose members had been Quakers for many generations. His father, Thomas B. Harvey, was a prominent physician in Indianapolis, and both he and Harvey's mother, Delitha Butler Harvey, were active in numerous philanthropic and charitable organizations. Harvey was known as a person with a "friendly disposition," who was seldom "too busy to exchange genial remarks with acquaintances." His colleagues often referred to him as "a gentleman of the old school."

Carrying on the family tradition of service, Harvey followed in the footsteps of his parents. He served for many years on the board of directors for the Bertha Esther Ballard Home Association, which provided "a comfortable

Christian home" at a minimal cost to young women who were self-dependent. Harvey was also on the board of directors of the Home for Friendless Colored Children. Both of these institutions were under the auspices of the Society of Friends for Indiana. He was active in his church and in various social and professional associations. Among these were the Chamber of Commerce, the Marion Club, the Columbia Club, and the Indianapolis Bar Association, for which he served as secretary and president. For several years he lectured on the subject of medical jurisprudence to classes at the Medical College of Indiana.

Born in 1856 in Plainfield, Indiana, Harvey and his family moved to Indianapolis at the age of eight. He attended public schools and the Indianapolis Classical School. He studied at Butler College in Indianapolis and Haverford College near Philadelphia. In 1882 he received his law degree from the Central Law School of Indianapolis and entered the private practice of law. That same year he married Kate P. Parott; they had three children—Thomas P., Horace F., and Jeannette. In 1894 Harvey was elected judge of the Marion County Superior Court, but chose to return to private practice after four years. He returned to the bench briefly in 1907 when he was appointed by Governor J. Frank Hanly to a newly created judgeship for the Superior Court for Marion County. A year later Harvey went back to private practice until his election to the Court.

Harvey maintained an active role in the Republican Party and in 1916 was nominated by the party for one of two judgeships that were open on the Supreme Court. He campaigned vigorously and was easily elected in a year in which Republicans trounced Democrats for most statewide offices. His election to the Court, along with that of David A. Myers, gave Republicans majority control. Despite his strong partisan ties, Harvey earned a reputation as an even-handed judge who was not swayed by ideological concerns.

He wrote forty-six majority opinions and participated in approximately seventy-five cases. Most of the opinions he wrote and the other cases in which he participated were decided unanimously, but on occasion he wrote a separate opinion. He wrote his only dissenting opinion in a case, *Board of Election Commissioners of City of Indianapolis v. Knight*, that involved a challenge to the Partial Suffrage Act of 1917, which granted women the right to vote in certain elections, mainly for municipal offices and school board positions. The majority ruled that the part of the act extending women the right to vote in municipal elections was invalid because it extended the franchise to persons who were not designated as electors under the constitution. The Court upheld the extension of suffrage for school elections. In his dissenting opinion, which was nearly as long as the majority's, Harvey carefully traced the history of the franchise in Indiana from the Constitutions of 1816 and 1851 and subsequent amendments. He determined that the general assembly had always had the power to determine who was eligible to vote in municipal elections. Demonstrating his adherence to judicial deference he wrote: "The power to declare a statute unconstitutional is one of the highest entrusted to a judicial tribunal, and is only to be exercised with the greatest of care, and only when there is no doubt of the unconstitutionality of the law. If there is any doubt in the mind of the court as to the constitutionality of a law, it must be resolved in favor of its validity."

Harvey was not as deferential to legislative authority in a case where the legislature had passed a statute calling for the election of delegates to a state constitutional convention. He joined with three other justices to invalidate the law on the grounds that the Indiana General Assembly lacked the authority to call for a constitutional convention. The majority opinion in *Bennett v. Jackson, Secretary of State et al.* stated that in a previous attempt to amend the constitution voters had rejected a proposal giving the legislature the power to initiate a call for a constitutional convention. Accordingly, only the voters themselves retained that power.

Harvey's service on the Court ended abruptly after he suffered a stroke in his Statehouse office and died on June 25, 1920. He had been in poor health since the death of his wife the previous December and had only returned to the Court a couple of months prior to his death. The outpouring of accolades following his death was a testimony to the high regard with which he was held. An editorial in the *Indianapolis Star* said about him: "Few men in city or state have ranked higher in his profession, few have been held in such uniformly high esteem as man and citizen."

LINDA C. GUGIN, PhD, is professor emeritus of political science, Indiana University Southeast. She is coauthor of *Sherman Minton: New Deal Senator, Cold War Justice* (1997) and *Chief Justice Fred M. Vinson of Kentucky: A Political Biography* (2002), coeditor of *The Governors of Indiana* (2006) and *Justices of the Indiana Supreme Court* (2010), and author of "Sherman Minton: Restraint against a Tide of Activism," *Vanderbilt Law Review* (2009).

SELECT BIBLIOGRAPHY

Adams, Wendy L., and Elizabeth R. Osborn, eds. *In Memoriam: Glimpses from Indiana's Legal Past*. Indianapolis: Indiana Supreme Court, 2006.

Dunn, Jacob Piatt. *The History of Greater Indianapolis: The History, the Industry, the Institution, and the People of a City of Homes*. Chicago: Lewis Publishing Company, 1910.

Indianapolis Star, June 26, 1920.

CASES CITED

Board of Election Commissioners of City of Indianapolis v. Knight, 187 Ind. 108 (1917).

Bennett v. Jackson, Secretary of State et al., 186 Ind. 533 (1917).

HOWARD L. TOWNSEND
October 5, 1917–November 1, 1923

DONALD D. DOXSEE

Before becoming a lawyer, Howard L. Townsend was a teacher of Greek, Latin, and mathematics at Tri-State College (now Trine University) in Angola, Indiana. This classic background must have instilled in him the clarity of thought and conciseness of language that resulted in his short and to the point legal opinions he wrote as the sixtieth judge of the Indiana Supreme Court.

Born on a farm in near Edon, Ohio, on December 1, 1869, Townsend and his family moved to Angola, where he graduated from high school. He went on to receive a bachelor's degree from Bethany College in West Virginia. Then, he returned to Angola to teach at Tri-State College. A few years later he turned to the law and attended Chicago-Kent College of Law, where he received his law degree.

After practicing law in Chicago for a few years, Townsend set up his practice in Fort Wayne, Indiana, in 1904. He practiced with Newton W. Gilbert, who was later appointed as vice governor of the Philippines from 1907 to 1908 by President Theodore Roosevelt. Townsend also practiced with Sol A. Wood, who became judge of the Allen County Circuit Court.

Active in Allen County Republican Party politics, Townsend received an appointment to the Court by Governor James P. Goodrich in October 1917. He filled a vacancy on the court left by the death of Richard K. Erwin of Fort Wayne. He won an election in 1918 to retain his seat and served until November 1, 1923, when he resigned to return to private practice.

Many of Townsend's criminal case decisions consisted of one or two lines. For example, at the end of a one-paragraph opinion, *Grose v. State of Indiana*, where the petitioner claimed that the trial court finding was not sustained by sufficient evidence, Townsend wrote: "The evidence is conflicting, and in these circumstances it is not our province to disturb the decision of the trial court." For more serious crimes such as murder and manslaughter, he wrote longer, more detailed decisions. Many of his civil case decisions were only a page or two long, but to the point. Until the judicial article of the Indiana Constitution was amended in 1970, all criminal appeals were heard by the Supreme Court. Today only death sentence cases are directly appealable to the Court.

During his service on the Court, Townsend wrote more than a hundred decisions and dissented in three. In one decision, *Heier v. State of Indiana*, he made reference to the "blind tiger law," a term that has long since passed into history. The term referred to a law that made it a violation of the criminal code for any establishment to sell illegal liquor. The term was an illusion to the fact that illegal liquor would likely make a person blind and as irrational as a drunken tiger. Even today, there are a few liquor establishments named "The Blind Tiger," although it is doubtful that most customers today know the origin of the name.

In an era when sterilizing persons in prison for certain criminal offenses and in mental institutions was a generally accepted practice and sanctioned by law, Townsend wrote the majority opinion in *Williams et al. v. Smith* that held that Indiana's sterilization law, which did not allow the prisoner an opportunity to object and present evidence against the procedure, was unconstitutional. "It is very plain that this act is in violation of the Fourteenth Amendment to the federal Constitution in that it denies appellee due process," Townsend wrote.

On the lighter side, Townsend was a member of the Illustrious Order of Scavengers of the World, a rather dubious organization dedicated to fun and the roasting of fellow members. Membership was limited and members had to be able "to take it" and "to give it." The membership was made up of the Indiana great and the near great. In addition to Townsend, the membership included a U.S. senator, a federal judge, an Indiana Appellate court judge, numerous Indiana trial court judges, and other dignitaries. They met once a year in Angola, to share a goose dinner and a little fun.

Townsend died of a stroke while vacationing in Florida on March 3, 1950. His body was returned to Fort Wayne for services. He was survived by his wife and two nephews. The honorary pallbearers included judges from Angola, Bluffton, and Auburn, as well as some of the leading lawyers and business people of Fort Wayne. He was cremated and his ashes turned over to his family.

DONALD D. DOXSEE, JD, is past president of the Allen County Bar Association. He is a board member of the Allen County Courthouse Preservation Trust. He practices in the association of Williams, Williams and Doxsee in Fort Wayne, Indiana

SELECTED BIBLIOGRAPHY

Archives, Carnegie Public Library, Steuben County.

CASES CITED
Grose v. State of Indiana, 193 Ind. 130 (1923).
Heier v. State of Indiana, 188 Ind. 172 (1919).
Williams et al. v. Smith, 190 Ind. 526, (1921).

BENJAMIN M. WILLOUGHBY
January 7, 1919–January 7, 1931

GREGORY M. HAGER

The 1920s was a dark time in Indiana politics when Ku Klux Klan-backed candidates were being elected to public office. Benjamin Milton Willoughby, the sixty-first judge of the Indiana Supreme Court, adamantly opposed the Klan and in return was vilified by the Klan and allied groups. Willoughby was one of three top state candidates in the 1924 election to overcome the oppositional influence of the Klan and win a second term on the Court.

Willoughby was born in Ripley County, Indiana, on May 8, 1855, the second child in a family of eight children. In 1873, at the age of eighteen, he traveled to Trimble County, Kentucky, where he worked as a teacher for two years before returning to Vincennes. He completed high school in Vincennes in 1876. There he taught school and served as a high school principal

while studying law in the offices of Captain George C. Reily in preparation
for entering the legal profession

Willoughby attended law school at Cincinnati College (now the University of Cincinnati), where he received his law degree in 1879. He returned to
Vincennes and was admitted to the bar that same year. In 1882 Willoughby
formed a successful law partnership with Lewis A. Meyer. Active in civic
affairs and service organizations, Willoughby held various leadership positions in the Vincennes Masonic Lodge and by the time of his death was the
oldest member of the lodge.

Between 1887 and 1898 Willoughby served as first the Knox County
deputy prosecuting attorney and later county attorney. He was active in
Republican politics and proudly cast his first vote ever for President
Rutherford B. Hayes. Willoughby was elected to the Indiana House of Representatives and served three terms from 1895 to 1899. In May 1899 Willoughby was the U.S. State Department's leading choice to replace John
Billheimer from Washington, Indiana, as U.S. consul to Zanzibar.
Billheimer's health had reportedly been negatively affected by the climate
of Zanzibar, prompting his resignation. Willoughby apparently considered
the consular position but turned it down after he "evidently secured some
inkling as to the undesirable quality of climate and decided to remain in
Indiana." Fellow Hoosier, Robert Mansfield of Marion, consequently was
named as consul to Zanzibar. Willoughby continued to practice law and in
1904 entered into a partnership with James House. Willoughby served as
judge of the Twelfth Circuit of Indiana from 1912 until his election to his
first Supreme Court term beginning in 1919.

The 1920s heralded an increase in Prohibition enforcement and a rise in
power of the Ku Klux Klan as a political force. The Klan was frequently allied
with the Indiana Anti-Saloon League, led by Methodist minister Edward
S. Shumaker. These two groups sought to support or oppose candidates
for office based on what they espoused to be correct American moral and
religious ideals. Shumaker's Indiana Anti-Saloon League was the dominant
organization in supporting Prohibition and upholding Prohibition laws,
even going so far as to draft and push through legislation referred to as the
bone-dry law, which made it illegal to consume or possess alcohol or to possess empty bottles, kegs, or cases that had once contained alcohol. Politicians who were not perceived by the league as being supportive of these and
other similar draconian measures were targeted for political opposition and
vilification.

A substantial portion of the Court docket during this decade consisted of ruling on matters arising from the result of the Indiana legislature's attempts to strengthen the federal Volstead Act, passed to enforce Prohibition. Literally hundreds of cases were heard and ruled on by the Court involving liquor law violations for possession of alcohol or illegal search and seizure related to the control of intoxicating beverages. Shumaker vociferously criticized Willoughby for being "bitterly hostile to prohibition" and encouraged voters to "give us a Supreme Court that is dry not wet."

In *State of Indiana v. Shumaker*, the Court concluded that Shumaker and his allies were deliberately trying to create a "false impression" of the Court's disposition of cases involving violations of liquor laws, and in so doing "garbled, falsified, and misrepresented the facts" about such cases. Thus the Court found Shumaker in contempt for his attacks on both Willoughby and the court at large and sentenced him to a fine of $250 and sixty days at the Indiana State Farm.

Shumaker was pardoned by Governor Edward L. Jackson, whose candidacy had been supported by both the Klan and the Anti-Saloon League. The Court overturned the governor's pardon because it determined he lacked the authority to issue a pardon for contempt of court. Shumaker served his time at the state farm, the first true defeat of the man many people of Indiana felt to be the most powerful figure in state politics.

On January 7, 1931, in declining health, Willoughby left the Court rather than pursuing a third term and returned to Vincennes, where he retired from the practice of law and from political life. After a long illness, Willoughby died on June 29, 1940, at Good Samaritan Hospital in Vincennes at the age of eighty-five.

GREGORY M. HAGER, MLS, is director, Willard Library of Evansville, Indiana. He is the president of the Vanderburgh County Historical Society.

SELECTED BIBLIOGRAPHY

History of Knox and Daviess Counties Indiana. Chicago: Goodspeed Publishing Company, 1886.
Indianapolis Journal, May 31, 1899.
Madison, James H. *Indiana through Tradition and Change: A History of the Hoosier State and Its People, 1920–1945.* Indianapolis: Indiana Historical Society, 1982.

CASES CITED
State of Indiana v. Shumaker et al., 200 Ind. 623 (1927).
State of Indiana v. Shumaker, 200 Ind. 716 (1928).

LOUIS B. EWBANK
January 1, 1920–January 3, 1927

DORIA M. LYNCH

Louis B. Ewbank, the sixty-second judge of the Indiana Supreme Court, led a life dominated by education. While he received little formal education, from his late teen years to his death he was active and influential in teaching others. Born on a farm on September 5, 1864, in Guilford, Indiana, he attended Dearborn County schools for a time, but primarily was expected to work on the family farmstead. As he grew to young adulthood, he began teaching in the same types of rural schools he had attended. In the course of his personal reading and self education, the law attracted his attention, and he prepared to enter the bar.

Ewbank's informal legal education began in Lawrenceburg, but he soon moved to Indianapolis to read law under William Watson Woollen. In 1891 Ewbank was admitted to the bar and practiced in Indianapolis with Benjamin F. Watson. Ewbank began teaching at the Indiana Law School in

Indianapolis in 1897 and continued to do so through 1914. He was also a frequent lecturer at Indiana University's law school.

Ewbank's lasting contributions to the education of lawyers were made through his publication of major law books: *Manual of Indiana Appellate Practice* (first edition 1900, second edition 1915), *Indiana Trial Evidence* (1904), and *Indiana Criminal Law* (1907). He coauthored *Modern Business Corporations* (1906) and edited the *Indiana Cumulative Digest* from 1904 through 1914. *Indiana Criminal Law* was popularly known as "the prosecutor's Bible." These books became standard in many Hoosiers' legal education.

While his publishing career grew, Ewbank remained active in his law practice. From 1910 to 1912 he was a partner in the Lagrange firm of Hanan, Ewbank and Hanan. He also maintained a practice in Indianapolis with his brother.

As a prominent author, teacher, and practicing attorney, the next logical career move for Ewbank was the bench. On November 12, 1914, he was elected to the Marion County Circuit Court. Upon his death, the bar recalled his service on the circuit court: "Not only were his decisions sound and eminently fair, but the bar of the period from 1914 to 1920, also remember him best for his patience and understanding of the problems confronting the young lawyer."

In 1918 Ewbank unsuccessfully sought nomination to the Supreme Court on the Republican ticket. Then, on August 1, 1920, Governor James P. Goodrich appointed Ewbank to fill a vacancy on the Court caused by the death of Lawson M. Harvey. Three months later Ewbank was elected to the Court in his own right by nearly 175,000 votes.

Ewbank's era on the Court was not noted for constitutional reform. However, the Court did take up some significant cases addressing the protection of citizens from unlawful searches and seizures, many of which stemmed from prosecutions for violations of Prohibition. *Callender v. State of Indiana* overturned the conviction of a man for possession and distribution of intoxicating liquors based on the improper procurement of a search warrant by the police. The Court held that the Prohibition Law of 1917 did not "authorize the search and seizure for the express and sole purpose of procuring evidence upon which to base a prosecution. Sections . . . of the act of 1917 were intended to provide a means of discovering and seizing liquors kept for an unlawful purpose. They are not intended to provide a means to disclose evidence in a criminal prosecution."

A similar case later that same year, *Flum v. State of Indiana*, also overturned a man's conviction under the Prohibition Act of 1917 on the basis of an illegal search warrant, this time because the warrant was excessively vague about the property to be searched. During this period the Court took a strong stance to protect individuals from falling victim to excessive and illegal searches, relying on the protection against unreasonable searches and seizures provided for in Article 1 of the Indiana Constitution.

In *Williams et al. v. Smith*, Ewbank and his fellow justices also declared unconstitutional the practice of compulsorily sterilizing convicted felons who were judged to be "unimprovable" and for whom "procreation was inadvisable" as had been allowed under a 1907 law, the first such law in the nation. An inmate, who was not given an opportunity to object or provide evidence against the procedure, sued to prevent his impending forced sterilization. The lower court ruled that the practice was unconstitutional. In 1921 Ewbank joined the Court's opinion that upheld the lower court ruling and declared the 1907 law unconstitutional on the grounds that the prisoner had been deprived of due process of law guaranteed by the Fourteenth Amendment of the U.S. Constitution.

While a member of the state's highest court, Ewbank was known for his sound legal reasoning and extensive research, with his friends noting that on a number of occasions "he worked far into the night in his legal research, to produce an opinion exhaustive of the questions presented by the case." He wrote more than three hundred opinions during his Court tenure, all of which are consistent in their clarity and refreshing in their logical, precise narrative of fact, law, and finding.

Upon the expiration of his term, Ewbank returned to private practice. During the administration of President Warren G. Harding, Ewbank's name was mentioned among the possible nominees to the U.S. Supreme Court, but he did not receive the appointment. Ewbank was also active in Indianapolis's historical community, writing various articles and books about his family's genealogy, Indiana's early laws, and Indiana history. In 1951 Ewbank retired due to ill health. He died on March 8, 1953, remembered throughout the community for his writings and instruction of young lawyers.

DORIA M. LYNCH, MA, is administrative specialist and historian at the United States District Court for the Southern District of Indiana. She is a contributor to *The Hoosier Genealogist: Connections* magazine, worked as an editorial assistant for *Finding Indiana Ancestors*, and compiled the Name Index to the *U. S. District Court Order Book, District of Indiana, 1817–1833*.

SELECTED BIBLIOGRAPHY

Brown, Paul Donald. "Indianapolis Men of Affairs," Indianapolis, Indiana, 1923. (Microfilm at Indiana State Library).

Citizens Historical Association. "Louis B. Ewbank, Attorney-at-Law." Indianapolis, Indiana, October 9, 1948. (From Indiana State Library Clipping File Biography, Ewbank).

Ewbank, Louis B. "A Real Pioneer: How an English Family Came to Indiana and How Its Members Built and Lived in the Early Days of the State." *Indiana Magazine of History* 38 (June 1942): 143–64.

Ewbank, Richard L., and Louis B. Ewbank. "John and Ann Ewbank Family," Indianapolis, Indiana, 1947.

Kothe, Herman W., et al. "In Memoriam." 231 *Indiana Reports* 44 (1953).

CASES CITED

Callender v. State of Indiana, 193 Ind. 91 (1923).
Flum v. State of Indiana, 193 Ind. 585 (1923).
Williams et al. v. Smith, 190 Ind. 526 (1921).

JULIUS C. TRAVIS
January 3, 1921–January 3, 1933

RAY E. BOOMHOWER

Julius Curtis Travis, the sixty-third man to serve on the Indiana Supreme Court, worked in journalism during his college days at the University of Michigan, but from an early age had set his sights on a legal career. Travis's time on the Court was highlighted by a decision that involved one of the most powerful men in the state during the 1920s, D. C. Stevenson, at one time the Grand Dragon of the Ku Klux Klan in Indiana.

Travis was born on July 31, 1868, in Pleasant Township, La Porte County. His father, Wesley, worked as a farmer, and his mother, Mary, served as a teacher before marriage. After graduating from the local high school in just three years, Travis entered the University of Michigan in 1888. When the university's student newspaper, the *University of Michigan Daily*, fell into financial trouble, he took over as its business manager and saved it from ruin. During his days at the university, Travis also helped establish a student-run magazine, *The Inlander*, and served as campus correspondent for newspapers in Chicago, Philadelphia, Detroit, and Brooklyn.

After earning a law degree from Michigan in 1894, Travis returned to La Porte to open his own law practice. On September 10, 1896, he married Ethel Closser, also of La Porte; the couple had four children. In 1898 Indiana Governor James A. Mount appointed Travis as prosecuting attorney of the Thirty-second Judicial Circuit. Travis also served on the city council and worked as city and county attorney. A longtime Republican, he served a number of years as secretary of the La Porte County Republican Committee, Travis also established several businesses in the area, including a furniture firm, a lumber and coal concern, a hardware company, and a livestock farm.

Travis's election to the Court in 1920 came at a time when the Ku Klux Klan was on its way to becoming a powerful force in the state; the organization claimed to have approximately 400,000 Hoosier members by 1923. Stevenson received credit for securing the governorship of the state for GOP candidate Edward L. Jackson in 1924, as well as having the Republican Party control both houses of the legislature. Stevenson fell from power following his conviction for second-degree murder on November 14, 1925, for the death of Madge Oberholtzer, a state government employee. Oberholtzer had taken poison after being raped and bitten by Stevenson aboard a railroad sleeping car. Before she died, she told of her harrowing ordeal to authorities.

Stevenson appealed his life sentence to the Court. His attorneys claimed that Stevenson had not been responsible for Oberholtzer's death. Travis joined three other judges of the five-member Court in rejecting Stevenson's appeal in *Stevenson v. State*. The majority per curiam opinion noted that when a suicide "follows a wound inflicted by a defendant," the act itself "is homicidal if deceased was rendered irresponsible by the wound and as the natural result of it." Years after leaving the Court, Travis noted that his research for the appeal "confirmed the fact that infection from human bites could kill."

Travis was also on the Court when it was under fire by Prohibition forces for being too easy on those who violated liquor laws. The Court often overturned these convictions because defendants had been denied constitutional rights such as protection against unreasonable search and seizure. One of the leading Court critics was Edward S. Shumaker, head of the Anti-Saloon League. Shumaker's attacks on the Court were so verbally virulent that the Court held him in contempt of court and sentenced him to sixty days in jail. Governor Jackson, who had been supported by the Anti-Saloon League, pardoned Shumaker. In *State v. Shumaker*, with Travis writing for the majority, the Court ruled that the governor lacked the authority to pardon for contempt of court and ordered Shumaker to serve the sixty-day sentence.

Travis lost his seat on the Court in the Democratic sweep in the 1932 election that saw the party take control of the Indiana House, Senate, and governor's office. After leaving the Court, Travis opened a law practice in Indianapolis. A member of the Indiana Bar Association for sixty-four years, Travis died on March 11, 1961, at the age of ninety-two. A few years before his death, Travis told a reporter that his secret to success: "If you want to live a long time, avoid hard work."

RAY E. BOOMHOWER is senior editor, Indiana Historical Society Press, and editor of *Traces of Indiana and Midwestern History*. He is the author of numerous books on Indiana history, including and *Gus Grissom: The Lost Astronaut* (2004) and *Robert F. Kennedy and the 1968 Indiana Primary* (2008). His articles have appeared in *Traces* and the *Indiana Magazine of History*.

SELECTED BIBLIOGRAPHY

Indianapolis Times, July 31, 1958.

Lutholtz, M. William. *Grand Dragon: D. C. Stevenson and the Ku Klux Klan in Indiana.* West Lafayette, IN: Purdue University Press, 1991.

Madison, James H. *Indiana through Tradition and Change: A History of the Hoosier State and Its People, 1920–1945.* Indianapolis: Indiana Historical Society, 1982.

Tucker, Richard K. *The Dragon and the Cross: The Rise and Fall of the Ku Klux Klan in Middle America.* Hamden, CT: Archon Books, 1991.

CASES CITED

State of Indiana v. Shumaker et. al., 200 Ind. 716 (1928).
Stevenson v. State of Indiana, 205 Ind. 141 (1932).

FRED C. GAUSE
November 1, 1923–January 5, 1925

JOHN L. KELLAM

Fred Carl Gause, the sixty-fourth judge of the Indiana Supreme Court, might best be remembered as a man who resigned to lead. A superficial review of his life might bring one to conclude that he regularly changed focus in his profession of law. One detects a theme, in his professional career, of resignation from one position of public service to assume another. During the course of his professional life, Gause displayed an exemplary resolve to assume positions of responsibility.

Of Quaker ancestry, Gause grew up in rural, east-central Indiana. The son of Doctor Thomas and Christine Boone Gause, he was born in Greensfork, Wayne County, Indiana, on August 29, 1879. His father died two years later in 1881, and his mother moved her family to Henry County. Gause graduated from New Castle High School in 1897. He attended Indiana University in 1898 and 1899, where he was a member of Beta Theta Pi Fraternity and graduated from the law department. After graduation he returned to New Castle and read law under the tutelage of John M. Morris and Eugene H. Bundy. He was admitted to the bar in 1900. Gause was a sole practitioner in New Castle from 1901 to 1914 and was county attorney of Henry County from 1902 to 1912. He married Mollie Brooks Cummins of Bluffton, Indiana, in 1904. They had one daughter, Katherine.

At the beginning of World War I, Gause, a Republican, was elected judge of Henry Circuit Court over Democrat Horace Yergin and Progressive Party candidate Albert Hammer. Gause assumed office in 1914, was reelected in 1920, and served until October 1923.

In 1918 citizens of Henry County sought Gause's legal expertise to resolve a community issue. In that year, citizens of each Indiana township contributed to a war chest for use by World War I soldiers to purchase cigarettes, candy, and entertainment. Henry County did its share and at the end of the war had a $21,000 balance. The legislature passed a bill enabling local governments to erect war memorials, and the Henry County War Chest Board sought the nonjudicial opinion of Gause as to whether its funds could be used for a county veterans memorial park. He opined that since the money was raised for a specific cause, contributors should be allowed to withdraw a prorata amount. His advice was followed, and after withdrawals the remaining $18,000 was used to create Henry County Memorial Park. The park in the rolling hills north of New Castle remains one of the most scenic attractions in east-central Indiana.

Gause was appointed to the Court on November 1, 1923, by Governor Warren T. McCray to complete the term of Howard L. Townsend of Fort Wayne, who resigned before his term expired. During his term, Gause was a prolific writer, second only to Louis B. Ewbank. Gause filed his first opinion on November 16, 1923, in the case of *Van Meter et al. v. Ridenour, Admin.*, a civil case pertaining to a will.

In a somewhat more notable case, Gause wrote the decision in *Diamond v. State* in which a man convicted of murder and sentenced to death in Porter Circuit Court filed a Petition for Insanity Inquest. He argued that following his conviction he became insane and was entitled to a jury determination of that issue, and asserted that a postjudgment ruling of insanity would preclude his execution. The Court's opinion held that Diamond's assertion of postjudgment insanity was a matter solely for the governor under Article 3 of the Indiana Constitution, and that the Court lacked the authority to stay the execution of a judgment. Eighty-three years later, this decision was overturned by the U.S. Supreme Court in *Panetti v. Quarterman*, a case pertaining to the same issue in the Texas courts. The Court ruled that the Eighth Amendment to the U.S. Constitution, which prohibits cruel and unusual punishment, bars a state from executing a person who is insane. Accordingly, state courts are responsible for ruling on petitions brought by prisoners claiming postjudgment insanity.

Upon completion of his term, Gause did not seek re-election, returning to private practice with the Indianapolis firm of Pickens, Gause, Davidson and Pickens. Gause's interest in public service did not wane. He served as commissioner of the Indiana State Election Board, a position he resigned immediately before his death. Gause was credited with knowing more about the state's election laws than anyone else.

Gause served as president of the Indiana State Bar Association in 1936 and president of the Indianapolis Bar Association in 1941. He was a member of the Broadway Methodist Church, American Bar Association, Columbia Club, Indianapolis Country Club, and the Indianapolis Chapter, Citizens Historical Association. Gause died at age sixty-four on February 15, 1944, in his home in Indianapolis and was buried in Crown Hill Cemetery.

JOHN L. KELLAM, JD, is trial judge and consultant, Indiana Supreme Court (2001–present). He is a member of the Indiana Supreme Court Commission on Race and Gender Fairness and the CMS Governing Board of Indiana Supreme Court Judicial Technology and Automation Committee, past president of the Indiana Judges Association, and a past member of the Board of Directors, Indiana Judicial Conference and Board of Managers, Indiana State Bar. Kellam is the author of "The Indiana Judicial System: An Analysis of Change," *Indiana Law Review* (1988).

SELECTED BIBLIOGRAPHY

Citizens Historical Association, biography, January 21, 1939.
Monks, Leander, J., ed. *Courts and Lawyers of Indiana*, vol. 3. Indianapolis: Federal Publishing Company, 1916.
New Castle Courier-Times, February 16, 1944.

CASES CITED

Diamond v. State of Indiana, 195 Ind. 285 (1924).
Scott Louis Panetti v. Nathaniel Quarterman, Texas Department of Criminal Justice, Correctional Institutions Division, 551 U.S. 930 (2007).
Van Meter et al. v. Ridenour, Administrator, 193 Ind. 615 (1923).

WILLARD B. GEMMILL
January 5, 1925–January 4, 1931

RICHARD E. HUMPHREY

Willard Beharrell Gemmill's dedication to justice and his commitment to the legal profession in Indiana are most notably recognized by the law school scholarships that bear his name. While recipients of these scholarships must be Grant County residents, they are not required to attend Indiana law schools. Gemmill's son, Robert A., also a prominent lawyer in Marion, Indiana, until his death in 1989, established the Gemmill Foundation, which funds the scholarships.

The sixty-fifth judge of the Indiana Supreme Court, Gemmill was born near the small town of Rigdon, Indiana, in southwestern Grant County, on August 7, 1875. The son of Andrew and Maria Covalt Gemmill, he was educated in the county schools and later attended DePauw University, where he was active in campus affairs. He served as class president, treasurer of the Orators Association, and was also a member of Delta Upsilon fraternity.

He received his bachelor's degree from DePauw in 1898, and then taught in the Rigdon public school system from 1898 to 1900 before continuing his education at the Indianapolis Law School. He earned his law degree in 1902, returned to Marion, and was subsequently admitted to the Grant County Bar Association. He married Florence Belle Jones on June 9, 1909. The couple's son, Robert A., was born in 1911.

In addition to practicing law, Gemmill was also active in Republican politics. He served one term in the Indiana House of Representatives from 1909 to 1911. He subsequently served one term in the Indiana Senate from 1914 to 1918. His legislative actions were marked by practicality and insight. In 1909 he introduced a resolution mandating the publication of biweekly House calendars, to be placed on each member's desk on Tuesdays and Fridays. The calendar was to include the number of each bill, the name of the introducing member, and enough information to indicate the bill's substance. He also sponsored legislation that prevented passing under or through railway crossing gates, mandating penalties for such behavior. In other legislation, he called for regulations preventing the waste of subterranean waters in Indiana and suggested penalties for such violations.

Before his election to the Court, Gimmell served briefly as the Marion city attorney and resigned that office to become Indiana special deputy attorney general, a position he held from 1918 to 1920. He was elected to the Court in 1924 on the strength of the Republican ticket that swept all statewide offices and took office on January 5, 1925. He served only one term, failing in his bid for re-election in 1930, a year of Democratic resurgence. During his six-year term, he authored some 132 opinions, 31 of them as chief justice. He served two terms as chief justice, from November 1926 to May 1927, and from May 1929 to November 1929. Cases upon which he rendered an opinion covered all aspects of the law, including both civil and criminal matters. In all his opinions, he demonstrated a keen grasp of the nuances of the law, while tempering his judgments with fairness and equity.

One of the most publicized controversies during Gemmill's tenure was the case of *State v. Shumaker* in which the Court found Edward S. Shumaker, head of the Indiana Anti-Saloon League, in contempt of court for his strong public verbal attacks on the Court's reputation and integrity. Shumaker was later pardoned by Governor Edward L. Jackson, but in a second case, *State v. Shumaker*, the Court ruled that the governor did not have the legal authority to pardon a conviction for contempt of court, and Shumaker was forced to serve his prison sentence. Gemmill, whose candidacy had been backed by the Anti-Saloon League, dissented in both Shumaker cases.

Upon retirement from the Court, Gemmill returned to Marion and formed the law firm of Gemmill, Browne and Campbell, with John R. Browne and John O. Campbell. In addition to his membership in the Grant County Bar Association, Gemmill was also a member of the Indiana State Bar Association and the American Bar Association. Active in civic affairs, he held memberships in the Marion Kiwanis and Mecca Clubs, the Meshingomesia Country Club, and the Columbia Club of Indianapolis. He was also a Scottish Rite Mason.

Gemmill died at home on May 24, 1935, of heart failure. Though he had been ill for several weeks, his death still came as a shock to his family and colleagues. The high regard in which he was held by his colleagues was demonstrated in the fact that the five sitting judges of the Court, including Chief Justice James P. Hughes, attended his funeral, as did several former members of the high court. The Grant County Bar Association attended his funeral en masse, and resolutions adopted by several bar associations were read during the service. Perhaps his greatest tribute came from the Kiwanis Club resolution, adopted upon his death. It labeled him, "[A] man of unimpeachable morality and high integrity, interested in the political life of the nation, state, and community, and as keenly alive to his civic obligations."

RICHARD E. HUMPHREY, is reference librarian, Ruth Lilly Law Library, Indiana University School of Law, Indianapolis. Coauthor of "Biographical Sketches of Indiana Supreme Court Justices," *Indiana Law Review* (1997), and he is the author of *Indiana Practice Materials: A Selective Annotated Bibliography*.

SELECTED BIBLIOGRAPHY

Club, Grant County Genealogy; "AncestryLibrary.com." *Indiana Marriage Collection, 1800–1941*. 2008. http://search.ancestrylibrary.com/cgi-bin/sse. dll?db=inmarr1880.

Indiana General Assembly. *Journal of the House of Representatives of the State of Indiana, 1909*. Indianapolis: Wm. B. Burford, 1909.

Indiana University School of Law-Bloomington. "Indiana Bar Proceedings." *Indiana Law Journal* (1934–35): 505.

———. "Indiana Bar Proceedings." *Indiana Law Journal*, (1935–36): 84.

JU (Gemmill), IN-CS: *Indiana & Westlaw*. September 29, 2008.

Marion Chronicle. May 27, 1935.

CASES CITED

State of Indiana v. Shumaker et. al., 200 Ind. 623 (1927).

State of Indiana v. Shumaker, 200 Ind. 716 (1928).

CLARENCE R. MARTIN
January 3, 1927–January 3, 1933

JAMES E. ST. CLAIR

"Justice long delayed is often justice denied," Clarence Reuben Martin wrote in an *Indianapolis Star* article shortly after his service as the sixty-sixth judge on the Indiana Supreme Court ended in 1933 and not long after he dissented in *Stevenson v. State*, in the case of D. C. Stevenson, the former grand dragon of the Ku Klux Klan in Indiana who was convicted of murder in one of the state's most lurid trials. Martin had publicly criticized the Court several times for its continued delay in deciding the Stevenson case, which had been pending for nearly six years before his sentence was upheld in a three-to-two decision announced in early 1932.

To prevent repeats of protracted criminal-case appeals and unclog congestion in the Court's docket, Martin advocated amending the state's constitution to expand the number of judges on the Court to eight or nine. Such an expansion, in Martin's view, would increase efficiency and also eliminate the need for the Indiana Court of Appeals because the Supreme Court would then be able "to take care of all the appellate business." While conceding that judges on the appellate court were equal in ability to Supreme Court judges, Martin said, however, that opinions of that court were not accorded the same weight in the legal community as those of the Supreme Court, and he argued that having one large court of last resort would result in "increased prestige outside the state." His proposed reforms were never adopted.

In his newspaper critique, Martin also took aim at the Court's obsession with technicalities, noting that at one time it was considered to be "the most technical court in the entire world." To illustrate the extremes the Court had once reached, Martin cited the famous "baled hay-thereby" case that involved a man who was badly injured after being thrown off a hay wagon by a low-hanging wire stretched across a road. The Court reversed a ruling in favor of the injured man because the complaint failed to insert the word "thereby" before the word "thrown" in describing the accident.

Martin, a Republican, was elected to a six-year term on the Court in 1926 at age thirty-nine, and he became chief justice in 1928. After losing his race for re-election in 1932, a casualty of the Democratic tidal wave that year, Martin resumed practicing law in Indianapolis. Martin, who was born on December 10, 1886, in Aberdeen, Ohio, began his legal career after graduating from the Indiana Law School in 1906, a proprietary school that eventually was taken over by Indiana University, and from the University of Michigan Law School in 1907.

Martin put his law practice on hold to serve in the U.S. Army during World War I. He attained the rank of major and commanded an infantry battalion in France and also performed special assignments for the offices of judge advocate general and inspector general. Following the war, Martin returned to his law practice in Indianapolis and became active in Republican politics. He was campaign manager for Albert J. Beveridge, a U.S. senator from 1899 to 1911, who defeated incumbent Senator Harry S. New in the Republican primary of 1922 but lost to Democrat Samuel M. Ralston, a former governor, in the general election. During the early 1920s, Martin also served as chairman of the speakers' bureau of the Republican State Committee and was legal counsel to a U.S. Senate subcommittee that undertook an investigation, at the urging of Indiana senator James E. Watson, into charges that employees of the Federal Trade Commission had been spreading radical, socialistic, and Bolshevist propaganda.

In 1922 Martin married Nellie L. Pape, also an attorney and the first female law clerk in Allen County. Their son, Edmund, better known as Ed, started selling cars as a young man from his parents' front yard, an enterprise that eventually grew into the Ed Martin Automotive Group, one of the largest dealerships in the state.

In addition to his legal career and political activities, Martin had long been active in the Masons, achieving considerable prominence, both statewide and nationally. In fact, when he died in May 1972 at age eighty-five, the obituary in the *Indiana Freemason*, called him "one of Indiana's Masonic giants." He held many leadership roles in the fraternal organization, including serving as grand master of Masons in Indiana in the early 1940s. Martin authored a small booklet titled *Traveling Military Lodges*, which traced the history of a system used to keep Masons connected to the order while they served in the armed forces. Martin presented the results of his research in a speech to the Conference of Grand Masters of Masons in North America in 1943. He also donated land that had been part of his family's farm for the construction of a new Masonic temple in northeast Indianapolis.

JAMES E. ST. CLAIR, MA, is professor of journalism, Indiana University Southeast. He is the coauthor of *Sherman Minton: New Deal Senator, Cold War Justice* (1997) and *Chief Justice Fred M. Vinson of Kentucky: A Political Biography* (2002) and coeditor of *The Governors of Indiana* (2006) and *Justices of the Indiana Supreme Court* (2010).

SELECTED BIBLIOGRAPHY

Indiana Freemason, June 1972.
Indianapolis Star, January 20, 1932, February 18, 1934.
Martin, Clarence R. *Traveling Military Lodges: Their History*. Reprint of a speech presented at the Conference of Grand Masters of Masons in the United States, 1943 (n.p.).

CASES CITED
Stevenson v. State of Indiana, 205 Ind. 141, (1932).

1912 ARBUTUS, INDIANA UNIVERSITY ARCHIVES

CURTIS W. ROLL
January 5, 1931–January 4, 1943

JAMES E. ST. CLAIR

At a memorial service held by the Howard County Bar Association in late 1970, Curtis William Roll, who served on the Indiana Supreme Court as its sixty-seventh judge from 1931 to 1943, was remembered as a man of conviction and principle who "always regarded himself as a Jeffersonian Democrat and until his death retained an interest in social and political problems." Over the course of a legal career that spanned nearly six decades, Roll, a native of Washington County, compiled a lengthy ledger of confronting and resolving social and political problems as a judge, private practitioner, and labor arbitrator.

Roll had been on the Court barely a month when he rendered his first opinion in *Owen v. Fortieth Judicial Circuit*, ruling invalid an act of the 1929 legislature separating the Lawrence-Jackson Circuit Court and creating the Lawrence Circuit Court because the bill went to the governor after the specified time period in which he was required to take action had expired. Another political case, though one that generated far bigger headlines because of its greater import, came before the Court not long after Roll had been reelected to a second six-year term. Raymond E. Willis, the defeated Republican candidate for U.S. Senate in 1938, and eleven other candidates on the statewide Republican ticket that year sought recounts in seven counties, claiming incidents of fraud, irregularities, and mistakes in the results. In *Robertson v. Circuit City of Lake County*, the Court, with only three members participating because two had been candidates for re-election, unanimously rejected the appeal, noting that recounts for state and senatorial races could be held only on a statewide basis.

A larger issue for Roll and his colleagues on the Court loomed a few years later when Republicans, now in control of the state legislature for the first time in more than a decade, passed in 1941 a series of "ripper bills" that were intended to strip the Democratic governor, Henry F. Schricker, of virtually all his powers. After the governor's vetoes of the bills were quickly overridden by the legislature, the confrontation between the executive and legislative branches of government moved into the courts, ultimately to the state Supreme Court. In the case of *Tucker v. State*, Roll and the three other Democratic members of the Court sided with Schricker, ruling that the legislature's attempts to eliminate the governor's powers were unconstitutional and violated the principle of separation of powers. The only dissent came from Frank N. Richman, a Republican judge.

While on the Court Roll also served as chairman of the Indiana Judicial Council, a body created in 1935 by the general assembly to study the operations of Indiana courts and to recommend ways of increasing efficiency in the state's judicial system. One of the council's recommendations, which was never adopted, called for the nonpartisan election of judges for local courts such as circuit and superior. Council members believed that such a change would result in attracting qualified candidates who were otherwise deterred from seeking these offices because of the political process.

Roll, who declined to seek a third term on the Court, returned to private practice, first in Indianapolis and then in 1948 back to Kokomo, where he had begun practicing law after graduation from the Indiana University School of Law in 1912. In short order, Roll went from deliberating the often weighty matters before the high court to appearing at meetings of city and county agencies for clients seeking zoning changes, objecting to annexation plans, or challenging board of health rulings. Roll also on occasion served on national arbitration panels hearing labor disputes, mainly those involving strikes by rail and airline unions in the late 1940s and early 1950s.

At age eighty-six, Roll remained active, and was counsel for the firm of O'Mahoney, Mahoney and Simmons in Kokomo and still taking an interest in social and political problems. He was speaking during a business meeting at his longtime church, Taylor Creek Primitive Baptist in Grant County, when he collapsed and died on November 8, 1970.

JAMES E. ST. CLAIR, MA, is professor of journalism, Indiana University Southeast. He is the coauthor of *Sherman Minton: New Deal Senator, Cold War Justice* (1997) and *Chief Justice Fred M. Vinson of Kentucky: A Political Biography* (2002) and coeditor of *The Governors of Indiana* (2006) and *Justices of the Indiana Supreme Court* (2010).

SELECTED BIBLIOGRAPHY

Kokomo Tribune, December 2, 1936, November 9, 1970.
Logansport Pharos Tribune, December 13, 1938.
The Rushville Republican, February 19, 1931.

CASES CITED

State ex rel. Owen v. Fortieth Judicial Circuit et al., 202 Ind. 354 (1931).
State ex rel. Robertson v. Circuit Court of Lake County et al., 215 Ind. 18 (1938).
Tucker v. State, 218 Ind. 614 (1941).

WALTER E. TREANOR

January 8, 1931–January 4, 1938

RALPH D. GRAY

Walter Emanuel Treanor was a gentleman and a scholar. The holder of four advanced degrees, three from Indiana University and one from Harvard University, he moved from a professorship at the IU School of Law in Bloomington to become the sixty-eighth judge of the Indiana Supreme Court and then to the U.S. Seventh Circuit Court of Appeals, where his premature death from cancer ended a brilliant career.

Treanor was born on November 17, 1883, the son of James Donnelly and Gertrude Summers Treanor, in Loogootee, Martin County, Indiana. The elder Treanor, a merchant in Loogootee, moved to Petersburg to become a schoolteacher in the late 1880s. Walter, a precocious student, received his formal education in the public schools of Petersburg. Upon his graduation from Petersburg High School in 1901, he began, immediately, at the age of eighteen, to teach Latin and history at the high school. In 1906, when he had saved enough money to marry and to attend IU, he moved to Bloomington. He graduated with honors in 1912. He then returned to Petersburg, becoming in 1915 a principal and then the superintendent of schools in Pike County. In addition to his administrative duties, Treanor was an exemplary teacher and football coach. A strict disciplinarian with a high moral standard, if not great ability at teaching the fundamentals of blocking and tackling, Treanor once canceled a game when he caught some of the players smoking cigarettes.

Called into military service in 1917, Treanor became an army lieutenant and went to France, where he was wounded. Upon returning to the United States in 1919, Treanor decided at age thirty-six to become a lawyer. He entered the IU School of Law in 1920, received a law degree in 1922, and then the Juris Doctor degree in 1923. He joined the faculty of the IU School of Law in 1922, where he remained until 1930, although he took a leave of absence from 1926 to 1927 to study at Harvard University, which awarded him a Doctorate in Juridical Science in 1927. In 1926 Treanor became the founding editor of the *Indiana Law Journal*, a position he held for four years, contributing a number of articles and book reviews.

A lifelong Democrat, Treanor was encouraged in 1930 to seek election to the Indiana Supreme Court. Successful in this initial effort, and again in 1936, Treanor was one of two newcomers to the court in 1931—he and fellow Democrat Curtis W. Roll of Kokomo replaced Republicans Willard B. Gemmill and Benjamin M. Willoughby. Treanor quickly established a reputation as an excellent jurist, a shrewd student of the law, and a gifted explicator of its principles. He wrote a number of significant decisions during his tenure on the court, including *In re Todd*, a landmark ruling that changed the way of interpreting the number of votes required to ratify constitutional amendments. Previously the Court had ruled that it required a majority of all voters in the election. In the *Todd* case the Court ruled that it required only a majority of those voting on the question. He also wrote the opinion upholding a controversial plan to reform the Gary school system in *State, ex rel. Cheeks v. Wirt, Superintendent of Gary Schools et al.* His dissent in *Storen et al. v. J.D. Adams Manufacturing Company*, regarding the collection of state gross revenue taxes on goods involved in interstate commerce, was upheld by the U.S. Supreme Court, as were some of his dissents as circuit court judge.

Soon after beginning a second six-year term on the Court in 1937, Treanor was named by President Franklin D. Roosevelt to the federal bench as Indiana's second member of the Seventh Circuit Court of Appeals, based in Chicago with jurisdiction over several midwestern states. He continued adding to his reputation as a scholar and independent-minded interpreter of the law, while also usually siding with the Roosevelt administration in cases carrying political overtones.

Sadly, the year after he joined the circuit court of appeals, Treanor was diagnosed with abdominal cancer. He courageously battled the disease and tried to keep up his work, but he was often hospitalized, both in Chicago and in Indianapolis. His death on April 26, 1941, at the age of fifty-seven, brought forth countless tributes including one from the president of the Indianapolis Bar Association, who said "as a teacher, [Treanor] was respected by his students, as a judge, he was respected by the bench and bar, as a citizen, he was respected by everyone."

Treanor's funeral was held in Bloomington, Indiana, where his law school students served as pallbearers, and he is buried in his adopted home city of Petersburg at the Walnut Hills Cemetery.

RALPH D. GRAY, PhD, is professor emeritus of history at Indiana University–Purdue University Indianapolis. His recent publications include *IUPUI: The Making of an Urban University* (2003) and *Meredith Nicholson: A Writing Life* (2008).

SELECTED BIBLIOGRAPHY

Gray, Ralph D. "An Indiana Man: Attorney Carl M. Gray of Petersburg." Unpublished manuscript. In author's possession.
Gugin, Linda C., and James E. St. Clair. *Sherman Minton: New Deal Senator, Cold War Justice*. Indianapolis: Indiana Historical Society, 1997.
Solomon, Rayman L. *History of the Seventh Circuit, 1981–1941*. Washington, DC: Bicentennial Committee of the Judicial Conference of the United States, 1981.
Walsh, Justin. *The Centennial History of the Indiana General Assembly, 1816–1978*. Indianapolis: The Select Committee on the Centennial History of the Indiana General Assembly, 1979.
Withered, Jerome L. *Hoosier Justice: A History of the Indiana Supreme Court*. Indianapolis: Indiana Supreme Court, 1998.
Indianapolis Star, April 28, 1941.

CASES CITED
In re Todd, 208 Ind. 168 (1935).
State, ex rel. Cheeks v. Wirt, Superintendent of Gary Schools et al., 203 Ind. 121 (1931).
Storen et al. v. J. D. Adams Manufacturing Company, 212 Ind. 343 (1937).

MICHAEL L. FANSLER

January 4, 1933–January 1, 1945

FRANK E. TOLBERT

Heroism may not be prerequisite to service on the Indiana Supreme Court, but it certainly could not hurt. During the Great Flood of 1913, Michael Louis Fansler, then prosecuting attorney of Cass County, was in a boat rescuing two women, each with babies in their arms, when it capsized in six feet of water. Fansler grabbed one of the women and her baby, caught a protruding telephone pole, permitting them to be pulled to safety by rope from a second-floor window by a man Fansler had recently tried for a felony. The other woman and her child were saved by another bystander.

The sixty-ninth judge on the Court, Fansler always seemed to be in the right place at the right time when it came to his political career. As a Democrat, he had the good fortune to live in Cass County, once described as a place that "always has been and always will be a bulwark of Democracy in Indiana," and to run for the Court in 1932, an election year in which the party ticket was headed by Franklin D. Roosevelt for president and Paul V. McNutt for governor. The Democrats were swept into office at all levels, carrying two new Democrats to the Court, including Fansler, giving the Democrats a four-to-one majority. Further, Cass County has had a rich legal history, contributing more than its fair share of Supreme Court judges: William Z. Stuart (1852–58), Horace P. Biddle (1875–81), Quincy A. Myers (1912–18), Moses B. Lairy (1915–21), David A. Myers (1917–34), and Frederick Landis Jr. (1955–65).

Born on July 4, 1883, Fansler attended public schools in Logansport and received his undergraduate and legal education at the University of Notre Dame. He graduated in 1905 and was admitted to the bar that same year. From 1908 to 1910, he served as part-time prosecuting attorney and then two terms as prosecuting attorney. He engaged in private practice until his election to the Court.

In 1932 Logansport attorney Frank McHale, who was instrumental in the election of McNutt as governor, persuaded Fansler to become a candidate for the Court. He won the Democratic nomination without opposition and in the general election beat Republican incumbent Julius C. Travis.

During Fansler's twelve years on the Court, he participated in approximately five hundred opinions, many of which he authored while serving as chief justice. Some of these dealt with major constitutional issues. In 1933, Fansler's first year on the bench, the Court adopted new rules governing admission to the bar. The Court was acting on the authority granted to it by an amendment to the state constitution approved by the voters in the 1932 election. The new rules changed the provisions in the constitution for admittance to the bar that required only that a person be twenty-one years of age and of good moral character. The Court added the stipulation that an applicant must also pass an examination to determine professional fitness. In 1935 these new rules were challenged in In re Todd on the grounds that the constitutional amendment under which the Court acted had not met the required majority for passage. Prior to Todd the Court had held that ratification of a constitutional amendment required approval by a majority of the voters who had voted for candidates in the general election. In Todd, the Court overturned precedent and ruled that ratification of an amendment required only a majority of the votes cast for and against its adoption. Fansler, the lone dissenter in the case, argued that "the importance of stable and settled rules of law is generally recognized and strong respect for precedent has become part of our legal system."

Fansler wrote the majority opinion in another significant constitutional case, *Tucker v. State*, that had partisan politics written all over it. The issue concerned bills passed by the Republican-controlled general assembly that sought to reduce the powers of the Democratic governor Henry F. Schricker. The laws, labeled "ripper bills" by the Democrats, eliminated many state agencies and reorganized others into new administrative departments, giving the governor authority over only one of these. In short order the Court invalidated the acts. Writing for the Court, Fansler said that under the Indiana Constitution the governor had sole and exclusive jurisdiction and authority to exercise executive powers, including the appointment and removal of executive officers, and these powers could only be altered by a constitutional amendment. The vote on the Court was along party lines, with the four Democrats voting to invalidate the "ripper bills" and the lone Republican, Frank N. Richman, voting to uphold them.

In another of his well-known decisions, *Opple v. Ray*, Fansler wrote an opinion that was still being cited in the 1950s by the Seventh and the Ninth Circuit Courts of Appeal as a guide to the measure of care required to avoid a charge of negligence. Fansler held that a motorist, driving in a reasonably prudent manner, who strikes an unlighted motor vehicle on a dark highway, cannot be charged with negligence resulting from collision with a vehicle that "a reasonably prudent person would not anticipate or expect to find in his path."

Fansler made contributions to the Court in other ways. He was instrumental in helping to end the backlog of cases coming from the appellate court to the Supreme Court, and later promoted improvements in the judicial system as chair of the Indiana Judicial Council from 1951 to 1960. Following Fansler's service on the Court, he formed the firm of Fansler, Fauvre, Dongus and Gemmer, the successor to the Indianapolis firm established by former President Benjamin Harrison.

Addressing the Cass County Bar Association two years before his death, Fansler paid tribute to the many Cass County lawyers and judges who had helped to shape his legal knowledge and skills. As a young lawyer attending court he said he "would hear the lawyers discuss their cases and argue their legal questions. It was the finest law school I ever attended." Fansler died on July 26, 1963.

FRANK E. TOLBERT, LLB, is a partner with, Miller, Tolbert, Muelhausen, Muelhausen, Groff and Damm. He is a member of the Cass County, Indiana, U.S. District

Court, Seventh Circuit, and U.S. Supreme Court Bar Associations, and the Indiana and American Trial Lawyers Association, a fellow of the Indiana Bar Foundation, and a member of the American College of Trial Lawyers and the Cass County and U.S. Supreme Court Historical Societies.

SELECTED BIBLIOGRAPHY

Letter of Thelma Conrad from 1913 Flood—America's Great Disasters. Files of the Cass County Historical Society.
Remarks of Michael L Fansler to Cass County Bar Association, April 5, 1961. In the author's possession.

CASES CITED

In re Todd, 208 Ind. 168 (1935).
Tucker et al. v. State of Indiana, 218 Ind. 614 (1941).
Opple et al. v. Ray, 208 Ind. 450 (1935).

JAMES P. HUGHES
January 3, 1933–January 1, 1939

MICHAEL J. SACOPULOS

A memorial tribute to James Peters Hughes, the seventieth judge of the Indiana Supreme Court, said that "his life was the law," and so it was. He was admitted to the bar in 1900, and for the next sixty-one years he was actively engaged in the legal profession in various ways. In particular he devoted himself to public service, holding offices at the local, state, and national levels. These positions were accessible to him in large part because of his active involvement in the Democratic Party.

Hughes was born on December 18, 1874, near Terre Haute, but three months later his family moved to Putnam County, which remained his home until his death. He attended Putnam County public schools and DePauw Preparatory School. He received his undergraduate degree from De-Pauw University in 1898 and a law degree from Indiana University in 1900, beginning the practice of law that same year. In 1902 he became the deputy prosecuting attorney for the Clay-Putnam Circuit Courts. Only two years later he was named prosecuting attorney for the same courts, a position he held for two terms.

In February 1911, when the Clay and Putnam County Circuit Courts were divided, Governor Thomas R. Marshall appointed Hughes as the first judge of the new Putnam County Circuit Court, and he was elected to this position four times, spending more than two decades on that bench. He repeatedly enjoyed wide election margins, often by several thousand votes. During these years, Hughes was a popular, hardworking member of the community. He served as special judge in fourteen different counties and commonly spoke at a variety of events.

Hughes only relinquished the Putnam County Circuit judgeship to become a judge on the Supreme Court in 1933. He served only one term. In 1938 he wanted to seek another term, but a fissure in the Democratic Party organization thwarted his desire. The state party organization slated another candidate, H. Nathan Swaim, for Hughes's seat on the Court. A group of lawyers in the party sought unsuccessfully to block that slate from being presented at the party nominating convention. As a result, Hughes refused to allow his name to be placed in nomination. This episode represented a rare occasion during the period when judges ran on partisan ballots when a party fought the nomination of an incumbent judge.

In his opinion writing Hughes often displayed a knowledge of history and literature. For example, in *Carroll Perfumers v. State*, the Court was asked to determine whether Carroll Perfumers came under the authority of the Indiana Board of Pharmacy and thus needed a permit to operate as such. In ruling that the business did meet the definition of a pharmacy, Hughes cited Exodus 30:25, English laws during the reign of Henry VIII, and act 5, scene 1 of Shakespeare's *Romeo and Juliet*. Hughes's opinion and the Shakespearian reference received national notice several weeks later in a *Time* magazine article. Literary and historical references aside, the essence of Hughes's opinion was that the statute in question was sufficiently clear as to what constituted a pharmacy, and that Carroll Perfumers fell within that definition.

At the conclusion of his term on the Court, Hughes moved on to the Indiana attorney general's office. He served until 1941, when he returned to private practice in Greencastle, Indiana, and was joined by his son, James G. Hughes, and had only one other law partner, John P. Allee, during his career. Allee's son ultimately won election to Hughes's first judgeship on the Putnam County Circuit Court.

Hughes's judicial skills and strong backing by Indiana Democrats did not go unnoticed at the national level. In 1945 President Harry S Truman appointed Hughes to the Federal Railroad Labor Panel, which was charged with mediating and resolving labor and wage disputes for railroad workers. During his tenure on this panel, Hughes was called upon to travel across the country to quell disputes and keep the railways functioning.

Following his retirement, Hughes lived the remainder of his days on his family farm in Cloverdale, Indiana. In an interview several years prior to his death, Hughes claimed: "My farming interests are my only hobbies." It was on this same farm a generation earlier that Hughes's uncle, Lee Wiley Sinclair, had been born in a log cabin. At the time Hughes was just starting his legal career, his uncle was constructing what became known as the "Eighth Wonder of the World." Sinclair rebuilt the West Baden Springs Hotel in 1902 with an atrium that was the largest freestanding dome in the world at that time.

Hughes married Putnam County deputy auditor, Mayme Gainor, in 1907. Their only child, James G., became a member of the bar as did their grandson, James E. Hughes. Mayme died in 1932. In 1935 Hughes married Margaret Conlin of Pennsylvania. Hughes died on his family's farm on August 30, 1961, at the age of eighty-six.

MICHAEL J. SACOPULOS, JD, is a practicing attorney in Terre Haute, Indiana. He is the author of numerous articles focusing upon medical malpractice and currently serves as general counsel for Medical Justice Services Inc.

SELECTED BIBLIOGRAPHY

Adams, Wendy L., and Elizabeth R. Osborn, eds. *In Memoriam: Glimpses from Indiana's Legal Past.* Indianapolis: Indiana Supreme Court, 2006.

Wesley Wilson, DePauw University Archivist. Interview with the author. September 15, 2008.

"Bard Cited," *Time,* May 10, 1937, http://www.time.com/time/magazine/article/0,9171,757794,00.html.

Greencastle Daily Banner, August 8, 1961.

Greencastle Putnam County Graphic, September 7, 1961.

Ginn, Ward L. "Lee Sinclair's Eighth Wonder of the World," http://www.clansinclairusa.org/.

Withered, Jerome L. *Hoosier Justice: A History of the Supreme Court of Indiana.* Indianapolis: Indiana Supreme Court, 1998.

CASES CITED

Carroll Perfumers, Inc. v. State of Indiana, 212 Ind. 455, (1937).

GEORGE L. TREMAIN
January 1, 1935–December 31, 1940

WILLIAM F. GULDE

A large crowd gathered at the small airstrip in Arlington, Virginia, on July 30, 1909, to watch Orville Wright land his new plane. The throng of visitors that historic day included President William Howard Taft and other important dignitaries. Nearby in the press section, with a school friend, stood thirty-five-year-old Greensburg attorney George Lee Tremain. Already a budding trial lawyer, Tremain's legal career, like Wright's new plane, was about to soar, achieving its highest honor as the seventy-first judge of the Indiana Supreme Court.

Born on April 6, 1874, near Hartsville, Indiana, Tremain was the first child of John W. and Eliza Jones Tremain. John moved to Jackson Township in Decatur County in 1868 and eventually bought a farm near the village of Alert. A loyal Democrat, John served as a justice of the peace, the Jackson Township trustee, and as a Decatur County commissioner. He eventually owned a prosperous farm south of Sardinia. George and his younger brother, Milton, and sister, Emma, attended one-room schoolhouses.

Tremain enrolled in the Central Normal School in Danville, Indiana, in 1894. He left campus for one year to teach school and then returned to complete his formal education in 1899. He later attended Indiana Law School in Indianapolis, was admitted to the bar in 1900, and opened a law office in Greensburg, Indiana.

Circuit Court Judge James K. Ewing served as an early mentor and partner for Tremain. In 1907 Tremain formed a partnership with Harvard University graduate Rollin A. Turner. The firm specialized in criminal law and quickly developed an impressive reputation, operating in Decatur County for the next twenty-seven years. On September 27, 1910, Tremain married Mary Littell, the daughter of a prominent Greensburg restaurant owner. Two years later, on January 10, 1912, Tremain made his first foray into politics when the Decatur County commissioners appointed him as the county attorney, a position he held for six years. In 1931 Governor Harry G. Leslie appointed him to the Indiana World War Commission, a post he held until 1934.

In his second attempt at public office, in 1932, Tremain was defeated in his bid for the Democratic nomination for judge of the Indiana Court of Appeals. A fistfight literally exploded on the floor of the convention in Indianapolis as angry delegates changed their votes from Tremain to William F. Dudine of Jasper. Tremain was not part of the melee, but many Democrats left the convention hall upset that Dudine was chosen as the party's nominee.

Tremain's third attempt at public office proved successful when he won the Democratic Party nomination in 1934 for the Supreme Court and went on to defeat Republican and fellow Greensburg native David A. Myers in the general election. Proud of both men, the local bar association hosted a four-course turkey dinner at the DeArmond Hotel in Greensburg after the election to honor the judges.

When Tremain arrived at the Court on January 2, 1935, he ran into Judge Curtis Roll in the Statehouse hallway. Tremain recounted to Roll that he had failed to make arrangements to be sworn in. Roll invited Tremain into his office and swore him in without any pomp or formal ceremony.

In his second year on the bench, Tremain became chief justice, a position that at the time was rotated among the justices according to district.

One important change during Tremain's tenure was the elimination of the Court's backlog of cases. For more than one hundred years, the Court had moved at a snail's pace. In 1937 the general assembly changed the Court's rules and procedures to reduce the time allotted for filing briefs and appeals from 180 days to 90. The new arrangements changed procedures dramatically, and for the first time in its history the Court cleared the docket of all older cases.

Tremain participated in a number of important cases. One that had political significance was *Robertson v. Circuit Court of Lake County*. In this case a number of defeated Republican candidates in the 1938 election had petitioned circuit courts in seven counties to recount the votes because of claims of fraud and voting irregularities. The successful Democratic candidates sued to prevent the recount. The case was heard by only three judges because two of the judges, Curtis G. Shake and Michael L. Fansler, had been candidates in the election. Tremain, who wrote the majority opinion, and the other two judges, both Democrats, ruled that the circuit courts had no jurisdiction under state law to conduct a recount, which they said was ministerial and not judicial in character.

Tremain was considered one of the two most liberal members of the Court at that time. The other was Walter E. Treanor. A good example of Tremain's liberal stance was his majority opinion in *Martin v. Loula*, when he ruled that the state's garnishee law was unconstitutional. He said it violated both the guarantee of equal treatment under the Bill of Rights of the Indiana Constitution as well as the equal protection clause of the Fourteenth Amendment of the U.S. Constitution because it did not treat all debtors the same. Tremain wrote that "the Constitution extends protection to the debtor at least equal to the protection it extends to the creditor."

He did not always take the liberal side on issues, however, as evidenced by his rulings affecting teachers' rights. A good example is his majority opinion in *Miller v. Barton School Township of Gibson County*. In this case he ruled against a teacher who claimed that the school administration violated the Teacher Tenure Act by denying him a continuing contract to which he was entitled. The facts of the case were such that Tremain concluded that school officials had acted properly under the law. Tremain said it was "the duty of the Court to adopt that construction [of the statute] best calculated to protect the public right as against the individual right, even though in individual circumstances such construction may work slight hardship."

As chief justice, Tremain's duties were not limited to official court business. In 1938 he administered the oath of office to thirty-seven-year-old Herman B Wells as the eleventh president of Indiana University. In 1940 Tremain was passed over by the Democratic Party for the nomination to run for his seat on the Court, one of the rare instances when a party chose not to renominate an incumbent, and he retired at the end of his term in 1940.

Tremain resumed his law practice in 1941 in Greensburg. His last public appearance occurred in June 1947 when he attended an alumni banquet at the Central Normal School. He died on February 8, 1948. Mary Littell Tremain outlived her husband by fourteen years. They had no children.

WILLIAM F. GULDE, is curriculum coordinator and former chair, Social Studies Department, North Central High School, Indianapolis. He is the author of *Hopes, Dreams, and Books: The Story of North Central High School 1956–2004* (2004).

SELECTED BIBLIOGRAPHY

Greensburg Daily News, June 22, 1932, November 7, 1934.
Harding, Lewis A. *A History of Decatur County Indiana*. Indianapolis: B. F. Bowen and Company 1915.
Indianapolis Star, March 25, 1937.
Indianapolis Times, April 12, 1937.

CASES CITED

Martin v. Loula, 208 Ind. 346 (1935).
Miller v. Barton School Township of Gibson County, 215 Ind. 510 (1939).
State ex rel. Robertson, et al. v. Circuit Court of Lake County, et al., 215 Ind. 18 (1938).

CURTIS G. SHAKE
January 4, 1938–January 7, 1945

SUZANNE S. BELLAMY

The seventy-second judge of the Indiana Supreme Court, Curtis Grover Shake was a colorful man known for his great storytelling ability. After his term on the bench ended in Indiana, Shake went to Nuremberg, Germany, where he presided over the war crimes trial of I. G. Farben, the most important of the cases brought against the German industrialists by the American military, and reportedly served as the model for the judge portrayed by Spencer Tracy in the movie *Judgment at Nuremberg*.

A lifelong Hoosier, Shake was born July 14, 1887, in his grandparents' log house in the southwestern Indiana town of Monroe City. In 1903 he headed off to Vincennes University, where he stayed for two years, taking courses to qualify him for a teacher's license. After two years of teaching at a one-room country school, Shake moved to Bloomington in 1907 to attend the Indiana University School of Law, graduating in 1910.

Shake relocated to the mining town of Bicknell, Indiana, to begin his legal practice, engaging mainly in suing coal companies and railroads. He also served as Knox County deputy prosecuting attorney and Bicknell city attorney. He moved to Vincennes in 1916 and formed a partnership with Joseph W. Kimmel, and also held the positions of city attorney, U.S. commissioner for the Southern Indiana Judicial district, and Knox County attorney. In 1926 Shake ran successfully for state senator on the Democratic ticket representing jointly Knox and Daviess counties. His adept public-speaking skills led to his nomination in 1928 as the Democratic Party's candidate for Indiana attorney general. In the last days before the election, Republicans claimed to have proof that Shake had formerly belonged to the Ku Klux Klan, producing a membership roster and card. While Shake never formally denied belonging to the Klan, he decried the "insinuations and false charges." Almost the entire Indiana Democratic slate, including Shake, lost its bid for election that year.

For the next ten years, Shake remained busy practicing law, speaking on behalf of Democratic causes, and writing several books about Vincennes. In 1937 President Franklin D. Roosevelt appointed Supreme Court judge Walter E. Treanor to the U.S. Court of Appeals for the Seventh Circuit, thereby opening a vacancy on the Court. Governor M. Clifford Townsend appointed Shake, describing him as a "middle of the roader."

After finishing out the remaining year of Treanor's term, Shake was elected in his own right in 1938 to a six-year term on the Court, a post he held until January 1945. He served as chief justice three times—1939, 1941, and 1944. Along with his judicial duties, Shake became involved on a national basis with the mediation of labor disputes. During the period 1938 to 1946, he mediated approximately four hundred labor clashes as a referee for the National Mediation Board. He served on six presidential emergency boards for the settlement of railroad strikes, chairing three of them from 1944 to 1947, gaining a national reputation in the process.

Shake wrote several significant opinions during his term on the Court. Perhaps the most important was *Warren v. Indiana Telephone Company*, which finally resolved a long-simmering debate over the role of the Indiana Court of Appeals. Throughout the state's history, the legislature had on occasion made the appellate court the court of last resort in certain types of cases, thus weakening the Supreme Court's ability to shape guiding legal principles. In the *Warren* case, Shake spoke for the Court when he rejected the legislature's authority under the state constitution to limit the Court's powers of review based on the need for consistency in interpretation of the state's laws. The Warren opinion in effect made the court of appeals an intermediate court of appeals and brought Indiana in line with a majority of the rest of the state court systems.

When his term on the bench expired in the beginning of 1945, Shake chose not to run for re-election and returned to Vincennes to practice law. In early 1947 he accepted an appointment to the war crimes trials in Nuremberg, where he was named presiding judge of the Farben case. Years later, Shake revealed his true feelings about the Nuremberg tribunals when he said that while he accepted their legitimacy, he questioned their makeup, objecting mainly to their American nature. He believed that an impartial tribunal from neutral countries would have been preferable since the judges then would be neutrals and not "the victor trying the vanquished."

After his return to Indiana in late 1948, Shake went back to Vincennes and the practice of law from which he did not retire until age eighty-eight. He served on the Vincennes University board of trustees from 1923 until 1966 and continued his involvement with federal mediation boards. In 1975 the Indiana Academy selected him for membership to honor his accomplishments on the national and state levels. On September 11, 1978, Shake's long and productive life came to an end at the age of ninety-one. The funeral and burial took place in Vincennes. The *Indianapolis Star* eulogized Shake by recounting his long career and concluded, "His death this week at the age of ninety-one ended a life recognized with many honors, a life in which he never ceased seeking useful things to do."

SUZANNE S. BELLAMY, JD, is a researcher and writer. She is the author of *Hoosier Justice at Nuremberg* (2010), a former editorial assistant of the Papers of Lew and Susan Wallace, and served as assistant general counsel, Anacomp Inc.

SELECT BIBLIOGRAPHY

Bellamy, Suzanne S. *Hoosier Justice at Nuremberg.* Indianapolis: Indiana Historical Society Press, 2010.

Borkin, Joseph. *The Crime and Punishment of I. G. Farben.* New York: Free Press, 1952.

DuBois, Josiah E., Jr. *The Devil's Chemists: 24 Conspirators of the International Farben Cartel Who Manufacture Wars.* In collaboration with Edward Johnson. Boston: Beacon Press, 1952.

Shake, Curtis G., Papers. Indiana State Library, Indianapolis, IN.

————. Byron R. Lewis Collection Library, Vincennes University, Vincennes, IN.
Withered, Jerome L. *Hoosier Justice: A History of the Supreme Court of Indiana*. Indianapolis: Indiana Supreme Court, 1998.

CASES CITED

Warren v. Indiana Telephone Company, 217 Ind. 93 (1940).

H. NATHAN SWAIM
January 1, 1939–January 1, 1945

GEORGE W. GEIB

Hardress Nathan Swaim, the seventy-third judge of the Indiana Supreme Court, enjoyed the distinction of serving on both the state and federal bench. A judge of the state Supreme Court from 1939 to 1945, he concluded his career between 1949 and 1957 as a judge of the U.S. District Court for the Seventh Circuit.

Swaim was born in Zionsville, Indiana, on November 30, 1890, to Charles R. and Alice Avery Swaim. He graduated from Zionsville High School and later supported himself teaching at the high school and working as a waiter on the dining cars of the Monon Railroad. He graduated from DePauw University in 1913 and then followed the Monon north to attend the University of Chicago Law School. There he was elected to the Order of the Coif and graduated cum laude in 1916.

Swaim enlisted in the army's Reserve Officer Training Program in the summer of 1917 and earned his commission at Fort Benjamin Harrison in Indianapolis. He was assigned to the Eighty-seventh and Eighty-eighth Infantry Divisions, rose to the rank of first lieutenant, and completed his tour of duty at Camp Dodge, Iowa. He was an organizer of an American Legion post in Indianapolis, the first to be formed in Indiana, and he served as its post commander from 1921 to 1922.

Admitted to the Indiana bar on July 1, 1916, Swaim established his legal practice in Indianapolis that year and returned to it in 1919 after he left the army. His only law partner was James M. Ogden. Swaim pursued a general practice and later took pride in his refusal to enter a single specialized branch of law. He did, however, show much interest in issues affecting youth. He headed the Indianapolis chapter of the National Foundation for Infantile Paralysis, served as president of the Indiana Sailors' and Soldiers' Children's Home in Knightstown, and served on the Indianapolis Board of School Commissioners.

Swaim was a natural politician, warm and affable, with a gift for conversation and storytelling. He knew the name of every coworker and customer when he worked on the Monon, and projected ease and confidence in social and political settings. He navigated the race-tinged issues of his school board service and the patronage-dominated concerns of his later political career with a skill that impressed many. Following in the footsteps of his father, a farmer who had been a highly partisan Democrat, Swaim soon became active in Democratic politics in Indianapolis. In 1930 he was elected to the first of his three terms as Democratic county chairman, where he participated in the implementation of the 2-percent system under Governor Paul V. McNutt, whereby the party collected 2 percent of the wages of salaries of state workers for the benefit of political campaigns.

In 1938 Swaim was chosen as his party's district chairman, and in the same year was nominated for the Third District seat on the Supreme Court. His selection as the party nominee, however, was not without controversy. The decision of the party organization to slate Swaim for the seat held by incumbent James P. Hughes did not sit well with the lawyers in the Democratic Party. They tried, but failed, to prevent Swaim from getting the nomination. In the general election he withstood the off-year Republican surge, and took his seat in January 1939.

Swaim's background was reflected in several ways in his service on the Court. As a practicing lawyer, he had always prided himself upon careful preparation and clear language, and he sought to convey these traits to his staff. He regularly commented to them that he did not want them to use a twenty-five-cent word when a ten-cent word was available. As a skilled politician, he sought to build consensus and unanimity for the Court's decisions. As a veteran of one world war, he served on the Court during another, and showed a special interest in issues of wartime service. His most visible activity was as a member of the American Bar Association's Committee on National Defense, reviewing the implementation of such defense measures as the Selective Service Act.

During Swaim's tenure the Court handed down one of its most significant constitutional decisions in the case of *Tucker v. State*. This landmark case grew out of challenges to statutes passed by the Republican-controlled legislature to strip Democratic governor Henry F. Schricker of most of his executive powers, such as the power to appoint and to reorganize departments of government. These "ripper bills," as they were popularly called, were overturned by the Court as violations of the constitutional principle of separation of powers. All four of the Democrats on the Court, including Swaim, ruled that these statutes were unconstitutional. The lone Republican, Frank N. Richman, dissented.

Upon the conclusion of his term of service, Swaim returned to his private law practice and a range of community activities. In 1949 Congress expanded the U.S. Court of Appeals for the Seventh Circuit by one member. A fellow veteran and Legionnaire, President Harry S Truman, appointed Swaim to the seat—first by recess appointment in October 1949, and then by permanent appointment in February 1950. The most significant appeal he heard involved the legal status of war brides. The lone Hoosier on that court, Swaim served until chronic health problems led to his death on July 30, 1957.

GEORGE W. GEIB, PhD, is professor of history at Butler University. He is the coauthor of *Federal Justice in Indiana: The History of the United States District Court for the Southern District of Indiana* (2007).

SELECTED BIBLIOGRAPHY

Beckwith, Edmund Ruffi. "Committee on National Defense: Comment on Current Activities." *American Bar Association Journal* 27 (1941).

Muncie Post-Democrat, October 14, 1938.

Solomon, Rayman L. *History of the Seventh Circuit, 1981–1941.* Washington, DC: Bicentennial Committee of the Judicial Conference of the United States, 1981.

United States Court of Appeals for the Seventh Circuit. "In Respect to the Memory of The Honorable H. Nathan Swaim." Proclamation, May 7, 1958.

CASES CITED

Tucker et al. v. State of Indiana, 218 Ind. 614 (1941).

FRANK N. RICHMAN

January 6, 1941–January 6, 1947

SUZANNE S. BELLAMY

The judicial career of Frank Nelson Richman, the seventy-fourth judge of the Indiana Supreme Court, did not end when he left the bench in Indiana. At the request of his country, he went to Germany after World War II to serve as a civilian judge in the subsequent Nuremberg proceedings convened by the United States to try secondary Nazi war criminals such as German industrialists.

Born July 1, 1881, in Columbus, Indiana, Richman grew up in various towns around the Midwest. He received his bachelor's degree from Lake Forest College in 1904. In 1906 he enrolled at the University of Chicago Law School, leaving there in 1908 after completing all his coursework and being elected to the Order of the Coif, but without the funds to pay for a sheepskin diploma. In 1940 the University of Chicago waived its fee and finally awarded Richman, by then a nominee for the Court, a Juris Doctor degree.

In 1908 the bar of Bartholomew County, Indiana, admitted Richman to the practice of law even without the formal degree.

Richman joined his uncle, Charles S. Baker, in the practice of law, naming their firm Baker and Richman, based in Columbus, Indiana. In 1931 Richman formed a law partnership with Julian Sharpnack that continued until 1941. Richman served as president of the Indiana State Bar Association in 1931 and 1932. In 1930 he served as chairman of its committee on legal education and led the campaign to rid the profession of incompetent lawyers by participating in the preparation of bar admission rules that the Court adopted in 1931.

A lifelong Republican, Richman successfully ran for election for the Supreme Court from the Second Judicial District in the general election of 1940. At the time he joined the judiciary in January 1941, Indiana politics were intensely partisan. In 1941 the Republican-controlled legislature passed more than twenty bills intent on reducing Democratic governor Henry F. Schricker's power to make executive appointments. Schricker vetoed the bills; the legislature overrode all the vetoes but one. Schricker next took his case to the courts. The Court at that time was made up of four Democrats and one Republican, Richman. In the case of *Tucker v. State*, the Court held "that the legislative reorganization of the executive branch deprived the governor of his legitimate constitutional authority and violated the state constitution's principles of separation of powers and checks and balances." Richman was the lone dissenting vote, writing an eloquent dissent in which he expressed "no approval of the governmental policy of the statutes in question" but rather a concern about "the purely legal question of validity under the Constitution."

While one might assume that Richman had endeared himself to the Republican Party by his dissenting vote in the *Tucker* case, the party clearly had other ideas. Throughout the 1940s, the conservative wing of the party grew in strength, based in large part on opposition to many of the programs of the New Deal and to the growing national obsession with communism. Richman became a victim of this ideological drift to the right when the state GOP failed to renominate him to his seat at its 1946 state convention due to his dissent from a Court opinion related to the 1945 liquor licensing law to which Republican governor Ralph F. Gates wanted no challenge. In *State ex rel. Zeller v. Montgomery Circuit Court*, the Court majority ruled in favor of a sheriff who sought to cancel the alcohol permit of a wholesaler. Richman's dissent in the three-to-two decision stated clearly that he did not disagree with the result reached by the majority in the case, only with "the method by which the result is reached." Richman thought that the Court, in issuing a permanent "order of prohibition" against the wholesaler, had usurped the power of the trial court in which the case was originally heard.

On June 13, 1946, the day the GOP convention was to begin, the *Indianapolis Star* reported that seventeen Republican attorneys, claiming to "represent the overwhelming sentiments of the lawyers of this state," had sent a telegram to the governor warning him that "his political future may be at stake if Judge Frank N. Richman is 'purged' from the Indiana Supreme Court for failure to follow party lines in writing an opinion." The telegram cited Richman's honorable and efficient service to the state and urged Gates to prevent a "miscarriage of political justice" and not jeopardize his own political standing.

Despite the pressure, the Republican Party refused to renominate Richman. He had previously taught part time at the Indiana University School of Law in Indianapolis during the Court's summer recesses, and he planned to return there as a full-time member of the faculty with the rank of full professor beginning in February 1947. Richman's plans changed when, in January 1947, he was offered the opportunity to become a member of a court in Nuremberg, Germany, organized by the War Department within the American occupation zone to try Nazi war criminals. He accepted the assignment and arrived in Germany in late February 1947, where his appointment was to hear the case against Friedrich Flick and his business associates, the first case brought by the Americans against German industrialists.

Richman returned to Indianapolis in January 1948, where he resumed his teaching career at the IU School of Law, teaching classes at both the Bloomington and Indianapolis campuses. The university named him professor emeritus after he retired in 1952. Richman remained active in the legal community, serving as an arbitrator in several labor disputes and as a special judge in Indiana circuit courts.

Unfortunately, Richman's retirement ended after only four years with his death on April 28, 1956, at his home in Indianapolis at the age of seventy-four. The funeral and burial took place in Columbus. The Bartholomew

County Bar Association passed a resolution that began: "The lives of great Americans are written in services—services to their communities, to their states, to their nation, and in all to their fellow men. Judge Frank N. Richman measured high in all these categories."

SUZANNE S. BELLAMY, JD, is a researcher and writer. She is the author of *Hoosier Justice at Nuremberg* (2010), a former editorial assistant of the Papers of Lew and Susan Wallace, and served as assistant general counsel, Anacomp Inc.

SELECTED BIBLIOGRAPHY

Appleman, John Alan. *Military Tribunals and International Crimes*. Indianapolis: Bobbs-Merrill, 1954.

Bellamy, Suzanne S. *Hoosier Justice at Nuremberg*. Indianapolis: Indiana Historical Society Press, 2010.

Madison, James H. *Indiana through Tradition and Change: A History of the Hoosier State and Its People, 1920–1945*. Indianapolis: Indiana Historical Society, 1982.

Mazal Library. "Trials of War Criminals before the Nuernberg Military Tribunals under Control Council Law No. 10." http: www.mazal.org/NMT-HOME.htm.

Richman, Frank N. Papers. Private Collection.

CASES CITED

State ex rel. Zeller v. Montgomery Circuit Court, 223 Ind. 476 (1945).

Tucker et al. v. State of Indiana, 218 Ind. 614 (1941).

MARTIN J. O'MALLEY
January 4, 1943–January 3, 1949

DAVID J. REMONDINI

The seventy-fifth Indiana Supreme Court judge, Martin "Mart" Joseph O'Malley was a classic "country lawyer" who served but a single term on the high court. He was elected as a Republican during World War II in 1942, when Republican fortunes were high in Indiana. He lost his seat in the election of 1948, when Democratic fortunes were on the rise.

Known as "Mart," even on the ballot when he ran for the Supreme Court, O'Malley was born September 17, 1890, in Pittston, Pennsylvania, and belonged to a family of eleven brothers and sisters. He dropped out of school to work at a local coal mine. Despite the lack of a high school diploma, he attended Saint Thomas College in Scranton, Pennsylvania, from 1910 to 1912. After graduating from Valparaiso University Law School in 1915, he was admitted to the bar. During 1922 he moved to Huntington, where he practiced law for more than five decades. During the 1930s he served as the Huntington County attorney, and twice as the Huntington city attorney, both before and after World War II.

Former Huntington circuit judge Mark A. McIntosh recalled O'Malley as "pretty much an 'office lawyer.' He was not the type of lawyer that people thought was slippery. He had an excellent upstanding reputation."

During O'Malley's legal career, he was involved in at least four cases that were heard by the Appellate Court of Indiana. Twice he was successful in winning appeals for his clients. His appellate work continued right up until the year he was elected to the Supreme Court. In 1942 the appellate court sided with O'Malley and held that his client, the city of Huntington, did not have to pay compensation to the widow of a fireman killed in the line of duty. However, the state Supreme Court overturned the appellate court ruling and affirmed the award for the decedent in *City of Huntington v. Fisher.*

One of the most famous people O'Malley defended was H. Allen Smith, a well-known author and humorist of his day. Smith, a Huntington resident, became involved in a legal matter surrounding the distribution of a risqué article titled "Stranded on a Davenport." It was never intended to be published, but it did find its way to a Huntington typing class, which drew the attention of school authorities and then the police. Smith was charged with "authorship and circulation of lewd, licentious, obscene and lascivious literature." He turned to O'Malley for his legal defense. He was able to offer him ten dollars up front and promised the rest later. O'Malley laughed and said, "The rest! There will be no rest. The ten dollars will cover immediate expenses, and I will have $500 worth of fun out of it." On O'Malley's advice Smith pled guilty and was fined $22.50. This episode prompted Smith's departure from Huntington.

O'Malley never held any state or local elective office prior to his election to the Court. He was active in local politics and ran for several local offices without success. In addition, he was involved heavily with Republican political activity in Huntington during the 1940 presidential campaign between President Franklin D. Roosevelt and Hoosier challenger Wendell Willkie. While losing nationally, Willkie scored a "solid" victory in Huntington and perhaps O'Malley's political legwork for Willkie helped him secure his position on the statewide ballot. O'Malley's son, John R., surmised that the desire to balance the statewide ticket with a Roman Catholic, along with his father's legal skills, earned him his spot on the ticket. In the year of his election, 1942, Republicans polled very well across Indiana, sweeping six statewide offices. Riding the GOP wave, O'Malley handily defeated Democrat Roscoe C. O'Byrne of Brookville. Shortly after his election, O'Malley and his family moved to the north side of Indianapolis, and at some point he taught evenings at the law school in Indianapolis.

During his six years on the Court, O'Malley penned eighty-one opinions. In the case of *Shephard v. Indiana*, he wrote for the majority in a somewhat unusual rape case. The defendant claimed that the intercourse was consensual. The rape victim claimed that she consented only "to prevent the ravishment of her younger sister after [the rapist's] own desires were satisfied." The Court ruled that there was not sufficient evidence to confirm this claim and ordered a new trial.

In one of his dissenting opinions, *City of Kendallville v. Twining*, O'Malley sided with the family of a voluntary fireman killed in the line of duty. The question was how the days that the fireman was "available to be called but didn't work" should be counted. O'Malley's view was that the majority had construed the Workmen's Compensation Act too narrowly and that a more liberal construction was necessary to achieve the purpose of the act and to help the dependents as well as society bear the loss of earnings of the injured or deceased workingman.

O'Malley was denied the opportunity to remain on the Court when he was defeated in the 1948 general election. O'Malley's son attributed his loss to the fact that the Republican presidential nominee, Thomas Dewey, confident that he would carry the state, made only one speech in Indiana. While Dewey won Indiana by a small margin, Henry F. Schricker, the Democratic candidate for governor, helped the Democrats sweep the state offices and win a majority of the congressional seats.

Following his term on the Court, O'Malley returned to Huntington to practice law. In 1949 he became the senior member of the firm of O'Malley and Brown. He also held several posts on the National Labor Relations Board and one appointment to the Presidential Emergency Board. O'Malley was also a literate man and belonged to a group of thoughtful local individuals known as the Cosmopolitan Club that was formed in 1894. Members wrote papers that debated the issues of the day. One essay that O'Malley wrote in 1963, "The Drift Away," focused on his political philosophy and bemoaned the size of the federal government, the size of the federal deficit, and the drift toward a more intrusive national government. He warned that the trend would move "toward government control of all ways of life."

O'Malley had married Cecile Phipps of northeast Indiana in 1916, and the couple had two sons, John and Norman. In 1965 O'Malley moved to Saint Petersburg, Florida. While visiting his son in Gainesville, Florida, in 1972, he became ill. He died there three weeks later on September 9, 1972, at the age of eighty-one.

O'Malley's impact on his community was quite long lasting. In an editorial commemorating his passing, the *Huntington Herald-Press* noted: "Mart O'Malley was a man of strong convictions and active nature. As an advocate representing a client or in support of an administrative policy he was vigorous and unrelenting. He was the kind of active citizen who became involved in civic issues and made his presence felt."

DAVID J. REMONDINI is chief deputy executive director, Indiana Supreme Court, Division of State Court Administration. He is former counsel to Chief Justice Randall T. Shepard. Remondini, a former reporter for the *Indianapolis Star*, is the author of more than 1,600 newspaper articles and several magazine articles for local, state, and national publications.

SELECT BIBLIOGRAPHY

"H(arry) Allen Smith." *Dictionary of Literary Biography.* http://www.bookrags.com/biography/harry-allen-smith-dlb2/4.html (accessed August 10, 2009).
Huntington Herald-Press, September 12, 1971.
Joan Keefer. Interview with the author, June 12, 2009.
John R. O'Malley. Interview with the author, July 27, August 3, 2009.
O'Malley, M. J. "The Drift Away." *Cosmopolitan Club*, March 5, 1963.
Smith, H. Allen. *Low Man on a Totem Pole.* Garden City, NY: Doubleday, 1946.

CASES CITED

City of Huntington v. Fisher, 111 Ind. App. 703 (1942).
City of Kendallville v. Twining, 224 Ind. 228 (1946).
Shephard v. State of Indiana, 224 Ind. 356 (1946).

HOWARD S. YOUNG SR.

January 1, 1945–January 1, 1951

RICHARD ANDREW YOUNG

Howard Sloan Young Sr., the seventy-sixth judge of the Indiana Supreme Court, was elected to and served on the Court for six years following forty years of private law practice and public service.

Young was born on August 7, 1879, in Indianapolis. His father, A. A. Young, was a successful politician and public servant, and public issues and affairs were daily fare at home. Howard received a bachelor's degree from the University of Chicago in 1898 at the age of nineteen and earned his law degree from the Indiana Law School in 1903, the same year that he was admitted to the bar.

From 1904 to 1944 Young practiced law during turbulent times, including World War I, the Roaring Twenties, the Great Depression, and World War II. He enjoyed the experience known as "riding the circuit," where lawyers and often the judge traveled from county to county, trying cases against each other by day and camping out as a group overnight. He represented railroads later in his practice and was a trial advocate throughout his legal career.

Young lived in Indianapolis all of his life. He married Elsie Street there, and they raised three children, a son and two daughters. Like his father, Young was active in community affairs and party politics, a necessity for judicial candidates who were nominated by political parties and elected in statewide general elections. He was a lifelong Republican and a member of the Columbia Club for fifty years. In 1920 Young was appointed a U.S. commissioner, a federal judicial position, working part time, largely in criminal matters. He also served as a member of the Indianapolis School Board, a position that was very important to him. He resigned both of these positions in 1944 when he was elected to the Court. From 1931 to 1932 he served as president of the Indianapolis Bar Association.

Young's election to the Court in 1944 was helped by the Republican sweep of all the statewide offices that year, plus the GOP winning the two senatorial seats and ten of the eleven congressional seats. Young defeated Democratic incumbent H. Nathan Swaim.

During his tenure on the Court, Young wrote 101 opinions, an average of seventeen per year. In 1949, when the Court had a particularly heavy caseload, Young wrote twenty-six opinions. In general his opinions tended to be direct and rather terse. He seldom dissented. World War II was ending and the nation's burst of growth was just beginning, but for the Court these were relatively quiet years in terms of cases that would change Indiana's future. However, Young participated in one very sensational case in 1950, *State ex rel. Purcell, Prosecuting Attorney v. Circuit Court of Sullivan County et al.*

The case grew out of a long-simmering feud between Sullivan County prosecutor John K. Purcell and Sullivan County Circuit Court judge Norvall K. Harris. The dispute erupted publicly in 1950 when Purcell succeeded in getting grand jury indictments against Harris for embezzlement, forgery, and issuing a fraudulent check. Harris fought back by appointing a special prosecutor to investigate Purcell. The Court first became involved when Purcell sought and obtained a temporary restraining order to prevent the investigation. It became more involved when Purcell filed a contempt of court citation against Harris, who had continued his legal harassment of Purcell. The Court issued a unanimous opinion that Harris was in contempt of court and ordered the sheriff to bring him to court for sentencing. Harris was fined $300 and sentenced to sixty days at the Indiana State Farm.

A debilitating stroke in 1950 prevented Young from running for a second term. After leaving the Court he returned to the private practice of law with his son, Howard, and his name carries on today in the firm of Young and Young. He died October 14, 1961, in Indianapolis. He was described in the Indianapolis Bar Association Memorial adopted by the Indiana Supreme Court: "Judge Young was always active in the civic and political life of the community and faithful as a member of the state and local Bar Associations. He was always fair in his dealings with his fellow lawyers and firm in his convictions in matters handled for clients. His thoroughness in preparation to the best of his ability gained for him a reputation of being an excellent advocate. His decisions were well reasoned, carefully and concisely expressed in accordance with rules of procedure and the law applicable."

RICHARD ANDREW YOUNG, JD, is civil trial lawyer with Young and Young, Indianapolis. He is a former Marion County deputy prosecutor (1971–72, 1980–81), past president, Indiana Trial Lawyers Association (1986–87), chairman, Marion County Election Board (1997–2003), and a former law clerk to the late Allen Sharp, Indiana Court of Appeals (1969–71). Young is also a trustee, Marian University (2008–present) and member of the Indiana Supreme Court Committee on Character and Fitness. He is the grandson of Judge Howard Young.

SELECTED BIBLIOGRAPHY

Adams, Wendy L., and Elizabeth R. Osborn, eds. *In Memoriam: Glimpses from Indiana's Legal Past.* Indianapolis: Indiana Supreme Court, 2006.

Withered, Jerome L. *Hoosier Justice: A History of the Supreme Court of Indiana.* Indianapolis: Indiana Supreme Court, 1998.

CASES CITED

State ex rel. Purcell, Prosecuting Attorney v. Circuit Court of Sullivan County et al., 228 Ind. 410 (1950).

OLIVER STARR
January 1, 1945–January 1, 1951

LORENZO ARREDONDO

Oliver Starr gained historical status as the seventy-seventh judge of the Indiana Supreme Court, but prior to his arrival on the Court he had gained statewide recognition for his role in prosecuting the most infamous theater bombing case in Indiana history.

Starr and his twin sister, Olive, were born December 10, 1883, in Wells County, Indiana. His parents were Benjamin and Sabina Nutter Starr. Oliver Starr obtained his bachelor's degree from Indiana University in 1905 and his law degree from the University of Michigan in 1908, where he served as an editorial assistant on the *Michigan Law Review*. He practiced law in Gary for many years and served as city attorney and then prosecuting attorney for Lake County at a time when few Republicans held public office in the county.

At one time Starr was a shareholder of the *Gary-Post Tribune* and represented the paper in legal matters. On June 23, 1913, he married Mary Helen Snyder, the sister of H. B. Snyder, the newspaper's editor and publisher. They had five children. Two were twins named Olive and Oliver, like their father and his sister. The other children were Benjamin, Thomas, and Mary. Mary Helen died in 1937, and two years later Starr married Ruth Schroeder in Fort Wayne.

In 1928 Starr prosecuted his most noted case, the trial of the bombers of the opulent State Theater. The bombing was the result of a business deal that went bad. The owner of the three other theaters in town felt threatened by the new competition and hired two bombers to "take care of business." They were so successful that the blast not only destroyed the theater but also caused more than a million dollars in damage to the surrounding neighborhood.

The state was represented by Starr as prosecutor and assisted by A. P. Draper, brother of future Supreme Court judge Floyd S. Draper, and Gerald Gillett, a relative of former Supreme Court judge John H. Gillett. The trial lasted more than a week, but it took only three ballots for the jury to reach a guilty verdict. The first ballot was eight to four for conviction; the second was ten to two; and the final ballot was unanimous. Starr was praised in the media for his skillful "legal strategy and masterly maneuvering," which had "never before been equaled in the annals of the criminal court."

Starr left the office of prosecutor in 1931, and from then until his election to the Supreme Court he made several unsuccessful attempts at public office. In 1934 he ran for judge of the appellate court, later was a candidate for U.S. representative, and in 1938 he was defeated in a race for U.S. Senate. He was not deterred by these defeats, and in 1944 he was elected to the Supreme Court. It was a good year to be a Republican candidate, as the party won all major offices, including governor, all but one congressional seat, and both U.S. Senate seats. This wave of popularity swept not only Starr onto the Court, but also two other fellow Republicans, Frank E. Gilkison and Howard S. Young Sr. Then every seat on the Court was held by a Republican.

During his six years on the Court, Starr wrote 124 opinions. While none dealt with major constitutional issues with long-lasting consequences, in his final year on the Court he wrote the majority opinion in a case that garnered a lot of publicity for the Court. It involved a bitter rivalry between

John K. Purcell, prosecutor of Sullivan County, and the Circuit Court Judge Norvall K. Harris. After Purcell obtained indictments against the judge for embezzlement, forgery, and writing fraudulent checks, Harris retaliated by appointing a special prosecutor to investigate Purcell. He in turn appealed to the Supreme Court and obtained a temporary restraining order to prohibit the judge from interfering with the performance of his official duties as prosecutor and attempting to influence or coerce the grand jury. The temporary restraining order did not deter Harris, who refused to suspend the special prosecutor's grand jury proceedings and in fact made statements that could prejudice the members of the grand jury against Purcell. The prosecutor then petitioned the Court to issue a contempt of court citation against Harris for these actions. In *State ex rel. Purcell, Prosecuting Attorney v. Circuit Court of Sullivan County et al.*, Starr showed little sympathy for the defendant. He said that the judge had relied on "suspicion and rumor" in calling the special grand jury and that "the judge is not acting judiciously but is attempting to hold an inquisition." The Court found the judge in contempt of court and ordered the sheriff to arrest him and bring him before the Court for sentencing. He was fined $300 and ordered to serve sixty days at the Indiana State Farm.

Starr chose not to run for re-election to the Court and retired from the bench in January 1951. He died on March 28, 1961.

LORENZO ARREDONDO, JD, is judge, Lake County Circuit Court. He is vice chair, Indiana Supreme Court Commission on Race and Gender Fairness, the author of "Combating Stereotypes," *American Judges Association Court Review* (1989), and the coauthor of "The Legacy of Hernandez v. Texas," *University of San Francisco Law Review* (1971).

SELECTED BIBLIOGRAPHY

Northwest Indiana Times, April 13, 2008.
"State Street Theatre Downtown—Date Line 1927." Hammond, Indiana, Twentieth Century Time Capsule. http://www.hammondindiana.com/20thcentury/time_capsule37.htm.

CASES CITED

State ex rel. Purcell, Prosecuting Attorney v. Circuit Court of Sullivan County et al., 228 Ind. 410 (1950).

FRANK E. GILKISON
January 1, 1945–February 25, 1955

FRANK E. GILKISON JR.

Frank Earl Gilkison was sworn in as the seventy-eighth justice of the Indiana Supreme Court on January 1, 1945, at age sixty-seven. His election to the Court in 1944 coincided with a Republican sweep of contested offices that brought two other Republicans to the Court. Their elections gave the party unanimous control of the Court. Gilkison, however, did not blindly follow the path of his colleagues, a trait lauded by fellow lawyers who observed that "his occasional dissenting opinions while on the Supreme Court proclaimed him to be a mental leader, and not a mere follower."

Gilkison was born November 3, 1877, the third of seven children of John and Matilda Inman Gilkison, in a home of rough-hewn timbers in Rutherford Township, Martin County. It was a family farm in the days of horse-drawn plows and wooden rail fences. His early education was in the Truelove one-room school half a mile from his home. High school education was sporadic and required boarding at the town of Loogootee, six miles to the north, and at the county seat at Shoals some fifteen miles away. Commuting was weekly or monthly by horse and buggy. The family was able to raise money for some college for most of the children. Two older brothers became physicians. Gilkison attended Indiana University School of Law in 1899 and graduated in the class of 1901. An undergraduate degree was not required for the two-year course for a law degree. He was admitted to the bar on June 19, 1901, and returned to Shoals and started practice with Hiram McCormick, an older attorney of local note.

After a few years Gilkison opened his own office and practiced law for thirty-five years until his election to the trial bench. As a trial lawyer Gilkison was described by his peers as a lawyer's lawyer with a natural love for the courtroom contest and as being especially well schooled in trial tactics. He was known as a competitive adversary who never neglected a client and as a person with a kind and warm personality.

Gilkison served as deputy prosecuting attorney from 1907 to 1909 and was elected judge of the Forty-ninth Judicial Circuit, composed of Daviess and Martin counties, in 1934 and again in 1940, giving up this position in 1944 when he won election to the Court.

Despite his modest education before entering law school, Gilkison was an intellectual and read extensively in the classics as well as the Bible. He was a fervent believer in the dignity and inalienable rights of the individual. Among others, this was reflected in his opinion in *Kirtley v. State*, holding unconstitutional as a violation of Kirtley's natural inalienable rights an Indianapolis ticket scalping law under which he had been convicted for selling a state finals basketball ticket for more than he paid for it. Gilkison, writing for the majority, said that the "personal liberty clause" in the state constitution "embraces the right of every one to be free in the use of their powers in pursuit of happiness in such calling as they may choose subject only to the restraints necessary to secure the common welfare."

Gilkison had a high regard for the human being and a keen understanding of human nature as shown in some of the dissents for which he was noted. His dissent in *Plotzki v. Standard Oil Co.* is a good example. In a suit for the wrongful death of an eleven-year-old boy who drowned in a pool of water in an excavation hole on Standard Oil property, the Court majority ruled that the company had not created an "attractive nuisance," thus absolving it for liability in the child's death. Gilkison's dissent, in which

James A. Emmert concurred, took exception to this narrow interpretation of the doctrine of attractive nuisance, noting: "Thereby the voice of property is made all powerful, and the lives and safety of little children are made subservient to that voice. This unnatural materialistic rule cannot endure." Gilkison's dissenting view in this case eventually became law.

A similar dissent in *Neal v. Home Builders, Inc.*, again with Emmert concurring, has also long since become the law. The majority held a three-year-old boy to be a trespasser to whom an owner had no duty of reasonable care, where the boy had become entrapped in an unsecured home under construction. Citing a previous ruling (*Young v. Harvey*) where the Court granted recovery to the owner of a horse killed by falling into an unguarded well on an unenclosed lot of a neighbor, Gilkison sharply criticized the majority opinion. He wrote: "A civilized Christian state cannot long tolerate such a perversion of the laws of nature, and of the experience of all civilized peoples." This means, he said, "that the law has greater respect for the rights of property than for the life and safety of little children."

One other notable dissent where both Gilkison and Emmert disagreed with the majority was *Yessen v. State. Yessen* was an appeal from a defendant convicted of raping a twelve-year-old girl. Her testimony was the main evidence used in the trial. The victim later recanted her testimony and said that the police had coerced her into making her statement by threatening to send her to a reformatory school. Gilkison said that the evidence on which the man had been convicted did "no more than raise a shadow, trace, possibility, opportunity or suspicion of guilt" and was "not sufficient to support a conviction."

Gilkison served on the Court until February 25, 1955, when he died suddenly, leaving his widow, the former Eva Edwards, and his son, Frank Jr., who is also a lawyer. Throughout his long career as a trial lawyer, prosecutor, circuit court judge, and Court judge, Gilkison made a significant contribution to the Indiana justice system. He was a man of the law.

FRANK E. GILKISON JR., LLB, JD, is a civil trial lawyer with Beasley and Gilkison. He is corporate counsel for the City of Muncie, Indiana, and a fellow of the American College of Trial Lawyers.

SELECTED BIBLIOGRAPHY

Adams, Wendy L., and Elizabeth R. Osborn, eds. *In Memoriam: Glimpses from Indiana's Legal Past*. Indianapolis: Indiana Supreme Court, 2006.

CASES CITED

Kirtley v. State of Indiana, 227 Ind. 175 (1949).
Neal Administrators, etc. v. Home Builders, Inc. et al., 232 Ind. 160 (1953).
Plotzki v. Standard Oil Co. of Indiana, 228 Ind. 518 (1950).
Yessen v. State of Indiana, 228 Ind. 316 (1950).
Young v. Harvey, 16 Ind. 314 (1861).

JAMES A. EMMERT
January 6, 1947–January 5, 1959

JOEL ROSENBLOOM

For some, the era in which James Allen Emmert served as the seventy-ninth judge of the Indiana Supreme Court marked the nadir of a system in which judges were elected, often served brief terms, and participated vigorously in partisan politics. For others, the Court during the same period was of high caliber generally and was dominated by Emmert by virtue of his integrity and intellect. This essay does not seek to judge between these views—much less to fix Emmert's position in the history of the Court or of Indiana law generally. It attempts, however, to convey the nature of Emmert's approach to judging and the flavor of the outsize personality that made him a favorite of the Indianapolis press in his day.

At the outset, Emmert was indeed a vigorous, partisan, Republican politician. Elected mayor of Shelbyville in 1925, he was elected judge of the Shelby Circuit Court in 1928 and reelected in 1934. In 1939 and 1940 he ran an extensive but unsuccessful campaign for the Republican gubernatorial nomination. In 1942 and 1944 he was elected and reelected state attorney general on the Republican ticket. On the day before the latter election, he sent a frankly political telegram, signed as attorney general, to county election boards, countermanding advice from the Democratic-controlled state election board on procedures for allowing voting by persons not on the registration rolls. There followed a heated hearing in Indianapolis before a committee of the Democratic-controlled U.S. Senate, but the committee chairman concluded that Emmert's legal position was correct and the controversy died.

Thus, when Emmert arrived at the Supreme Court in 1947, he did so as a veteran Republican politician. He remained one thereafter. In the fall of 1956 Israel, France, and Great Britain jointly attacked Egypt because of its seizure of the Suez Canal. On the next morning, Emmert chortled that Israeli Premier Ben Gurion should be given "the royal Republican tomahawk," because the threat of war would cement a victory in the November election for incumbent President Dwight D. Eisenhower and Republicans generally.

Emmert was not, however, a typical southern Indiana Republican. Although he was born in Laurel, Indiana, on September 26, 1895, and raised in Clarksburg, Indiana, where his grandfather had established a flour mill, Emmert obtained a bachelor's degree from Northwestern University in 1920 and a law degree from Harvard Law School in 1923. U.S. Supreme Court Justice Felix Frankfurter, a leading figure in President Franklin D. Roosevelt's New Deal administration, once said that Emmert was "the best research student" he had ever had as a professor at Harvard Law.

Nonpolitical experiences, moreover, had a major impact on Emmert's approach to appellate judging. His twelve years as a trial court judge, for example, left him with an abiding respect for trial court judges and the trial court process generally. In criminal cases before the Court, he often called for a complete trial transcript in order to understand the full context of an appeal. He once remarked that he regularly did so in death-sentence cases because he felt a need to assure himself that there was no doubt, reasonable or not, of the accused's guilt.

Similarly, where a trial judge had found after hearing that pretrial publicity made a fair criminal trial impossible without a change in venue, Emmert argued powerfully in dissent that the Indiana statute forbidding more than one change of venue could not constitutionally prevent the trial judge from carrying out his duty to ensure a fair trial (*State ex rel. Fox v. La Porte Circuit Court*). The U.S. Supreme Court subsequently adopted Emmert's position on the Indiana statute and the role of the trial judge (*Irvin v. Dowd*).

The same sense that courts have a major, independent role to play in protecting the rights of individuals led Emmert to argue in dissent that, while the legislature had the right to make reasonable classifications, "[r]easonableness must be fair, just [and] conscionable." On that basis, he concluded that a statute treating adopted and natural children unequally for purposes of inheritance violated both the U.S. and the Indiana constitutions (*Scott v. Scott*).

This is not to say that Emmert was a consistent wielder of judicial power to second-guess the work of other branches of government. A World War I veteran who served in France for twenty-two months and who helped to organize the Indiana State Guard in 1940, he dissented at length from a decision holding that the grant of free hunting and fishing licenses to veterans violated constitutional guarantees of equal treatment (*Hanley v. State*).

Nor was he what today would be termed a "liberal." Emmert was a lifelong devotee of rifle and pistol shooting, a president of the Indiana State Rifle Association, and a director of the National Rifle Association. When a majority of the Court upheld a statute that required a license for the carrying of an unconcealed pistol outside the bearer's home, he dissented vigorously, invoking the Indiana Constitution, which explicitly granted an individual right to bear arms, and tracing the history that gave the right meaning (*Matthews v. State*). So, too, he wrote an opinion for the Court that effectively banned convictions for rape based on the uncorroborated testimony of the alleged victim, unless she had been subjected to a psychiatric examination, and he dissented sharply when that opinion was later overruled in *Burton v. State*.

In short, his opinions do not form an integrated, consistent whole. They reflect, rather, the differing phases of a strong personality, which was itself not all of a piece. He could be pugnacious in the defense of a position. He had, for example, a long-running duel over the Court's budget with an Indiana legislator who owned several peony farms and who persuaded his colleagues to replace the zinnia with the peony as the Indiana State Flower. Emmert uniformly referred to the man, not by name, but as "that peony growing b-st--d." He was unafraid, moreover, of being thought eccentric. To avoid commuting to Shelbyville during the week, he slept on a couch in his office, and it was notorious that "early arrivals to the statehouse would sometimes see him walking down an upper hallway in his bathrobe." And he never hid his enthusiasms. He talked at length to anyone who would listen about the importance of tombstone inscriptions as a source for family history.

Above all, he had an inordinate talent for friendship. At noon or in the late afternoon, he welcomed one or more of his newspaper or other buddies for "a cup of tea"—bourbon and branch water served in heavy, china tea cups. These sessions were filled with gossip about law, politics, history and, most of all, laughter and good fellowship. Those in the late afternoon were often carried over into dinner at the Indianapolis Press Club or a nearby restaurant. Small wonder that his retirement from the bench—forced by a Democratic sweep of statewide offices in 1958—and his death in 1974 were marked by an outpouring of affection and respect.

JOEL ROSENBLOOM, JD, is a retired partner with Wilmer Hale and practices in communications law. He is the author of "Authority of the Federal Communications Commission" in *Freedom and Responsibility in Broadcasting* (1961), coeditor and author of a chapter on cable television in *The Communications Act: A Legislative History of the Major Amendments, 1934–1996* (1999), and the author of two articles in the *Federal Communications Law Journal*, "On the 60th Anniversary of the Communications Act" (1994) and "The 'Vast Wasteland' in Retrospect" (2003).

SELECTED BIBLIOGRAPHY

Bodenhamer, David J., and Randall T. Shepard. "The Narrative and Counternarratives Indiana Legal History." In *The History of Indiana Law*. Edited by David J. Bodenhammer and Randall T. Shepard. Athens: Ohio University Press, 2006.
James Emmert Clippings File. Indiana State Library, Indianapolis, IN.
   "James Allen Emmert, Jurist." Arts and Humanities Commemoration Collection of the Shelbyville Rotary Club, June 7, 1979.
   "Newspapermen call him Jim and think he is a great guy." June 1, 1947 (file p. 90).
Indianapolis Star, January 6, 1959, April 21, 1974.
Withered, Jerome L. *Hoosier Justice: A History of the Supreme Court of Indiana*. Indianapolis: Indiana Supreme Court, 1998.

CASES CITED

Burton v. State of Indiana, 232 Ind. 246 (1953).
Hanley v. State Indiana, 234 Ind. 326 (1955).
Irvin v. Dowd, Warden, 366 U.S. 717 (1961).
Matthews v. State of Indiana, 237 Ind. 677 (1958).
Scott v. Scott, Administrix et al., 238 Ind. 474 (1958).
Wedmore v. State of Indiana, 237 Ind. 212 (1957).
State of Indiana ex rel. Fox etc. v. La Porte Circuit Court et al., 236 Ind. 69 (1959).

The author was a law clerk to Emmert from 1956 to 1957 and included personal reminiscences of his time with the judge.

PAUL G. JASPER
January 3, 1949–March 31, 1953

ANGELA M. QUINN

Paul George Jasper served less than one full term as the eightieth judge of the Indiana Supreme Court. He was the lone Democrat on the Court at a time when partisanship played a role in elections to the Court as well as decisions that were made. Described as a quiet and pensive man, Jasper was said to be troubled by the animosity on the Court and the sharp criticism directed at it. In his second year on the Court he was already thinking about leaving to take another position. He ultimately left the Court with nearly two years left in his term.

Jasper was born in Fort Wayne on December 15, 1908, and completed his education there before entering Indiana University at Bloomington, where he obtained a law degree in 1932. At IU he excelled in athletics, lettering in basketball and football. One of his basketball teammates was Branch McCracken, the starting center, who was renowned for scoring

30 percent of the team's points during his career at IU. Jasper also played center and stood six feet, two inches tall. Although he did not attain Mc-Cracken's scoring record, he was perhaps the greatest athlete to serve on the Court.

Besides his athletic prowess, Jasper excelled in other ways at IU. He was president of the senior class and president of the Board of Aeons. He had a strong relationship with IU throughout his life. He was a lifetime member of the IU Alumni Association and served as its president in 1960. Other IU-related organizations to which he belonged included the I-Men's Club, the Woodburn Guild, and the Varsity Club. He served as class agent for the School of Law and as a judge of the school's Moot Court Program. The IU Alumni Association recognized his many contributions to the university, the state, and the nation by presenting him with its Distinguished Alumni Service Award in 1970.

Jasper practiced law in Fort Wayne until World War II, when he served in the Ninety-eighth Infantry in the central Pacific during the last part of the war and rose to the rank of major. After the war he resumed his law practice. From 1946 to 1948 he was chair of the Allen County Democratic Party. In 1948 he won the party nomination for the Court and beat incumbent judge Martin J. O'Malley by a solid margin. No doubt he was helped by the strong showing of the Democratic Party in that election. He was only forty years old, the youngest person, at that time, to sit on the Court since 1899. His fellow justices were all Republicans, a situation that may have contributed to his apparent discontent about the Court.

The Court had a particularly heavy caseload when Jasper came on board. He wrote seventy-eight opinions in his four years on the Court. During his tenure the Court was the subject of extensive publicity and criticism, and Jasper himself was the object of criticism. In one particular case, a deputy attorney general criticized one of Jasper's opinions to a reporter, in remarks that he thought were off the record. The remarks were printed, however, creating embarrassment for both Jasper and the lawyer. Jasper was said to be "magnanimous in his assessment of the situation and in his treatment of the young lawyer." After chiding him to be wary of confiding to reporters, Jasper "apparently forgot about the matter."

During the 1950s President Harry S Truman appointed Jasper on six separate occasions to serve on the President's Emergency Board to settle railroad labor disputes. This service may have contributed to rumors that Jasper was in line for a federal judgeship, but that did not materialize. Three months into his fifth year on the bench, March 23, 1953, Jasper resigned to become assistant general counsel for the Public Service Company of Indiana, the largest public utility in the state. In 1974 he joined the Indiana Electric Association, a group of investor-owned utilities in the state, and remained active in that association until his death.

After he left the Court, Jasper still remained involved. He served as a special judge in numerous cases, as a disciplinary hearing officer for the Court, and as chair of a Court committee studying the Indiana judiciary. When Jasper died, Chief Justice Randall T. Shepard said of him: "He was the soul of civility and grace, and I always looked forward to seeing him. Even after he left the Court, he continued to be a forceful advocate for improvements to our judicial system."

In addition to the service to the judicial system, Jasper served his state and community. For more than sixteen years he was a member of the Indiana State Police Board, to which he was appointed by four different governors. He was active in the Allen and Marion County, Indiana, and American Bar associations. He was also a member of the American Judicature Society and participated in various philanthropic and civic activities in both Fort Wayne and Indianapolis.

Jasper died on October 23, 2001, at the age of ninety-two. Earlier that year he had been selected for the IU Academy of Law Alumni Fellows, the highest honor the law school bestows upon its graduates. His family attended the dinner to accept the award in his name. He was survived by his wife, Mary Tucker, his two children, Paul and Jamia Jasper Jacobsen, eight grandchildren, and thirteen great-grandchildren. He was also an uncle to Marilyn Tucker Quayle, wife of former vice president Dan Quayle.

ANGELA M. QUINN, MA, is executive director of ARCH, Fort Wayne's historic preservation nonprofit organization, since 1996. She is the author of *The Underground Railroad and the Antislavery Movement in Fort Wayne and Allen County, Indiana* (2001), several National Register nominations, and articles in *History of Fort Wayne and Allen County*.

SELECTED BIBLIOGRAPHY

Dale, Julie, ed. "Alumni in the News: Academy of Law Alumni Fellows Inducts Five." *Bill of Particulars*. Bloomington: Indiana University School of Law, 2002. http://129.79.131.64/publications/particulars/2002winter/alumninews.shtml.
Indianapolis Star. October 5, 2001.
Withered, Jerome L. *Hoosier Justice: A History of the Supreme Court of Indiana*. Indianapolis: Indiana Supreme Court, 1998.

ARCH N. BOBBITT
January 2, 1951–January 7, 1963

FREDERIC C. SIPE

Arch Newton Bobbitt, "Archie" to his friends, had long been active in politics before he became the eighty-first judge of the Indiana Supreme Court, and his many years of work as a lawyer and in state government made him feel at home in the Statehouse. As a World War I navy man, he had many friends and even more acquaintances and was uniformly regarded as a top-notch lawyer. He could not walk down the street without being greeted every few steps.

Bobbitt was born in Eckerty, Crawford County, Indiana, on September 3, 1895. He graduated from Birdseye High School and attended Central Normal College at Danville. A lifelong Republican, he began his career of public service in 1918 when he was elected Crawford County clerk, but he resigned that office to join the navy in World War I. After the war he returned to Crawford County and in 1920 was elected to a four-year term as county auditor.

During his work as auditor, Bobbitt became acquainted with court proceedings and decided to become a lawyer. In those days, law school was not required to be admitted to the bar, nor was a bar examination. The only requirement was for two witnesses to swear in court that you were of good moral character. That was no problem for Bobbitt. In 1925 he was admitted to practice before the Indiana Supreme Court. Nevertheless, he chose to attend Benjamin Harrison Law School at night for three years, graduating in 1927.

Starting in the 1920s, Bobbitt began to work his way up the political ladder, beginning with his selection as Republican county chairman, followed by his election as Third District chairman. These positions helped him to attain public office. In 1925 he was appointed director of the state gasoline tax department, and in 1928 he was elected to a two-year term as state auditor. In 1930 he began practicing law full time.

His star continued to rise when he became state GOP chair in 1937. It was in this position that Bobbitt became a powerbroker in state politics. Following the 1940 election, the Republicans took control of both houses of the state legislature with large majorities. Bobbitt's suite in the Claypool Hotel churned out bills for legislative action. Bobbitt said of his operations: "If ever there ever was a legislature that was run from the Claypool Hotel, this was one." Former Indiana Supreme Court Judge Fred C. Gause served as one of the principal draftsman for the bills. One of this groups major initiatives were four bills aimed at reducing the power of Democratic governor Henry F. Schricker. These measures, which became known as the "ripper bills," were declared unconstitutional by the Court in 1926. Bobbitt acknowledged later that these proposals were a mistake. He came to recognize that these bills "would have destroyed our form of government entirely, and we would have had a commission form of government instead of an executive representative."

In 1950 Bobbitt won election to the Court, replacing Howard S. Young Sr., who was retiring. At that time, the judges did not have a law clerk and paid "research boys" out of their own pockets or did the research themselves. Some judges worked quickly, while others took quite a long time to write a decision. To Bobbitt, correctness, not time, was of the essence of an appeal. Unlike today, he believed that a lawyer should have the right to control the progress of his case. If the lawyer was not ready to have it heard, Bobbitt thought he should be given an extension. "Because it's his case," Bobbitt said, "He's the one I thought ought to control it." He also felt that if a case was worthy of an appeal, it deserved an oral argument.

Although politics brought him to the Court, it was also the cause for his departure. He lost his bid for re-election in 1962. Some have speculated that an opinion he wrote limiting the bonding authority for schools might have contributed to his defeat. In *Allen v. Van Buren Township of Madison County* the Court held that limits set by the Indiana Constitution for school bonds was based on 2 percent of the net assessed property valuation, not actual property value, thus reducing considerably the amount of bonding authority available. The opinion quashed school construction plans throughout the state and resulted in retaliation by the Indiana State Teachers Association, which circulated copies of the opinion to teachers throughout the state accompanied by a strong critique by the association. Bobbitt later blamed the teachers for his defeat and advocated removing judges from politics.

Bobbitt also blamed his loss on two rulings unfavorable to a certain politician. A newspaper reporter later told Bobbitt that the politician in question had said to him, "Yes, I defeated the [so-and-so] and took a great deal of pride in it." Years later, in a speech presenting a portrait of Bobbitt to the Indiana University School of Law in Indianapolis, Harvey A. Grabill said: "I have no doubt but what if Indiana selected its judges on a non-partisan basis that [Bobbitt] would have spent the rest of his life on the Court."

After his departure from the Court, Bobbitt continued to practice law for many years with his well-regarded firm, Ruckelshaus, Bobbitt and O'Connor. He also took time to continue his legal scholarship, writing and updating the venerable attorneys' practice manual, *Works' Indiana Practice*, which was originally penned in 1882 by John D. Work.

Bobbitt often visited the Statehouse and the judges and staff of the Supreme Court and Court of Appeals in his later years. Although today it may seem odd to say about any one person, Bobbitt was at the same time, a partisan politician, a lawyer, a scholar, and a gentleman. His experiences demonstrate the logic and necessity of the nonpartisan judicial appointment system that Indiana enjoys today. Bobbitt died on January 24, 1978.

FREDERIC C. SIPE, JD, is an attorney. He is a former law clerk to Chief Judge George B. Hoffman Jr., Indiana Court of Appeals and, with Arch N. Bobbitt, the coauthor of *Works Indiana Practice*.

SELECTED BIBLIOGRAPHY

Bobbitt, Arch N. Interviews with Jesh Randall. August 3, September 11, 17, 1974. Oral History of Judge Bobbitt, Indiana State Library, Indianapolis, IN.

Grabill, Harvey A. *Remarks on Presentation of Portrait of Judge Arch N. Bobbitt to Indiana University School of Law*. Indianapolis, n.d.

Walsh, Justin E. *The Centennial History of the Indiana General Assembly, 1816–1978*. Indianapolis: Select Committee on the Centennial History of the Indiana General Assembly, 1987.

Withered, Jerome L. *Hoosier Justice: A History of the Supreme Court of Indiana*. Indianapolis: Indiana Supreme Court, 1998.

CASES CITED

Allen v. Van Buren Township etc., et al., 243 Ind. 665 (1962).

FLOYD S. DRAPER

January 2, 1951–January 10, 1955

LORENZO ARREDONDO

Floyd Stanley Draper was first and foremost a public servant. He served continuously in public office from 1923, when he became chief deputy prosecutor for Lake County, until 1960, when he served as judge of the Lake County Criminal Court. He was one of a few justices who served at all three levels of the state judicial system. However, his judicial career was even more unusual because he served first on the court of appeals and then as the eighty-second judge of the Indiana Supreme Court before becoming criminal court judge.

Born October 17, 1893, in Fulton, New York, Draper was educated in public schools and graduated from Watertown High School. He received his law degree from Valparaiso University in 1915 and began private practice in Gary in 1917. Although he was a Republican in a highly Democratic area, he managed to thrive. He served two terms as chief deputy prosecutor in Lake

County—from 1923 to 1924 and 1927 to 1931. He was the city attorney for Gary in 1939. He began his judicial career in 1942 when he was elected to the Court of Appeals. He was reelected to a second term on that court in 1946. Then in 1950 he handily won a seat on the Indiana Supreme Court. Republican candidates that year were aided by having the popular incumbent U.S. Senator Homer E. Capehart at the top of the ticket. Two other Republicans in addition to Draper were elected to the high court—Arch N. Bobbitt and Frank E. Gilkison, giving the Republicans a four-to-one majority on the Court.

His former law clerk, Richard M. Givan, who later became chief justice of the Supreme Court, described Draper as being "on the conservative side. He took a harder line with criminals than some of the other justices." Draper's conservatism in criminal cases is evident in a dissenting opinion he wrote in the case of *Taylor v. State*. The case involved lengthy judicial proceedings against a man who pled guilty to armed robbery, but whose sentencing was delayed for more than three years due to various hearings regarding his mental competency and his indefinite incarceration at either the Indiana Hospital for the Insane or the Village for Epileptics. He finally escaped from the epileptic center, and in his final appearance before the trial court was sentenced to ten to twenty years in prison, despite his plea for a new trial. The majority opinion overturned the trial court's ruling with instructions to enter a judgment for the defendant. The majority opinion stated that there must be some "recognized legal purpose" for unusual delays in sentencing, and that even then the termination of the delay had to be fixed. Accordingly, "an American citizen is entitled to live without a Damocles sword hanging over his head." Draper, perhaps drawing upon his experience as a prosecutor, wrote a strong dissent. He said: "I am afraid that the legendary sword which the Court has removed from the heads of the culprits now dangles over the heads of trial court judges."

Draper's conservatism was evident in other ways. In 1952 he joined the consensus of the other Court judges responding to questions posed by the *Indianapolis Times* that Americans were "losing their freedom," and that terms of judges, at both the federal and state level, should be limited. Also, Draper said he thought that the outstanding legal problem confronting the nation was "increasing government controls."

Draper decided not to complete his full term on the Court. After four years, he resigned from the bench, reportedly because of his brother's ill health. His departure initiated a chaotic episode in the history of judicial appointments that included four different appointments for two open positions. Following Draper's resignation in January 1955, Governor George N. Craig quickly appointed Isadore E. Levine to fill the vacancy. In less than a month the Court lost another member when Frank E. Gilkison died suddenly. One month later Craig appointed George W. Henley Jr. to fill Gilkison's vacancy. It was widely reported that Craig intended his appointment of Levine and Henley to be interim appointments. Indeed, in April the governor announced the appointment of Norman F. Arterburn to fill Levine's position and Frederick Landis Jr. to fill Henley's position, and in short order Henley and Levine resigned. Two days after the Court ended its term, Arterburn and Landis were sworn in.

For Draper, his role as a judge did not end with his departure from the Court. For three years he engaged in private practice in Gary before retiring, but fate intervened to bring him back to the bench. In 1960 Lake County Criminal Court Judge William J. Murray died in office. Governor Harold W. Handley tapped Draper to fill the vacant position.

Following his stint on the criminal court, Draper retired once again, this time for good. He moved to Bradenton, Florida, where he died on March 20, 1980. The Lake County Bar Association, remembering his willingness to give up his retirement to serve as criminal court judge, said of him: "Whether he did it out of Republican loyalty, he and Handley being GOP activists, or out of a desire to restore more faith to the Lake County judicial system . . . it was the action of a man possessed of a keen sense of duty."

LORENZO ARREDONDO, JD, is judge, Lake County Circuit Court. He is vice chair, Indiana Supreme Court Commission on Race and Gender Fairness, the author of "Combating Stereotypes," *American Judges Association Court Review* (1989), and the coauthor of "The Legacy of Hernandez v. Texas," *University of San Francisco Law Review* (1971).

SELECTED BIBLIOGRAPHY

Adams, Wendy L., and Elizabeth R. Osborn, eds. *In Memoriam: Glimpses from Indiana's Legal Past*. Indianapolis: Indiana Supreme Court, 2006.
Indianapolis Star, March 22, 1980.
Indianapolis Times, April 21, 1952.

CASES CITED
Taylor v. State of Indiana, 233 Ind. 398 (1954).

DAN C. FLANAGAN
April 1, 1953–December 31, 1954

SCOTT M. BUSHNELL

Few Indiana Supreme Court judges have had as varied a career in law and politics as did Fort Wayne's Dan Collins Flanagan, the eighty-third judge to serve on the Court. Lawyer, Republican county chairman, prosecutor, judge, teacher, and author, Flanagan was said to possess a keen understanding of the law and an unusual gift for politics.

The son of a lawyer, Flanagan was born on April 23, 1899, in Lafayette, Indiana. After graduating from the Frankfort public schools, he enlisted in the U.S. Army as the nation entered World War I and rose to the rank of sergeant in the field artillery. His tour of duty included seven months in France, where he served with distinction. Flanagan attended Butler University and the University of California before earning his law degree in 1921 from Benjamin Harrison Law School, which is now the Indiana University School of Law, Indianapolis.

Flanagan opened a solo practice in Frankfort in 1921 and became deputy prosecutor in Clinton County the following year. He moved in 1924 to Fort Wayne, and in 1928 he became Allen County deputy prosecutor. In 1925 he married Mabelle Cass, and they had one son, Dan Jr. During the 1930s Flanagan rose to chairman of the Allen County Republican Central Committee, where he played a significant role in developing one of the strongest Republican organizations in the history of Allen County.

Flanagan was the unsuccessful Republican candidate for judge of the Indiana Appellate court twice in the 1930s before winning election in November 1940 when the Republican slate, led by presidential nominee and Hoosier native Wendell Willkie, was victorious in Allen County. Flanagan was elected by his five fellow judges as chief justice of the appellate court in May 1943 and gained another four-year term in the November 1944 election. It was reported some years later that Flanagan had been the only candidate for the appellate court to be nominated four times by acclamation at the Republican state convention.

In 1949 Flanagan returned to private practice. He began lecturing at Valparaiso University and at the University of Notre Dame and wrote the two-volume *Indiana Trial and Appellate Practice* (1952) with F. Leroy Wiltrout and Frank Hamilton. Flanagan's earlier book, *Indiana Pleading and Procedure* (1947), was said to be "one of the most widely accepted legal works used by practicing attorneys in the state" by the *Fort Wayne Journal-Gazette* on October 8, 1952.

Flanagan's dedication to the practice of law did not diminish his love of politics. He played a pivotal role garnering Midwest support for the presidential candidacy of Dwight D. Eisenhower in 1952, serving as Indiana chairman of the candidate's advisory committee.

Flanagan was appointed to the Court by Governor George N. Craig in April 1953 to complete the term of Paul G. Jasper, who resigned to accept a post as counsel for a public utility. Jasper also hailed from Fort Wayne and had served as the Allen County Democratic chairman a decade after Flanagan had led the county's Republican Committee.

In his final year on the Court, Flanagan served as chief justice before his term ended on December 31, 1954. His opinions were well regarded for their clarity and conciseness. He was not without a "flowery" moment or two in his judgments, however. In one case, *Taylor v. State*, where he ruled in favor of an appellant who claimed to have been denied reasonable promptness in sentencing, Flanagan concluded his opinion: "An American citizen is entitled to live without a Damocles sword dangling over his head." The opinion prompted two other justices to write separate concurring opinions and two others to write separate dissenting opinions, one of whom observed "that the legendary sword which the court has removed from over the heads of culprits now dangles over the heads of our trial judges."

In 1954 Flanagan advised Craig that he did not intend to seek another term on the Court. He returned to private practice and became well known in northeastern Indiana for his willingness to help young attorneys. Flanagan's "keen insight into the law" made him a valuable consultant, the Allen County Bar Association observed in its memorial tribute to him, adding that when Flanagan "appeared in court, the court was always well pleased to see him representing a client inasmuch as he knew that his client would have skilled representation, and that the legal points involved would remain clear-cut."

Flanagan died on February 28, 1960, in Fort Wayne. Although he had been ill for two months, the death of the fifty-nine-year-old was unexpected. He had announced he would seek the Republican nomination for judge on the Allen Circuit Court only a few weeks earlier. "He was a good trial lawyer, an excellent judge, an eloquent orator and a talented writer of clear, readable prose," the *Fort Wayne Journal-Gazette* wrote in its editorial on March 1, 1960.

SCOTT M. BUSHNELL is a former Associated Press writer and editor. He is the author of *Hard News, Heartfelt Opinions: A History of the Fort Wayne Journal-Gazette* (2007), *Historic Photos of Fort Wayne* (2007), *Historic Photos of Indiana* (2010), and coauthor of *Roanoke: The Renaissance of a Hoosier Village* (2003).

SELECTED BIBLIOGRAPHY

Adams, Wendy L., and Elizabeth R. Osborn, eds. *In Memoriam: Glimpses from Indiana's Legal Past*. Indianapolis: Indiana Supreme Court, 2006.
Fort Wayne Journal-Gazette, October 8, 1952, March 1, 1960.

CASES CITED
Taylor v. State, 233 Ind. 398 (1954).

INDIANA SUPREME COURT

HAROLD E. ACHOR
January 3, 1955–December 12, 1966

JOHN R. LEAL

Harold Edward Achor, the eighty-fourth judge of the Indiana Supreme Court, had a legal career that spanned thirty-five years, including ten years in private practice and nearly twenty-five years as a judge on three different courts. Ill health prevented him from serving longer.

He was born in Coffeeville, Kansas, on November 16, 1907, and while he was still an infant his parents moved to Kosciusko County, Indiana. He attended public schools in Atwood and graduated from Indiana Central College, now the University of Indianapolis, in 1928. Three years later he earned a law degree from Indiana University. In 1932 Achor entered private practice in Anderson, while also taking time to teach speech and political science at Anderson College from 1932 to 1937.

Achor took his first step up the judicial ladder in 1942 when he was elected Madison Superior Court judge, a position he held for two terms. He was then elected to the Indiana Appellate court and served a four-year term. In 1954 he was elected to the Indiana Supreme Court. His election occurred in a year in which the Republican Party swept all major offices. Achor had barely begun his term in January 1955 when the Court underwent a rapid turnover in its composition. Floyd S. Draper resigned his seat in January and Frank E. Gilkison died suddenly in February. In March Governor George N. Craig named two interim appointments to the Court to fill these vacancies—Isadore E. Levine and George W. Henley Jr. These two appointees then resigned in May, and in short order Craig appointed Norman F. Arterburn and Frederick Landis Jr. as their replacements.

While Achor was on the Court he commuted from nearby Anderson, where his family lived. During the week, he usually stayed overnight in his private chambers to read briefs scheduled for oral argument. A work day of ten to twelve hours was not unusual for him or his law clerks. Often Achor had his law clerks research and update cases not cited in the briefs which, in his opinion, merited examination for principles of law that he considered might have some bearing on the issues at hand. On cases assigned to him, he asked his law clerks to submit memoranda on the application of "rules of the court" and whether such were followed in order for the court to have proper jurisdiction. Achor further required that all cases cited in the briefs be researched, and he would thereafter scrutinize the cases in order to determine whether or not they had a bearing on the legal issues presented before the Court.

Achor was soft-spoken, considerate, charismatic, had a tenacious grasp of the law, and an excellent memory for cases that upheld certain principles of law. He was always well prepared for oral argument by counsel. Although initially setting counsel at ease, he nonetheless questioned, invariably at great length, to narrow the issues at hand. He held a strong belief that rules of the Court must be followed in order to obtain jurisdiction and to properly present issues to the Court for deliberation. Many cases failed because the rules were not followed. Achor believed that without strict adherence to rules, there could be no orderly administration of justice and that rules exist for the conduct and reliance by society in all walks of life.

To Achor, the rules and evidence went hand in hand. This is illustrated by his majority opinion in one case in particular, which held that the trial court had erred in failing to determine that a defendant was no longer a minor whose parents were obligated to pay for a transcript of the court record for an appeal. The Court ruled that as an indigent adult he was entitled to have a transcript provided for him at public expense and ordered that one be provided. This resulted in the Court granting a rehearing of the case (*State ex rel. Butler v. Allen Superior Court*).

After oral argument, Achor worked undisturbed in his chambers to dictate the first draft of his opinion. He was very particular with his written opinions, which often his secretary retyped until he felt it expressed his true opinion on the issues for consideration before the Court. He wrote a total of 264 opinions.

Court decisions at that time were typically unanimous, but a case that stirred much controversy and produced three separate concurring opinions and a partial dissent illustrates that this was not always true. The case, *State ex rel. Indiana State Bar Association v. Indiana State Real Estate Association*, was initiated by lawyers seeking an injunction against realtors to prevent them from "practicing law" in real estate transactions. The Court granted partial injunctive relief to the lawyers in ruling that only lawyers could execute certain legal documents such as deeds and mortgages. However, the Court also held that it was permissible for real estate brokers and agents to complete certain forms generally used in standard real estate transactions, even if the forms had been created by lawyers. Arterburn wrote a concurring opinion in which he agreed with the Court's interpretation of the law, but took his own profession to task for "bringing an action . . . that was ill-considered from a public relations point of view." He said, "the image of the lawyer is not enhanced by this proceeding." Amos W. Jackson, the Court's only Democrat, wrote a separate opinion in which he concurred in part and dissented in part. His point of disagreement with the Court was with the notion that a hard and fast line could be drawn in a class-action suit to determine which profession was best suited to handle a specific process. Instead, he said, these issues should be determined by the circumstances in each transaction, and should be "resolved by the parties themselves with judgment, good will and a clear and constant regard for the protections of the client."

In his final year on the Court, Achor was frequently absent due to ill health. He worked at home a good deal of the time. He chose not to run for re-election and retired from the Court on December 12, 1966. He died on February 5, 1967, at the age of fifty-nine.

JOHN R. LEAL, JD, is an attorney. He is the author of "Five Questions," an article on end-of-life directives. Leal is past president Fort Wayne Estate Planning Council.

SELECTED BIBLIOGRAPHY

Withered, Jerome L. *Hoosier Justice: A History of the Supreme Court of Indiana.* Indianapolis: Indiana Supreme Court, 1998.

CASES CITED

State ex rel. Butler v. Allen Superior Court, 241 Ind. 627 (1961).

State ex rel. Indiana State Bar Association et al. v. Indiana State Real Estate Association Inc. et al., 244 Ind. 214 (1963).

The author was Achor's law clerk from 1961 to 1962 and included personal reminiscences in the essay.

ISADORE E. LEVINE
January 13, 1955–May 23, 1955

DONALD B. KITE SR.

Isadore Edward Levine was Indiana's first Jewish Supreme Court judge, and while Levine had many roles in his life both before and after his brief service on the Court as its eighty-fifth judge, one constant and important influence throughout his adult life was his involvement with the American Legion.

Levine was born in Michigan City, Indiana, on March 25, 1897, the son of Morris and Dora Wortell Levine. Levine's parents immigrated to England, and ultimately to the United States from Russia or Poland. They resided in New York for a short time before moving to Boston, then to Michigan City. They raised six children, two sons and four daughters. In the 1890s Levine's father started a chain of clothing stores called the Boston Stores (which were so-named because Boston was then a center of the fashion industry). Levine became president of the Boston Stores after the death of his uncle in 1958.

After graduating from high school in Michigan City, Levine received his bachelor's degree from the University of Michigan in 1919, and his law degree from the same institution in 1921. He participated in ROTC in college and was scheduled to go overseas during World War I, but the Armistice was declared before he went. This enabled him to complete his education, and on the day following his graduation from law school he married Rose Anne Hubar of Detroit, Michigan. Levine and his wife had two children, Maurice and Barbara.

Prior to his appointment to the Court, Levine served for twelve years as La Porte County's chief deputy prosecutor. He lost his bid for La Porte County prosecutor in 1932 and an extremely close primary election for La Porte County Circuit judge in 1952. He also had a private law practice both before and after his appointment to the Court with Robert Gettinger, a fellow American Legion member. Levine often returned home from his law practice at the end of the day and announced, "Well kids, I had a good day at the office. I took in a $10 fee, a $5 fee, and couple of small ones."

Levine was a Republican at a time when the state party was split between the Theodore Roosevelt progressives, led by Governor George N. Craig, and the more conservative forces led by Senators William Jenner and Homer E. Capehart. Levine was a big supporter of Craig. Both men had been involved, at the national level, in the affairs of the American Legion. Craig had been the organization's National Commander, and Levine had served as Indiana's representative to the organization's national executive committee for a total of eight years, which at that time was said to be the longest period a Hoosier had served on the committee. Levine was a charter member of a private fund-raising group formed by Craig called the Republican Victory Committee. On January 13, 1955, Craig announced Levine's appointment to the Court. Levine's son said this was the "crowning moment" in his career. The *South Bend Tribune* published a photograph of the jubilant Levine being kissed by his wife just after the swearing-in ceremony. Levine succeeded Floyd S. Draper, whose term was to expire on December 31, 1956.

Newspapers reported that Levine's tenure on the Court was expected to be short, and that he and George W. Henley Jr., who had been appointed to replace Frank E. Gilkison, had only agreed to serve due to the prestige associated with the position. Records of Craig's correspondence verify that the governor viewed the appointments of Levine and Henley as temporary.

The press reported that Levine, unlike Henley, would not say whether his appointment was temporary or whether he would resign, but on May 20, 1955, both men submitted their resignations effective May 23, 1955. According to the family history, Levine resigned from the Court to care for his wife, who was recovering from a massive heart attack. Her physician advised her to return to La Porte from Indianapolis to recover.

During Levine's brief tenure the Court handed down a number of interesting decisions. One example is *Echterling v. Kalvaitis* for which Levine, speaking for a unanimous court, wrote the majority opinion. In *Echterling* the Court applied the doctrine of adverse possession, which recognizes a kind of "squatters' right," allowing an individual who has established himself on someone else's land for an extended period of time to claim legal title to the land. Another interesting case was *Hanley v. State*, which involved a rehearing of a case decided prior to Levine's arrival on the Court. A divided Court determined, both initially and after the case was reargued, that a 1945 state law exempting former members of the U.S. armed forces from paying fees for hunting and fishing licenses was unconstitutional. James A. Emmert wrote a stirring dissent, noting the many sacrifices routinely made by veterans and cautioning that the Court's ruling endangered a number of other veterans' enactments. The Indiana Department of the American Legion had supported the law, and Levine concurred wholeheartedly with Emmert's dissenting opinion.

In addition to his significant involvement in American Legion activities, Levine was president of several civic organizations, including the La Porte Kiwanis Club, the YMCA Board, and the Chamber of Commerce. He was a member of Temple Beth-El in South Bend, several Masonic organizations, the Jewish War Veterans of America, the World War I Barracks, the Greater La Porte Development Corporation, the Elks Lodge, the Little Theatre Club, the Beatty Memorial Hospital Advisory Board, and the Levine Foundation.

Levine served as La Porte County attorney for the Indiana Toll Road Commission, a role that resulted in a La Porte exit being added to the toll road. He was also the La Porte County Rationing Board chairman, and consequently was granted a C designation on his ration card. However, Levine "would not be seen driving" with his C card displayed in his window.

Levine died of a heart attack on April 5, 1963. His funeral included military honors by the American Legion. Levine was survived by his wife and two children and was buried in the B'Nae Zion Jewish Cemetery in La Porte.

Nancy Gettinger, daughter of Levine's longtime law partner, remembered Levine as a kind and generous man who enjoyed smoking cigars and who at Christmas gave Boston Store dresses to her and one of her sisters.

DONALD B. KITE, SR., JD, is a partner with the Indianapolis law firm of Dean-Webster, Wright and Kite, LLP. He is coauthor of *Federal Justice in Indiana: The History of the United States District Court for the Southern District of Indiana* (2007), recipient of Defense Trial Counsel of Indiana Defense Lawyer of the Year Award (2005), and corecipient of the Indianapolis Bar Association's Dr. John Morton Finney Jr. Award for Excellence in Legal education (2007).

SELECTED BIBLIOGRAPHY

Governor Craig to Attorney David W. Dennis, Richmond, Indiana, April 28, 1955. Papers of Governor George Craig, Personal Correspondence, 1954–1955, Indiana State Archives.
Hammond Times, May 7, 1939.
Indianapolis News, January 18, 1955.
La Porte Herald-August, January 13, 1955.
Levine, Maurice G. *The Levine Family of La Porte Story*.
Michigan City News, April 6, 1963.

CASES CITED

Echterling et ux. v. Kalvaitis et ux, 235 Ind. 141 (1955).
Hanley v. State of Indiana, Indiana Department of Conservation et al., 234 Ind. 326 (1955).

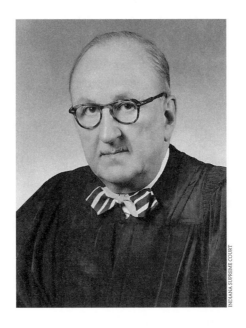

GEORGE W. HENLEY JR.

March 15, 1955–May 23, 1955

COLLEEN KRISTL PAUWELS

Serving only sixty-nine days, George Washington Henley Jr. had the second shortest tenure as a judge of the Indiana Supreme Court. Filling the unexpired term of Judge Frank E. Gilkison, who died in office, Henley accepted the appointment as the Court's eighty-sixth judge with the understanding that it would be for no longer than the remainder of that term of the Court, which was to conclude on May 21, 1955. A director of the Monon Railroad at the time, Henley commented that he was "deeply appreciative of the appointment to the highest court of my state, [but] such a period is far longer than I care to be divorced from a busy and pleasant law practice." Governor George N. Craig said he made the temporary appointment to give himself time to find permanent appointees to the two openings then on the Court.

Earlier that January, Floyd S. Draper of Gary resigned from the Court to return to private practice. When Gilkison died, the Court was no longer able to do its work. This was during a period when the annual salary of the Court judges was $13,500, and the governor remarked that it was difficult to find the "kind of men we want" because of the low pay and need for them to move to Indianapolis.

Henley was born to a prominent Bloomington family with its roots tracing back to colonial days. His ancestors included pioneer stone men in Indiana, a distinguished Civil War captain, and leaders in both the legal and business community in the area. After graduating from Indiana University, his father, George Sr., moved the family to Washington, D.C., to accept an appointment with the U.S. War Department and later a position with the Office of the Surgeon General. While in Washington, George Sr. married Flora Abell of Maryland in 1884, and on May 13, 1890, George Jr. was born. When George Jr. was five years old, the family returned to Bloomington.

Entering Indiana University after attending public schools in Bloomington, Henley graduated with a bachelor's degree in 1913 and a law degree 1914. While at the university, he was a director of the Indiana Union, as well as the Indiana Revue. He was a member of the Phi Delta Phi, a honorary legal fraternity, and the Phi Kappa Psi, a social fraternity. Upon graduation, he began practicing law in Bloomington in the office of his uncle, Joseph Henley. He married Elba Amelia Fickel, an IU classmate, in 1917. They had two daughters.

In 1937 Henley was elected to the Indiana House of Representatives, serving until 1949. In 1943, 1945, and 1947 he was majority leader of the House. He served on the Wendell Willkie Notification Committee in 1945 and was the permanent chairman of the 1946 Republican State Convention.

After serving as the attorney to the IU Board of Trustees beginning on July 1, 1940, Henley was elected by the State Board of Education to the IU Board of Trustees in 1945, serving until 1951.

Through the years, Henley was on the boards of directors for the Monon Railroad, the Indiana Bell Telephone Company, Showers Brothers, Public Service Indiana, and Fagan Brothers Stone Company. He was a member of the Indiana Commission on Interstate Cooperation, the Indiana Legislative Advisory Commission, the National Bill Drafting Committee, and the Council of State Governments.

Active in many area civic organizations, Henley served as president of the Kiwanis Club and was the exalted ruler of the Elks Lodge. In addition, he was a member of the First Methodist Church, Masonic Lodge, Scottish Rite, the Indianapolis Press Club and the James Whitcomb Riley Memorial Association.

Henley died in Bloomington on February 19, 1965 at the age of seventy-three. In a eulogy delivered by Indiana University chancellor, Herman B Wells, he said of Henley: "He was proud of his distinguished pioneer ancestors and quick to acknowledge his debt to them. His position of influence and power was used to further innumerable good causes. By his leadership he made the power structure of the community a beneficent force. As a member of an old and highly respected family, he felt that it was his duty to accept an uncommon amount of civic responsibility. . . . We who had the good fortune to know him will always remember his rare capacity for friendship."

COLLEEN KRISTL PAUWELS, JD, MLS, is associate professor of law and director of the Law Library, Indiana University Maurer School of Law, Bloomington. She is the author of *Hepburn's Dream: The History of the Indiana Law Journal* and coauthor of *Trustees and Officers of Indiana University, 1982 to 2010* (forthcoming) and *Legal Research Today: Traditional Sources, New Technologies.*

SELECTED BIBLIOGRAPHY

Indianapolis Star, March 17 1955.
Indianapolis Times, March 20, 1955.
"Press Release, Death of George W. Henley." News Bureau, Indiana University, February 19, 1965. George W. Henley File, Indiana University Archives, Bloomington, IN.
Roehr, Eleanor L. "George Washington Henley, 1890–1965." *Trustees and Officers of Indiana University 1950 to 1982*. Bloomington: Indiana University, 1983.
Walsh, Justin E., ed. *A Biographical Directory of the Indiana General Assembly, 1900–1984*. 2 vols. Indianapolis: Select Committee on the Centennial History of the Indiana General Assembly, 1984.

FREDERICK LANDIS JR.
May 23, 1955–November 8, 1965

FRANK E. TOLBERT

One might think that the role of a judge of the Indiana Supreme Court was solely the interpretation of the law on the bench, but when Frederick Landis Jr., the eighty-seventh judge to serve on the Court, was still commuting to Logansport in 1960, he detected a northbound speeding trucker on Michigan Road. He pulled him over, identified himself, and slated him in to Monday's 8 a.m. session of the Logansport City Court. The defendant pled "guilty." Justice is a multifaceted thing.

Landis was born on January 17, 1912, into a family of notable individuals. He was the son of Frederick Landis Sr., who served as a congressman, and Bessie Baker Landis. His uncle was the renowned Kenesaw Mountain Landis, whose father lost a leg at the Civil War battle at Kennesaw Mountain, Georgia. He later became a federal district judge in Chicago and baseball's first commissioner in 1921, barring eight Chicago White Sox players for bribery in the famous Black Sox Scandal.

Landis attended high school in Logansport, Indiana, and Great Neck, New York, and then Wabash College before obtaining a bachelor's degree in 1932 and a law degree in 1934 from Indiana University. He was admitted to the Indiana bar in 1934. Landis enlisted in the navy in World War II and rose to the rank of lieutenant. From 1942 to 1946 he was a member of the naval reserve. He married E. Joyce Stevenson on July 4, 1945, and they had five children: Diana, Frederick, Susan, Gilliam, and Kenesaw Mountain Landis III.

Landis had a distinguished political career before his elevation to the Court. He was the prosecuting attorney in Logansport from 1938 to 1940 and also a general practitioner. He was known as a formidable advocate. He served in the Indiana House of Representatives from 1951 to 1953, followed by two full terms in the Indiana Senate. In his first year as a state senator, he received an award from the state, county, and municipal employees "for statesmanship, honesty, and integrity in the Eighty-eighth Indiana General Assembly."

He was a close ally of Governor George N. Craig, who was instrumental in advancing Landis's career in several ways. In 1954 Craig appointed Landis to a blue-ribbon committee to formulate policies on the state level that would conform to recommendations of the national committee on intergovernmental relations. As a senator, Landis participated in Craig's sweeping agenda that included the erection of a state office building and an increase of weekly benefits for workmen's compensation and unemployment. He was instrumental in bringing about passage of a law that resulted in the codification of the state's overlapping, conflicting, and unclear enactments that constituted probate law.

On April 13, 1955, Craig announced his intention to appoint Landis and another Republican, Norman F. Arterburn, to the Court. The handling of these appointments created something of a controversy because of two interim appointments that Craig had made upon the retirement of Floyd S. Draper and Frank E. Gilkison. Craig had appointed Isadore E. Levine to replace Draper and George W. Henley Jr. to replace Gilkison. Although it was widely reported that both judges had agreed to serve only on an interim basis, there are indications that Levine gave up his seat reluctantly. However, he did resign on May 20, 1955, along with Henley, and on May 23, 1955, Landis and Arterburn were sworn in. In 1956 both Landis and Arterburn stood for election and won. With Dwight D. Eisenhower at the top of the ticket it was a banner year for Republicans. The GOP ended up with every seat on the Court. Landis was elected to a second term in 1962.

From 1955 to 1965 Landis participated in more than 1,075 cases and wrote 197 opinions. In terms of political consequences, one of the most significant was *State ex rel. Handley v. the Circuit Court of Marion County*, a case that settled a political conflict within the Republican Party. In 1958 Governor Harold W. Handley announced his intention to seek his party's nomination for the U.S. Senate. His Republican opponent for the nomination sought a judicial remedy to prevent Handley from running because of a state constitutional provision declaring the governor ineligible to run for any other office during his term of office. The Court rendered a per curiam decision on the eve of the party convention declaring Handley eligible to run because the state constitution could not prescribe qualifications for federal offices.

Landis concurred in another case, *Tinder v. Music Operating Co.*, of lasting significance, this one pertaining to gambling. The issue was whether pinball machines were in violation of the prohibition against gambling in the state constitution and the subsequent statutes enacted in pursuance of that prohibition. The Court determined that to the extent that playing pinball machines involved a degree of skill in manipulating the pinball flippers, it entailed more than chance and therefore was not gambling. However, the Court further ruled that playing pinball machines could be considered gambling, and therefore illegal, if a player could exchange free replays for cash or other items. This precedent was used in 1979 to invalidate a state law permitting pari-mutuel horse track betting.

In 1965 Landis resigned his seat on the Court to accept an appointment to the U.S. Court of Customs Appeals. He was recommended for that position by Logansport native Frank McHale, a national Democratic committeeman, who said, in proposing Landis for that position to President Lyndon B. Johnson, that native talent should always overcome party politics. Landis served eighteen years on this court and took senior judge status on December 31, 1983. He died on March 1, 1990, in Carmel, Indiana, and is buried in Logansport.

FRANK E. TOLBERT, LLB, is a partner with Miller, Tolbert, Muelhausen, Muelhausen, Groff and Damm. He is a member of the Cass County U.S. District Court, Seventh Circuit and U.S. Supreme Court bar associations, the Indiana and American Trial Lawyers Association, a fellow of the Indiana Bar Foundation, and a member of the American College of Trial Lawyers and the Cass County and U.S. Supreme Court historical societies.

SELECTED BIBLIOGRAPHY

Withered, Jerome L. *Hoosier Justice: A History of the Supreme Court of Indiana.* Indianapolis: Indiana Supreme Court, 1998.

CASES CITED

State Board of Tax Commissioners, et al. v. Indianapolis Lodge #17, Loyal Order of Moose, Inc., 245 Ind. 614 (1964).
State ex rel. Handley v. the Superior Court of Marion County, etc., 238 Ind. 421 (1958).
Tinder v. Music Operating Inc., 237 Ind. 33 (1957).

NORMAN F. ARTERBURN

May 23, 1955–May 13, 1977

LINDA C. GUGIN

Norman Frank Arterburn often proclaimed that he wanted to be remembered first and foremost as a country lawyer, but he will be remembered for far more than that. The eighty-eighth judge of the Indiana Supreme Court, Artberburn was the first permanent chief justice of Indiana, an outspoken critic of U.S Supreme Court rulings, and the architect of legal and ethical reforms adopted during his tenure as chief justice.

Arterburn was born in Bicknell, Indiana, in 1902. As a young boy he spent Saturday mornings dusting the office of a local lawyer, Curtis G. Shake, who later served as chief justice of the Court. Arterburn graduated cum laude from Indiana University in 1923 and received his law degree from the University of Chicago in 1926. He taught at Washburn University School of Law in Topeka, Kansas, before settling down in Vincennes and later taught part time at the IU School of Law in Bloomington. In 1926 he entered private practice and in 1928 was elected prosecuting attorney for Knox County. Two years later, defeated by the same candidate whom he beat in 1928, he returned to private practice. In 1955 Arterburn began his long judicial career when Governor George N. Craig appointed him to the Court to succeed George W. Henley Jr., who resigned from the Court after serving four months. Arterburn was then elected to the Court in 1956, and reelected every term thereafter.

Prior to 1971 Arterburn served ten terms as chief justice, a position that was rotated among the sitting judges. Then, in 1971, he was selected by the newly established Judicial Nominating Commission to be the first chief justice of Indiana. His selection was the result of a 1970 amendment to the Indiana Constitution (Article 3) that changed the way that the chief justice, as well as justices of the Supreme Court and judges of the court of appeals, are selected and retained. The new title of chief justice of Indiana replaced the title chief justice of the Indiana State Supreme Court. Arterburn's term as chief justice, which began on January 1, 1972, ended on December 1, 1974, but he remained on the bench until May 1977 when he reached the mandatory retirement age of seventy-five. At the time of his retirement, he had served longer than any other member of the Court except for Isaac N. Blackford, the preeminent nineteenth-century jurist.

Artberburn wrote more than one thousand opinions and generally followed a conservative approach to the law. He described himself as a "law and order judge believing in discipline when it comes to the criminal side of the law." For example, in 1972 the Court decided in *State of Indiana v. Robert Lee Dusch et al.*, that as a general rule, when police are serving a search warrant, they must knock and announce the purpose of their entry, except in particular circumstances. The opinion overturned the conviction of the defendant in the case. The majority opinion cited a U.S. Supreme Court ruling as the basis of its decision. In a stinging dissent, Arterburn said that he found nothing in the constitution that requires police to knock before entering with a search warrant. "The interest of society in the prevention of crime is too great to free guilty persons on such trivialities," he said.

Arterburn did not always rule against the defendant. In 1973 he wrote the majority opinion in *Harry Adams v. State of Indiana*, reversing the conviction of a defendant who was found guilty on the basis of bullet fragments surgically removed from his body and used as evidence against him. Arterburn said the intrusion was of "the most serious magnitude" and that the Court "could not sanction a surgical operation forced on the defendant for this purpose."

In 1972, dutifully following a U.S. Supreme Court ruling in *Furman v. Georgia* that the death penalty as practiced throughout the states at that time was unconstitutional, Arterburn wrote the unanimous decision in *Charles Wayne Adams v. State of Indiana* declaring that the Indiana death penalty statute was unconstitutional. His opinion bemoaned the lack of standards established by the U.S. Supreme Court for determining when the death penalty might be constitutional. Just five years later, Arterburn was forced once again to declare in *Lester French v. State of Indiana* that a new death penalty statute passed by the general assembly in 1973 was unconstitutional. He made it clear he did not agree with the U.S. Supreme Court's reasoning but that he "had taken an oath to support the Constitution as interpreted by that Court" and therefore had no alternative but to declare the state statute unconstitutional.

Arterburn developed a reputation over the years for his sharp public criticism of rulings by the U.S. Supreme Court, which he claimed were responsible for coddling criminals and increasing crime rates. He even presented a resolution to the Annual Conference of Chief Justices chastising the Court for transgressing sound legal principles and usurping fact-finding functions in the weighing of evidence in certain cases. He also proposed a constitutional amendment to establish a Court of Constitutional Definition with the authority to decide questions of constitutional interpretation that the U.S. Supreme Court would have to rely on in its rulings.

A self-described conservative Republican, Arterburn had been active in Republican Party politics prior to his Court tenure. Partisan interest was an issue in one of his most noted opinions, which declared that vetoes cast by Democratic governor Matthew E. Welsh were invalid because he failed to take action within the specified amount of time allotted by the constitution. At issue was whether the legislature was technically still in session during a special session. Welsh argued that it was not. Arterburn and the two other Republicans on the Court ruled in *Hendricks v. Northwest Indiana Crime Commission, Inc.* that it was, giving the governor an opportunity to return the bill to the legislature. The decision meant that the vetoes were invalid, and the two pieces of legislation favored by the Republican legislature—a reapportionment bill and a bill providing for special prosecutors—were valid laws.

Arterburn is credited with helping to bring about important legal and ethical reforms. He participated in the expansion of the Court's authority over local trial courts as well as the expansion of the court of appeals and its jurisdiction. He was instrumental in improving the standards for the education and examination of candidates for admission to the law profession and in establishing effective procedures for disciplining lawyers who did not measure up to standards of the legal profession. He also was a strong advocate for Vincennes University and significantly boosted its fate in a 1970 opinion that ruled it was a part of the state educational system, making it eligible for state funding. He received an honorary degree from VU in 1971.

Arterburn married Lois Richards in 1926, and they had four daughters—Joan, Joyce (deceased), Linda, and Faith. In 1971 he married Loretta Vieck. He died February 10, 1979, in Fort Meyers, Florida, and was buried in Vincennes.

LINDA C. GUGIN, PhD, is professor emeritus of political science, Indiana University Southeast. She is coauthor of *Sherman Minton: New Deal Senator, Cold War Justice* (1997) and *Chief Justice Fred M. Vinson of Kentucky: A Political Biography* (2002), coeditor of *The Governors of Indiana* (2006) and *Justices of the Indiana Supreme Court* (2010), and author of "Sherman Minton: Restraint against a Tide of Activism," *Vanderbilt Law Review* (2009).

SELECT BIBLIOGRAPHY

Arterburn Family Scrapbook. Loaned to the author by Mrs. Loretta Arterburn Holl.
"Judge Norman F. Arterburn." *Knox County History*. Vincennes: Vincennes Historical Society and Antiquarian Society in cooperation with Turner Publishing Company, 1988.
Louisville Courier-Journal, May 15, 1977.
Norman F. Arterburn Papers. Lewis Historical Collections Library. Vincennes University. Vincennes, Indiana.
Vincennes Sun-Commercial, January 1, 1977.

CASES CITED

Charles Wayne Adams v. State of Indiana, 259 Ind. 164 (1972).
Furman v. Georgia, 409 U.S. 902 (1972).
Harry Adams v. State of Indiana, 260 Ind. 663 (1973).
Hendricks, Secretary of State of Indiana v. State ex rel. Northwest Indiana Crime Commission, Inc. et al., 245 Ind. 43 (1964).
Lester French v. State of Indiana, 266 Ind. 276 (1977).
State of Indiana v. Robert Lee Dusch et al., 259 Ind. 507 (1972).

AMOS W. JACKSON
January 5, 1959–January 4, 1971

GEORGE T. PATTON JR.

Amos Wade Jackson, the eighty-ninth judge of the Indiana Supreme Court, represented the end of an era on the Court in several important ways. He was the last person to serve on the Court with out attending law school. He also retired from the bench in 1970, the year the voters of Indiana approved the constitutional amendment that replaced partisan elections with a merit system for selecting justices, coupled with nonpartisan retention elections. Had Jackson chosen to run again in 1970, he would have participated in the last election based on partisan judicial ballots. A change in the titles of Court members from judge to justice was also ushered in by this judicial reform amendment.

Jackson was born on June 25, 1904, in Ripley County, Indiana. He graduated from Versailles High School and then attended Hanover College. In his senior year in college he became a member of the Ripley County bar.

He graduated from Hanover with a bachelor's degree in June 1926. He and his father formed a partnership in the general practice of law in Versailles under the name of Jackson and Jackson that continued for more than fifty years. They also operated Jackson and Jackson Abstract Company.

On August 20, 1927, Jackson married Lola M. Raper, with whom he had two daughters. He became president of the Bank of Versailles, and served as prosecuting attorney for Ripley County from 1937 to 1940. Later, he was a county probation officer leading him to advocate for prison and penal reform, and these sympathies were often reflected in his opinions. Jackson served as an associate attorney for the U.S. War Department during 1942 and 1943. He was a member of the Ripley County Selective Service Board during 1952.

Jackson was an outdoorsman who enjoyed boating and fishing in Indiana and Kentucky. He was a member of the National Rifle Association and frequently wrote members of Congress against efforts to impose gun control. He played a part in the creation of Versailles State Park, served as secretary of the Ripley County Park Board, and was a member of the Southeastern Indiana Park Association.

In 1958 Jackson won election as a Democrat to the Court by beating the venerable incumbent James A. Emmert. Jackson was the lone Democrat on the high bench until 1963, when Walter Myers Jr. joined the Court. Jackson wrote 245 opinions, with his first being on January 29, 1959, and his last on December 31, 1970. His opinions were direct, concise, and to the point.

The case of Robert John Dowlut is a good example of Jackson's work. In 1963 the police, without a warrant, arrested the seventeen-year-old Dowlut at the home of his parents in South Bend. At the police station they interrogated him about the murder of Anna Marie Yocum. The police did not advise Dowlut of his constitutional rights, refused his request to call an attorney, and precluded him from talking to his father. He was interrogated over a two-day period. They told him that his father's gun was used in the shooting and unless he confessed his father would go to prison or even the electric chair. Pressured to confess by these tactics, Dowlut finally told them that the gun was buried in a cemetery. There the police took pictures of him digging up the gun and holding it.

At trial, Dowlut's counsel moved to suppress the evidence based on violations of procedural rights guaranteed under the Indiana and United States constitutions. The trial court denied the motion. A jury convicted Dowlut of murder, and he was sentenced to prison for life. His attorney appealed.

Writing for the Court in *Robert John Dowlut v. State of Indiana*, Jackson said: "The record in this case is so voluminous, consisting of two volumes of transcript and eight briefs that only the bare essentials necessary for consideration in this appeal can be touched upon." Jackson addressed only the motion to suppress: "The record clearly shows that all of the evidence [Dowlut] sought to have suppressed was obtained as a result of an unlawful incarceration." Jackson reversed the ruling on the motion to suppress and remanded the case for a new trial. Dowlut was never retried.

An example of Jackson's sympathy for prison and penal reform can be found in an opinion written near the end of his tenure in *Anthony Edward Graham v. State of Indiana*. Graham was convicted for attempting to cash a stolen check for $145 at a liquor store. The offense carried a possible prison term of from two to fourteen years with a fine of no less than ten dollars nor more than one thousand dollars. After conviction, Graham challenged on appeal the sufficiency of the evidence. Jackson had little trouble rejecting this claim, but he wrote that he wanted "to call attention to a fact that should be given attention by the legislature." The penalty was what Jackson addressed:

> At the last account, the end of the 1969–70 fiscal year, it cost the State of Indiana approximately six dollars and six cents per day to maintain an inmate in the state prison. Assuming an inmate sentenced . . . serves the minimum sentence of two years, with no time off for good behavior, he has cost the taxpayers of the state directly the sum of $4,423.80; this at a time when our penal institutions are over-crowded, under-staffed, inadequately equipped, and utterly failing their assigned role of rehabilitating the inmate. In addition to the direct cost, if the inmate be a married man with a family, the day the prison doors open to admit him, the doors to the welfare office in the county of his residence must of necessity open to his wife as a welfare recipient in order that she may be sure her family is housed, fed, and clothed until her husband's return.

The penalty for this nonviolent crime was greater than the penalty for assault and battery with intent to commit a felony. Jackson suggested that the severity of the penalty could violate protections in both the Indiana and U.S. constitutions against cruel and unusual punishment.

Jackson finished his second six-year term on the Court during 1970 in poor respiratory health. He passed away on September 30, 1972, in King's Daughters Hospital in Madison, Indiana.

GEORGE T. PATTON JR., JD, is cochair Appellate Services Group, Bose McKinney and Evans LLP, Indianapolis/Washington, D.C. He is a former law clerk for Chief Justice Randall T. Shepard (1987–89). Patton is the author of "Political Pragmatism and Common Sense: Leading Cases of the Indiana Supreme Court," in *The History of Indiana Law* (2006) and *Indiana Practice: Appellate Procedure* (West Group 2001 and 2009 Supp.).

SELECTED BIBLIOGRAPHY

"Obituary of Amos W. Jackson." *Res Gestae,* 17 (1972).

CASES CITED

Dowlut v. State of Indiana, 250 Ind. 86 (1968).
Graham v. State of Indiana, 255 Ind. 237 (1970).

The personal papers of Amos W. Jackson are at the Indiana State Library Indiana Division, Manuscripts Section, Indianapolis.

WALTER MYERS JR.
January 7, 1963–June 2, 1967

THOMAS E. WHEELER II

Walter Myers Jr., the ninetieth judge of the Indiana Supreme Court, was a Renaissance man. Myers was offered a scholarship to the Herron School of Art in Indianapolis while in eighth grade. He enjoyed drawing charcoal sketches and painting in oils and was described by his brother as "quite an accomplished cartoonist." In addition to being an artist, Myers also enjoyed music, both classical and modern, and was actively involved with the Indianapolis Symphony.

Born on June 9, 1914, Myers was a lifelong resident of Indianapolis and joined a family of prominent attorneys devoted to public service. His father was a former Speaker of the Indiana General Assembly, assistant U.S. postmaster general, and practiced law in Indianapolis for more than sixty years. His younger brother, Joseph, was a judge on the Marion County Municipal Court for thirty-five years, and his maternal grandfather was a judge in

Virginia. Myers was a devoted family man. He married Jane Weldon Kinghan on November 26, 1952, and had a son, Dennis, and a stepson, John R. Kinghan.

Myers attended public schools in Indianapolis and was the pitcher for the Shortridge High School city championship softball team. He graduated from Shortridge in 1931, after just three and a half years. After high school, he followed his father to Yale University, where he received an undergraduate degree in 1935 and a law degree in 1938. During his junior year at Yale, Myers missed one-half of the school year due to a ruptured appendix. Despite this he was able to graduate on time with his classmates and in the top 10 percent of his class. The numerous surgeries that Myers had as a result of his ruptured appendix precluded him from serving in the military during World War II, but he was active in bond drives and various other home-front activities.

After his graduation from Yale in 1938, Myers returned to Indianapolis and began practicing with his father at the firm of Myers and Smith. He later practiced with the firm of Myers, Northam and Myers. James Northam was married to Myers's sister, Katharine. Like his father, Myers was actively involved in Democratic politics, serving as precinct committeeman, ward chairman, and eventually Marion County chairman. Longtime Congressman Andrew Jacobs Jr. credits Myers, when he was Marion County Democratic Chair, with getting him his first job as a deputy at the Marion County Jail. Myers also served as deputy prosecuting attorney under Indianapolis mayor Al Feeney.

Myers's first foray into the electoral process was a run for a seat on the Superior Court of Marion County in 1952, but he was defeated. He was also unsuccessful in his bid for the Marion County Circuit Court four years later, being defeated by Judge John Niblack in the 1956 election. Undeterred, he ran for and was elected to the Indiana Court of Appeals in 1958, serving as presiding judge for the May 1959 term and chief judge for the November 1959 term. He was a member of the appellate court until his election to the Indiana Supreme Court in 1962.

He was elected to a six-year term to replace Arch N. Bobbitt, who had received negative publicity for his decision regarding the constitutional limitation on the ability of cities to issue bonds for construction projects. Myers began serving on January 7, 1963. Although very active in partisan politics,

Myers was frequently described as a "truly friendly man" who "genuinely liked people." He was nonpartisan in the discharge of his judicial duties and "demonstrated keenness of intellect, a sound understanding of the law, and an ability of expression which has been of great assistance" to his fellow judges and the attorneys who practiced before him. He maintained friendships with people from diverse backgrounds and cultivated these friendships during his tenure on the bench. As a judge, he was focused on promoting efficiency in the courts through modernizing the manner in which they did business.

Myers also had a keen interest in service to his community, acting as a member of the Pentalpha Masonic Lodge, Scottish Rite, Murat Shrine, and the Tau Kappa Epsilon fraternity. He was also a member and president of the Board of Managers for the YMCA Central Branch and served on the Board of the Marion County Tuberculosis Association. He took great pride in his service on the board of the Suemma Coleman Home and was very active in advocating the adoption of orphaned children. Myers and his wife were also heavily involved in the parish life at Second Presbyterian Church, where he served as an elder.

After a lengthy illness, Myers passed away on June 2, 1967, just four years into his six-year term on the Court. Governor Roger D. Branigin appointed David M. Lewis of Indianapolis, a former Marion County Prosecutor and unsuccessful 1940 gubernatorial candidate, to serve the remainder of Myers's term.

THOMAS E. WHEELER II, JD, is a member, Frost Brown Todd LLC. He is an author/ speaker on the subjects of civil rights and constitutional law. Wheeler is a two-time winner of the Indiana State Bar Association's Benjamin Harrison Writing Award and a winner of the Burton Award for Legal Achievement cosponsored by the Library of Congress for his article "Slamming in Cyberspace: The Boundaries of Student 1st Amendment Rights"(2003).

SELECTED BIBLIOGRAPHY

Adams, Wendy L., and Elizabeth R. Osborn, eds. *In Memoriam: Glimpses from Indiana's Legal Past,* Indianapolis: Indiana Supreme Court, 2006.

J. N. Meyers to Chief Justice Richard M. Givan. October 19, 1978. On file in the Indiana Supreme Court Library.

RAKESTRAW FAMILY COLLECTION

FREDERICK E. RAKESTRAW
January 7, 1966–January 2, 1967

DOUGLAS B. MORTON

As Indiana's ninety-first judge, Frederick Eugene Rakestraw served only 360 days, the fifth-shortest term in the Indiana's Supreme Court history. Having been appointed by Governor Roger D. Branigin early in 1966, he had to stand for election the following November. In losing that election, he became the last victim of Indiana's system of popularly elected judges and the poster boy for merit selection on the high court.

Born in Lima, Ohio, on August 29, 1923, his parents divorced just before the birth of his third sister when he was only five. Rakestraw was always a capable student, excelling at extemporaneous speaking. In his senior year of high school his debate team won the Ohio state championships.

In 1941 Rakestraw attended Manchester College, completing two years before he was called for military duty. He served in the Signal Corp in the European theater. While his unit was ostensibly in charge of storage of communications gear, much of his service time was actually spent supervising German prisoners of war. He attained the rank of staff sergeant. He later commented that he could not understand how the United States had won the war in the face of the overwhelming incompetence that he saw.

On December 25, 1943, while on leave, Rakestraw married Wilodean (Billie) Weimer. He returned home in January of 1946 and began his legal studies, completing five years of combined college and law school in just three and a half years. He received his bachelor's degree from Indiana University at Bloomington in 1947 and his law degree in 1949. He was admitted to the bar that same year.

Rakestraw began the private practice of law in Akron, Indiana, where he joined a firm operated by William Deniston. As a Democrat in a heavily Republican area, Rakestraw was defeated for Fulton County prosecutor in 1952 by his future law partner, Lawrence Brown. In 1954, however, he was elected circuit court judge, defeating the two-term incumbent. He became the first Democrat elected to any position in Fulton County in eighteen years. Reelected in 1960, he served as circuit court judge until 1965.

While Rakestraw was on the trial court bench, he and his wife suffered an event that would terrify the family of any public servant. One morning while walking to school, their daughter, Lynne, was taken at knifepoint by a deranged man who thought that this was the only way to force others to listen to him. The abductor offered to trade her for the prosecutor, who had been notified and was on his way to the house where she was being held before a relative of the abductor negotiated Lynne's release. Lynne was unharmed and the entire event was over before Rakestraw knew it was occurring.

As a rising star in the Democratic Party, Rakestraw was selected as the nominee for the Supreme Court in 1962 but lost in what proved to be a Republican year. The political landscape changed, however, when Branigin was elected governor in the Democratic landslide of 1964, and Frederick Landis Jr. of Logansport resigned from the Court in late 1965 to accept a federal position on the Court of Customs. Rakestraw, from the same geographic area as Landis, was one of the few serious contenders for the position. He claimed that he was appointed because he happened to be in Indianapolis and inquired about the position at the right time.

During his service on the Court, Rakestraw quickly built a reputation as one of its most productive members. He served six months as chief justice, due to regular rotation of that office. He penned forty-seven majority opinions, two concurring opinions, and two dissenting opinions. Most prominently, he authored *Elder v. Fisher*, a well-reasoned opinion that applied common law principles of concurrent liability and ruled that a pharmacy that sold liquor to a seventeen-year-old could be held responsible when the boy became intoxicated, drove, and caused an accident that left a young girl a paraplegic. Until Rakestraw's opinion, the proximate cause of an intoxicated person causing injury was always the consumption of the alcohol by that person. The *Elder* opinion eventually led to the passage of Indiana's Dram Shop Act, over which the general assembly had previously been deadlocked.

Rakestraw won the Democratic nomination for re-election in 1966, but in the Republican rout that year Donald R. Mote was swept into office and Rakestraw swept out. Feeling the obligation to complete the term of office for which he had been appointed, Rakestraw was the only Court member in the building on December 31, 1966, when the Democratic Party sought a stay order on the election recounts demanded by Republicans over extremely close races for the Marion County Council. Rakestraw not only declined to make the political decision that his party leaders asked of him, he also commented unfavorably on the propriety of the request. His last judicial act thus impressed courtwatchers with its obvious high ethical standard and favorably impressed Republican observers, but it damaged his chances for further Democratic Party support.

He was passed over for appointment in 1968 when Mote died, and in 1970 he sought and was denied the nomination of his party. This saga was a setting for the ongoing discussions of amending the Indiana Constitution to remove Supreme Court judges from the ballot and was one of the compelling arguments supporting a change to merit selection instead of popular election.

At the age of forty-three Rakestraw returned to private practice. In 1967 he joined in partnership with Albert Chipman and future Court of Appeals judge Eugene Chipman. In 1971 he formed a new partnership with Jesse and Lawrence Brown in Rochester, where he continued to practice until his retirement in 2002.

A father of five, Rakestraw remained involved in his community through his church, as Kiwanis District lieutenant governor, and as Democratic county chairman. Rakestraw also remained active with the bar association through various committees that pertained to rules of professional conduct. He was elected a Fellow of the Indiana Bar and the American Bar Foundations. In 1999 he was the recipient of the Indiana State Bar Association's Golden Career Award.

Rakestraw died August 18, 2004, after a period of declining health. He is buried in Rochester. The Fulton County Community Foundation annually gives scholarships in his name to area students attending law schools.

DOUGLAS B. MORTON, JD, was judge, Fulton Circuit Court 1979–2008, and is now senior judge. In 2001 he was the winner of the Kinsey Award for Juvenile Judge service and from 1994 to 2008 appeared as a regular guest on WROI's Legal Program.

SELECTED BIBLIOGRAPHY

Chipman, Eugene N., Sr. Memorial Resolution for the Fulton County Bar Association, Courtroom Memorial Service, August 20, 2004. In author's possession.
Rakestraw, Wilodean. Interviews with the author. June–September, 2008.
Ted A. Wagoner to the Dean of the Indiana Law School, February 17, 1999. Nomination of Frederick E. Rakestraw for the Alumni Fellow Award. In author's possession.

CASES CITED

Elder v. Fisher etc., 247 Ind. 598 (1966).

The author enjoyed a long personal and professional friendship with Rakestraw and included personal reminiscences in the essay.

DONALD R. MOTE
January 1, 1967–September 17, 1968

DONALD J. MOTE

Donald Roosevelt Mote was a small-town farm boy who rose from the fields of Randolph County to become the ninety-second judge of the Indiana Supreme Court over the course of a forty-year legal career. His term on the Court was cut short when he died from cancer at the age of sixty-eight.

Mote was born in Crete, Indiana, on April 23, 1900, the son of Oliver P. and Emma A. Mote. He attended Spartanburg High School and began undergraduate studies at DePauw University in 1919. During the previous year, however, a coal strike caused a fuel famine, and DePauw faced having to close its doors. Mote was among 150 male students who answered a call from the school to assist in cutting wood for a day in order to keep the doors of the school open. The men worked all day, and by nightfall they had cut and corded more than a 150 cords of wood. Their efforts, along with a coal preservation policy implemented by the administration, permitted the university to keep its doors open.

For reasons unknown, Mote transferred to Wabash College in Crawfordsville, Indiana, for his senior year of undergraduate study. A varsity letterman in football, Mote played left tackle for Wabash and was described as, "a bit light for the line, but makes up what he lacks in weight, with speed and fight." Mote was required to take one course at Wabash in the fall of 1924 in order to complete his credit hours and received his degree in June 1924.

In January 1924, before receiving his degree from Wabash, Mote enrolled in the George Washington University Law School in Washington, D.C., then known as the National Law School. In Washington he worked for Herbert Hoover, then the U.S. Secretary of Commerce, and was also a pardon deputy at the U.S. Department of Justice. During his first year of study, Mote held both jobs and worked nights. Unfortunately, he fell ill and was unable to continue his studies at George Washington.

In 1926 Mote returned to Indianapolis to continue his legal career. On June 30, 1927, he was admitted to the practice of law in the Marion Circuit Court. During his time in Indianapolis, Mote worked with Judge Milton B. Hottel, former member of Indiana Court of Appeals, and they later formed the firm Hottel, Mote and Smith, which specialized in probate and insurance law. Mote's work with Hottel is said to have stimulated his interest in the appellate bench.

Mote became active in Republican politics in Indianapolis. He served as a Republican precinct committeeman, and for a time, before entering private practice, was employed as a deputy to then Indiana Attorney General Arthur Gilliam. Mote continued to practice law in the city for ten years.

In the spring of 1932, Mote became engaged to Flora Hunter of Indianapolis. In one instance his devotion to the law came to odds with his devotion to those he loved. Two days before his scheduled wedding to Flora, Mote traveled to New Albany for a hearing in federal court. After waiting all day he was dismayed to learn that his case would be carried over to the following morning. He wrote to his fiancée that his return might be delayed. Although he tried to reassure her that he would arrive in time for the rehearsal, he told her that if he did not, "perhaps you had better go ahead and then tell me just what I have to do." Mote did make it back in time, and he and Flora were married on April 20, 1932. The couple had two children, Virginia and Thomas.

In 1937 Mote moved to Manchester, where he continued to practice law for twenty-one years. In 1958 he moved, once again, to Wabash, and started a practice with Merl M. Wall. Later he joined in a practice with Robert F. Gonderman and William H. Tallman. Mote remained politically active, serving as chair of the Wabash County Republican Finance Committee, and in 1960, as an alternate delegate to the Republican National Convention. He also served as the Wabash county attorney from 1957 to 1962. He enjoyed spending his spare time at the Wabash Country Club or playing gin rummy at the Elks Club. Deeply religious, Mote regularly attended church.

In the fall of 1962, Mote ran for the Indiana Appellate court under the campaign slogan, "Vote for Mote." He was elected and later praised for his work on that court. It was said of Mote, "As a member of the Appellate court of Indiana, he proved himself well qualified for the position. He was diligent in his work, aggressive in the presentation of his views, and his opinions were logical and well-written."

Mote served on the Court of Appeals until he was elected to the Supreme Court in 1966, defeating incumbent Frederick E. Rakestraw by a margin of nearly 115,000 votes. At the time he joined the Court, Mote was suffering from cancer. Despite his illness, he was a prolific writer and staunchly supported his positions through many dissenting opinions. Not long after his election to the Court, Mote was hospitalized for further treatment, where he continued to write opinions from his hospital bed. The Wabash County Bar Association later described Mote as "a person of strong convictions and always fought vigorously for the principles in which he believed, even though the position he took was at the time an unpopular one."

On September 17, 1968, Mote lost his battle with cancer. A memorial service was held prior to Mote's funeral in the Wabash Circuit Courtroom. Dignitaries from the Indiana Supreme and Appellate courts, the Indiana Bar Association, and several other bar associations were in attendance. Indiana Chief Justice David M. Lewis eulogized Mote as a "studious guardian of the law." Alluding to his cancer, Lewis said, "If you all knew the great effort Judge Mote made to serve as judge at the time of his suffering, it would be complete testimony to a fine gentleman."

DONALD J. "D.J." MOTE, JD, is chief deputy prosecutor, Jefferson County, Indiana (2007–present). He was deputy prosecutor, Marion County Homicide Division (2006), deputy district attorney, Arapahoe County, Colorado (2005), deputy prosecutor, Marion County (2000–04), and staff attorney, Indiana Supreme Court Disciplinary Commission (1998–2000).

SELECTED BIBLIOGRAPHY

Adams, Wendy L., and Elizabeth R. Osborn, eds. *In Memoriam: Glimpses from Indiana's Legal Past*. Indianapolis: Indiana Supreme Court, 2006.
The Bachelor (Wabash College), November 24, 1923.
The Mirage (DePauw University), 1920.
Donald R. Mote to Flora Hunter, April 18, 1932.

INDIANA SUPREME COURT

DAVID M. LEWIS
June 21, 1967–January 6, 1969

STEPHEN A. CLAFFEY

David Meriwether Lewis, a third-generation nephew of the historic explorer Meriwether Lewis, made history in his own right throughout a distinguished career as an Indiana trial lawyer, a prosecutor, a bar association leader, and his relatively brief service as the ninety-third judge of the Indiana Supreme Court.

Born March 15, 1909, to Frank T. and Ann McLeod Lewis, he was raised on a farm in Lawrence just outside Indianapolis. Lewis graduated from Lawrence High School, and then earned his way through DePauw University by running his own pig farm, rather than accepting family financial support. Following graduation from DePauw, he received a law degree in 1932 from the University of Chicago, graduating with honors. After a brief stint practicing law in Chicago, Lewis returned to Indianapolis, where he remained throughout his legal career.

Lewis became a prominent Democrat at a young age, and remained active in politics throughout his adult life. He was elected Marion County prosecutor in 1938 at the age of twenty-nine, making him one of the youngest lawyers to be elected to that prominent position. During his two-year term as prosecutor, he was elected president of the Indiana Prosecuting Attorneys Association. He also ran unsuccessfully for the Democratic Party nomination for governor in 1940. He served two terms in the mid-1940s as an Indiana state election commissioner, and an eight-month term in 1952 as Marion County Democratic Party chairman. He served as vice president of the Indianapolis Bar Association in 1956 and president in 1958.

Lewis was a respected, seasoned, and successful trial lawyer and a Fellow of the American College of Trial Lawyers. His private practice covered general civil and criminal law, as lawyers in that time rarely specialized. Nonetheless, having gained considerable trial experience as Marion County prosecutor, in his private practice he tried a number of highly publicized criminal cases, including the successful defense of two individuals charged in connection with a sensationalized alleged bribery of state highway officials. Colleagues said he "relishe[d] most a difficult criminal case."

On June 21, 1967, Governor Roger D. Branigin appointed Lewis to the Indiana Supreme Court to complete the term of Judge Walter Myers Jr., who died earlier that month. Myers was chief justice at the time of his death, so Lewis became chief justice of the Court. This was not an easy role to fill, for there were three Republican judges and two Democrats then serving and a substantial backlog of undecided cases. Lewis took the lead in clearing the backlog, and privately to his family he said the elimination of the backlog was his most satisfying achievement while on the Court.

The Court handed down 365 reported decisions during Lewis's term, of which he authored ninety-one. This production of decisions was a major feat considering that Judge Donald R. Mote was ill during a significant part of the Lewis's short term, and it was long before word processors and computer research tools.

On the bench Lewis shied away from enforcing strict compliance with technical appellate rules, where the violation had not prejudiced the fairness of the appeal and especially if the consequence of requiring adherence was that a lawyer would be at risk of malpractice or loss of face with a client. He reminded his clerks of the difficulties that confronted lawyers in trying to make a living in private practice.

Harris v. YWCA of Terre Haute, which abolished the common law doctrine of charitable immunity in Indiana, is considered by some historians to be Lewis's most notable opinion. This doctrine, which now seems antiquated, gave charitable organizations immunity from tort liability. The Indiana decision was not, however, a cutting-edge judicial decree, as the Indiana Supreme Court joined the wave of other state courts striking down the immunity defense, with ultimately all but a few states rejecting the defense.

Lewis enjoyed telling his law clerks at the Court about strategies he used in various trials. One recounting that he told with obvious glee was of his closing argument in a civil trial where a policeman, whom Lewis was defending, was accused of viciously and repeatedly striking the plaintiff with his police baton. Lewis secreted a police baton under his jacket during his closing statement, took it out without warning, and struck the rail of the jury box. He exclaimed as he did so that he was striking that rail just as the plaintiff claimed he was struck by the officer. With an explosion of sound and flying wood from the blows, the old jury box rail splintered into countless pieces. Lewis then turned to the jury and quietly observed that the plaintiff would be at the mortuary and not in the court room if his story was true. The policeman was found not guilty. The trial judge gave Lewis a private chewing out. According to Lewis, the judge was not upset about the damages or the outcome, but was unhappy about not having been warned of the stunt. The judge told Lewis that he was as shocked as the jurors were when Lewis attacked the rail.

Known for his personal warmth and easygoing personality, Lewis was uncomfortable being called Judge or Justice Lewis while sitting on the Court or following his retirement. He was, by his preference, called "Dave" by his colleagues and fellow lawyers.

Lewis chose not to stand for election to the Court when his term ended, and he retired from the bench on January 6, 1969. He returned to his private law practice, from which he retired three years later. Lewis died on September 24, 1985, having completed an active and diverse life of political, governmental, and professional service. He was survived by his wife, Elizabeth (Betty) Lapp Lewis, and three sons, David M. Jr. and twins, Frank T. and Charles Stanford.

STEPHEN A. CLAFFEY, JD, is a partner with Baker and Daniels, LLP. He is a former law clerk for Chief Justice David M. Lewis and the author of numerous articles for attorneys on commercial law, creditor's rights, and financial restructuring topics.

SELECTED BIBLIOGRAPHY

Indianapolis News, November 6, 1965.
Indianapolis Star, September 25, 1985.

CASES CITED

Harris v. YWCA of Terre Haute, 250 Ind. 491 (1968).

The author was a law clerk for Lewis and drew upon his personal reminiscences in preparing this essay.

DONALD H. HUNTER
January 2, 1967–September 6, 1985

SARAH M. FRANK

Donald Herbert Hunter, the ninety-fourth judge of the Indiana
Supreme Court, was one of a few judges to serve on all levels of the judiciary, and he presided on the bench for thirty-seven years before he reached
the mandatory retirement age. Hunter was a leading proponent of judicial
reform and modernization of the Indiana courts. At the time of his election
to the Court, there was much debate about a proposed amendment to the
Indiana Constitution that would dramatically change the method by which
members of the appellate courts were chosen. The amendment removed
judges from partisan elections, and instead provided for appointment by
the governor, subject to approval of retention votes every ten years. Hunter
strongly supported this amendment, as he thought it would remove judges
from political pressure and bring more respect to the judiciary. The amendment was approved by the voters in 1970. Hunter was the first member of

the Court to appear on a statewide ballot for retention in 1972, and then to serve a ten-year term under the new amendment. He was approved for a second ten-year term in 1982, but he retired in 1985 when he reached the mandatory retirement age of seventy-five.

Hunter was a true Hoosier and a World War II hero, as well as an outstanding jurist. He was born in Anderson, Indiana, on October 21, 1911, and graduated from Anderson High School. He then worked his way through Lincoln Law School in Indianapolis and received his law degree in 1937. Hunter soon began his private practice in Lagrange and also served as deputy attorney general. From 1943 to 1944 he served one term in the Indiana House of Representatives.

Hunter joined the army in 1943, was trained as a combat medic, and served on the front lines in Europe. He showed his courage during the battle for the bridge at Remagen, Germany, the only bridge remaining over the Rhine River in 1945. The American army was attempting to cross this bridge while the German army was told to hold the bridge at all costs or to destroy it. Many soldiers did not make it across, but Hunter did. He was awarded many honors for his wartime valor, including the Combat Infantry Badge, the Combat Medic Badge, five Campaign Stars, the Bronze Star, and the Purple Heart. The Belgian government awarded him the Belgique Four-ragere.

When Hunter returned to Indiana, he resumed his legal career. He was elected judge of the Lagrange Circuit Court, where he served for fourteen years from 1948 through 1962. He was elected to the Indiana Appellate court in 1963 and served three years, which included two terms as chief justice. He was elected to the Indiana Supreme Court in 1966 and remained there until he reached the mandatory retirement age in 1985. He served three terms as chief justice of the Court, a position that rotated among the judges until 1972, when judicial reform created a permanent chief justice-ship that was selected from among the sitting justices by the Judicial Nominating Commission.

Hunter was always a strong advocate of judicial reform. From 1967 to 1971 he served on the Constitutional Revision Commission that initiated the judicial reform amendment. For his work on the commission he was awarded a Certificate of Commendation from Speaker of the House Otis R. Bowen. Hunter wrote several law review articles about the need for judicial reform. In one article, he explained that the judiciary would have more respect if judges were appointed by an executive officer. He approved the Judicial Amendment proposed for Indiana, which provided that the governor would appoint the judges for the Supreme Court and the court of appeals, but appointments would be from nominations submitted by an independent nonpartisan screening body. Hunter believed such a system would not only help to insure that judges were independent from political pressure, but also that the people would be afforded a voice in the Court's ultimate composition. As he wrote, "Respect for our judicial system and its functions must be a constant force in our constitutional republic if it is to survive. Judicial reform is essential to accomplish that respect."

During his eighteen years on the Court, Hunter was known as a progressive judge in civil matters and a champion of the rights of common working men and women. He was the author of many significant majority opinions, including an important 1969 case, *State ex rel. Mass Transportation Authority v. Indiana Revenue Board*, in which the Court found that the Indiana Constitution did not allow the governor to exercise a pocket veto. Hunter argued that to determine gubernatorial powers it was "necessary for this Court to look to the history of its adoption particularly with a view toward discerning the intentions of the drafters of our present Constitution." His lengthy and detailed examination of the debates at the Constitutional Convention in 1850 established that the expressed intention of the delegates was to deny the governor the right of a pocket veto.

Hunter also wrote strong dissenting opinions. In *American National Bank & Trust Co. v. Indiana Department of Highways*, he disagreed with the majority opinion that found a statute transferring bonding authority from the Toll Road Commission to the Department of Highways to be unconstitutional because it violated the prohibition against the state going into debt. He wrote that "a statute comes before this Court clothed with a presumption of constitutionality," and that the party challenging the statute has the burden of proving it unconstitutional. Based on his analysis of the constitution and the statute Hunter concluded that burden had not been satisfied and therefore any doubt about the validity of the statute had to be resolved in favor of its constitutionality.

Hunter had a great respect for the rights of all individuals and wrote a particularly strong concurring opinion in a case, *Petition of Hauptly*, holding that a married woman had the same right to be granted a change of name as any other individual, married or unmarried.

Hunter served on numerous committees to improve the legal profession. In 1971 he was chairman of a special committee creating the Disciplinary Commission and giving effect to the Code of Professional Responsibility for lawyers. In 1974 he served as a member of a commission to formulate and adopt codes of ethics for judges. He also worked for revision of the adoption laws and for upgrading judicial salaries. A lifelong scholar of Abraham Lincoln, he gave many speeches and addresses on the life of Lincoln.

Held in highest esteem by his colleagues, Hunter in May 1976 received a Sagamore of the Wabash honor from Bowen for his unselfish dedication and service to his fellow Hoosiers and the state of Indiana. During his years on the Indiana Appellate and Supreme courts, Hunter and his wife resided in Anderson. They had two children and three grandchildren. Hunter died on October 27, 1991, in Lagrange. He left a legacy in his life and in his judicial opinions that reflects the values, bravery, and aspirations of his fellow Hoosiers.

SARAH M. FRANK, JD, is a private attorney in general civil practice. Frank is a legal researcher and writer and an adjunct faculty member, Department of Mathematics, Indiana University–Purdue University Indianapolis.

SELECTED BIBLIOGRAPHY

Hunter, Donald H. "Some thought about Judicial Reform." *De Paul Law Review* 19, no. 3.

CASES CITED

State of Indiana ex rel. MTA v. Indiana Revenue Board et al., 250 Ind. 607 (1969).
American National Bank & Trust Co. v. Indiana Department of Highways, 439 N.E.2d 1129 (Ind. 1982).
Petition of Hauptly to change her name, 262 Ind. 150 (1974).

The author, a former law clerk to Hunter, drew upon her personal reminiscences for this essay.

ROGER O. DeBRULER
September 30, 1968–August 8, 1996

FRANK SULLIVAN, JR.

Roger Owen DeBruler, the ninety-fifth judge of the Indiana Supreme court, was the longest-serving member of the Court during the twentieth century. Appointed the youngest justice ever at age thirty-four, he could easily have been the longest-serving ever, but he had new worlds to conquer and retired at the age of sixty-two.

DeBruler was born August 5, 1934, in Evansville and attended public schools there. He served as a military intelligence officer in Germany and earned undergraduate and law degrees at Indiana University in Blooming-ton. In 1963 Governor Matthew E. Welsh appointed DeBruler to fill a vacancy in the Circuit Court of Steuben County, his wife Karen's home county.

Governor Roger D. Branigin appointed DeBruler, a Democrat, to the Supreme Court on September 30, 1968, following the death of Donald R. Mote, a Republican. At that time, judges appointed to fill vacancies had to stand for election at the next election following appointment, but a vacancy had never arisen so late in an election year. The Republicans pressed to have the contest on the 1968 ballot. The State Election Board, controlled by Democrats, argued that the ballots had already been printed and taxpayers should not have to pay reprinting costs. The appellate court rejected the Republican challenge after the Supreme Court refused to intervene. The Supreme Court also rejected collateral litigation that would have required reprinting.

Upon moving to Indianapolis, DeBruler took a deep interest in the restoration of the city's historic Lockerbie neighborhood. Devoid of owner-occupied housing, the DeBrulers, Kenneth M. Stroud, DeBruler's closest friend, and a few others became pioneers in what has become one of India-napolis's premier neighborhoods.

While chief justice in 1969, DeBruler secured legislative repeal of a plethora of statutes obligating circuit court judges to appoint members of local government boards. Such duties were in "no way connected with [the] functions [of] a judge," he maintained.

In 1970 DeBruler ran for election and won a six-year term on the Court by a narrow margin over his Republican opponent, Frank V. Dice. That year the voters approved a constitutional amendment that changed the system for selecting and retaining members of the Court. Following appointment, justices would now stand for a periodic "yes-no" retention vote at the first statewide general election following two years on the Court and, if retained, every ten years thereafter. DeBruler himself was retained in 1976 with 65 percent of the vote and in 1986 with 57 percent of the vote.

During his twenty-eight-year tenure, DeBruler wrote nearly nine hundred majority opinions and six hundred dissents, a contribution to Indiana's jurisprudence that a biographical sketch of this length can only touch upon.

Arriving at the Court only two years after the U.S. Supreme Court's *Miranda* ruling had banned unwarned custodial confessions, DeBruler wrote opinions enforcing its mandate (*Mims v. State*) and provided additional safe-guards when police interrogated juveniles (*Lewis v. State*) or sought consent to conduct searches (*Pirtle v. State*). Several of his early dissents arguing for exclusion of certain evidence—evidence demonstrating "depraved sexual instinct" (*Kerlin v. State*) and certain out-of-court statements (*Patterson v. State*) were later adopted by the Court. DeBruler's dissent in *Jackson v. State*, challenging the constitutionality of the indefinite incarceration, on grounds of incompetence to stand trial, of a man accused of petty theft was vindicated by the U.S. Supreme Court in *Jackson v. Indiana*.

DeBruler wrote many opinions about the duties of a judge when considering whether to impose a death sentence. Over time, his opinions came to comprise the canon of sentencing law in Indiana capital cases, addressing the need to prove aggravating circumstances (*Dillon v. State*), separately consider any mitigating circumstances (*Lowery v. State*), and weigh the aggravating and mitigating circumstances (*Spranger v. State*).

Other notable opinions by DeBruler included cases that allocated costs of unfinished nuclear power plants to utility shareholders rather than customers (*Citizens Action Coalition v. Northern Ind. Public Service Co.* and *National Rural Util. Co-op Finance Corp. v. Public Service Comm.*), the definitive Indiana decision holding that comprehensive general liability insurance policies covered environmental damage (*American States Ins. Co. v. Kiger*), and a landmark opinion upholding the constitutionality of one of the nation's first tort reform statutes, the Indiana Medical Malpractice Act (*Johnson v. St. Vincent Hosp.*). His dissent in *Thomas v. Review Bd. of Ind. Emp. Security Div.*, supporting unemployment benefits for a man who had quit his job rather than work on a munitions assembly line in violation of his religious beliefs, was adopted by the U.S. Supreme Court.

Since his retirement on August 8, 1996, DeBruler has led an active life of travel, study, and devotion to his wife, children, and grandchildren, including lengthy excursions in France and the Yukon and deep immersion in French language and the works of authors such as William Faulkner and James Joyce. An unfailingly courteous and kind man, DeBruler described Hoosiers as people who "always valued neighborliness, hospitality, and concern for others, even those who may be strangers" (*Moran v. State*). In doing so, he certainly described himself.

FRANK SULLIVAN JR., JD, LLM, is a justice of the Indiana Supreme Court. He served on the Court with DeBruler from Sullivan's appointment in 1993 until DeBruler's retirement in 1996.

SELECTED BIBLIOGRAPHY

DeBruler, Roger O. "Non-Judicial Duties of Indiana Trial Judges." *Indiana Legal Forum*, vol. 3 (1969).
Indianapolis News, September 25, 30, October 1, 5, 1968.
Indianapolis Star, August 8, 1996.
Kueterman, Greg. "Leaving the Bench." *Indiana Alumni* (July/August 1996).
Sullivan, Frank, Jr. "A Tribute to Justice Roger O. DeBruler." *Indiana Law Review* 30 (1997).

———. "A Tribute to Justice Roger O. DeBruler." *Indiana Law Journal* 72 (1996).

Withered, Jerome L. *Hoosier Justice: A History of the Supreme Court of Indiana.* Indianapolis: Indiana Supreme Court, 1998.

CASES CITED

American States Ins. Co v. Kiger, 662 N.E.2d 945 (Ind. 1996).

Citizens Action Coalition of Indiana, Inc. v. Northern Indiana Public Service Company, 485 N.E.2d 610 (Ind. 1985).

Dillon v. State, 454 N.E.2d 845 (Ind. 1983). (DeBruler dissenting).

Jackson v. State of Indiana, 255 N.E. 2d 515, 518 (Ind. 1970). (DeBruler dissenting).

Johnson v. St. Vincent Hospital Inc., 404 N.E. 2d 585 (Ind. 1980).

Kerlin v. State of Indiana, 265 N.E. 2d 22, 25-27 (Ind. 1970). (DeBruler dissenting).

Lewis v. State of Indiana, 288 N.E. 2d. 138 (Ind. 1972).

Lowery v. State, 478 N.E.2d 1214 (Ind. 1985). (DeBruler dissenting).

Mims v. State of Indiana, 262 N.E. 2d 638 (Ind. 1970).

Moran v. State of Indiana, 644 N.E.2d 536 (Ind. 1994).

National Rural Utilities Cooperative Finance Corp. v. Public Service Commission of Indiana, 552 N.E.2d 23 (Ind. 1990).

Patterson v. State of Indiana, 324 N.E. 2d 482,488 (Ind. 1970). (DeBruler dissenting).

Pirtle v. State of Indiana, 323 N.E. 2d 634 (Ind. 1975).

Spranger v. State, 498 N.E.2d 931 (Ind. 1986). (DeBruler dissenting).

Thomas v. Review Board of the Indiana Employment Security Division, 391 N.E. 2d 1127 (Ind. 1979). United States Reports.

Jackson v. Indiana, 406 U.S. 715 (1972).

Miranda v. Arizona, 396 U.S. 715 (1972).

Thomas v. Review Board of the Indiana Employment Security Division et al., 450 U.S. 707 (1981).

RICHARD M. GIVAN
January 6, 1969–December 31, 1994

JEROME L. WITHERED

He flew airplanes and was a flight instructor, rode motorcycles, raised and trained Arabian show horses, was a photographer at the Indianapolis 500, served in the Indiana legislature, and was a successful lawyer. And then he became the ninety-sixth judge of the Indiana Supreme Court and chief justice. That was Dick Givan.

Born June 7, 1921, Richard Martin Givan was a fourth-generation Hoosier lawyer, his great-grandfather having started the family legal tradition in Dearborn County around the turn of the twentieth century. Givan grew up in the Indianapolis area, where his father practiced law. Following high school, he was a pilot in the U.S. Army Air Corps during World War II. After the war, Givan attended Indiana University and then law school at the IU School of Law, Indianapolis. During law school, he had the distinction of being appointed as the first law clerk for the Indiana Supreme Court, serving all five judges.

After law school and admission to the bar in 1951, Givan received an appointment from the Court as deputy state public defender. He later served as a deputy attorney general and as the assistant attorney general of Indiana. In this capacity, he argued the case of *Irvin v. Dowd*, a seminal death penalty case, before the U.S. Supreme Court. The case involved constitutional questions of whether adverse pretrial publicity and predetermined opinions of guilt by most prospective jurors deprived the defendant of a fair trial. Following the Court's decision reversing the conviction, Givan teamed with the local prosecuting attorney to retry and convict Irvin. In 1959 he became a partner in the law firm of Bowen, Myers, Northam and Givan, and maintained a private law practice until he assumed the bench in 1969. He also served as a Marion County deputy prosecutor.

One of his most important cases as a private practitioner was the Indianapolis Mass Transit Authority case, *State ex rel. Mass Transp. Authority of Greater Indianapolis v. Indiana Revenue Board*, in which he, along with a team of one other Republican and two Democratic lawyers, challenged the pocket veto by Governor Roger D. Branigin of a bill that funded the Indianapolis MTA through 90 percent of inheritance tax collections. The Indiana Constitution specifically provided procedures for the governor to sign and veto legislative enactments. By neither signing nor vetoing the MTA bill, Branigin had attempted a pocket veto of the bill, which arguably was not permitted by the constitution. The result of the court challenge led by Givan was a ruling that the Indiana Constitution did not allow the governor the option of a pocket veto, and since the governor had not properly vetoed the bill, it became law. Hence, the MTA was entitled to 90 percent of inheritance tax collections.

After being elected to the legislature in 1966 and serving one term, Givan in 1968 sought and obtained the Republican nomination for the Supreme Court, and was elected in the fall. He entered the race only after the candidate he had pledged to support died of a heart attack before the Republican State Convention.

As a judge, Givan was plainspoken, straightforward, and frugal in his use of words. His reasoning was that lawyers do not have the time and clients do not have the money to pay lawyers to take the time, to read through a judge's long-winded philosophizing on the law. State the law, state the facts, apply the law to the facts, and finish—that was his view of how an appellate opinion should be written. He also disliked and avoided footnotes, using only fourteen of them in 1,571 opinions during his twenty-six years on the bench. His rationale: if the comment is not important enough to be in the body of the opinion, then it should not be there at all.

When Chief Justice Norman F. Arterburn, Indiana's first permanent chief justice, decided to retire from the office in 1974, Givan—who had a long history of trying cases and arguing before the Indiana courts, and who had personally known every Court justice since the 1940s—was the obvious choice of the Judicial Nominating Commission. He was reelected as chief justice in 1979. When his second term was about to expire, he expressed a desire to have another member of the Court take over the reins. He was a strong believer in term limits, holding the view that turnover, new blood, and fresh ideas were important in any endeavor, and especially so in government and the judiciary. But the commission prevailed on him to stay on for another term. He remained chief justice another two and a half years, until 1987, when he retired from the post.

As chief justice, Givan led the fight to upgrade bar admissions standards by requiring certain core legal classes in law school, and he significantly enhanced the Division of State Court Administration. He also worked tirelessly on behalf of the Indiana judiciary, vastly improving, among other things, the Indiana Judicial Center and its assistance and research programs for trial judges.

But the most endearing, and enduring, trait of Givan was his sense of the common person. He could relate to a factory worker or a corporate executive just the same. And in the eyes of the law, they were the same. He likened his role as a judge to that of a baseball umpire: call the balls and strikes as you see them, without regard to who the pitcher, batter, team, or team owner is.

All who knew Givan knew that he was the most down-to-earth, unpretentious judge they ever met. He introduced himself to everyone as "Dick Givan." Even as chief justice, when calling on the telephone, he would tell the receptionist, who oftentimes had no idea who he was, that it was Dick Givan calling for the individual. He was also, without a doubt, the best legal storyteller of his generation. Having known many lawyers and judges around the state, and having tried cases in all corners of Indiana, his vast knowledge of the judiciary was legendary, as was his ability to tell the stories of lawyers, judges, and legal cases.

Givan retired from the Court in 1994, but remained active in legal and judicial affairs until in his eighties. He died on July 21, 2009. His wife of sixty-two years, Pauline, preceded him in death in 2008. The family legal tradition is carried on by his daughter, Libby Givan Whipple, a former Indiana deputy attorney general, and by his grandson, Jonathan Chenoweth, currently a state deputy public defender.

JEROME L. WITHERED, JD, is a partner with Withered Burns and Persin, Lafayette, Indiana. He is the author of *Hoosier Justice: A History of the Supreme Court of Indiana* (1998) and coauthor of *Indiana Trial Practice* (1996).

SELECTED BIBLIOGRAPHY

Kuesterman, Greg. "Justice Givan nearing end of Brilliant Legal Journey." *The Indiana Lawyer* (July 13, 1994): 6.
Withered, Jerome L. *Hoosier Justice: A History of the Supreme Court of Indiana.* Indianapolis: Indiana Supreme Court, 1998.
———. "Richard M. Givan: Justice, Indiana Supreme Court." *Indiana Law Review* 30 (1977): 35–41.

CASES CITED

Irvin v. Dowd, Warden, 366 U.S. 717 (1961).
State of Indiana ex rel.MTA, etc. v. Indiana Revenue Board et al., 251 Ind. 607 (1969).

The author was Givan's law clerk from 1977 to 1979 and drew upon his personal reminiscences for this essay.

INDIANA SUPREME COURT

DIXON W. PRENTICE
January 4, 1971–January 6, 1986

MICHAEL G. NAVILLE

Although joining in 693 legal opinions as majority drafter, or as a concurring or minority opinion, Dixon Wright Prentice, at the age of eighty-nine, says that none really stand out to him that he feels characterizes his career on the bench. Rather, Prentice, the ninety-seventh judge of the Indiana Supreme Court, seems most proud of the fact that he was one of the driving forces behind the adoption of Trial Rules 53.1 and 53.2, known as the "lazy judge rule." He said:

> I did it actually in response to a problem we were having in my own county, when we had a judge who would listen to two attorneys argue over a two day trial, and then tell them to 'work it out' when we were all finished. Heck, if we could have worked it out, we wouldn't have been trying it in the first place. That lazy judge rule made them make a decision. One judge wanted to give them notice before we did it first, but I said "No." I also added that whoever got called on the "lazy judge" mo-

tion, had to have it certified to the Supreme Court, so that there would be a record. No judge wants that on their resume, so I think I helped out in that regard.

Prentice was born on June 3, 1919, in Sellersburg, Indiana, and when he was seven years old he moved to Jeffersonville, where he resided for the rest of his life. He attended Indiana University as an undergraduate in prelaw back when it was not a requirement to have an undergraduate degree prior to applying for law school. He received his law degree in 1942 from IU. During World War II, he served in the navy from 1942 to 1946 and stayed with the U.S. Naval Reserve, rising from a third-class seaman to a commission as an ensign and retired as a lieutenant commander. He then practiced law in Sellersburg and in Jeffersonville from 1946 to 1970. During that time he was president of the Clark County Bar Association.

In 1970 Prentice won the Democratic nomination for the Supreme Court, and went on to win the seat held by retiring judge, Amos W. Jackson, another Democrat. His election, along with that of Roger O. DeBruler, was historic in that it was the last time that Supreme Court judges were elected on partisan ballots. In 1970 the voters ratified an amendment to the state constitution that abolished partisan election of judges for the court of appeals and the Supreme Court, and put in place a merit system of selection for initial appointment coupled with retention elections.

Prentice's route to the high bench was atypical of those who reached the Court. Often, those who sat on the Court before 1970 did so after previously serving as prosecutor or circuit court judge or both, and as a rule they were active in party politics, almost a necessity to obtain the party nomination, which was decided at the state party convention. Prentice, however, had no judicial experience and very little political experience, stating that he was "so green it was unbelievable." Just prior to running, he and his brother had spent four years developing a major shopping mall in Clarksville. This endeavor had taken its toll on his law practice. Nonetheless he decided to seek the party nomination. His only opponent eventually dropped out of the race, and Prentice won the nomination and then the election in a year that favored Democratic candidates.

In 1976 Prentice won his retention election and served another nine years, before retiring from the bench with one more year to serve. He says the reason he chose to retire early is that he found it increasingly difficult to keep up with the caseload, and thought it was time to let someone else have his seat. Governor Robert D. Orr appointed Brent E. Dickson to complete the last year of Prentice's term.

Although Prentice never served as a judge until he joined the Court, he exhibited a judicial temperament, as illustrated in a story told by Kenneth Nunn, a prominent southern Indiana attorney. He said that when he was in high school and a self-proclaimed "pretty bad kid," he had been walking the streets one day when he saw a "fancy car in a driveway with its trunk open and a set of golf clubs inside." He stole the golf clubs, went out and hit all the balls out of it, and then tried to sell it. He was caught in short order and put in jail. Upon his release a few days later, he was told the clubs "belonged to Mr. Prentice," and that he should go and apologize. When he did as advised, Prentice did not castigate or yell at him in any way. Instead, he pulled out fifty cents and tossed it towards him on the desk and said, "Here, you need a haircut. Don't do this anymore." Several years later, Nunn was at the pinnacle of his profession and getting ready to present an oral argument in front of the Court when Prentice walked out to the bench with the other justices. He said, "my hands started shaking. He never brought it up, or even said anything about it, but as I recall, I lost that case!"

Of the nearly seven hundred opinions that Prentice wrote, one that stands out because of its political impact is *State v. Nixon*, which declared the Indiana pari-mutuel law permitting horse track betting unconstitutional. Speaking for a sharply divided Court, Prentice said that when they framers wrote the constitutional prohibition against "lotteries," they intended it to embrace "all forms of gaming." This opinion produced two dissenting opinions, one from Justice Donald H. Hunter and one from Justice DeBruler. These responses were relatively mild in comparison to the angry reaction by the Indiana General Assembly, which had passed the pari-mutuel wagering act in 1977. The *Nixon* decision was in effect invalidated by the voters in 1988 when they approved a constitutional amendment removing the state's ban against lotteries.

In addition to serving as a commissioner of the National Conference on Uniform State Laws, Prentice was also on the spearheading committee that instituted continuing legal education for the state of Indiana, a requirement that most, if not all, states now have adopted to varying degrees. Widely hailed as one of the most effective ways to insure the populace that attorneys are maintaining minimum standards of competence, Prentice's efforts have served the Indiana legal population admirably.

When pressed about his favorite memories on the bench, Prentice stated: "It would have to be my relationship with my clerks. I was always very fortunate to have outstanding clerks. They were all just fine people. I have two now that still call me every year on my birthday and I just feel so good about that."

Prentice currently resides in Tucson, Arizona, with his wife of sixty-seven years, Phyllis Ropa Prentice.

MICHAEL G. NAVILLE, JD, is managing partner with Lorch and Naville, New Albany, Indiana. He is a U.S. Magistrate Judge for Southern District of Indiana.

SELECTED BIBLIOGRAPHY

Fifer, Ronald R. Interview with the author. September 3, 2008.
Kelso, Robert A. Interview with the author. September 1, 2008.
Nunn, Kenneth. Interview with the author. September 3, 2008.
Prentice, Dixon W. Interviews with the author. September 16, 2008, October 22, 2009.

CASES CITED

State of Indiana; Hoosier Horse Industries v. Joseph H. Nixon, 270 Ind. 192 (1979); 384 N.E. 2d 152.

ALFRED J. PIVARNIK
May 13, 1977–December 14, 1990

MARK A. BATES

Alfred Joseph Pivarnik was a pioneer by virtue of becoming the first person appointed by merit selection to the Indiana Supreme Court. Selecting Pivarnik to become the ninety-eighth person to sit on the Court, Governor Otis R. Bowen said, "I think we'll have a splendid Supreme Court justice. He's known for hard work." Bowen's words proved prophetic as Pivarnik's work ethic served Indiana well during his time on the Court.

Born January 20, 1925, in Valparaiso, Indiana, Pivarnik grew up on a farm in Porter County. His father worked in Lake County and Pivarnik, along with his brothers and sisters, helped run the family farm, which left little time for extracurricular activities. Because World War II was raging, Pivarnik, like many others, joined the army after graduating from Valparaiso High School in 1943. He attended Creighton University as part of a college training detachment in the U.S. Army Air Corps.

Inducted on July 17, 1943, Pivarnik served with the 301st Bomb Group, 352nd Bomb Squadron. Based in Foggia, Italy, he saw combat in bombing raids during the North Apennines and Po Valley campaigns as a radio operator gunner on a B-17 Flying Fortress. Pivarnik was awarded the American Theater Ribbon, the Good Conduct Medal, the Air Medal, the Mediterranean Theater Ribbon with two Bronze Stars, and the Victory Medal, World War II. He reached the rank of corporal and was honorably discharged in 1946.

Returning to civilian life, Pivarnik attended Valparaiso University and obtained his law degree in 1951. Admitted to the bar on June 6, 1951, he worked for Aetna Insurance Company and then State Farm Insurance. In 1952 he began his lengthy public service by working as Porter County deputy prosecutor. The prosecutor and Pivarnik were the county's only prosecutors. Pivarnik continued to work as a deputy prosecutor for Frederick Crumpacker when Crumpacker was elected in 1954.

Pivarnik was elected prosecutor in 1958 and ran for circuit court judge in 1962. His opponents were Professor James S. Savage from the Valparaiso Law School and Crumpacker, his former boss. During a community forum, Savage stated that he had taught Pivarnik everything Pivarnik knew about the law while Pivarnik was a student, and Crumpacker insisted he had taught Pivarnik everything about being a prosecutor. Displaying his great sense of humor, Pivarnik spoke last and told the audience to vote for him because, "I know everything they both know." Pivarnik won the election.

Pivarnik was circuit court judge for fourteen years until sworn in to replace retiring Justice Norman F. Arterburn on May 13, 1977. By selecting Pivarnik over two other nominees, Bowen based his decision solely on merit, passing up an opportunity to make history by appointing the first woman to sit on the Court. He said: "Although each of the nominees demonstrated exceptional ability and talent, Judge Pivarnik was especially impressive in a personal interview. I previously stated that I would select the individual whom I judged to be best qualified to fill this important judicial post," said Bowen.

Bowen's faith and trust in Pivarnik were more than repaid through the new justice's dedication to the Court. "A position such as this is not given for some honor. It is not given for some gift or reward," said Pivarnik. "I've been placed here to accept the responsibility and duty of the highest order. I will give a full measure of devotion to this job."

The work ethic instilled in him as a child came to fruition on the Court. In thirteen and a half years, Pivarnik authored nearly one thousand majority opinions, a tremendous output for his term. He wrote an average of seventy opinions a year, more than one a week.

From 1977 until 1990, the Court's caseload consisted overwhelmingly of criminal appeals because defendants whose sentences were greater than ten years had the right to directly appeal their convictions to the Court. Pivarnik remained true to his conservative principles, but never ignored the facts or the law. In *Sears v. State* he wrote the unanimous decision to reverse a criminal conviction because the trial took place in the wrong county, the first time the Court had reached this result in more than forty years. In *Peterson v. State*, a question of first impression, Pivarnik barred the identification testimony by a witness who could only identify the defendant after first being hypnotized.

In the civil arena, Pivarnik held in *Barnes v. A.H. Robins, Co., Inc.* that the statute of limitations begins to run for a Hoosier upon discovery of an injury, not when the person is first exposed to the defective product or foreign substance. He also wrote in *Kellogg v. City of Gary* in 1990 that Indiana's constitution allowed Hoosiers to carry guns, a right that was not recognized for all Americans under the U.S. Constitution until *District of Columbia v. Heller*, eighteen years later.

Pivarnik worked hard and handled the cases before him with fairness and dignity, but still retained a sense of humor and a hearty laugh. Each morning he would enter his office, make a cup of coffee and talk with his staff about a variety of topics before tackling his work.

When Pivarnik was sworn in he said, "To an Indiana lawyer, the highest honor you can pay him is to put him on the Supreme Court. I am very humbled and very proud, and I have feelings I cannot put into words as to what it means to have Indiana do that for me." Pivarnik promised the citizens of Indiana to "give a full measure of devotion to this job, and . . . the highest measure of dedication that my ability permits." True to his word, he retired from the Court on December 14, 1990, after becoming seriously ill, because he could no longer devote the time and energy that he believed was required of a Court justice.

After his lengthy public service, Pivarnik returned to Porter County, where he was content to be a husband to Catherine, a father to Dan, Alana, Ed, Tim, and Laura and a grandfather to eleven. He died on June 3, 1995.

MARK A. BATES, JD, is an attorney in private practice, Schererville, Indiana. He is a former law clerk, Indiana Supreme Court (1981–84), an assistant administrator, Indiana Supreme Court (1984–91) and wrote, author's comment, "Trial Rule 61 Harmless Error" 4 *Indiana Practice: Rules of Procedure Annotated* (Harvey, 1991, ed.).

SELECTED BIBLIOGRAPHY

"Ceremonies Induct New Supreme Court Associate Justice—and Pay Tribute to Retiring Justice Arterburn." *Res Gestae* 21 (1977): 239.
Crandall, Colleen. Interview with the author. July 26, 2008.
Indianapolis Star, June 5, 1995.
Kokomo Tribune. March 16, May 14, 1977.
Personal papers of Alfred J. Pivarnik (in possession of family).
Pivarnik, Catherine. Interview with the author. September 26, 2008.

CASES CITED

Barnes v. A.H. Robins, Company, Inc., 476 N.E.2d 84 (Ind. 1985).
District of Columbia v. Heller, 128 S. Ct. 2783 (2008).
Kellogg v. City of Gary, 562 N.E.2d 685 (Ind. 1990).
Peterson v. State, 448 N.E.2d 673 (Ind. 1983).
Sears v. State, 456 N.E.2d 390 (Ind. 1983).

The author was a law clerk to Pivarnik from 1981 to 1984 and drew upon his personal reminiscences of the justice in preparing this essay. The author is grateful to Catherine Pivarnik for sharing her memories and allowing access to personal papers and photographs as well as to fellow law clerks Colleen Crandall, Tim Guiden, and Jim McCune, who generously gave of their time to review this brief profile and shared their remembrances of working for the justice.

RANDALL T. SHEPARD

September 6, 1985–Present • Chief Justice 1987–Present

KEVIN W. BETZ • KRISTIN LAMB AND AMELIA DEIBERT

From Pope John Paul II to famous American appellate attorneys, to his own political party, to friends and supporters from his hometown, Chief Justice Randall Terry Shepard, the ninety-ninth justice of the Indiana Supreme Court, has addressed these advocates and their legal and personal appeals, with wisdom, plain English, and independence. As his close friend, attorney and lifelong supporter from his hometown, Ted Lockyear, said with a smile: "I've had a lot of cases in front of the Supreme Court during Randy's time—and he's voted against me every time!"

Through these challenging cases and various leadership roles, Shepard has puffed a second wind of progress into the Indiana state judicial system. While the Court had a prestigious past in the 1800s, by 1925 it had lost its way. In 1885 *West's Reporting* of cases grouped Indiana into the most progressive supreme courts, finding that in 1910, the Indiana Supreme Court was the fifth most cited court in the nation. But a decline started in 1925 that was uninterrupted until Shepard began his leadership in 1987. While adhering to its traditional roots, the Court has transformed itself into a beacon of progressive opinions in all areas of the law.

Shepard, known to family and friends as Randy, was born in Lafayette on December 24, 1946. His seventh-generation Hoosier family soon moved to Evansville, where Shepard grew up. He graduated cum laude from Princeton in 1968 and received his law degree from Yale University Law School in 1972. After serving briefly as a special assistant at the U.S. Department of Transportation, he returned home. Shepard served as the top assistant to Evansville mayor Russell G. Lloyd, and later as an Evansville trial court judge at the age of thirty-three. From 1980 to 1985 he was as a Vanderburgh Superior Court judge.

In 1985, at the age of thirty-eight, Shepard was appointed by Governor Robert D. Orr to the Indiana Supreme Court. Less than two years later he was selected chief justice of Indiana. A member of the Indiana Judicial Nominating Commission who chose the chief justice in 1987 later said: "We thought [Justice] Pivarnik would get the job, but when we interviewed Randy, he just knocked all of our socks off."

Soon after becoming chief justice, Shepard led a reform movement to make the Court truly a supreme court. The reform gave the Court discretion over which cases to hear and allowed the Court the opportunity to hear more civil cases instead of mainly criminal cases. Because the Court now has time to thoroughly research and analyze a smaller number of cases, the Court is once again well-known throughout the nation.

A controversial political issue came before the new chief justice and the Court in early 1988. The Indiana Republican Party challenged the residency of Evan Bayh, the Democratic Party's candidate for governor, who was the son of the former U.S. senator from Indiana, Birch Bayh. Even though the case was initiated by Orr, who had appointed him to the Court, Shepard authored the unanimous opinion in *State Election Board v. Bayh*, which found that Bayh had met the state constitution's residency standard. When Bayh became governor at the age of thirty-three, he was the youngest governor in the nation, and Shepard was the youngest chief justice in the country.

In 1989 a case of international significance came before the Court. Paula Cooper, a fifteen-year-old girl, had been convicted for murdering a seventy-eight-year-old Bible school teacher and sentenced to death. When the case came before the Indiana Supreme Court, no less an advocate than John Paul II, along with an array of national and international associations, conservative and liberal, besieged the Court over this death penalty case. Shepard wrote the unanimous opinion in the case of *Cooper v. State*, holding that the Indiana Constitution prohibited the execution of a teenager, no matter the gruesome nature of the murder. The *New York Times* wrote in its editorial page: "[T]he court deserves credit for a wise and courageous decision." Standing in front of the Eiffel Tower in Paris, CBS News anchor Dan Rather led his broadcast with the news of the *Cooper* decision.

This case is only one of the more than eight hundred majority opinions and fifty law journal articles or legal commentaries that Shepard has contributed during his tenure. One of his most pronounced points of focus is on the Indiana Constitution. In his seminal 1989 *Indiana Law Review* article "Second Wind for the Indiana Bill of Rights," Shepard made a call for federalism to reinvigorate the state's constitution, and that has happened. Indiana lawyers now venture to make arguments based on the Indiana Constitution, rather than the U.S. Constitution, a rarity before 1989.

The chief justice has also brought innovations with his innate gift for plain yet elegant expressions, as well as his warmth as a person. His list of accomplishments in moving Indiana's judiciary forward is highlighted by the adoption of cutting-edge alternative rules of resolution that allow citizens to settle their disputes instead of litigate them, comprehensive rules that allow jurors far more involvement and understanding of the process than ever before, a statewide program that was the first of its kind to promote scholarships for minority law school graduates, and a statewide pro bono model that is the envy of other states. He also helped forge judicial pay raises that took Indiana judges from the cellar of judicial pay to the median. In 2008 Shepard was presented the Diversity in Practice Award by the *Indiana Lawyer* recognizing those in the legal community who have demonstrated a commitment to diversity and inspired others to work for diversity as well. In addition, he has increased public interaction with the Court by holding far more oral arguments and by expanding the use of techniques suited to the information age (such as webcasting the Court's sessions, creating pages of self-help legal tools, and providing electronic access to Court news and decisions). All of these innovations have been achieved through his leadership and work with many others, including the Indiana General Assembly. As State Senator Vaneta Becker said: "When he speaks, the Legislature listens."

Shepard has also become a national judicial leader. From 1989 to 1999, he was a chair of the American Bar Association's Section of Legal Education and Admissions to the Bar, which governs accreditation for all 175 law schools in the country. From 2005 to 2006 he served as the president of the Conference of Chief Justices. In 2006 U.S. Supreme Court Chief Justice John G. Roberts appointed Shepard to the prestigious U.S. Judicial Conference Advisory Committee on Civil Rules—a unique honor for a state court justice. Governor Mitch Daniels, a close friend of Shepard's since college, selected him as cochair of the Indiana Commission on Local Government Reform in 2008. Because of these and other appointments Shepard is widely viewed as one of the most prominent judges in the nation.

In October 2009 Shepard was the recipient of the prestigious Dwight D. Opperman Award for Judicial Excellence. The chair of the selection committee said that Shepard "is a shining star of the American justice system, the pride of lawyers and judges—especially state court judges—in and well beyond Indiana."

Shepard's passion and leadership extends beyond the law. He is a national and state advocate for historic preservation, a passion he shares with his wife, Amy MacDonell. He is a trustee on the National Trust for Historic Preservation and has led many efforts nationally and in Indiana to preserve significant historic sites.

The Indiana Constitution defines his job title broadly and grandly as "Chief Justice of Indiana" and Shepard has filled it fully and superbly. Before even completing his tenure on the Indiana Supreme Court, he is already the longest-serving chief justice in Indiana history. As of 2010, he had served as chief justice of Indiana for more than twenty years. He once said, "My Mom always told me that if you're doing a job that they don't need to pay you for, you're probably in the right job."

KEVIN W. BETZ, MS, JD , is principal partner at Betz and Associates, Indianapolis, a litigation boutique law firm. He was the lead author from 1990 to 2002 of a law review article that analyzed the Indiana Supreme Court's docket, dispositions, and voting, published annually in the *Indiana Law Review*, see, for example, "An Examination of the Indiana Supreme Court Docket, Dispositions, and Voting," (2002).

SELECTED BIBLIOGRAPHY

Evansville Courier-Press, May 29, 2008, December 9, 2009.

Lopeman, Charles S. *The Activist Advocate: Policy Making in State Supreme Courts*. Westport, CT: Praeger Publishing, 1999.

New York Times, July 17, 1989.

Shepard, Randall T. "Second Wind for the Indiana Bill of Rights." *Indiana Law Review* 22 (1989).

CASES CITED

State Election Board v. Bayh, 521 N.E. 2d, 1313 (Ind. 1988).

Cooper v. State, 540 N.E. 2d 1216 (Ind. 1989).

The author was law clerk to Chief Justice Shepard from 1988 to 1990 and drew upon his personal reminiscences for this essay. As employees of Betz and Associates, Kristin Lamb and Amelia Deibert assisted Betz as coauthors.

BRENT E. DICKSON
January 6, 1986–Present

MICHAEL J. DeBOER

"The American dream is very much alive in Indiana." These words, spoken by Brent E. Dickson at his robing ceremony, reflected the perspective he would bring to his service as Indiana's one hundredth justice. His life story is, in many ways, a typical story like that of many Hoosiers. It is a story of being born with few privileges, working hard, making the most of opportunities, doing the right thing, and catching a break every now and then. As a consequence, his appointment was the realization of the American dream for an ordinary Hoosier.

Dickson was born in Gary, Indiana, on July 18, 1941, to Ray and Nola Dickson, but his family moved to Hobart a few years later. His father was a businessman, and his mother was a steady force in the home. His maternal grandfather, an immigrant dairy farmer with a farm near Lowell, never missed a milking in more than forty-seven years, providing Dickson with a model work ethic.

Dickson graduated from Hobart High School in 1959 and Purdue University in 1964. To finance his college education he received scholarship help and worked summers at U.S. Steel Gary Works, at a Hobart pizza restaurant, and as a professional pianist. He lived in the Chauncey Cooperative House, which permitted students to limit their costs by sharing expenses and household duties. He was a member of the student senate, a managing editor of Purdue's daily student newspaper *The Exponent*, a member of the senior honorary organization Iron Key, and a piano player in the Salty Dogs student Dixieland band.

At Purdue, Dickson met Jan Ellen Aikman of Terre Haute, whom he married on June 8, 1963. They had three sons, Andrew, Kyle, and Reed. In 1964 Dickson began his education at Indiana University School of Law at Indianapolis. He attended at night and worked full time as an insurance claims adjuster. He wrote an article on Indiana zoning law that was published in the school's law review. In 1968 he received his law degree and was admitted to the Indiana bar and the federal courts in Indiana. In 1975 he was admitted to the U.S. Supreme Court.

Dickson's legal career began at a two-person law firm in Lafayette. In 1970 he opened his own general practice law office. In 1977 he joined several Lafayette attorneys to form a new firm, eventually known as Dickson, Reiling, Teder and Withered. In addition to being certified as a civil trial advocate, he was an active member of the Indiana State Bar Association and served on the board of directors of the Indiana Trial Lawyers Association. In his community, he was active in many service organizations and served as president of the Tippecanoe County Historical Association.

On December 18, 1985, Governor Robert D. Orr appointed Dickson to the Supreme Court. In his announcement, Orr remarked that he had "all the confidence in the world that Brent Dickson will make a fine Supreme Court Justice. . . . He is an outstanding attorney and legal scholar with a good dose of common sense and practical judgment." He also noted that Dickson's "legal expertise and experience in matters ranging from insurance and corporate law to criminal cases will make him a valuable member of the court."

In his investiture speech on January 6, 1986, Dickson expressed his "profound respect for our legal system" and "those crucial elements of jurisprudence which have made our system great." He noted that the judiciary fills a number of vital social functions, including "foster[ing] social harmony and order by assuring fair and just forums for the peaceful resolution of disputes," applying "the principles of the common law in a[n] ever-changing world," and "protecting citizens from government infringement upon their liberties and from criminal conduct of others." He also expressed hope that the sense of humanity embedded in him by his clients would keep him "aware that the everyday nitty-gritty business of this Supreme Court does affect the real lives of people."

Dickson's regard for the legal system is evident in his opinions that narrowly interpreted the barriers to access, such as statutes of limitations and repose that obstruct claimants who seek peaceful redress for harms suffered. Similarly, his opinions reflect a philosophy that the burden a citizen must carry to challenge the constitutionality of legislation must not be too heavy. In addition, he believed that the burden a party must carry to obtain summary judgment must not be so light that it precludes being heard by a jury of peers. He has also promoted private efforts and alternative forms of dispute resolution and refined the judicially administered tools to ensure the orderly, fair, peaceful, and efficient resolution of disputes.

Dickson's noteworthy contributions include his work in Indiana constitutional law. In his opinions, he has expounded fundamental constitutional values, including the rights to exercise religion freely, to obtain remedy for injury by due course of law, and to have a jury trial, as well as the right against double jeopardy and the freedom from unreasonable searches and seizures. In one of his most important opinions, *Collins v. Day*, he explained the prohibition against the general assembly granting privileges or immunities that are not equally available to all. In his opinions in *Boehm v. Town of St. John* and *State Board of Tax Commissioners v. Town of St. John* he elaborated on the requirement that the legislative and executive branches provide a property tax system characterized by uniformity, equality, and just valuation of property.

For more than a decade, Dickson taught Indiana constitutional law at the IU law schools at Bloomington and Indianapolis, and he has written several articles recounting Indiana's constitutional history and discussing the role of lawyers and judges in writing the constitution. Dickson also has served as chair of the Records Management Committee and the Task Force on Access to Court Records and as liaison to the Disciplinary Commission and the Board of Law Examiners. He has promoted civility as a professional value among lawyer and judges, and he cofounded and served as the first president of the Sagamore chapter of the American Inns of Court, which fosters lawyer excellence, professionalism, and civility. For Dickson, the families of judges have been an important concern, which led to his assistance in the founding and development of the national Judicial Family Institute.

During his investiture address, Dickson expressed gratitude to friends and family, colleagues and clients. He acknowledged the small and large investments of so many people in his life who shared in his accomplishments. Thus, in his appointment, Dickson saw the American dream fulfilled in his own his life and in the lives of so many others who shared in his achievements.

MICHAEL J. DeBOER, JD, is law clerk to Theresa L. Springmann, U.S. District Court Judge, and adjunct professor of law, Valparaiso University School of Law. DeBoer was a former law clerk to Justice Brent E. Dickson (1998–2000) and the author of "Equality as a Fundamental Value in the Indiana Constitution," *Valparaiso University Law Review* (2004).

SELECTED BIBLIOGRAPHY

Dickson, Brent E. Investiture address, January 6, 1985. In the author's possession.
Fisher, Barbara M. "Brings Keen Perception to Hoosier Court." *The Purdue Alumnus* 74 (October 1986).
Orr, Robert D. Press release, December 18, 1985. In the author's possession.

CASES CITED
Collins v. Day, 644 N.E.2d 72 (Ind. 1994).
Boehm v. Town of St. John, 675 N.E. 2d 318 (Ind. 1996).
State Board of Tax Commissioners v. Town of St. John, 702 N.E.2d 1034 (Ind. 1998).

JON D. KRAHULIK
December 14, 1990–October 31, 1993

GRETA MORRIS SCODRO

All who knew Jon David Krahulik describe him as a skillful trial lawyer who "had a deep and abiding faith in the jury system." He spent three "brief but energetic" years, in Chief Justice Randall Shepard's words, as Indiana's 101st justice. He wrote several opinions that helped to reshape the parameters of tort liability in Indiana.

Appointed December 14, 1990, Krahulik, the first Democratic appointee in more than twenty years, was chosen via the merit selection process by Governor Evan Bayh. Although new to judging, Krahulik was no stranger to the courtroom. He had been trying cases and arguing criminal and civil appeals for more than twenty years, representing plaintiffs and defendants, businesses, doctors, and other diverse individuals. Arguing a case before the Court he soon joined, Krahulik had represented candidate Bayh in *State Election Board v. Bayh*, the highly publicized "residency challenge" by the Republicans to keep Bayh from running for governor. Krahulik won the case, and Bayh won the election.

Krahulik's appointment in 1990 coincided with the reduction of the Court's mandatory criminal docket, allowing the justices more time to focus on cases of most interest to Hoosiers. He authored 141 majority opinions, nearly evenly split between criminal and civil cases. *Webb v. Jarvis* articulated a framework for analyzing whether a defendant is liable for a wrongful action, and is still cited as a starting point for discussion in tort cases. Several opinions he wrote for the Court moderately expanded a tort plaintiff's opportunity to recover damages for wrongful acts of negligence. *Erie Insurance Co. v. Hickman* recognized a tort cause of action when insurance companies act in bad faith; *Walker v. Rinck* said physicians may owe a duty to children not yet conceived; and *Valinet v. Eskew* encouraged landowners to inspect property for potential hazards to passersby.

Two opinions began the transition away from the traditional "impact rule." *Cullison v. Medley* allowed recovery for emotional distress, even in the absence of physical assault, in a wrongful trespass. *Shuamber v. Henderson* established that the reasons for the traditional "impact rule" regarding emotional distress in the absence of physical injury, were no longer valid.

Some opinions removed vestiges of outdated practices, such as *Huffman v. Monroe County School Corporation* that ended the rule that allowed the release of one person who committed a wrongful act of negligence to release others. In others, the court rendered opinions that put a stop to trial tactics that seemed unfair. For example, *Modesitt v. State* overturned the "Patterson Rule," a controversial hearsay exception that allowed prior out-of-court statements by witnesses to be admitted as evidence under certain circumstances, and set new more limiting rules about when such statements should be allowed. Krahulik was interested in medical malpractice cases, and his majority opinion in *Culbertson v. Mernitz* set the standard for reviewing informed consent cases. A host of Krahulik's opinions argued that certain matters are best left to juries to decide, whether the question was a death sentence, as in *Kennedy v. State*, or vacating a summary judgment by the Court in civil cases.

Krahulik stepped down as a justice in 1993 to become president and chief operating officer of the Chemed Corporation, a publicly traded company based in Cincinnati, Ohio. Having served in the judiciary, he said, he wanted to try his hand as an executive. He returned to law, though, ultimately at Yosha Krahulik and Levy, where he practiced with both of his sons, achieving another of his life's goals.

Born during World War II on December 31, 1944, Krahulik grew up in Indianapolis. His mother was a schoolteacher and his father was a man of several occupations. After Krahulik graduated from Indiana University in 1965 with a major in history, he married Irene Duncan. He then obtained his law degree at IU School of Law at Indianapolis, in 1969, cum laude, having served as an editor on the law review. For the first two years after law school, he was an associate at Baker and Daniels. He then began his long relationship with Bingham Summers Welsh and Spilman (now Bingham McHale), including a term as the managing partner.

Keeping fit was integral to his view that one should be strong in body, mind, and spirit. Throughout 1992 his lightweight racing bike could be seen parked in the Court's robing room, ready for a lunchtime training ride as the forty-eight-year-old Krahulik prepared for Hawaii's Ironman Triathlon. As a college sports fan, he loyally selected IU to win the NCAA men's basketball tournament every year, no matter the odds. He wore IU's cream and crimson to counter Justice Brent E. Dickson's display of the black and gold of Purdue when the rival teams played one another.

Krahulik's eyes lit up when he talked about his family. The family visited chambers often, and after his retirement, Krahulik led field trips to the statehouse with grandchildren in tow. With all, he was generous with his time and talents, and in giving young attorneys an opportunity to do trial work.

Numerous awards came Krahulik's way for service to community and the legal profession, including the Indianapolis Inns of Court Lifetime Professionalism Award in 2004, only the second time it had been given, in recognition of "his distinguished career, and exemplifying the highest standards of skillful advocacy, character, integrity, and civility." IU law school gave him the Distinguished Alumni Service Award in 2005. He also was named a Sagamore of the Wabash. His former law firm established a scholarship in his name. He was appointed a commissioner for the Indiana Lobbying Registration Commission in 2005. At the Jordan YMCA, he served on the board of managers. As an adjunct professor at the IU School of Law at Indianapolis, he taught a course on Indiana constitutional law. He chaired the committee responsible for drafting the Indiana Rules of Evidence that were adopted by the Court in 1993. As a director on the Indiana Lawyers

Commission in the late 1970s, he recommended changes to Indiana's criminal justice system.

Krahulik died on September 6, 2005, at the age of sixty. He often said, in public and in private, that he had been very lucky in his life: lucky convincing Irene to marry him, lucky to have three wonderful children, and lucky to have worked with so many fine people.

GRETA MORRIS SCODRO, JD, is deputy administrator and staff attorney for the Indiana Supreme Court (since 1995). A native Hoosier, she is distantly related to Judges Jehu T. Elliott and Douglas J. Morris.

SELECTED BIBLIOGRAPHY

Hogsett, Joseph H. "Indiana's 1988 Gubernatorial Residency Challenge." Master's thesis, Indiana University, June, 2007.
Indianapolis Star, September 8, 2005.
"Inns of Court Honor Krahulik," *Indiana Lawyer*, April 21, 2004.
Krahulik, David (son of Justice Krahulik). Interview with the author. N.d.
Shepard, Randall T. "Reflections on a Decade at the Indiana Supreme Court." *Indiana Law Review* 30 (1997).
Steck, Hans W. (former law partner of Krahulik). Interview with the author. N.d.
Sullivan, Frank Jr. "A Tribute to Justice Jon D. Krahulik." *Indiana Law Review* 39 (2006).
Tittle, David O. (former law partner of Krahulik). Interview with the author. N.d.

CASES CITED

Culbertson v. Mernitz, 602 N.E.2d 98 (Ind. 1992).
Cullison v. Medley, 570 N.E.2d 27 (Ind. 1991).
Erie Insurance. Co. v. Hickman, 622 N.E.2d 515 (Ind. 1993).
Huffman v. Monroe County Community School Corp., 588 N.E.2d 1264 (Ind. 1992).
Kennedy v. State of Indiana, 620 N.E.2d 17 (Ind. 1993).
Modesitt v. State of Indiana, 578 N.E.2d 649 (Ind. 1991).
Shuamber v. Henderson, 579 N.E.2d 452 (Ind. 1991).
State Election Board v. Bayh, 521 N.E.2d 1313 (Ind. 1988).
Valinet v. Eskew, 574 N.E.2d 283 (Ind. 1991).
Walker v. Rinck, 604 N.E.2d 591 (Ind. 1992).
Webb v. Jarvis, 575 N.E.2d 992 (Ind. 1991).

The author was a law clerk for Krahulik from 1990 to 1993 and drew on her personal reminiscences for this essay.

FRANK SULLIVAN JR.
November 1, 1993–Present

ROBERT A. PARRISH

Upon his appointment as the 102nd justice of the Indiana Supreme Court on November 1, 1993, by Governor Evan Bayh, Frank Sullivan Jr. pledged that "the court [would] be stable, yet not stand still." Lauded by his peers as "an intelligent, fair-minded, and hardworking lawyer," Sullivan brought these qualities to his work at the Court and has kept his pledge to push Indiana law forward, while also helping to provide stability during his tenure.

Sullivan was born in South Bend, Indiana, on March 21, 1950. After graduating from Dartmouth College in 1972, he returned to Indiana to serve as a caucus assistant in the Indiana House of Representatives through 1973. He spent the next six years serving the state in Washington, D.C.; first as a legislative assistant to U.S. Representative Edward Roush in 1974, and as an aide to U. S. Representative John Brademas from 1974 to 1979.

Sullivan returned to Indiana to attend law school, graduating from the Indiana University School of Law at Bloomington in 1982. Upon his graduation from law school, he entered private practice at the Indianapolis law firm of Barnes and Thornburg, where he practiced corporate and securities law between 1982 and 1989. In 1989 Bayh persuaded Sullivan to return to public service by appointing him the state's budget director. Sullivan served in that capacity until December 1992, when he became the governor's fiscal policy adviser shortly before his appointment to the bench.

Sullivan's tenure on the bench has indeed been marked by jurisprudential progress and stability. Since 1999 the Court's membership has remained relatively unchanged, allowing for continuity while also affording the Court a broad perspective in approaching and solving legal issues.

Beyond the stability of the Court during his tenure, Sullivan has made a number of significant contributions to the state's legal landscape. Most notable, according to one of his colleagues, has been his jurisprudence in the areas of administrative law, where, in *Austin Lakes Joint Venture v. Avon Util. Inc.*, "he staked out a strong position in favor of requiring exhaustion of administrative remedies before resorting to the courts" and corporate law in *Barth v. Barth*, where he took "the view that close corporations have some characteristics shared with true partnerships . . . [a position that has] significantly affected corporation law."

In addition to his jurisprudential contributions, Sullivan has devoted himself to a number of causes that seek to "improve the image of the legal system and profession." He has served as chair of both the American Bar Association's Appellate Judges Conference and its Judicial Clerkship Program. He has also served as the Judicial Division liaison to the ABA Commission on Racial and Ethnic Diversity in the Profession and has demonstrated his commitment to promoting diversity in the profession by routinely hiring judicial clerks from diverse racial and ethnic backgrounds.

Sullivan's contributions have extended beyond the bench and to the academy as well. In 2001 he received a master's of law degree from the University of Virginia. His published scholarship ranges from an examination of the extradition and trial of former Chilean dictator Augusto Pinochet under the principle of separation of powers, to a critique of whether administrative adjudicative decisions are sounder when derived from specialized courts or centralized offices with more general expertise. Drawing upon his prior experience as state budget director, Sullivan officially joined the ranks of the IU School of Law at Indianapolis faculty in 2007 to teach a course on the legal aspects of government finance.

Perhaps the capstone to Sullivan's tenure on the bench has been his work on the state's Judicial Technology and Automation Committee. The Indiana Supreme Court established this project in 1999 "to provide leadership and governance regarding the use of technology in Indiana Courts." Its goal has been "to equip every Indiana trial court with a twenty-first century case management system and to connect individual courts' case management systems with each other and with law enforcement, state agencies and other users of court information." The resulting system has promised to streamline and increase the efficiency of the legal system throughout the state. Since JTAC's inception, Sullivan has been the committee's chair and principal steward. In many ways, it is his work with JTAC that has allowed Sullivan to fulfill his pledge of both providing the legal community with greater stability, while allowing it to move forward by continually taking into consideration the realities of the present and the state's future needs.

ROBERT A. PARRISH, JD, is a lecturer in law, Indiana University Maurer School of Law, Bloomington. He is coeditor of *Remembering Jim Crow: African Americans Tell About Life in the Segregated South* (2001) and a former law clerk to Justice Frank Sullivan Jr.

SELECTED BIBLIOGRAPHY

Boehm, Theodore. Interview with the author. September 17, 2008.
Indianapolis Star, October 10, November 2, 3, 1993, September 5, 2008.
Sullivan, Frank, Jr. "A Separation of Powers Perspective on Pinochet." *Indiana International and Comparative Law Review* 14 (2003).
———. "Some Questions to Consider before Indiana Creates a Centralized Office of Administrative Hearings." *Indiana Law Review* 38 (2005).

CASES CITED
Austin Lakes Joint Venture v. Avon Utilities Inc., 648 N.E.2d 641 (Ind. 1995).
Barth v. Barth, 659 N.E.2d 559 (Ind. 1995).

MYRA C. SELBY
January 4, 1995–October 7, 1999

LINDA C. GUGIN

When Myra Consetta Selby was appointed to the Indiana Supreme Court by Governor Evan Bayh on December 19, 1994, she became the first female and the first African American justice on the state's highest court. She said of her appointment: "It is important for this institution to, as closely as possible, reflect society. Having a woman and having a minority member got it closer to that. It is my deepest hope that this institution will continue to reflect society as it is and not as it once was." On the bench she sought to make the Court, as well as the judicial system as a whole, fairer and more just. Although she served slightly fewer than five years before resigning to return to private practice, she left her mark in many ways.

Selby was sworn in as the 103rd justice on January 4, 1995, after a career that included private practice and government service. She was born on July 1, 1955, in Bay City, Michigan. She graduated from Kalamazoo College in 1977 and received her law degree from the University of Michigan in 1980. She practiced law in Washington, D.C., with the law firm of Seyfarth Shaw Fairweather and Geraldson. In 1983 she joined the Indianapolis law firm of Ice Miller Donadio and Ryan, where she specialized in health law. She became Bayh's Director for Health Care Policy in 1993 and served in that position until her appointment to the Court. After her initial two years on the Court, she won her retention election and another ten-year term. However, for reasons that she said pertained to family concerns, she resigned from the Court in 1999 and returned to Ice Miller.

Selby wrote 105 opinions, averaging twenty-one opinions per year. Frequently she was the justice who was most in agreement with fellow justices. Her arrival on the Court was marked by a high degree of overall consensus, a trend to which she contributed when she replaced Richard M. Givan, who was a prolific dissenter. Her high degree of agreement with the majority position led one Court observer to speculate that she could become the swing vote on the bench.

Despite the honor of being the first African American and female justice, she said it was a role she did not seek. "What I sought," she said, "was the opportunity to represent the people of Indiana on the Court." While she represented all of the people of the state, her service was perhaps the most significant for women and minorities, as evidenced by some of her groundbreaking opinions.

She wrote three opinions for a unanimous Court in her final year on the bench pertaining to the obligation of a landowner to protect an invitee from the criminal actions of third parties when those crimes are foreseeable. To determine this, the Court relied on the "totality of the circumstances" principle. The lead case in the trilogy resulted from a lawsuit brought by a young woman who was sexually assaulted at the Delta Tau Delta fraternity house at Indiana University by a former fraternity member. Selby's opinion noted that in the two years prior to the attack there had been two specific incidents in which females had been assaulted at the fraternity house and that one month prior to the assault the national organization had sent the campus chapter information that rape and sexual assaults were more likely to occur in fraternities. Applying the "totality of the circumstances" principle to the case of *Delta Tau Delta v. Johnson*, Selby said that "DTD owed to (the plaintiff) a duty to take reasonable care to protect her from a foreseeable assault."

The Court applied the "totality of the circumstances" test to two other similar cases. In *Vernon v. The Kroger Store*, the Court determined that a grocery store owed a duty to a customer who was attacked in the store's parking lot following a shoplifting incident. In *L. W. v. Western Golf Association*, a Purdue University student brought suit after being raped in the building where she lived, which was owned by the Western Golf Association and a scholarship foundation. In this case the Court held that the organizations did not owe a duty to a female member who was raped on the premises because that crime was not foreseeable.

Selby wrote three opinions relating to medical care, each of which favored the plaintiffs. In one case the court decided that certain applications of the two-year statute of limitations under the state's Medical Malpractice Act were unconstitutional. The plaintiff was a woman whose physician had misdiagnosed a case of breast cancer that was not discovered until after the two-year statute of limitations had passed. In *Martin v. Richey*, Selby wrote that "to require a plaintiff to bring a claim for medical malpractice before becoming aware of her injury and damages . . . would be boarding the bus to topsy-turvy land." The import of this decision was applauded by one constitutional expert, who said, "It lets people know this Supreme Court isn't your grandfather's Supreme Court . . . [It] is very serious about what it is doing."

In 1997 the Women and Law Division of the Indianapolis Bar Association awarded Selby the Antoinette Dakin Leach Award, given to women lawyers whose efforts have forged a path for others. In October 1999, shortly before Selby left the Court, Chief Justice Randall T. Shepard named her as chairwoman of the Court's Commission on Race and Gender. The commission was established to assess the status of race and gender issues within the legal profession and the court system. Selby helped to lay the groundwork for the commission with an article on race and gender she wrote for the 1999 *Indiana Law Review*. In 2002 the commission released its Executive Report and Recommendations, outlining its finding on the treatment of women and minorities in the Indiana judicial system and proposing far-reaching recommendations for change. Most of the commission's recommendations were approved by the Court, which committed itself to implement as many of them as possible.

When Selby left the Court in 1999, Shepard summed up the essence of her many contributions to the Court and the legal profession. He said she had been a "one-woman wrecking crew bringing down glass ceilings."

LINDA C. GUGIN, PhD, is professor emeritus of political science, Indiana University Southeast. She is the coauthor of *Sherman Minton: New Deal Senator, Cold War Justice* (1997) and *Chief Justice Fred M. Vinson of Kentucky: A Political Biography* (2002), coeditor of *The Governors of Indiana* (2006) and *Justices of the Indiana Supreme Court* (2010), and the author of "Sherman Minton: Restraint against a Tide of Activism," *Vanderbilt Law Review* (2009).

SELECTED BIBLIOGRAPHY

Indiana Lawyer, November 27, 1996, July 21, October 27, 1999.

Indianapolis Star, July 9, 16, October 10, 1999.

Patton, George T., "14 Appellate Civil Case Law Update," *Res Gestae* 43 (September 1999): 14.

Selby, Myra, "Examining Race and Gender Bias in the Courts: A Legacy of Indifference or Opportunity?" *Indiana Law Review* 32 (1999): 1167

CASES CITED

Delta Tau Delta, Beta Alpha Chapter v. Johnson, 712 N.E.2d 968 (1999).

Martin v. Richey, 711 N.E.2d 1273 (1999).

L.W. v. Western Golf Ass'n, 712 N.E. 2d 983 (1999).

Vernon v. The Kroger Co., 712 N.E. 2d 976 (1999).

PHOTO BY JOHN GENTRY

THEODORE R. BOEHM
August 8, 1996–September 30, 2010

JOEL M. SCHUMM

Before taking the bench in 1996 as the 104th justice of the Indiana Supreme Court, Theodore Reed Boehm was not just a highly accomplished attorney, he was a leading architect of the successful strategy "to use amateur
sports as a way to spark development and put Indianapolis on the map." His
preappointment accomplishments were replicated in a distinguished judicial
career, marked by comprehensive, common sense, and often clever opinions
on a wide range of important issues.

Born in Evanston, Illinois on September 12, 1938, Boehm moved with
his family to Indianapolis when he was four. He attended public school,
graduating from Shortridge High School in 1956. Boehm attended Brown
University from 1956 to 1960. He spent his junior year abroad, studying
mathematics at the University of Munich. Boehm graduated from Brown
with a bachelor's degree in philosophy with high honors, and was inducted

into Phi Beta Kappa. He enrolled at Harvard Law School from 1960 to 1963, graduating magna cum laude and serving as an editor of the *Harvard Law Review*.

Boehm spent his entire legal career in a variety of distinguished and challenging legal positions. He began as a law clerk at the U.S. Supreme Court for Chief Justice Earl Warren, serving there from 1963 to 1964. He then returned to Indianapolis to work at Baker and Daniels, becoming a partner in 1970 and the firm's first managing partner in 1980. He was heavily involved in complex corporate law cases, including representing Eli Lilly against insurers who refused coverage of multimillion dollar lawsuits brought by women who had used Diethylstilbestrol (DES). He also argued the landmark Supreme Court reapportionment case of *Davis v. Bandemer*, where the Court broke new ground by indicating a willingness to use the U.S. Constitution as a tool to prevent gerrymandering of electoral districts for partisan political purposes.

Boehm left Baker and Daniels in 1988 to become general counsel of the appliances division of General Electric. He was promoted to the aircraft engines division just seven months later, prompting a senior vice president to demand he "clone himself" before leaving. Boehm left GE in 1991 and served as deputy general counsel at Eli Lilly until 1995, when he returned to Baker and Daniels.

Outside the legal realm, Boehm was heavily engaged in community development in Indianapolis beginning in the late 1970s. As the first president of the Indiana Sports Corporation, he played a leading role in bringing national and international sporting events to Indianapolis, including the National Sports Festival in 1982 and the Pan American Games in 1987. Hundreds of amateur sporting events followed. These events necessitated the construction of state-of-the-art sporting venues and hotels and downtown development. With a big assist from Boehm, a city described by some in the 1970s as "a cemetery with lights" was transformed into the amateur sports capital of the world.

Boehm's remarkable legal and community work brought national recognition, such as an appointment to the inaugural board of editors of the prestigious *National Law Journal* in 1978 and as the subject of a lengthy "heavy hitter" article in the *American Lawyer* in 1987. As Indiana Supreme Court justice Frank Sullivan Jr. aptly remarked in a speech to the American Bar Association, Boehm's "Harvard Law degree, U.S. Supreme Court clerkship, distinguished law practice, and record of civic leadership make him one of the most highly qualified persons ever to sit on our court."

When Governor Evan Bayh appointed Boehm to the Indiana Supreme Court in 1996, he praised Boehm's "unparalleled understanding and appreciation of the law," while Chief Justice Randall T. Shepard commended Boehm's impressive legal credentials and his "long track record in community service." Boehm's service on the Court included the webcasting of all oral arguments, the adoption of a coherent set of new appellate rules, and a 2000 constitutional amendment that made the Court's jurisdiction almost entirely discretionary. In addition, Boehm took a lead role in the Court's Jury Pool Project that created "the most comprehensive, accurate list of jurors ever compiled," and led the 2007 negotiations for office space for ancillary Court operations that saved taxpayers nearly a million dollars.

Boehm's tenure on the Court was marked by a great deal of consensus, with Boehm authoring unanimous opinions on a wide range of topics. Despite his lack of criminal practice experience, many of his opinions addressed significant issues of criminal law and procedure. For example, *Woods v. State* resolved the longstanding confusion regarding when a claim of ineffective assistance of counsel must be brought, holding it should usually be brought in a postconviction proceeding when a supporting record exists. In *Sales v. State* Boehm drew on his wit and knowledge of mathematics in confronting a change to the use of the term "percent" in the operating-while-intoxicated statute. He gave the term its logical meaning in context, explaining the contrary view "would long since have produced not an impaired driver but a corpse, indeed one perhaps needing no embalming." The most notable exception to unanimity in criminal cases came in death penalty cases, where Boehm wrote several powerful dissents joined by Justice Robert D. Rucker. Governors later granted clemency to death row inmates in three of these cases, relying at least partially on the dissent or its rationale.

Boehm also authored scores of opinions in civil cases on topics as prosaic as family law and torts to more complicated corporate law issues involving securities and insurance. When there was division on the court, Boehm was often the swing vote. For example, in *Martin v. Richey* he joined the majority in holding the statute of limitations in medical malpractice cases, which required suits to be filed within two years of the occurrence of the event, unconstitutional. A year later he wrote the opinion upholding the requirement that products liability claims be brought within ten years in *McIntosh v. Melroe*.

In big stakes cases of statewide significance, the court often relied on Boehm for a comprehensive, common sense, and quick opinion. In the 2003 case *D & M Healthcare v. Kernan*, challenging the longstanding practice of gubernatorial vetoes allegedly returned too early, Boehm relied on the doctrine of *de minimis non curat lex*, "the courts' way of saying, 'So what?'" He also authored the 2006 opinion *Bonney v. Indiana Finance Authority*, rejecting a challenge to the impending lease of the Indiana Toll Road. The decision was issued just a week after oral argument and just days before the lease was to commence.

In addition to his impressive work on the Court, Boehm continued his involvement in community development and sporting events. He served as cochair of the World Basketball Championships in 2002, chair of the Indianapolis Cultural Development Commission since 2002, and chair of the Nominating and Governance Committee of the United States Olympic Committee from 2004 to 2006.

On May 25, 2010, Boehm announced his decision to leave the Court. Chief Justice Randall T. Shepard said, "While it is disappointing to lose Justice Boehm as a colleague, we are all grateful for his fourteen years of service to our state's judiciary. He has brought powerful insight to our deliberations and enormous energy to the goal of making Indiana a better place for its citizens."

JOEL M. SCHUMM, JD, is a clinical professor of law, Indiana University School of Law, Indianapolis. He is the director and founder of the Appellate Clinic and a former law clerk to Justice Theodore Boehm (1998–2000).

SELECTED BIBLIOGRAPHY

Borden, Anthony. "Heineman's In-House Revolution." *The American Lawyer* (September 1989).

Browning, Ron. "Governor Spares Life on Way Out." *The Indiana Lawyer* 15 (2005).

———. "Olympic Judge." *The Indiana Lawyer* 14 (2004).

Hoskins, Michael W. "Supreme Court Operations Move." *The Indiana Lawyer* 18 (2007).

Indianapolis Star, October 3, 1999, August 31, 2001, December 26, 2004, November 20, 2005.

Kueterman, Greg. "Boehm: High Court Next–and Last–Stop." *The Indiana Lawyer* 6 (1996).

Weinstein, Claudia. "Calling the Plays at Baker & Daniels." *The American Lawyer* (April 1987).

Sullivan, Frank, Jr. "Twelve Years on the Indiana Supreme Court." Speech to the American Bar Association 2006 Annual Meeting.

CASES CITED

Bonney v. Indiana Finance Authority, 849 N.E.2d 473 (Ind. 2006).
D & M Healthcare, Inc. v. Kernan, 800 N.E.2d 898 (Ind. 2003).
Davis et al. v. Bandemer et al., 478 U.S. 109 (1986).
Martin v. Richey, 711 N.E.2d 1273 (Ind. 1999).
McIntosh v. Melroe Company, 729 N.E.2d 972 (Ind. 2000).
Sales v. State of Indiana, 723 N.E.2d 416 (Ind. 2000).
Woods v. State of Indiana, 701 N.E.2d 1208 (Ind. 1998).

ROBERT D. RUCKER
November 19, 1999–Present

RAY E. BOOMHOWER

A decorated combat infantryman in the Vietnam War, Justice Robert Dennis Rucker, the 105th justice to serve on the Indiana Supreme Court, is the first African American male to sit on the state's highest court. Appointed by Governor Frank O'Bannon, Rucker replaced Justice Myra C. Selby, the first African American and female to serve on the Court, who resigned from office to return to private law practice. Upon his ascension as justice, Rucker said: "There is an old Negro spiritual that has as its refrain, 'My soul looks back and wonders.' Twenty years ago, when I left law school, never in my wildest dreams did I anticipate that one day I would sit as a member of this court."

Born in Canton, Georgia, on January 19, 1947, Rucker was the oldest of eleven children. He grew up in Gary, Indiana, raised from the age of fourteen by his stepmother, Arlisa Rucker Patterson, who noted that Rucker was an obedient and hardworking youngster. He attended Indiana University Northwest on a part-time basis while working at Inland Steel. Before he could finish his college studies, Rucker was drafted in military service and sent to Vietnam. He served as radio operator with the First Cavalry Division (Airmobile) and rose to the rank of sergeant. Rucker participated in Operation Pegasus, the relief of besieged marines at Khe Sanh in northwestern Quang Tri Province in South Vietnam. He described the experience as "tough and scary." Twice wounded in action, he received the Purple Heart and Bronze Star for meritorious service, but does not dwell on his time in combat. "You're there, you do your job, and you come home," he once told a reporter. "It was a traumatic experience. Not one I like to talk about."

Upon his return home to Indiana, Rucker, who had married before leaving for his army service, had "no plans other than raising a family." He returned to work at Inland Steel, but left soon after for such occupations as bank teller and counselor for a jobs training program. Rucker decided to resume his studies at IU Northwest. In those days, he had plans of graduating and attending medical school. He was inspired in part by the chairman of the school's chemistry department, who told Rucker a challenging course of studies would be five hours each in chemistry, physics, and German. "That got me started in a pre-med program," Rucker noted. "And that made me really appreciate long, long hours of study, spending a lot of time in the library."

Before Rucker graduated, he met Alton Gill Jr., a Gary attorney, who convinced him he could make a difference if he pursued a legal career. After receiving his bachelor's degree in sociology in 1974, Rucker, with the help of a Woodrow Wilson/Martin Luther King Jr. Fellowship, entered law school at Valparaiso University. "I was motivated most of the time I was in law school by absolute fear of failure," recalled Rucker, who earned his law degree in December 1976. Rucker passed the bar on his first try and joined the East Chicago law firm of African American attorney W. Henry Walker, for whom he had clerked during his last year of law school. Rucker later earned a master of laws degree in the judicial process from the University of Virginia Law School in 1998.

Rucker ran for the office of state representative in 1978. Although he lost the race, he met Jack Crawford, a candidate for Lake County prosecutor. Crawford won the election and hired Rucker as a deputy prosecutor. His time with the prosecutor's office included a case that Rucker said gave him

the most satisfaction as an attorney. The trial involved the successful prosecution of two men, Herbert and Randall Dellenbach, who had defrauded
numerous consumers purchasing heating systems. Rucker was also able to
take the Dellenbachs to civil court to remove liens they had placed on their
victims' homes. Rucker, who lost a 1980 election for a Lake County judgeship, left the prosecutor's office to return to private practice with Walker. He
later served as the deputy city attorney for Gary from 1987 to 1988 before
opening his own law practice.

Rucker broke new ground for the state when in 1990 Governor Evan
Bayh appointed him to serve as the first African American judge on the Indiana Court of Appeals. "I think my appointment does mean a lot of things
to a lot of different people—male, female, black and white," Rucker said at
the time. "And I hope that the appointment can serve as a beacon of inspiration to our children, certainly to other African-American lawyers, and to
the legal community in general." In one precedent-setting decision he made
while on the appeals court, Rucker wrote the majority decision on a 1998
case from Fort Wayne involving a passenger who left a car halted by police
during a traffic stop in a high-crime neighborhood. In his opinion, Rucker
wrote that the police officer that had detained the passenger had not been
justified in his action. "The fact that one turns away from the police in a
high-crime neighborhood is not sufficient to establish reasonable suspicion
of criminal activity," Rucker noted.

In 1999 O'Bannon, filling the vacancy left by Selby's resignation, appointed Rucker to the Court from a list of three candidates provided him
by the Judicial Nominating Commission. O'Bannon noted that Rucker had
proven his ability while on the Indiana Court of Appeals and praised him for
being a "careful, thoughtful, thorough and independent judge." The governor also said that Rucker brought to the state's highest court "a wealth of
experience as an appellate court judge, a deputy prosecutor, a city attorney
and a general practitioner."

When he was named to the Court, Rucker described himself as a moderate who did not know if he was "liberal or conservative, left or right. I think
I take a centrist approach to most things and hope to continue that on the
Supreme Court." The Court on which Rucker serves has earned a reputation
as nonideological, with few defined voting blocks, basing their decisions
instead on the merits of each case. Still, a study of the voting patterns in
criminal cases of the Court found that although the Court overall has been

overwhelmingly proprosecution, Rucker voted in favor of the defendant "58 percent of the time, and was by far the most pro-defendant justice on the court." Rucker wrote the majority decision in *Bader v. Johnson* whereby the court granted parents the right to seek damages for distress under malpractice law when physicians negligently fail to warn them of possible or likely birth defects, and also gave workers the opportunity for greater court awards if their employers had not paid them the full amount of their normal paychecks in *St. Vincent Hospital and Health Care Center, Inc. v. Steele.*

RAY E. BOOMHOWER is senior editor, Indiana Historical Society Press, and editor of *Traces of Indiana and Midwestern History.* He is the author of numerous books on Indiana history, including *Gus Grissom: The Lost Astronaut* (2004) and *Robert F. Kennedy and the 1968 Indiana Primary* (2008). His articles have appeared in *Traces* and the *Indiana Magazine of History.*

SELECTED BIBLIOGRAPHY

Cherna, Jason A. "The Indiana Supreme Court's Voting Patterns in Criminal Decisions." *Albany Law Review* 70, issue 3 (June 22, 2007).

Fort Wayne Journal-Gazette, December 20, 2004.

Hoskins, Michael. "A Year of Stability for Court: Annual Analysis Mulls Justices' Voting Patterns, Workloads in 2007." *Indiana Lawyer* (June 11, 2008).

Indianapolis Star, December 2, 1990, August 21, October 26, November 20, 1999, July 26, 2000, April 23, 2002, November 11, 2004.

Kaelble, Steve. "Finally Convinced to Pursue Legal Career, Rucker Climbs to Supreme Heights." *Indiana Alumni Magazine* (July/August, 2001).

CASES CITED

Patricia Bader M.D. and Northeast Indiana Genetic Counseling, Inc. v. Ronald Johnson and Connie Johnson, 732 N.E. 2d 1212 (Ind. 2000).

St. Vincent Hospital and Health Care Center, Inc. v. Robert J. Steele M.D., 766 N.E. 2d 699 (Ind. 2002).

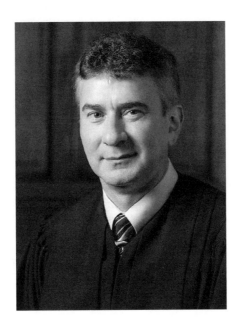

STEVEN H. DAVID
October 18, 2010–Present

LINDA C. GUGIN

When Governor Mitch Daniels appointed Steven Howard David to be the 106th justice of the Indiana Supreme Court he said that he chose him for his "diversity and breadth of experience," which included a lengthy career in the military, six years as counsel and senior attorney for a corporation, and fifteen years as a trial judge in Boone County. Among the four justices he joined on the Court, only one—Justice Robert D. Rucker—had served on active duty in the military, and none had experience in the business sector. Only two other justices—Chief Justice Randall T. Shepard and Rucker—had prior judicial experience, Shepard as trial court judge and Rucker as an appellate court judge.

David's experience added diversity to the Court, although not the kind of diversity some had hoped. Some wanted the governor to name a woman. At the time of David's appointment Indiana was one of two states without a female member on its highest bench. Daniels, however, said that "gender equality" might have been a tiebreaker, but that in the end he deemed David to be the "best person on the merits."

David was born in Fort Wayne on April 22, 1957. His father was in the U.S. Air Force, and he lived in many different places growing up, but most of his life he lived in Bartholomew County. He graduated from Columbus North High School in 1975, and attended Murray State University on an ROTC scholarship and was named Distinguished Military Graduate and Outstanding Senior in Finance. After graduating magna cum laude in 1979, he was commissioned into the U.S. Army as a second lieutenant but deferred his military service to attend Indiana University School of Law in Indianapolis. Following his graduation in 1982 he was admitted to the Indiana bar.

Before entering the private practice of law, David fulfilled the commitment of his ROTC scholarship and served on active duty in the army. From 1982 to 1986 he was in the Judge Advocate General's Corps at Fort Benning, Georgia and Fort Benjamin Harrison, Indiana. From 1986 to 2009 he served continuously in the Army Reserves. He retired from the reserves in 2010 with the rank of colonel. During his distinguished military career he served as an active military judge, as a unit commander, and as chief defense counsel for the Office of Military Commissions at Guantanamo Bay. Daniels said that David's defense of Guantanamo detainees "stood for the rule of law in one of the most challenging assignments I can imagine any lawyer has been given." Testifying before the U.S. House Armed Services Committee, in July 2008, David said his role as chief defense counsel was to serve as "the conscience of the United States government" to ensure that the military commissions trying Guantanamo detainees "abide by the fundamental law of the land applicable in every other American judicial proceeding where life and liberty are at stake."

For his service in behalf of Guantanamo detainees David received the Defense Superior Service Medal, the nation's third-highest noncombat award. He also was awarded the Military Meritorious Service Medal four times and the Army Commendations Medal five times.

When David left active duty he practiced law in Columbus with the firm of Cline, King and King from 1986 to 1987 and from 1987 to 1988 with the firm of Richard S. Enyon. In 1988 he became corporate counsel and then senior attorney and assistant secretary for Mayflower Transit Company in

Carmel, Indiana. In 1994 he was elected judge of the Boone County Circuit Court, a position he held until his appointment to the Indiana Supreme Court. In this position he was especially devoted to issues involving juveniles, both inside and outside the court. He was a member of the board of Indiana Council of Juvenile and Family Court Judges, serving as its president. In this capacity he testified on several occasions before the Indiana General Assembly on such matters as education reform for placement of children outside their homes and the shift of child welfare funding from county property taxes to the state general fund. David received the Judge Robert E. Kinsey Award given for outstanding efforts of members of the Judiciary with juvenile jurisdictions.

His work as trial court judge was familiar to the justices on the Court. On numerous occasions he was appointed by the Court to serve as special judge, and two of these were death penalty cases. One for which he served as special judge, ended up three times before the Indiana Supreme Court. In that case, *The State of Indiana v. Zolo Agona Azania* the defendant had been convicted in 1981 for killing a police officer. On an appeal, the Court twice upheld his conviction but set aside the recommendations of two juries that he should receive the death penalty because of procedural concerns. On his third appeal the Court appointed David to preside over the case as special judge.

Twenty-four years had elapsed between his first conviction and his third appeal. David ruled in favor of the defendant. He said that "fundamental constitutional principles of fairness, due process and speedy justice warrant this court prohibiting the State to seek the death penalty against this defendant in this case under these circumstances." In a three-to-two opinion, written by Justice Frank Sullivan Jr., the Court ruled against David's decision after finding "that the delay and any resulting prejudice in the case did not violate Azania's due process rights." *Azania* was the only criminal case in which David was reversed by the higher court. His overall record of reversals was a good one, having been reversed only six times out of thirty-three cases.

David said he sought the position on the Court because "my life has been about public service." The validity of this claim is borne out by his twenty-seven years of military service and fifteen years as a circuit court judge. In addition to his government service he has been involved in numerous community organizations, serving on the board of directors of the Community Foundation of Boone County, the Zionsville Area Boys and Girls Club, and the Lebanon Area Boys and Girls Club. He has been a member of the Lebanon Kiwanis Club and the Zionsville American Legion.

Following the announcement of David's appointment, Chief Justice Shepard said that he and his colleagues "were pleased to have Judge David join us. He showed exceptional talent during the application and interview process." In response, David said "I am looking forward to working with the absolute best supreme court in the United States, the absolute best court of appeals, and the trial judges and all of the trial judges and every lawyer. Most importantly I look forward to serving the citizens of the state of Indiana."

SELECTED BIBLIOGRAPHY

David, Steven. Testimony, U.S. House Armed Service Committee. http://armedservices. house.gov/pdfs/FC073108/David_Testimony073108.pdf.
The Indiana Law Blog: Ind.Courts—How have the judges fared? Judge Steve David. http://indianalawblog.com/archives/2010/07ind_courts_how_8.html.
The Indiana Law Blog. "Daniels selects Steven David to join Indiana Supreme Court (from the Governors Press Office). September 17, 2010. www.indianalawblog.com/.
Schnedier, Mary Beth. "Governor appoints 'best person' to top court." http://www.indy-star.com/article/2010918/LOCAL/9180331/Governor-appoints-best-person.
Shepard, Randall. Supreme Court Web site

CASES CITED

State of Indiana v. Zolo Agona Azania, "Order Barring The State From Seeking the Death Penalty," Superior Court of Allen County, Indiana, Cause No. 02D04-9-8109-CF-401 (2005).
State of Indiana v. Zolo Agona Azania, 865 N.E. 2d 994 (2007).

Photographs

Top: *The 1892 Indiana Supreme Court. Left to right: Robert W. McBride, Walter Olds, Byron K. Elliott, John D. Miller, and Silas D. Coffey.* **Bottom:** *The Indiana Supreme Court circa 1910. Left to right: James H. Jordan, Oscar H. Montgomery, John V. Hadley, Leander J. Monks, and Quincy A. Myers.*

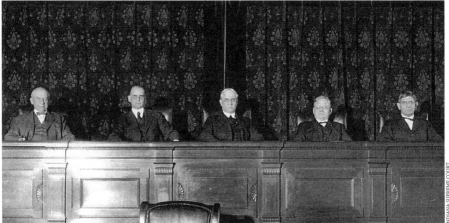

Top: *The 1912 Indiana Supreme Court. Left to right: Douglas J. Morris, Charles E. Cox, Leander J. Monks, Quincy A. Myers, and John W. Spencer.* **Bottom:** *The Indiana Supreme Court circa 1925. Left to right: David A. Myers, Willard B. Gemmill, Julius C. Travis, Benjamin M. Willoughby, and Louis B. Ewbank.*

Top: *The 1930 Indiana Supreme Court. Left to right: Clarence R. Martin, Willard B. Gemmill, Julius C. Travis, Benjamin M. Willoughby, and David A. Myers.* **Bottom:** *The Indiana Supreme Court circa 1941. Left to right: Curtis W. Roll, Frank N. Richman, H. Nathan Swaim, Michael L. Fansler, and Curtis G. Shake.*

Top: *The Indiana Supreme Court, 1951–53. Seated: James A. Emmert, Arch N. Bobbitt, and Paul G. Jasper. Standing: Floyd S. Draper and Frank E. Gilkison.* **Bottom:** *The 1959 Indiana Supreme Court. Left to right: Amos W. Jackson, Arch N. Bobbitt, Frederick Landis Jr., Harold E. Achor, and Norman F. Arterburn.*

Top: *The 1963 Indiana Supreme Court. Left to right: Harold E. Achor, Norman F. Arterburn, Amos W. Jackson, Walter Myers Jr., and Frederick Landis Jr.* **Bottom:** *The 1968 Indiana Supreme Court. Left to right: Norman F. Arterburn, Amos W. Jackson, David M. Lewis (chief justice), Roger O. DeBruler, and Donald H. Hunter.*

The 1974 Indiana Supreme Court. Front row: Norman F. Arterburn (chief justice), Richard M. Givan, and Donald H. Hunter. Back row: Dixon W. Prentice and Roger O. DeBruler.

The 1987 Indiana Supreme Court.
Left to right: Richard M. Givan,
Brent E. Dickson, Randall T. Shepard
(chief justice), Roger O. DeBruler, and
Alfred J. Pivarnik.

The 1995 Indiana Supreme Court. Front row:
Brent E. Dickson, Randall T. Shepard (chief
justice), and Myra C. Selby. Back row: Roger O.
DeBruler and Frank Sullivan Jr.

The 2010 Indiana Supreme Court. Left to right: Frank Sullivan Jr., Brent E. Dickson, Randall T. Shepard (chief justice), Robert D. Rucker, and Theodore R. Boehm.

Top left: *Judge Horace P. Biddle was one of seven justices with ties to Cass County who have served on the Court. During his lifetime, Biddle was as well known for his volumes of poetry as for his legal career. In this photo, Biddle is standing in front of his retirement home, The Hermitage, located on Biddle's Island in the Wabash River near Logansport.* **Top right:** *One of twelve children, Judge Jehu T. Elliott is pictured here with his surviving brothers and sisters circa 1870. Front row, left to right: Mary Elliott Bradbury, Elizabeth Elliott Peed, Amanda Elliott Bundy, and Teresa Elliott McCready. Back row, left to right: Stephen Elliott, Judge Elliott, and Abraham Elliott.* **Bottom:** *Judge Walter E. Treanor began his career as a teacher and then superintendent for the Petersburg school system. He left the school when he joined the army during World War I. This photo captures "Coach" Treanor (far left) and the 1914 Petersburg High School football team.*

Top: *Judge John W. Spencer moved to the Vanderburgh County area and began practicing law in 1885 when he was just twenty-one years old. This photo, found in a collection held by the Willard Library in Evansville, captures Spencer on Wabash Woods Ferry in 1921. After his retirement from the Court, Spencer was well known for purchasing farm and bottomlands in and around Posey County.* **Center:** *Judge Louis B. Ewbank was first appointed to the Court by Governor James P. Goodrich, and later that year was elected in his own right. His brothers Jim and Richard were also lawyers. However, it was said that when all the brothers got together, Loebo (a farmer) could out argue all of them. Here he is pictured with his brothers at the Smith Reunion in 1938. Left to right: Loebo, Louis, Dick (Richard), and Jim.* **Bottom:** *Over the years, members of the Court have taken periodic retreats. In November 1941 judges (left to right) Michael L. Fansler, Curtis W. Roll, Curtis G. Shake, and Frank N. Richman met at Judge H. Nathan Swaim's cottage on Freeman Lake.*

Top: *The bulk of the Court's work takes place outside of public view. The justices meet regularly in their Indiana Statehouse conference room to discuss cases and other Court business. Pictured here is the 1958 Court: (clockwise beginning in foreground) Frederick Landis Jr., Harold E. Achor, Arch N. Bobbitt, James A. Emmert, and Norman F. Arterburn.* **Bottom:** *In 1951 Indianapolis area media frequently speculated on the potential appointment of Indiana Supreme Court Judge Paul G. Jasper to the federal bench. While the highly anticipated new federal district never materialized, Jasper still had the opportunity to meet with President Harry S. Truman in person.*

PHOTO FROM COURT OF INTERNATIONAL TRADE

GIVAN FAMILY COLLECTION

Opposite, top: *Judges Frank Richman and Curtis Shake were both asked by President Harry S. Truman to serve on the military tribunals held in Nuremberg, Germany, following World War II. In their free time Richman and Shake took advantage of the opportunity to visit local sites with the help of their driver. This photo was taken in 1947.* **Opposite bottom:** *Judge Howard S. Young Sr. headed a family of lawyers that has practiced continuously in Indianapolis since he opened his office in 1904. Young's son (Howard Jr.), daughter-in-law, and their five sons are all lawyers. This photo captures three generations of Young family lawyers around the dinner table. Left to right: Judge Young's grandsons Thomas and Drew (only top of head is barely visible), nephew Jack, son Howard Young Jr. carving the turkey, Judge Young, brother Byron Young, and Nancy (Howard Jr.'s wife).* **Top:** *Many of Indiana's Supreme Court justices have served on other courts as well. Frederick Landis Jr. sat on the Indiana Supreme Court from 1955 to 1965. He resigned on November 8, 1965, and on the same day accepted an appointment as judge of the U.S. Court of International Trade. He served in that position until 1983.* **Above right:** *Some of Justice Richard M. Givan's well-known passions included raising horses and photography. Each May he could often be spotted trackside taking pictures at the Indianapolis 500.*

Top left: *Indiana Supreme Court justices enjoy a wide variety of activities outside the Court. Justice Jon D. Krahulik was especially interested in keeping fit. He took this to the extreme in 1992 when he completed the world famous Iron Man Triathlon in Kona, Hawaii.*
Top right: *Justices come to the court with a wide variety of backgrounds. In this picture, chairman and CEO of the Pan American Games in Indianapolis, and future justice, Theodore R. Boehm (far right), joins Lieutenant Governor John M. Mutz, Amigo (mascot of the games), and Indianapolis Mayor William H. Hudnut in a celebration on Monument Circle after the announcement that Indianapolis was chosen as host city for the 1987 Pan American Games.* **Above:** *In Indiana there was no required attorney license fee until 1971. Pictured here are Judges Roger O. DeBruler, Norman F. Arterburn, Dixon W. Prentice, Richard M. Givan, and Donald H. Hunter paying their $15 licensing fee to the Clerk of the Supreme Court, Billie R. McCullough, on June 23, 1971. The fee is now $115.*

PHOTO BY ED MOSS

D. TODD MOORE, *INDIANAPOLIS STAR*

Top: *On November 20, 1998, nine justices and more than a hundred law clerks gathered for the first ever Law Clerk Reunion. The event was held at Fletcher Pointe on Indianapolis's near south side. Attending justices included (front row, left to right) Randall T. Shepard, Frederick E. Rakestraw, Dixon W. Prentice, Richard M. Givan, and Jon D. Krahulik; as well as (back row, left to right) Frank Sullivan Jr., Paul G. Jasper, Brent E. Dickson, and Theodore R. Boehm.* **Right:** *In addition to the more formal weekly meetings in the Court's conference room, the justices often meet in more informal venues. One longstanding tradition was lunch at the Block's Department Store's restaurant, located just east of the Statehouse. In this photo (left to right) Alfred J. Pivarnik, Brent E. Dickson, Randall T. Shepard, Roger O. DeBruler, and Richard M. Givan enjoy one last lunch on the day Block's closed its doors, January 29, 1988.*

Above: *While an undergraduate at Purdue University, Justice Brent E. Dickson was the pianist for the Salty Dogs, a student Dixieland jazz band originally founded on campus in 1947. The membership of the group often changed and it continued for more than twenty years. This photo was taken at a September 2001 reunion jam session with Dickson at the piano.* **Left:** *At the Indiana University School of Law–Indianapolis, Justice Frank Sullivan Jr. (left) talks with former American Bar Association President Dennis Archer and law clerk Jimmie McMillan.* **Opposite, top:** *Oral arguments are heard in the Indiana Supreme Court Courtroom and are open to the public. Media is granted permission to be in the courtroom during Supreme Court arguments with prior approval.* **Opposite, right:** *At its discretion, the Court can ask appellate counsel to appear before the Court for oral arguments. In a room directly behind the courtroom, the Robing Room, the justices gather to don their robes before taking their places on the bench. From left to right, Justices Sullivan, Dickson, Randall T. Shepard, Robert D. Rucker, and Theodore R. Boehm prepare for an oral argument in 2003.* **Opposite, left:** *Indiana Supreme Court justices spend considerable time discussing each case in both formal and informal settings. Here Justices Shepard and Boehm are caught in a discussion near one of the four marble staircases in the Statehouse.*

Appendix, Indiana Supreme Court 1816–1853; 1853–1872; 1872–Present

"The Old Supreme Court"
1816–January 3, 1853

	Thomas L. Smith (1847–1853)	Samuel E. Perkins (1846–1865)
	Charles Dewey (1836–1847)	Jeremiah C. Sullivan (1837–1846)
Isaac N. Blackford (1817–1853)	Stephen C. Stevens* (1831–1836)	John T. McKinney* (1831–1837)
John Johnson (1816–1817)	James Scott (1816–1830)	Jesse L. Holman (1816–1830)

*Governor James B. Ray appointed Stevens and McKinney on January 28, 1831. *The Green Bag* (1892) indicates that McKinney was nominated to replace Holman.

Indiana Supreme Court Justices
January 3, 1853–December 16, 1872

			John Pettit (1871–1877)
			Robert C. Gregory (1865–1871)
James L. Worden (1871–1882)			James M. Hanna (1857–1865)
James S. Frazer (1865–1871)	Alexander C. Downey (1871–1877)	Samuel H. Buskirk (1871–1877)	Samuel B. Gookins (1855–1857)
James L. Worden (1858–1865)	Jehu T. Elliott (1865–1871)	Charles A. Ray (1865–1871)	Alvin P. Hovey (1854–1855)
William Z. Stuart (1853–1858)	Andrew Davison (1853–1865)	Samuel E. Perkins (1846–1865)	Addison L. Roache (1853–1854)

Indiana Supreme Court
1872–Present

				Steven H. David (2010–Present)
				Theodore R. Boehm (1996–2010)
				Roger O. DeBruler (1968–1996)
		Robert D. Rucker (1999–Present)		Donald R. Mote (1967–1968)
		Myra C. Selby (1995–1999)		Frederick E. Rakestraw (1966–1967)
		Richard M. Givan (1969–1994)	Randall T. Shepard (1985–Present)	Frederick Landis, Jr. (1955–1965)
		David M. Lewis (1967–1969)	Donald H. Hunter (1967–1985)	Isadore E. Levine (1955)
	Brent E. Dickson (1986–Present)	Walter Myers, Jr. (1963–1967)	Harold E. Achor (1955–1966)	Floyd S. Draper (1951–1955)
Frank Sullivan, Jr. (1993–Present)	Dixon W. Prentice (1971–1986)	Arch N. Bobbitt (1951–1963)	Dan C. Flanagan (1953–1954)	Oliver Starr (1945–1951)
Jon D. Krahulik (1990–1993)	Amos W. Jackson (1959–1971)	Howard S. Young Sr. (1945–1951)	Paul G. Jasper (1949–1953)	Michael L. Fansler (1933–1945)
Alfred J. Pivarnik (1977–1990)	James A. Emmert (1947–1959)	H. Nathan Swaim (1939–1945)	Martin J. O'Malley (1943–1949)	Julius C. Travis (1921–1933)
Norman F. Arterburn (1955–1977)	Frank N. Richman (1941–1947)	James P. Hughes (1933–1939)	Curtis W. Roll (1931–1943)	Moses B. Lairy (1915–1921)
George W. Henley Jr. (1955)	George L. Tremain (1935–1940)	Clarence R. Martin (1927–1933)	Willard G. Gemmill (1925–1931)	Quincy A. Myers (1909–1915)
Frank E. Gilkison (1945–1955)	David A. Myers (1917–1934)	Louis B. Ewbank (1920–1927)	Fred C. Gause (1923–1925)	John H. Gillett (1902–1909)
Curtis G. Shake (1938–1945)	Douglas J. Morris (1911–1917)	Lawson M. Harvey (1917–1920)	Howard L. Townsend (1917–1923)	Francis E. Baker (1899–1902)
Walter E. Treanor (1931–1938)	Oscar H. Montgomery (1905–1911)	Charles E. Cox (1911–1917)	Richard K. Erwin (1913–1917)	Timothy E. Howard (1893–1899)
Benjamin M. Willoughby (1919–1931)	Alexander Dowling (1899–1905)	John V. Hadley (1899–1911)	Leander J. Monks (1895–1913)	Robert W. McBride (1890–1893)
John W. Spencer (1912–1919)	Leonard J. Hackney (1893–1899)	J. James McCabe (1893–1899)	Joseph S. Dailey (1893–1895)	Joseph A. S. Mitchell (1885–1890)
James H. Jordan (1895–1912)	John D. Miller (1891–1893)	Byron K. Elliott (1881–1893)	Walter Olds (1889–1893)	Edwin P. Hammond (1883–1885)
Silas D. Coffey (1889–1895)	John G. Berkshire (1889–1891)	John T. Scott (1879–1881)	Allen Zollars (1883–1889)	William A. Woods (1881–1883)
William E. Niblack (1877–1889)	George V. Howk (1877–1889)	Samuel E. Perkins (1877–1879)	William H. Coombs (1882–1883)	Horace P. Biddle (1875–1881)
Samuel H. Buskirk (1871–1877)	Alexander Downey (1871–1877)	John Pettit (1871–1877)	James L. Worden (1871–1882)	Andrew L. Osborn (1872–1875)

Index

Page numbers in italics refer to illustrations